The Origins of Racism in the West

Is it possible to speak of western racism before the eighteenth century? The term "racism" is normally only associated with theories, which first appeared in the eighteenth century, about inherent biological differences that made one group superior to another. Here, however, leading historians argue that racism can be traced back to the attitudes of the ancient Greeks to their Persian enemies and that it was adopted, adjusted and reformulated by Europeans until the dawn of the Enlightenment. From Greek teachings on environmental determinism and heredity, through medieval concepts of physiognomy, down to the crystallization of attitudes to Indians, Blacks, Jews and Gypsies in the early modern era, they analyse the various routes by which racist ideas travelled before maturing into murderous ideologies in the modern western world. In so doing this book offers a major reassessment of the place of racism in pre-modern European thought.

MIRIAM ELIAV-FELDON is Professor of Early Modern European History at Tel Aviv University. Her previous publications include *Realistic Utopias: The Ideal Imaginary Societies of the Renaissance* (1982), *The Protestant Reformation* (1997) and *The Printing Revolution* (2000).

BENJAMIN ISAAC is Fred and Helen Lessing Professor of Ancient History at Tel Aviv University. His books include *The Limits of Empire: The Roman Army in the East* (1990), *The Near East under Roman Rule* (1998) and *The Invention of Racism in Classical Antiquity* (2004).

JOSEPH ZIEGLER is a senior lecturer at the Department of General History, University of Haifa. He is the author of *Medicine and Religion c. 1300: The Case of Arnau de Vilanova* (1998).

The Origins of Racism
in the West

Edited by

Miriam Eliav-Feldon,

Benjamin Isaac

and

Joseph Ziegler

CAMBRIDGE UNIVERSITY PRESS
Cambridge, New York, Melbourne, Madrid, Cape Town, Singapore,
São Paulo, Delhi

Cambridge University Press
The Edinburgh Building, Cambridge CB2 8RU, UK

Published in the United States of America
by Cambridge University Press, New York

www.cambridge.org
Information on this title: www.cambridge.org/9780521888554

First published 2009

Printed in the United Kingdom at the University Press, Cambridge

A catalogue record for this publication is available from the British Library

ISBN 978-0-521-88855-4 hardback

Contents

Illustrations

Notes on contributors

ROBERT BARTLETT is Wardlaw Professor of Mediaeval History, University of St Andrews, Scotland. His recent publications include *The Natural and the Supernatural in the Middle Ages* (2008) and *The Hanged Man: A Story of Miracle, Memory and Colonialism in the Middle Ages* (2004). *The Making of Europe* (1993) was joint winner of the Wolfson Literary Award for History.

PETER BILLER is Professor of History, University of York. His research interests are the medieval history of heresy, inquisition, proto-racial thought, and medicine. His recent publications include *The Measure of Multitude: Population in Medieval Thought* (2000); 'A "Scientific" View of Jews from Paris around 1300', *Micrologus* 9 (2001); *The Waldenses 1170– 1530: Between a Religious Order and a Church* (2001); 'Black Women in Medieval Scientific Thought', *Micrologus* 13 (2005); and 'Goodbye to Waldensianism?', *Past and Present* 192 (2006).

DENISE KIMBER BUELL is Professor of Religion at Williams College (Williamstown, MA, USA). She is the author of *Why This New Race: Ethnic Reasoning in Early Christianity* (2005) and *Making Christians: Clement of Alexandria and the Rhetoric of Legitimacy* (1999). Her current work explores early Christian ideas of agency and transformation in relation to negotiations of difference among humans and between 'human' and 'non-human'.

JORGE CAÑIZARES-ESGUERRA, Alice Drysdale Sheffield Professor of History at the University of Texas, is the author of the award-winning *How to Write the History of the New World* (2001) and *Puritan Conquistadors* (2006). He is also the author of *Nature, Empire, and Nation* (2006) and co-editor with Erik Seeman of *The Atlantic in Global History, 1500–2000* (2006). He is currently studying historical narratives of Atlantic colonization understood as the fulfillment of prefigurations in four different types of texts (nature, the Bible, the classics, and indigenous sources).

MIRIAM ELIAV-FELDON teaches early-modern European history at Tel Aviv University. Her research interests include Renaissance utopias, pacifism and peace plans, and post-Reformation heresies. She is now working on impostors and the development of means of identification during the sixteenth and seventeenth centuries.

DAVID GOLDENBERG is Cohen Professor in Jewish Religion and Thought at the University of Cape Town and a Visiting Scholar at the University of Pennsylvania. His research interests are in the field of Judaism in Late Antiquity, and his recent publications include a chapter on Josephus's 'Mosaic Constitution' in *The Lost Bible: Ancient Jewish Writings Outside of Scripture*, ed. Louis Feldman, James Kugel and Lawrence Schiffman (forthcoming) and 'Babatha, Rabbi Levi and Theodosius: Black Coins in Late Antiquity', *Dead Sea Discoveries* 14 (2007).

VALENTIN GROEBNER teaches Medieval and Renaissance History at the University of Lucerne, Switzerland. His books include *Defaced: The Visual Culture of Violence in the Middle Ages* (2005) and *Who Are You? Identification, Deception, and Surveillance in Early Modern Europe* (2007). He is currently working on medieval and modern narratives of organ transplantation.

BENJAMIN ISAAC is Fred and Helen Lessing Professor of Ancient History at Tel Aviv University. His books include *The Limits of Empire: The Roman Army in the East* (1990), *The Near East under Roman Rule* (1998) and *The Invention of Racism in Classical Antiquity* (2004). He is a member of the Israel Academy of Sciences and Humanities and of the American Philosophical Society. He was awarded the Israel Prize for History in 2008.

CHARLES DE MIRAMON is a researcher at the Centre National de la Recherche Scientifique, Centre de Recherches Historiques, École des Hautes Études en Sciences Sociales (Paris), working in an interdisciplinary group on medieval scholasticism. He specializes in canon law and is now working on a book on the legal revolution of the twelfth and thirteenth centuries. His publications include a work on the 'semi-religious' and on conversion to religious life (*Les donnés au Moyen Âge*, 1999) and he is co-editor of a volume on the history of heredity (*L'hérédité entre Moyen Âge et Époque moderne: Perspectives historiques*, 2008).

DAVID NIRENBERG is Professor in the Committee on Social Thought and the Department of History at the University of Chicago. His work focuses on the co-production of Jewish, Christian, and Islamic cultures: that is, on how these cultures each constitute themselves by inter-relating with or thinking about the others.

ANTHONY PAGDEN is Distinguished Professor in the Department of Political Science, University of California, Los Angeles. His most recent publications include *Peoples and Empires: Europeans and the Rest of the World, from Antiquity to the Present* (2001); *La Ilustración y sus enemigos: Dos ensayos sobre los orígenes de la modernidad* (2002); *Worlds at War: The 2,500-Year Struggle between East and West* (2008); and as editor *The Idea of Europe from Antiquity to the European Union* (2002), all of which have been translated into numerous European and Asian languages. He is currently completing a book on Enlightenment and Cosmopolitanism.

RONNIE PO-CHIA HSIA, Edwin Earle Sparks Professor of History at Pennsylvania State University, was elected in 2000 to the Academia Sinica (Taiwan) and is currently researching the history of Sino-European relations from the sixteenth to the eighteenth centuries. His books include *The World of Catholic Renewal 1540–1770* (1998) and recently he edited the *Blackwell Companion to the Reformation World* (2004).

H. A. SHAPIRO is the W. H. Collins Vickers Professor of Archaeology in the Department of Classics, The Johns Hopkins University. A scholar of Greek art and archaeology, he is the author of *Art and Cult under the Tyrants in Athens* (1989) and the editor, most recently, of the *Cambridge Companion to Archaic Greece*.

JOSEPH ZIEGLER is Senior Lecturer at the Department of General History, University of Haifa. He is the author of *Medicine and Religion c. 1300: The Case of Arnau de Vilanova* (1998). He is currently studying the rise of physiognomic thought *c.*1200–*c.*1500.

Acknowledgements

'Racism in Western Civilization before 1700' was the title of the Howard Gilman International Conference held at Tel Aviv University on 13–15 December 2005. The present collection of essays is based mostly on the lectures which were delivered during those three days. In the organization of the conference and in the preparation of this volume we incurred many debts of gratitude to participants, sponsors, and to persons who assisted us in various ways.

First and foremost we are very grateful to the distinguished scholars, from Israel, Europe and the USA, who made the effort to come to Tel Aviv and to contribute knowledge and new insights to the discussion on the origins of racism in the West. Some of them, for different reasons, chose not to submit an article for publication, and thus we should like to take this opportunity to thank them here for their active participation and valuable contribution: Joseph C. Miller from the University of Virginia, Mechal Sobel from the University of Haifa, Paula Fredriksen from Boston University, as well as Gideon Bohak and Ehud Toledano from Tel Aviv University. We are also most grateful to David Nirenberg, who had been unable to attend the conference yet agreed to offer us the important essay included in this volume. In addition we wish to express our thanks to our colleagues who served as chairpersons of the conference sessions and offered many comments and valuable insights of their own: Shulamit Shahar, Gadi Algazi, Ron Barkai, Maurice Kriegel, Irad Malkin, Margalit Finkelberg and Ora Limor. The good will and efficient organizational skills of Ms. Ronit Spiegel, Head of the President's Office, and of Ms. Ayelet Triest, were major components in ensuring the success of the conference.

The generous financial support of the Howard Gilman Foundation, allocated to us by the then President of Tel Aviv University, Prof. Itamar Rabinovich, and the additional funds granted by the Dean of the Lester and Sally Entin Faculty of Humanities, Prof. Shlomo Biderman, by Mrs. Beverley and Dr. Raymond Sackler, by the Tel Aviv University School of History, as well as by the Fred W. Lessing Institute of European

Civilization, the S. Daniel Abraham Center for International and Regional Studies, the Morris E. Curiel Institute for European Studies, the Goldstein-Goren Diaspora Research Center, and the Stephen Roth Institute for the Study of Contemporary Antisemitism and Racism, made the conference possible and also helped with financing some of the costs of the present volume.

Finally, we should like to thank warmly Mr. Michael Watson and the editorial staff of Cambridge University Press, whose encouragement and meticulous work on the texts were invaluable.

1   Introduction

Benjamin Isaac, Joseph Ziegler and
Miriam Eliav-Feldon

Preliminary remarks

Racism is condemned in our times on moral and scientific grounds and in the twenty-first century there is no major movement anywhere that openly describes itself as racist. That certainly was not true for the first half of the twentieth century when racism was a central tenet in the ideology of major and ruling movements in many countries to the extent that racism itself was sometimes regarded as an inborn characteristic protecting the better races from contamination.[1] It lost its legitimacy not only because of the excesses to which it led, but, no less importantly, because it was associated with the cause of the losers in world history: Nazism, colonialism, apartheid, and the heritage of slavery. 'Racist', like 'fascist' and 'Nazi', is commonly used as a random pejorative – particularly convenient, because it places the target of the invective on the defensive, requiring her or him to prove that s/he is not a racist, fascist or Nazi. While racism certainly has not disappeared, it operates nowadays mostly in disguise and under different names. Before its demise as an officially enforced policy, however, it was a clearly defined ideology, based on elaborate theories and a pseudo-scientific apparatus that often resulted in precisely formulated legislation. In its fully developed form therefore it was a combination of group hatred and an extensive mechanism justifying such hatred as rational and based on an objective reality. Historically and as a phenomenon in social relations, the term 'racist' is to be distinguished from ethnic and cultural stereotypes and prejudice. It is more than an attitude or a set of attitudes; it is an ideology which claims to be based on scientific truth. History shows

---

[1] Sir Arthur Keith, *Ethnos or the Problem of Race Considered from a New Point of View* (London: K. Paul, Trench, Trubner & Co., Ltd, 1931), pp. 72–4: 'Race prejudice is inborn; it is part of the evolutionary machinery which safeguards the purity of a race. Human prejudices have usually a biological significance.' Thus not just race, but even racism is part of a grand natural scheme leading towards the improvement of man. It is the ultimate argument of the racist: prejudice is a natural protective mechanism. Keith, Rector of Aberdeen University, also regarded war as a natural, inborn mechanism to further the means and opportunities of life.

that it was a distinct phenomenon that could lead, and in some cases has led to, *sui generis* forms of discrimination and persecution. Racism, including its development over time, must therefore be studied as a separate phenomenon, distinguished clearly from other forms of hostility.

The most obvious characteristic of racism is the attempt to rationalize the irrational – and this is where it differs from other forms of group prejudice. Rudiments of racist thinking continue to exist in western bureaucracies without many people noticing. A traveller may encounter a questionnaire in which s/he is asked to declare 'race', a concept few serious contemporary biologists regard as having any validity. One of the possible answers may be 'Caucasian', a term widely used to indicate people with a light skin. Yet nobody nowadays attaches the slightest scientific value to it, for it was introduced by chauvinist eighteenth-century scholars who maintained that only people of so-called 'Caucasian stock' were truly beautiful.[2] Those who today describe themselves as Caucasian think they mean no more by this term than that they have a light skin. Yet it is a remnant of a pseudo-scientific edifice, more than two centuries old, which divided humanity into superior and inferior categories on the basis of physical characteristics, the best of them presumably originating in the Caucasus. All this is not to deny the social reality of social groups, some of them distinguished by skin colour.

The difficulty of studying the history of racism is compounded by profound differences in the perception of the phenomenon, determined as they are by specific historical experiences and social realities. Racism in the United States is associated with groups that are physically different. Skin colour is an essential aspect and slavery is a crucial element in the history of the relationship. In Europe the targets of racism were minorities that were not physically distinguishable from other groups of the population. They were victims of discrimination and persecution, but were not usually exploited as slaves. Thus, in the US physical characteristics are usually regarded as an essential feature of racism, while in western Europe they are not. In the US those who were discriminated against usually looked different from the discriminators; in Europe they were mostly indistinguishable and hence, in some periods, were made to wear special clothes or markings. An important result of this distinction is that in Europe the concept 'race' is no longer accepted as a valid subdivision of mankind. However, in the US 'race' is a term widely used to distinguish

---

[2] Christoph Meiners, *Grundriss der Geschichte der Menschheit* (Lemgo: Meyer, 1785), p. 43; Johann Friedrich Blumenbach, *Über die natürlichen Verschiedenheiten im Menschengeschlecht* (Leipzig: Breitkopf und Härtel, 1798), pp. 135–7. See Benjamin Isaac, *The Invention of Racism in Classical Antiquity* (Princeton, NJ: Princeton University Press), pp. 105–6.

population groups such as African Americans, Native Americans, etc. Physical differences, notably skin colour, are an essential part of the distinction. In twentieth-century Europe the Jews were major victims of racist persecution although they were not physically different from the rest of the population; in the US anti-Semitism exists, but the Jews are not regarded as a separate race.

Another difficulty in gaining an understanding of racism and its history is the disparity of the various disciplines and conceptual tools involved in the analysis of the subject. One frequently feels that the biologists, philosophers, sociologists, literary critics and various kinds of historians writing about race and racism have little in common apart from a basic disapproval of discrimination. What one group of scholars regards as a significant advance in understanding is regarded by another as entirely irrelevant. The shelves full of thematic volumes of essays, many of them cited in the notes to this introduction and elsewhere in this book, show to what extent the field is dominated by groups (not to say 'networks') of scholars representing specific disciplines or approaches who share a common perspective even if they disagree on specifics.

Given these differences in outlook it is not easy to find common ground for those who want to study the historical development of racism, for there is no consensus on what racism is or whether races exist at all. Since the subject arouses strong emotions and touches on acute sensitivities, it is also especially hard to maintain the level of dispassionate argument appropriate in an academic exchange. Those incapable of doing so sometimes attempt to de-legitimize opinions contrary to their own, for instance by dismissing as racist views of racism they do not share. This may happen even in academic exchange.[3]

The present book proceeds from a number of general premises, the first of them being that it is worth studying the history of racism. This may not be obvious to all. A distinguished historian of antiquity has asked: '*is* racism, as opposed to other ills such as economic imperialism or religious fanaticism (of several different brands), really the most urgent moral and social issue in the contemporary world?'[4] The first answer to this question

---

[3] E.g. Michael Lambert, 'Review of B. Isaac, *The Invention of Racism in Classical Antiquity*', *Classical Review* 55 (2005), 658–62, at 661; Shelley P. Haley, 'Review of B. Isaac, *The Invention of Racism in Classical Antiquity*', *American Journal of Philology* 126 (2005), 451–4, at 452. As already observed, 'racist' is now often used as a convenient pejorative.

[4] Fergus Millar, 'Review Article: The Invention of Racism in Antiquity', *The International History Review* 27 (2005), 85–99, at 86. Similarly, Joseph Geiger, *Zion* 70 (2005), 553–8 (Heb.), at 558, argues that there is no justification for the study of racism in itself, since there are also non-racist forms of discrimination and persecution. By the same token one could argue that there is no point in studying lung cancer since people also die of diabetes and cardio-vascular diseases.

is that, being historians, we are studying the history of a significant phenomenon in social history without claiming that it is *the most urgent* issue in the contemporary world. We may note also that other studies have been published on the same general theme without a defence of the relevance of the question.[5] The second answer is that, as already noted, racism may be regarded as illegitimate in our times, but has by no means disappeared. It occurs under different names and in different guises. It is our contention that this variability has been one of the characteristics of the phenomenon through the ages and it is precisely this point that, we hope, will be elucidated in the present work through the perspective of its development over a long period.

The second assumption is that it is intellectually sound and morally justified to study racism as a topic in the history of ideas; in other words, to study its conceptual development over time, rather than its practical application or the social relationships which lay at the root of the phenomenon.[6] It has been asked whether racism is an idea or an attitude. It should be regarded as an idea that leads to and justifies certain attitudes. We do not ignore the reality to which it has led through the ages: social and economic discrimination, violent persecution and slavery. It must be kept in mind, however, that other forms of prejudice and group hatred have led to similar practices. To put it bluntly, discrimination, genocide and slavery have never been the exclusive prerogative of racists. Of course they have been an essential ingredient of racism, but that does not make it futile to clarify the specific conceptual nature of racism and trace it over time.

Our third assumption is that racism essentially is a form of rationalization and systematization of the irrational, an attempt to justify prejudice and discrimination through an apparently rational analysis of presumed empirical facts. While group prejudice in general has been known at all times and by all peoples everywhere, the attempt to legitimize it by rational and systematic analysis is not universal. It developed in the West, in Europe and the Americas, even if it spread and made its adherents and victims elsewhere over time. Conflicting assertions occur frequently: either it is claimed that group prejudices have been rationalized always and

---

[5] E.g. Thomas F. Gossett, *Race: the History of an Idea in America* (Dallas: Southern Methodist University Press, 1963); Imanuel Geiss, *Geschichte des Rassismus* (Frankfurt am Main: Suhrkamp, 1988); Albert Memmi, *Le racisme. Description, définitions, traitement*, second edition (Paris: Gallimard, 1994); Christian Delacampagne, *L'invention du racisme: Antiquité et Moyen Age* (Paris: Fayard, 1983); Christian Delacampagne, *Une histoire du racisme. Des origines à nos jours* (Paris: Le livre de poche: France-Culture, 2000); George M. Fredrickson, *Racism: A Short History* (Princeton, NJ: Princeton University Press, 2002).

[6] Naomi Zack, *Philosophy of Science and Race* (New York and London: Routledge, 2002) for the modern period from Hume and Kant onwards.

everywhere in a form resembling that which they acquired in nineteenth-century Europe, or, alternatively, it is maintained that racism is a phenomenon of the past few centuries, connected with colonialism. We disagree with both ideas. Even if Europeans applied it elsewhere and even if it was taken over by non-Europeans in recent times, we claim that the origins of racism, as a form of rationalized group prejudice subject to systematic thinking, are to be sought in the West, as the title of this book indicates.

One often encounters a vague sense that racism is basically the same as ethnic prejudice and discrimination, but in a more malicious and serious form. We regard this as an erroneous view: there are mild or even seemingly kind manifestations of racism while the vilest acts have been perpetrated in ethnic and religious conflicts where racism did not play a role. It may be said that racism has led to the most widespread systems of discrimination and persecution in history, but it will not clarify our understanding of these topics if we assume that racism is merely a more virulent form of discrimination in general or that it is somehow worse for the victims than other forms of prejudice. The present book is based on the assumption that racism is to be distinguished conceptually from other forms of collective discrimination. Thus religious persecution need not be associated with any form of race hatred, to mention one obvious form of non-racist group conflict. Nobody doubts the importance of religion in the struggle between the Jews and the Seleucids in the Hellenistic period or between Protestants and Catholics in the sixteenth and seventeenth centuries, whatever political and social tensions were also part of these conflicts. Ethnic hostility can be fierce, but it will not be conducive to clarity if we claim that racist hatred and conflict between ethnic groups are one and the same. The Spartans kept their neighbours, the Messenians, in perpetual collective submission and categorized them as 'between free men and (chattel) *douloi*'.[7] The helots were treated with notorious brutality and their hatred for the Spartans was commensurate,[8] yet there is no suggestion they were ever seen as anything but Greek, nor is there evidence that they were seen as inferior by nature. Any study of racism must be based on a clear idea of what it is, what it is not, and what distinguishes it from other forms of inequality and discrimination. The aim of this

---

[7] Pollux, *Onomasticon* 3.83. The literature is vast. For the helots, see among others Paul A. Cartledge, in Paul A. Cartledge and F. David Harvey (eds), *Crux: Essays in Greek History presented to G. E. M. de Ste Croix on his 75th Birthday* (London: Duckworth, 1985), pp. 16–46; Yvon Garlan, *Slavery in Ancient Greece* (Ithaca, NY: Cornell University Press, 1988); Annalisa Paradiso, *Forme di dipendenza nel mondo greco: Ricerche sul VI. Libro di Ateneo* (Bari: Edipuglia, 1991).
[8] Thucydides 4.80; Xenophon, *Hellenica* 3.3.4–11. One dissatisfied Spartan asserted that the helots even wanted to eat their Spartan masters raw (Xenophon, *Hell.* 3.3.6).

collection of studies, then, is to see whether we can trace a pattern of such forms of rationalized prejudice, originating in the western world, in various periods before 1700.

Ethnic identity and race

For the sake of clarity in discussing racism and its development, it is essential to avoid discussions of identity. The concept of identity is a complex notion: it involves how a person, or a group of persons, thinks about her/himself or themselves; how others see him/her or them; how this affects the person or persons, and so on.[9] It attempts to understand how a person or a group reaches an answer to the question: 'Who am I?' or 'Who are we?' If we want to understand the history of racism we must concentrate on the question of how one group saw another.[10]

Also, we discuss *racism*, not race. As already noted, while European society including its academics did not consider 'race' a respectable concept after World War II, the term never died out in the US and is still used there widely. To cite a few examples: 'To argue that the concept of race is badly abused and exaggerated does not, of course, alter the fact that some racial differences exist. Scientific research is backward in telling us precisely what they are.'[11] Another work goes even further: 'Whereas racial

[9] David Joël de Levita, *The Concept of Identity* (Paris and The Hague: Mouton & Co., 1965), continues the seminal study of Erik H. Erikson, *Childhood and Society* (New York: Norton, 1950).

[10] Emma Dench, *Romulus' Asylum: Roman Identities from the Age of Alexander to the Age of Hadrian* (Oxford: Oxford University Press, 2005), ch. 4, 'Flesh and Blood', pp. 222–97, discussing ideas of blood and descent, proceeds from the opposite assumption and considers all these topics: how Romans saw themselves and their relationship with other Italian peoples, how Greeks saw them through the ages, how Romans saw others, the meanings they attached to descent and culture, the way in which they saw the body, physiognomy, abnormal appearances, physical transformation and modern interpretations of all this. In passing the chapter discusses the Athenian views of their pure lineage (also in ch. 2) and much more. It is hard to distill any clear-cut conclusions from the text, but her point seems to be that '"culture" and physiognomy, or "culture" and descent are by no means universally treated as mutually exclusive categories in ancient explanations and judgments of human difference' (p. 224). Thus she denies that modern notions of race are applicable in Roman thinking (p. 280). These are answers to questions which we are not asking in the present volume. A general account of integration and discrimination in Greece and Rome has recently been published by Fik Meijer, *Vreemd volk, Integratie en discriminatie in de Griekse en Romeinse wereld* (Amsterdam: Athenaeum-Polak & van Gennep, 2007).

[11] Gordon W. Allport, *The Nature of Prejudice* (1954, repr. Reading, MA: Addison-Wesley, 1979), pp. 110–11. In the US much academic work concentrates on the extent to which races are objective facts, while the two main opposing groups are called objectivists or essentialists and constructionists or constructivists. See e.g. Leonard Harris (ed.), *Racism* (Amherst, NY: Humanity Books, 1999), introduction.

groups are distinguished by socially selected physical traits, ethnic groups are distinguished by socially selected cultural traits ... It is only when social and cultural attributes are associated with physical features that the concept "racial" and hence that of racial groups takes on special significance.'[12] The existence of both ethnic and racial groups is taken for granted in this approach and the mix of social, cultural and physical features results in serious confusion.[13]

Recent developments in genetics have revived the discussion of whether race exists at all. It is not the aim of this volume to contribute to this debate and none of its contributors are taking part in it. Recent publications are mostly cautious in their conclusions.[14] The subject is highly charged and attracts lively attention in the news media.[15] There is, however, encouraging resistance to this tendency.[16] 'There is no conceptual basis for race

[12] William J. Wilson, *Power, Racism, and Privilege: Race Relations in Theoretical and Sociohistorical Perspectives* (New York: Macmillan, 1973), p. 6.

[13] Denise K. Buell, *Why this New Race: Ethnic Reasoning in Early Christianity* (New York: Columbia University Press, 2005), pp. 13–21, uses the term intentionally and purposely employs both race and ethnicity interchangeably in her analysis of early Christian attitudes. She gives her reasons with copious references. The terminology in Buell's work is therefore quite different from that in the present book, but the general aims and approach are related and even similar, although the focus is on religion in particular which is central in only some of the papers here.

[14] See references in Isaac, *The Invention of Racism*, pp. 30–3. A work that early on denied the validity of the concept of race, and thus its applicability to the Jews, is Karl Kautsky, *Rasse und Judentum* (first edition: Stuttgart: J. H. W. Dietz, 1914; second edition: 1921); English translation: *Are the Jews a Race?* (London: Jonathan Cape, 1926).

The anti-racist UNESCO statement on the nature of race and racial differences of 1950 still assumes the existence of races in some form. See *The Race Concept: Results of an Inquiry* (No authors, Westport, CT, 1952, copyright: Paris, UNESCO), p. 99. For more recent discussions: Michael J. Bamstead and Steve E. Oleson, 'Do races exist?' *Scientific American*, December, 2003: their answer is '"no" if races are defined as genetically discrete groups, but researchers can use some genetic information to group individuals into clusters with medical relevance'; see further the special issue of *Nature Genetics* 36 (2004) with at least seven useful articles. Particularly helpful is Charles N. Rotimi, 'Are medical and nonmedical uses of large-scale genomic markers conflating genetics and "race?"' (43–7). See now Zack, *Philosophy of Science and Race*, p. 7: 'The case for the scientific nonexistence of biological race is straightforward and consistent with (accepted) scientific cases for the nonexistence of many other things.'

[15] For instance, an editorial in the *New York Times* of July 30, 2005: 'Debunking the concept of "race"'; and an article in *The Economist* of April 15– 21, 2006, 79–80: 'Race and medicine, Not a black and white question'. Note also the review article by the Race, Ethnicity, and Genetics Working Group, 'The Use of Racial, Ethnic, and Ancestral Categories in Human Genetics Research', *American Journal of Human Genetics*, 77(4) (October 2005), 519–32.

[16] For instance, Joseph L. Graves, *The Emperor's New Clothes: Biological Theories of Race at the Millennium* (New Brunswick, NJ: Rutgers University Press, 2001); *The Race Myth: Why We Pretend Race Exists in America* (New York: Dutton, 2004); Charles Hirschman, 'The Origins and Demise of the Concept of Race', *Population and Development Review* 30(2)

except racism.'[17] We are satisfied quoting the anonymous author of a brief article: 'The process of using genetics to define "race" is like slicing soup. You can cut where you want, but the soup stays mixed.'[18]

Another approach, now widely accepted in the US, redefines race as a social reality in contemporary society. Thus it is denied that race, defined as a biological concept, reflects reality, but it is claimed that it can profitably be used as a social concept.[19] A recent study of the history of modern racism states:

> Race [i.e. racist] science, although undergoing many changes in the course of its history, nevertheless is best understood not in terms of changing stages, but in terms of an underlying continuity ... To a large extent, the history of racial science is a history of accommodations of the sciences to the demands of deeply held convictions about the 'naturalness' of the inequalities between human races.[20]

This is a radically different manner of justifying prejudice and it is therefore useful to investigate whether all or only some stages of this development served to justify far-going persecution and oppression.

Racism and the West

Some critics claim that an historical study of racism should not be centred exclusively on western, European society, ignoring Turkish, Chinese,

---

(2004), 385–421. Hirschman discusses the current confusion, mostly in the US, over the meaning of race between a biological concept which is untenable and a social category for which there is no logical basis. The term continues to be used, even if there is no longer a theory to justify this. See now: Charles Loring Brace, *'Race' is a Four-Letter Word: The Genesis of the Concept* (New York: Oxford University Press, 2005, inaccessible to us).

[17] Hirschman, 'Origins and Demise', 401.

[18] Anonymous, 'Slicing Soup', *Nature Biotechnology* 20 (2002), 637. Cf. Pat Shipman, *The Evolution of Racism: Human Differences and the Use and Abuse of Science* (New York: Simon & Schuster, 1994): 'drawing a line around an ephemeral entity like a human race is an exercise in futility and idiocy.' See also: Kwame Anthony Appiah, 'Why There Are No Races' in Harris (ed.), *Racism*, 267–77. For an early and authoritative, critical discussion: Julian S. Huxley and A. C. Haddon, *We Europeans: A Survey of 'Racial' Problems* (New York and London: Harper, 1936), introduction and p. 215: '[the concept of] race turns out to be a pseudo-scientific rather than a scientific term.' The works of Robert Miles, published since the 1980s, also argue that the subject to be studied is racism, not race. See his *Racism after 'race relations'* (London and New York: Routledge, 1993), ch. 1 and 'Apropos the Idea of "Race" ... Again', in: Les Back and John Solomos (eds.), *Theories of Race and Racism: A Reader* (London and New York: Routledge, 2000), pp. 125–43. See now: Robert Miles and Malcolm Brown, *Racism*, second edition (London and New York: Routledge, 2003) with a new Introduction.

[19] Michael Omi and Howard Winant, *Racial Formation in the United States: From the 1960s to the 1980s* (New York: Routledge & Kegan Paul, 1986; second edition New York: Routledge, 1994). See especially the Introduction, pp. 1–6 and the definition, pp. 60–5.

[20] Nancy Stepan, *The Idea of Race in Science: Great Britain 1800–1960* (Hamden, CT: Archon Books, 1982), p. xx.

Japanese, Hindu and African societies and their prejudices.[21] Fredrickson gives three reasons why he concentrates on racism in Europe and its colonial extensions, and two of them apply to this volume as well: 'The varieties of racism that developed in the West had greater impact on world history than any functional equivalent that we might detect in another era or part of the world.' And: 'the logic of racism was fully worked out, elaborately implemented and carried to its ultimate extremes in the West'.[22] We furthermore assert that the opinion that racism needs to be discussed also in respect of non-western cultures rests on a confusion of racism and other forms of prejudice. The mythology and sagas of numerous peoples contain stories about their own separateness and superiority. However, prejudice expressed as myth is radically different from prejudice elevated to the level of scientific truth, even though both are expressions of chauvinism and group prejudice. We do not assume that prejudice and bigotry were invented in the West; we claim rather that the specific form of rationalizing these prejudices and attempting to base them on systematic, abstract thought was developed in antiquity and taken over in early modern Europe. Racism, the nineteenth- and twentieth-century ideology familiar to us, developed in Europe, not in China, Japan or India. It is generally accepted that Greek civilization was the first to raise abstract, systematic thought to a level that we now recognize as approaching our own.[23] They were the first to develop abstract concepts in their thinking about nature and to systematize those ideas. It is therefore worth considering whether the Greeks not only pioneered attempts to think systematically about concepts such as political systems and freedom, but also made the first effort to find a rational and systematic basis for their own sense of superiority and their claim that others were inferior. In other words, they subjected their prejudices to systematic analysis, looked for a firm basis for them in nature and sought to justify them at a rational level.

The subject of this study is precisely the conceptual mechanisms that the Ancient Greeks developed towards this purpose and that were taken over with alacrity by later thinkers. Our aim is not to write the history of injustice all over the world, or of prejudice in world history. It is to trace

---

[21] Millar, 'Invention of Racism', 86–7; Lambert, 'Review of B. Issac', 660; Denise McCoskey, 'Naming the Fault in Question: Theorizing Racism among the Greeks and Romans,' *International Journal of the Classical Tradition* 13.2 (2006), 265. Ronnie Po-chia Hsia, in his contribution to this book, p. 265, clearly states that in ancient China it was language, culture and lifestyle that mattered, all of them features that could be changed and adapted and are therefore not to be regarded as racism.

[22] Fredrickson, *Racism*, pp. 6, 11. Fredrickson assumes that racism 'did not infect Europe itself prior to the period between the late mediaeval and early modern periods'.

[23] Henri Frankfort *et al.*, *Before Philosophy: the Intellectual Adventure of Ancient Man* (Chicago: University of Chicago Press, 1946).

the development in Europe and its colonies of a particular form of prejudice, characteristic of western culture, namely racism. If after all a similar pattern remains to be discovered in China or in India or anywhere else in the non-western world before the modern period, that is a separate and independent issue and for others to describe. However, the schemas and specific manifestations of racism represent a form of rationalization that was unknown and could not have existed before the Greeks developed those forms of abstract and systematic thinking which we usually call philosophy. In this sense we still believe racism originated in the West, for nothing comparable existed in ancient Egypt, Babylonia or China, all societies saturated with prejudices and chauvinism.

Definition

It is essential to be both precise and flexible in the definition of racism. Any definition we use should exclude forms of prejudice and persecution that are not strictly racist, such as discrimination on a religious or social basis, but it should include any systematic attempt to rationalize the division of human beings into groups based on presumed inborn physical and other characteristics. This means we would exclude the expulsion of the Jews from Spain, but include even positive statements claiming, for instance, that the French are born cooks. The former was a form of religious persecution; the latter is an innocuous form of racism.

Albert Memmi defines racism as follows: 'Racism is the valuation, generalized and definitive, of differences, real or imaginary, to the advantage of the accuser and the disadvantage of his victim, in order to justify privilege or aggression.'[24]

The merit of Memmi's definition is the absence of an insistence that the differences should be biological. As he remarks: 'The difference is real or imaginary. If there is no difference the racist invents it; if it exists he interprets it to his advantage ... The racist can utilize a real feature, biological, psychological, cultural or social: the colour of the skin of a Black or the cultural tradition of the Jews.'[25] Memmi describes the essential features of racism as follows:

---

[24] Albert Memmi, 'Le racisme est la valorisation, généralisée et définitive, de différences, réelles ou imaginaires, au profit de l'accusateur et au détriment de sa victime, afin de légitimer une aggression ou un privilège.' *Le Racisme* (revised edn Paris: Gallimard, 1994), p. 193; this was adopted by the *Encyclopaedia universalis* and, in modified form, by UNESCO. In an earlier publication, 'Essai de définition du racisme', *La Nef* 19–20 (1964), 41–7, Memmi still refers to *biological* differences.

[25] Memmi, *Le Racisme*, p. 184.

(1) the differences between groups may be real or imaginary;

(2) they are assigned values;

(3) they are applied to all members of a given group;

(4) they are held to be constant and unchanging;

(5) It entails a justification of the accuser/aggressor: 'By an accurate or a falsified characterization of the victim, the accuser attempts to explain and to *justify* his attitude and his behaviour toward him.'[26]

Isaac prefers the following definition: 'An attitude towards individuals and groups of peoples which posits a direct and linear connection between physical and mental qualities. It therefore attributes to those individuals and groups of peoples collective traits, physical, mental and moral, which are constant and unalterable by human will, because they are caused by hereditary factors or external influences, such as climate or geography.'[27]

It has been claimed that a proper definition of racism necessarily includes a reference to oppression and to 'irrational and usually violent hostility directed at individuals or groups, who typically become victims of the dominant group'.[28] It goes without saying that this is often an aspect of racism, but it is not a necessary aspect. If individuals, belonging to a tiny minority, claim – as often happened in history – that those belonging to the majority are inferior by nature, that is still racism even though the minority does not persecute the despised majority. Equally, there are many forms of persecution that have nothing to do with racism, as we have noted above.

Racism must be defined sufficiently broadly to cover different manifestations over time, and must be sufficiently sharp not to include a rag-bag of forms of discrimination or chauvinism.[29] It should include ideas, whether or not these are applied in practice, and it should exclude non-racist hatred of groups, based on ethnic and religious prejudice even if this hatred resulted in active discrimination and persecution.[30] Our definition

---

[26] Albert Memmi, *Dominated Man: Notes towards a Portrait* (New York: Orion Press, 1968), pp. 187–95.

[27] Isaac, *The Invention of Racism*, p. 23.

[28] James H. Dee, *Bryn Mawr Classical Review*, 'Review of B. Isaac, *The Invention of Racism in Classical Antiquity*', 49 (June 2004). Dee gives an example of what he regards as the correct approach, represented by Ian Haney López, *New York Times* op.-ed., May 22, 2004. In a discussion of two Supreme Court decisions related to discrimination, the question is asked under what circumstances some groups deserve constitutional protection. The answer given in this case, to James Dee's satisfaction, was: when groups suffer subordination.

[29] Dick Howard, 'The Roots of Racism. Review of "The Invention of Racism in Classical Antiquity"', *The Journal of Blacks in Higher Education* 46 (Winter 2004/2005), 126–8, at 127: 'This summary definition of racism … avoids the twin dangers of overextension and hyper specificity. Racism subsumes the individual within the group; it leaves no room for plurality, difference, or escape from one's determination.'

[30] We refrain from using the term 'racialism' which is not helpful for our purposes. It has been defined as follows: '*Racialism* must be distinguished from *racism*, which adds value

must encompass all mild and even innocuous forms of racism, including those cases where there are 'positive feelings about a group to which common (admirable) characteristics might be attributed and considered unalterable by reason of hereditary or other determinism'. After all, the racists normally ascribe to themselves such positive characteristics. Thus Miles and Brown have argued that 'rather than assent to an ever-broadening concept of racism, it should be more narrowly defined as an ideology if it is to be of serious analytical value'.[31] They further observe: 'the inflation of the concept has resulted in it being used to connote a [too] wide range of practices and processes'. Thirdly, they note that 'there is no necessary logical correlation between cognition and action'.[32] Racism, in other words, can be understood profitably only if it is seen in precise terms as an idea, or set of ideas, and an ideology. In other words, the essential difference between racism and other forms of prejudice and chauvinism is that the former claims that the characteristics of the other are determined by nature while the latter attributes them to custom, social forces or education and the like. The former unlike the latter thus claims that human characteristics are unalterable and passed on from one generation to the next.

Theory and practice

The supposition that it is profitable to study racism as an idea was denied apparently by at least one ancient historian who disagrees with the *Economist* of December 3–9, 2005, p. 84: 'Ideas matter in politics; no one disputes that.' He argued that it was pointless to analyze racism as a set of ideas: 'but if we are going to discover a Roman mood, or as we might better say a set of attitudes, we have to look beyond particular texts and consider the patterns in what people actually did'.[33] Power, it is said here, is an essential component of racism or even *the* essential component. Racism is an instrument in

judgements (mostly negative, but sometimes positive)'; Eduard Machery and Luc Faucher, in Henri Cohen and Claire Lefebvre (eds.), *Categorization in Cognitive Science* (Amsterdam: Elsevier, 2005), p. 2, n. 2.

[31] Miles and Brown, *Racism*, p. 112.   [32] Miles and Brown, *Racism*, p. 103.

[33] William V. Harris, *Times Literary Supplement*, September 10, 2004, p. 9. See also Israel Shatzman, *Historia* 16 (2005), 115–26 (Heb.), at 124. Lambert, 'Review of B. Issac', 658–62 at 660, curiously states that the reality of modern racism is best understood by viewing and discussing the film *Schindler's List*. Schindler's story is fascinating, particularly as told in the novel by Thomas Keneally, *Schindler's Ark*. However, it is salutary to consider that a South African classicist, writing in a British journal, here advises the public on the best way to understand Nazi racism, namely through an American film, based on a novel produced by an Australian author which deals with an altogether exceptional episode in the Nazi persecution of the Jews, an episode, it may be noted, with a happy ending, thanks to the genuinely heroic activities of an Austrian entrepreneur.

the struggle for power and part of a political process. This is a curiously simplistic view, ignoring the fact that racism is found in equal measure among those with and without power.[34] As an approach it fails to explain essential features of racism. To mention just one instance: after World War II anti-Semitism was much stronger in many countries formerly occupied by Germany than before the war. This was most notoriously the case in Poland where Jews continued to be persecuted and killed for years, and also, at a far subtler level, in the Netherlands,[35] despite the fact that the German occupation, which made anti-Semitism a central element in its policies, had been destroyed and discredited. Why this should have been the case is a question still awaiting a satisfactory answer.[36] The least that can be said is that years of racist rule continued to have an impact after the occupier had been defeated.

As already noted, racism is not restricted to majorities in a society. It exists among minorities or can be aimed at foreign peoples. Racist ideas have been used, and are still used, by political bodies and organizations to further their own ends, but this does not mean we are justified in regarding racism as nothing but a tool in the hands of politicians or demagogues.

Interestingly, the opposite suggestion has also been advanced: racism is not a component of power politics, but of anti-politics.[37] The difficulty here is that 'anti-politics' is one of those imprecise terms whose meaning does not emerge from a definition but from the way it is used. After decades of frequent use we read: 'To begin with, we do not even quite know what anti-politics actually is.'[38] It is often used by authors who see

---

[34] The idea goes back to Ruth Benedict, *Race: Science and Politics* (New York: Modern Age Books, 1940), p. 151 and *Race and Racism* (London: Routledge, 1942), pp. 111–27: 'Racism and Class Conflicts'. It is found also among some Marxist authors: Oliver Cromwell Cox, *Caste, Class and Race: A Study in Social Dynamics* (New York: Monthly Review Press, 1970); Etienne Balibar and Immanuel Wallerstein, *Race, Nation, Classe: Les identités ambigues* (Paris: La Découverte, 1988); English translation: *Race, Nation, Class: Ambiguous Identities* (London and New York: Verso, 1991). For discussion: Hubert M. Blalock, *Power and Conflict: Toward a General Theory* (Newbury Park, CA: Sage Publications, 1989).

[35] Poland: Jan T. Gross, *Fear: Anti-Semitism in Poland After Auschwitz: An Essay in Historical Interpretation* (New York: Random House, 2006). For the Netherlands this is sadly illustrated, for instance, by the work by Michal Citroen, *U wordt door niemand verwacht: Nederlandse Joden na kampen en onderduik* (Utrecht: Het Spectrum, 1999).

[36] Former Israeli prime minister Yitzhaq Shamir asserted that 'Poles suck in anti-Semitism with their mother's milk.' That is a racist explanation for racism. Gross argues that Poles were feeling guilty: so implicated were they in the Jewish tragedy, aiding the Germans and expropriating Jewish property. That may not be sufficient as an explanation.

[37] Howard, 'Roots of Racism'.

[38] Andreas Schedler (ed.), *The End of Politics? Explorations into Modern Antipolitics* (Basingstoke: Macmillan; New York: St. Martin's Press, 1997), p. 1.

no need to define it at all.[39] One political thinker, in his introduction to a collection of papers on anti-politics, describes anti-political ideologies as a rejection of at least one of four basic premises of politics. These are, in his opinion, the acceptance by the members of a community of their mutual interdependence and of their internal differences; the ability to act in concert; and their preparedness to accept authoritative decision.[40] If racism is to be connected with anti-politics, this has to refer to the fact that racism denies to groups of people (for example slaves, but also women and resident foreigners) participation in political life.[41]

A historical study

No two social conflicts are exactly the same and there would be little point in trying to write a history of racist conflict purely as a social phenomenon. However, in this book we deal with the history of ideologies, not with social structure. The supposition that the prejudices and ideas of one period influence those of another is not fanciful and cannot be dismissed as a form of essentialist naivety. A work about eighteenth-century British culture states as a matter of course: 'The authority of Greek and Roman texts should not be underestimated in providing ruling-class men, in particular, with the distinction between themselves and barbarians.'[42] The same work observes: 'most histories of race [sc. racism] have not adequately acknowledged the power of residual proto-racial [sc. proto-racist] ideologies, or older conceptions of national and religious difference that persisted despite the fact that the socio-economic conditions which gave birth to them changed'. The author calls this 'the sedimentation of racial [sc. racist] ideology'.[43] It is this approach which underlies, for instance, the work of Léon Poliakov.[44]

Our aim in producing the present work is to offer a number of selected studies that discuss the presence or absence of racist ideas and ideology in

---

[39] Trevor Smith, *Anti-Politics: Consensus, Reform and Protest in Britain* (London: C. Knight for the Acton Society Trust, 1972), does not trouble to define the term although it appears in the title of his book.
[40] Schedler (ed.), *The End of Politics?*, pp. 2–3.
[41] Howard, 'Roots of Racism', 128.
[42] Roxann Wheeler, *The Complexion of Race: Categories of Difference in Eighteenth-Century British Culture* (Philadelphia: University of Pennsylvania Press, 2000), p. 15.
[43] Wheeler, *The Complexion of Race*, p. 9. See, for a rather similar observation, Imanuel Geiss, *Geschichte des Rassismus* (Frankfurt am Main: Suhrkamp, 1988), pp. 49 and 79.
[44] Léon Poliakov, *Le mythe aryen: essai sur les sources du racisme et des nationalismes* (Paris: Calmann-Lévy, 1971), translated as *The Aryan Myth* (New York: Basic Books, 1974) and his four-volume *Histoire de l'anti-sémitisme* (Paris: Calmann-Lévy, 1955–77; English trans.: Philadelphia: University of Pennsylvania Press, 2003).

the West from classical antiquity till 1700. It is by no means our intention or ambition to provide a systematic history of the subject, but rather to stimulate constructive consideration of the issue. We have chosen a number of topics that we considered to be of central importance for the matter at hand. Each of the authors has her or his views on the subject and there was no attempt to reach a common conclusion, but merely to consider a broad common theme. The aim was, first of all, to stimulate the discussion concerning the existence of racism and development of racist ideas and ideology in various forms before its broadly acknowledged appearance in the modern period.

Topics according to periods

Antiquity

While Isaac responds to some of the reactions to his own book on the subject the three other historians of antiquity address fields that were not treated in Isaac's work: attitudes towards blacks (Goldenberg), early Christianity (Buell) and the evidence from images (Shapiro).

Shapiro discusses a specific topic: the image of the Persians in Greek visual arts. He concludes that this reflects a different outlook from the one found in the contemporary Greek literature. He recognizes that there is a form of racism to be found in Athenian public oratory of the fourth century, but that is not his subject. His point is that the imagery on household objects, produced for the private market in Greece, belongs to a sphere different from that of the public oratory, and conveys another attitude towards Persians and eastern peoples. While the public oratory represents ideology, the imagery he analyzes depicts an invented world of exotic foreigners. Shapiro's Persians were for the Greeks the major foreign power in the fifth and fourth centuries, the enemy in the wars of the early fifth century and the later fourth. As such they appear in the literature. The point of Shapiro's paper is that, at another level, they come across as a largely imaginary people, who were no more 'real' or historical than the Amazons or the Trojans to whom the Persians are most often likened. Thus a hostile ideological view could co-exist with a world of fantasy.

Like Shapiro, Goldenberg concentrates on a specific subject within the realm of attitudes towards foreigners in the classical world, namely black Africans. He considers attitudes towards blacks in the classical world, in ancient Jewish literature and Early Christian texts. Similar to Shapiro's Persians in Greek eyes, the blacks belonged in Greek and Roman views, according to Goldenberg, more to a world of fantasy than to one of confrontation with actual people. The Greek, Roman, Jewish and Early

Christian position was not genuinely racist, he argues, because black was a metaphor, not associated with real people with an actually dark skin. Black people, he says, became real, rather than abstract beings, only in Christian literature from Origen onwards. As observed by Goldenberg, in classical Greece and Rome black people probably were not strongly represented and therefore less noticed as a real minority and more as a curious, but rare phenomenon. Whatever their numbers in the Greek and Roman world, there never was a part of the Roman Empire that was inhabited exclusively or even primarily by black people, nor was there any such people situated in the immediate sphere of influence of the Empire. Yet Goldenberg argues that the Christian literature of the third century and afterwards contained ideas about blacks which influenced the West's later developing racism against black Africans, where it was an aspect of conquest and empire.

Furthermore, argues Goldenberg, in antiquity it was the blacks' physical being, and in particular the skin colour of black people, that was found objectionable, not their customs or what were believed to be their innate characteristics. He agrees that racism existed in Greece and Rome, but claims that attitudes towards black Africans were of a different kind. He reaches this conclusion because he does not recognize any negative associations in the mental sphere that go together with the real and visible physical difference. The latter was regarded as distasteful by various authors – and aesthetic prejudice certainly is a feature of later racism. However, Goldenberg emphasizes that the presumed link between physical and mental characteristics is a prerequisite for genuine racism. Even so he recognizes the prominence of colour symbolism in antiquity: the negative moral value of black versus white. In Greece and Rome black is associated with death and the underworld; it is the colour of ill omen and sin. White, in the poets, is a mark of divinity and beauty. The words for white and black develop connotations of 'lucky' and 'unlucky', 'happy' and 'unhappy'. It is probably a matter of choice whether one wishes to see this as racism or not, when it is applied to people with a dark skin. In any case, however, Goldenberg agrees that racism can be recognized in the Christian position from Origen onwards (*c.* 185–284). Origen, in controversial assertions, consistently and emphatically refers to Ethiopians as living in the dark, i.e. in sin. He was highly influential and his approach became generally accepted in the patristic literature. The Ethiopians, not having received a Christian baptism, are black in spirit and without divine light. In Christianity the abstract evil became real in the form of an identifiable human being, the black African, a statement which Buell also accepts. These ideas then influenced the West's developing racism against black Africans.

Racism as ideology is central to the paper of Buell, who analyzes religious sources that are deeply ideological in nature and develop their notions of ethnicity with a practical aim, namely to make conversion to Christianity possible and, more than that, imperative, with the end result that there is a firm barrier between the converted Christians and the non-believers. We should note that conversion to Christianity and its concomitant change of ethnicity, as in the case of the transmission of acquired characteristics, well represented in Greek and Latin literature, is a one-way process. There is no question of apostasy or conversion of Christians to other religions in the sources cited by Buell. We could also see this in traditional Greek terms: there is a basic contrast between *nomos* and *physis*, between custom and nature. The idea of the transmission of acquired characteristics is a concept to get around this opposition and turn *nomos* into *physis*, or to change unalterable *physis* all the same by changing *nomos*. This is easily applied in the case of Christianity because it focuses on religion, a spiritual phenomenon, rather than physical features.

What Buell does not say in so many words, but is implied by her arguments, is the following: her interpretation of early Christianity has the advantage that it makes it easier to understand why Roman imperial power found it convenient to adopt Christianity as state religion; a religion with claims of universality suited an empire with similar ideological notions, because the Empire, in principle, encompassed all of the inhabited world, even if in practice this ideal always remained unfulfilled. As Buell says: '*Acts* clearly argues that it is through the apostles that God will restore the rule of Israel – but not simply in the earlier geographical territory, but over the entire world.' Conversely – but that is not our topic – Christianity was typically a religion that could spread in an empire and be used as an instrument of empire by its rulers.

The Middle Ages

Is the concept of racism applicable to western societies in the Middle Ages? By using it, are we not importing a modern concept into a medieval reality which we thus gravely distort?[45] The articles in the medieval section of this book should guide us to possible answers to these questions and chart the map for future research into the history of racism in the Middle Ages.

---

[45] Similar questions have already been asked in Peter Biller, 'Black Women in Medieval Scientific Thought', *Micrologus* 13 (2005), 477–92 at 492 and William C. Jordan, 'Why Race?', *The Journal of Medieval and Early Modern Studies* 31 (2001), 165–73.

The issues of race and racism in western medieval societies have recently received the attention of several scholars studying the history of the British Isles in the Middle Ages. Three vignettes could serve to illustrate the problematic question of racism as a category applicable to English society at any time during the Middle Ages, not forgetting Susan Reynolds's words urging us to be cautious when using the term race (invented, as we shall see in Charles de Miramon's paper, in fourteenth-century France and in a non-ethnic context) for medieval nations or people. 'Medieval *gentes* were not races in any sense in which the word can be used without misunderstanding in the late twentieth century', asserts Reynolds, and warns that using the word 'race' in modern historical narratives invites confusion between what people in the past believed about their common descent and history and what we believe about them. The sources do not suggest that physical differences, even where they existed, were as important to them as they are to modern racists. The *gentes*, although they believed in their common descent and culture, were in reality defined primarily by their political allegiances and not by their biological uniqueness.[46]

But how to explain Bede's (d. 735) use of the vernacular name *Bretonnes* instead of the Roman *Britanni*? Alexander Murray in a recent article suggested that this betrayed a 'racial animus' and that Bede may have expressed here contempt towards the Britons as the word 'Yank' might do in modern English towards an American.[47] Bede's further allegation, that the Britons originated in Armorica, on the north-western coast of Gaul, and could thus have been newcomers to Britain, and that they were *barbari* (implying cruelty, arrogance and ignorance), was intended perhaps to justify the Britons' elimination.

The Norman Conquest and the encounter between Normans and English in the eleventh and twelfth centuries was another crucial event in British history raising the issue of racism. A group of foreign people took the country by force and extreme violence, devastated the country-side, slaughtered, exiled or dispossessed almost all of the most powerful pre-Conquest landholders, and took full control of the land and all main

[46] Susan Reynolds, *Kingdoms and Communities in Western Europe 900–1300* (Oxford: Oxford University Press, 1984), p. 255 and 'Our Forefathers? Tribes, Peoples, and Nations in the Historiography of the Age of Migration', in *After Rome's Fall: Narrators and Sources of Early Medieval History. Essays Presented to Walter Goffart*, ed. Alexander Callander Murray (Toronto: University of Toronto Press, 1998), pp. 17–36, at 25–6, 31. Many contributors to the important collection 'Race and Ethnicity in the Middle Ages', ed. Thomas Hahn, *The Journal of Medieval and Early Modern Studies* 31 (2001), 1–173 are less cautious when translating *gens* and its vernacular cognates as 'race'.
[47] Alexander Murray, 'Bede and the Unchosen Race', in *Power and Identity in the Middle Ages: Essays in Memory of Rees Davies*, ed. Huw Pryce and John Watts (Oxford: Oxford University Press, 2007), pp. 52–67.

political and religious institutions. Yet by the end of the twelfth century the bitter hostility between the native English and the invading Normans waned dramatically. Ethnic distinctions had not only broken down, but something more profound had happened: despite Norman victory and the concentration of power and wealth in the hands of the conquerors, English identity triumphed. Analyzing the processes of conquest and assimilation, Hugh Thomas recently pressed the case that essentially a non-racist sentiment is a key variable for understanding the remarkable speed of assimilation of Normans and *Normanitas* into the English and Englishness and the latter's subsequent triumph.[48]

A similar non-racist instinct was characteristic of the Norman conquerors. Pragmatic prejudice leading to discrimination on behalf of the Normans was not ideologically based or founded on deep-seated biases. The Normans did harbour an ethnocentric feeling of cultural superiority to the English, but it was insignificant when compared to the prejudices against the Jews or against the Celts and Slavic people. Thomas stresses the limits to the extent to which medieval thinkers connected descent and identity and the total lack of interest in developing a consistent, systematic theory of assimilation or ethnic distinction based on cultural or genetic inheritance. For medieval people, descent was only one factor to be considered when they thought about ethnicity and culture, and in the particular case of England, ancestry was rarely noted as a factor in the post-Conquest discussions of distinctions between peoples. Thus Goscelin of Saint-Bertin, a pre-conquest immigrant who sympathized with the conquered, wrote of the English daughter of a Danish father and a Lotharingian mother, without any indication that there was anything bizarre or unnatural in the girl's ethnic shift. Lanfranc (*c.* 1010–1089), the first Norman archbishop of Canterbury, born in Pavia and educated in North Italy, was one of many regarded as English, by a manner other than birth. Medieval writers clearly accepted that there was more to ethnicity than ancestry, and they would not automatically link ethnicity and descent. Obviously, broad similarities of the two cultures, particularly in religion, eased the process of assimilation. When it came to others, however, such as Jews, Celts or Slavs, things were somewhat different.

The third episode in the history of the British Isles that has called for the use of the terms 'race' or 'racism' was the violent encounter in the twelfth and thirteenth centuries between the English and the Welsh and Irish. Robert

---

[48] Hugh M. Thomas, *The English and the Normans: Ethnic Hostility, Assimilation, and Identity 1066 – c. 1220* (Oxford: Oxford University Press, 2003), pp. 236–7. For a different reading of this encounter see Thomas Hahn, 'The Difference the Middle Ages Makes: Color and Race before the Modern World', *The Journal of Medieval and Early Modern Studies* 31 (2001), 1–37, at 7–8.

Bartlett's article in the present volume addresses the debate surrounding the nature of this encounter. Was labelling the Irish as fickle (*leves*, i.e. unreliable and governed by emotion rather than by reason), in the statutes of the 1297 Dublin Parliament, or describing Englishmen who resort to Irish fashions as *degeneres* (i.e. those who are degenerate by birth or character), proof of English racist thought?[49] If Gerald of Wales called the Irish a barbarous people, should he be named a racist? There is plenty of evidence that what we might call 'a language of racism' was employed for political purposes at the official level by both sides in medieval Ireland in the thirteenth and fourteenth centuries. For the English *gens* in Ireland, such language was used to bolster its identity and purity and to classify the Irish as an inferior nation, contact with whom might lead to degeneracy. Rees Davies compared Welsh legal texts, which proclaimed that an individual born to Welsh parents on both sides was by definition a gentleman, thus defining membership of a people by purity of blood-descent, with the privileges exempting an Englishman from being convicted in Wales other than by fellow Englishmen 'by birth and by blood' – both, he believed, being part of a general discourse of identity shared at the time by all peoples of the British Isles.[50]

These were encounters between co-religionists belonging to different ethnicities, which were only partially characterized by significant physical distinctions. However, what about encounters with groups of people who did not share in the dominant religion and who were marked by distinctive bodily characteristics (different skin-colour, shape of eyes, noses and lips)? Geraldine Heng asserts that a racializing discourse, positing religion, colour, and bodily difference, emerged in thirteenth-century England and was instrumental in the formation of the English nation. Ideas and behaviours implying the immutability of Jews and Jewishness as well as of Saracens, originating in religious thought and not from biological distinctiveness, could hint at a powerful proto-racist sentiment current at that time.[51] In any case, whether one may impute racism to

[49] James F. Lydon, 'Nation and Race in Medieval Ireland', in Simon Forde, Lesley Johnson and Alan V. Murray (eds.), *Concepts of National Identity in the Middle Ages* (Leeds: School of English, University of Leeds, 1995), pp. 103–24, at 104.

[50] Rees R. Davies, 'The Peoples of Britain and Ireland 1100–1400: 1. Identities', *TRHS* 6th ser. 4 (1994), 1–20, at 6; Lydon, 'Nation and Race', p. 106.

[51] Geraldine Heng, 'The Romance of England: Richard *Coeur de Lion*, Saracens, Jews, and the Politics of Race and Nation', in Jeffrey J. Cohen (ed.), *The Postcolonial Middle Ages* (New York: St. Martin's Press, 2000), pp. 135–71, at 139 and *Empire of Magic: Medieval Romance and the Politics of Cultural Fantasy* (New York: Columbia University Press, 2003), pp. 63–113, at p. 70. Jonathan M. Elukin, 'From Jew to Christian? Conversion and Immutability in Medieval Europe', in James Muldoon (ed.), *Varieties of Religious Conversion in the Middle Ages* (Gainesville: University Press of Florida, 1997), pp. 171–89, at 171, 184.

English medieval society at a certain period or in a certain political context or not, the very use of the concept in historical discourse is valuable because it generates novel insights and debates.

In one of the more famous scenes in Chrétien de Troyes' *The Story of the Grail*, composed in the 1180s, the hero Perceval, who passed five glorious and heroic years of successful combats but never remembered God, meets a group of penitents who reveal to him the secrets of Christianity and the true object of his unfulfilled quest. Perceval is unaware that the day is Good Friday and the penitents tell him in detail the story of the crucifixion. Their story ends with a direct reference to the Jews:

> In their hatred the wicked Jews, who should be killed like dogs, forged their own evil and our great good when they raised Him on the cross. They damned themselves and saved us.[52]

With the spirituality engulfing the scene, such harsh and abusive language directed at the Jews seems grossly offensive, yet it was quite common when depicting other ethnic or religious groups. Christian sources, both literary and pictorial, often referred to Muslims and Mongols as dogs.[53] Marco Polo, for example, refered to the Saracens of Abyssinia as 'these Saracen dogs' and celebrated their massacre 'for it is not fitting that Saracen dogs should lord it over Christians'.[54] Abusive, vulgar, stereotyped utterances about various European realms, regions, settlements and their populations were common in a variety of medieval writings even among Jews depicting Christians as pigs.[55]

But some hundred years after Chrétien, in a quodlibet about Jews from the faculty of arts in Paris, they were treated not *secundum theologiam* but *secundum naturam*.[56] A cold scientific air engulfs their representation. A question about the flow of blood typical of Jewish men leads to a biological explanation: the dominance in them of the melancholic humour.

---

[52] *The Complete Romances of Chrétien de Troyes*, trans. David Staines (Bloomington and Indianapolis: Indiana University Press, 1990), p. 415.

[53] Debra Higgs Strickland, *Saracens, Demons and Jews: Making Monsters in Medieval Art* (Princeton and Oxford: Princeton University Press, 2003), pp. 159–60, 204–6, 223–4; Alexandra Cuffel, *Gendering Disgust in Medieval Religious Polemic* (Notre Dame, IN: University of Notre Dame Press, 2007), pp. 216–20.

[54] Marco Polo, *The Travels*, trans. Roland Latham (London: Penguin, 1958), pp. 306–7.

[55] Len E. Scales, '*Germen Militiae*: War and German Identity in the Later Middle Ages', *Past and Present* 180 (2003), 41–82, at 41–3; Paul Meyvaert, '"Rainaldus est malus scriptor Francigenus" – Voicing National Antipathy in the Middle Ages', *Speculum* 66(4) (1991), 743–63; Cuffel, *Gendering Disgust*, pp. 224–6.

[56] Peter Biller, 'Views of Jews from Paris around 1300: Christian or "Scientific"?', in D. Wood (ed.), *Christianity and Judaism* (Oxford: Blackwell, 1992) (Studies in Church History 29), 188–90, 202–5 and 'A Scientific View of Jews from Paris around 1300', *Micrologus* 9 (2001), 137–68, at 160–1.

Associated with this biological 'fact' were the Jews' diet, their medical practice, their physical appearance, and their psychological and social characteristics. The Jewish body was inherently different from other bodies and the anti-Jewish stereotype was woven into a complex scientific frame. Using Benjamin Isaac's definition of racism as 'an attitude towards individuals and groups of peoples which posits a direct and linear connection between physical and mental qualities', this debate – from a modern perspective – clearly reflected proto-racist attitudes.[57] The co-existence of discussions of Jews suffering a flux of blood and of the superior quality of black women's milk and sex, reinforces the impression that something did happen between 1190 and 1300 to enable a proto-racist shift in Latin Europe. The scientific language of the debate about Jews and black women clearly suggests a specific form of rationalizing prejudices and attempting to base them on systematic, abstract thought (humoral and elemental theories). But are we doing these medieval writers justice by labelling certain of their ideas 'racist', or are we thus projecting onto them our modern experience?

And from the opposite direction: does the similarity between the attitudes which appeared around 1300 to the innumerable examples of proto-racist expressions in antiquity collected by Benjamin Isaac indicate continuity, a clear lineage of ideas? Many of the texts which were the vehicles of proto-racist attitudes among the learned in the classical age were unknown in Latin Christendom until the twelfth century. When they began to re-emerge as part of the translation project and later became assimilated into the academic curricula, these classical proto-racist ideas became available to the European mind once more. Was there any immediate or long-term influence of these texts on attitudes to specific groups within or around Western Christendom? For example, was the deterioration in Christian–Jewish relations from the twelfth century onwards related to the growing exposure of learned and unlearned circles to proto-racist ideas and sentiments? Questions such as these need to be tackled systematically if we are to understand the processes of transmission and reception of proto-racist ideas migrating from the classical pagan world to medieval Christian society.

Indeed, the fact that the early medieval period is hardly mentioned in the articles in this volume suggests that the rediscovery of the classical corpus of biological, medical and environmental texts should be regarded as a watershed. Christianity, with its missionary zeal and the claim of

---

[57] Biller, 'Black Women in Medieval Scientific Thought'. See also T. F. Earle and Kate J. P. Lowe (eds.), *Black Africans in Renaissance Europe* (Cambridge: Cambridge University Press, 2005).

possessing the keys to universal salvation, often thought to be a barrier against virulent racism and racial thought, apparently performed this function successfully until the twelfth century or so. Moreover, the number of encounters with non-Europeans was quite small until the late eleventh century, minimizing the need to cope with otherness. *Circa* 1100, however, Europeans began to meet new ethnic groups, and not only on the battlefield, whether in Southeast Asia or on the streets of Mediterranean cities, in missionary and commercial contexts. It was then that the language describing such foreign groups seemed to change, becoming more biological and stressing the inherent physical and mental characteristics of these peoples. Were these feelings and sentiments hitherto unknown in Europe, or were these records of new encounters revealing sediments of classical proto-racist perceptions?

The rhetorical change coincided with a biological shift that became apparent in western religious thought (philosophical as well as theological). On the basis of the assimilation of Aristotelian biology and Galenic medicine, the human body acquired a central place as the locus of individuality, as a source of significant influence on behavioural patterns, and as a treasure-trove of information to be applied to a series of philosophical and theological questions. In a society which increasingly thought of Christ biologically (with special reference to the condition of his body), how did this shift affect the reception of biological (often proto-racist) ideas about the behaviour of ethnic groups?

Some of the articles in the medieval section of this collection highlight other debates arising from different interpretative strategies adopted by researchers. Scholars of medieval literature have recently come to stress the hegemonic impulse of pre-colonial western Christianity revealed in European travel literature from *circa* 1300 onwards.[58] The view of the harmonious diversity of mankind expressed by John Mandeville has been depicted as an ambivalent approach containing elements of an intellectual system based on the relation of climate to physiology, a connection which could be used to justify the subjugation of other peoples and would be used, eventually, as part of the justification of slavery.[59] Suzanne Akbari maintains that the account of the bodily diversity of mankind in medieval encyclopaedic and travel literature should be regarded as a full-blown discourse of race, which would facilitate and rationalize the exercise of

---

[58] Andrew Fleck, 'Here, There and In Between: Representing Difference in the *Travels* of Sir John Mandeville', *Studies in Philology*, 97 (2000), 379–400, at 390.

[59] Suzanne Conklin Akbari, 'The *diversity of mankind* in The Book of John Mandeville', in Rosamund Allen (ed.), *Eastward Bound: Travels and Travellers 1050–1550* (Manchester: Manchester University Press, 2004), pp. 156–76, at pp. 164–6.

power in the colonial setting. Such discourse included naming and categorizing groups of people in order to specify what was normal and beautiful in contradistinction to what was pathological and ugly. She also
asserts that the medieval categories of bodily difference, yoking together
environmental/climatic theories and heredity, should be regarded as
equivalent to early-modern and Enlightenment definitions of race.
Indeed, Aristotelian notions concerning the role of climate in human
development were applied in the sixteenth century to the subjugation of
the native populations of America – but does this allow us to assume
automatically that these texts were read in the same way in the thirteenth
and fourteenth centuries?

By considering texts other than the romance literature and the travel
narratives (real or imaginary) most often used to underscore the importance
of racism in the medieval West, the articles in the medieval section of this
volume deal with the question of the nature and the importance of classical
heritage in transmitting proto-racism into Latin Christendom. The picture
which emerges is a mixed one: on the one hand, a powerful impact and a
quick reception of key texts and ideas that revived proto-racism in the western
psyche (Biller); on the other hand, a peculiar reading of some scientific texts
in a way that neutralized their proto-racist potential (Ziegler). According to
medieval natural philosophy and medicine, individual and group inborn
characteristics (physical and mental) were liable to change (albeit with great
difficulties), while traits predetermined by astral and environmental influences could always be avoided through the practice of free will.

At the same time, however, the sources reveal the growing importance
of the body and its functions as a primary cause of behaviour and as a
marker of typical group characteristics. This is manifested in the increasingly physiological manner in which ethnic differences were portrayed in
twelfth- and thirteenth-century pictorial sources (Bartlett), in the growing
presence of blood as a major determinant of nobility (Miramon), and in
the almost obsessive preoccupation with black–white coitus in Italy during
the fifteenth and sixteenth centuries (Groebner).

Thus, in many respects the medieval period differs from both antiquity
and the early modern period. It reintroduced to Western Christendom
many texts containing proto-racist ideas; it adopted a material approach to
the human being underlying the direct, causal relationship between bodily
constitution and moral, behavioural and mental condition; but at the
same time it mitigated the proto-racist potential by diluting it with
Christian humanistic approaches. By allowing the transmission and en-
abling the reception of these classical texts among the learned, the medieval period played a crucial role in the revival of proto-racist ideas and
concepts in the pre-modern world.

Robert Bartlett surveys pictorial sources (mainly manuscript illuminations to texts which discuss an ethnic encounter) from the twelfth and
thirteenth centuries and argues that an increasingly racist depiction of
ethnic differences began to emerge in the second half of the twelfth
century. The strategy of illustrating ethnicity relied on a physiological
approach that stressed bodily features such as skin colour, shape of eyes,
size and shape of nose and lips, or on non-physiological bodily markers
such as hair-style, clothes or weapons.[60]

Peter Biller provides a detailed account of the translation, transmission,
and reception of the proto-racist ancient scientific texts into thirteenth-
and fourteenth-century academic circles in the arts and medical faculties.
In particular he stresses the importance of environmental thinking stemming from the Hippocratic *Airs, Waters and Places* as a vehicle of a proto-
racist outlook that affected the European intellectual scene. This outlook
became common knowledge that infiltrated medical, philosophical and
theological discourses. The sheer density of such ideas and texts from the
thirteenth century onwards and the varied contexts in which they
appeared lead Peter Biller to suggest that these new biological and environmental materials were converted into the commonplaces of the minds
and vocabulary of the literate. It seems that students of arts and medicine
were emphatically encouraged to think of the superiority of northern
European bodies, to show an almost obsessive preoccupation with the
black/white physical dichotomy and especially with black female bodies,
and to develop a growing interest in the peculiarities of Jewish bodies.
Through Albertus Magnus's commentary on Aristotle's *Politics* as well as
his environmental treatise *On the nature of place* (*De natura loci ex latitudine
et longitudine eiusdem proveniente*) and some natural philosophical questions, Biller attempts to approach a mental event in the individual histories
of an average late-medieval student who was systematically fed with proto-
racist ideas. According to Biller, such texts not only diffused ancient ideas,
they also added new emphases such as the naturalness of whiteness, the
hot black woman, and the scientific account of Jewish characteristics (the
dominance in their bodies of melancholic humour).

Joseph Ziegler surveys the ethnic references in various treatises of
learned physiognomy produced in the Latin West from *c.* 1200 to
c. 1500. He shows that despite the growing presence of stereotypical
biological characteristics attributed to various ethnic groups (Irish, Jews

---

[60] See his earlier treatment of the topic in Robert Bartlett, *The Making of Europe: Conquest,
Colonization and Cultural Change 950–1350* (London: Allen Lane, 1993), pp. 236–42 and
'Medieval and Modern Concepts of Race and Ethnicity', *The Journal of Medieval and
Early Modern Studies* 31 (2001), 39–56.

and Saracens) in a variety of literary sources, scientific, learned physiognomy was largely non-ethnic. Unlike their classical predecessors, medieval physiognomers (physicians and philosophers alike) did not realize the ethnic, even racist potential of physiognomy.

Attempting to explain a significant discontinuity between classical and medieval physiognomy, Ziegler suggests that in addition to Christianity's strong universalistic and humanistic influences (an explanation challenged by Denise K. Buell in her contribution to this collection), in this particular case of learned physiognomy, scientific theory constituted a major obstacle on the road to turning medieval physiognomy into a significant proto-racist tool. Analyzing the philosophical and medical discourse regarding the transmission of bodily and behavioural traits (using theories of embryology, environmental determinism, and commentaries on Avicenna's discussion of complexions in his *Liber canonis*) he shows that the key explanatory concept of complexion (both natural and radical) available to these scientists could not provide them with a stable and solid foundation for a coherent doctrine of biological continuity and determinism. Without such a doctrine medieval physiognomy could hardly become racist.

Valentin Groebner looks at the topic of race and sex in late-medieval literary imagination and daily practice. He investigates the changing categories in which carnal relations between Europeans and non-Europeans were described in literature between the thirteenth and sixteenth centuries. Concentrating on German and Italian material, the paper explores the development of the sexualized figures of Asians and Blacks from courtly epics and fantastic tales of the thirteenth and fourteenth centuries to travel accounts and novellas of the fifteenth and sixteenth centuries. He shows how in the fourteenth century the theme of sex with the exotic other (a common and traditional literary topos) was transformed into a grotesque and comical relationship with the female slave, and he links the change to the growing awareness of the increase in the numbers of Asian slaves present in the streets of Mediterranean Europe. With the arrival of ever larger numbers of slaves from Northern and Western Africa in the second half of the fifteenth century, the sexualized black woman, the seductive Moorish princesses, and the sexually hyperactive princes from African or Oriental lands gave way to a new paradigm that expressed a deep-seated anxiety. The new narratives came to emphasize the sexual contact between Christians and Moors as grotesque, appalling and menacing – the black-and-white coitus becoming the centre of the plot against Christianity.

Charles de Miramon investigates the genealogy of the concept of race in French sources of the fourteenth and fifteenth centuries. He shows how the word 'race' first emerged in France, not in Spain or Portugal. It was not coined to denigrate a despised minority or an alien people with a strange skin colour or to justify colonization or enslavement. The word emerged in the context of the discourse on nobility in the fourteenth and fifteenth centuries and was hence not initially racist. It was linked to the transformed and growing importance of blood in defining and describing nobility in general and royal nobility in particular. Hunting literature and treatises on dogs and birds of prey became a vector promoting a notion linking the animal world, nobility and reproduction. Miramon scans practical and theoretical political texts, learned feudal law and literary works, zoological treatises and lexicographical literature, and tries to evaluate how they modified older representations of kinship and heredity. The most visible change in the social and political significance of blood in the 1330s was the emergence in the two French-speaking cultures, France and England, of the concept of *Princes de sang* (Princes of royal blood) and the coining of a new proverb: *Bon sang ne saurait mentir* ('Good blood would not know how to lie', i.e. a worthy nature cannot conceal itself).

The following century would bring a new development in the Iberian setting: the extension of the power of these ideas about heritability found in the discourses of animal breeding and of aristocratic genealogy to new corners of culture and society. As far as medieval Iberia is concerned, David Nirenberg has already shown that before the mass conversion of Jews in 1391, anxiety about the reproduction of racial categories, or even evidence for such categories, is difficult to find.[61] There is little evidence that descendants of converts were stigmatized as 'racially impure' before the fifteenth century. Marriage to converts went unhindered, reflecting a certain confidence in the efficacy of conversion. Things, however, changed dramatically during the first third of the fifteenth century. Nirenberg reflects on the use of race and racism in the historiography of the Jews in medieval Spain and illustrates the cognitive benefits that may be gained from emphasizing, rather than eliding, the medieval vocabularies through which 'naturalizations' of difference were expressed. He studies the sudden application to Jews of words such as *raza*, *casta* and *linaje*, which emerged in the 1430s in discussions of animal breeding and reproduction. This coincided with the appearance of an anti-*converso* ideology which sought to establish new religious categories and discriminations, and legitimate these by naturalizing their reproduction. This 'genealogical turn' was successful also because it appealed to medieval common knowledge about nature. The doctrine of 'limpieza de sangre'

---

[61] David Nirenberg, *Communities of Violence: Persecution of Minorities in the Middle Ages* (Princeton, NJ: Princeton University Press, 1996), pp. 149–50.

(purity of blood) which emerged in 1449 was one of the clearest expressions of this genealogical turn, maintaining that the reproduction of culture was embedded in the reproduction of the flesh. Religious difference created a theory of biological essence which was indivisible from religion.

The early-modern period

While the official policy in Spain was vacillating between attempts at complete assimilation of its minorities (forced conversions and expulsions of those who would not convert), and attempts at discrimination and separation on the basis of lineage and 'blood', ideas about the inherent qualities of members of certain groups of people were fast spreading outside the Iberian peninsula.

Ronnie Po-chia Hsia accepts the position that by the sixteenth century traditional anti-Judaism evolved in some cases into an attitude which could be defined as racist anti-Semitism, i.e. regarding religious differences between Christians and Jews not only as a question of beliefs and customs but as a matter of essential identity. By analyzing Lutheran texts of the sixteenth century, he shows how these novel attitudes towards Jews became part and parcel of an acceptable discourse in Protestant Europe as well. Similar concepts were then exported to European spheres of influence in other continents, hindering the recruitment of indigenous converts to the clergy. No amount of baptismal waters or of Christian-European education could change the essential nature of a former pagan (particularly if he were dark-skinned) – thus stressed some missionaries, basing their claims on what they believed was the European experience with former Jews.

As in the early Christian centuries (analyzed by Denise K. Buell), the question whether religious conversion transforms a person's essence was again high on the theological agenda. The Reformation, and the ensuing waves of mass conversions, increased and spread the obsession with religious dissimulation and with 'true' identity throughout Europe, and thus the Iberian concern with the inherent qualities of New Christians would acquire additional racist elements and become first an all-European and then a global issue.

Still within Europe, however, a new ethnic minority was forcing authorities and observers to contend with foreign social elements. Although strangely devoid of religious content, the attitudes towards the Gypsies, writes Miriam Eliav-Feldon, should also be seen as containing seeds of racist thought. These small groups of nomads, rarely discussed by scholars in the context of the early history of racism but most often viewed only as part of the early-modern concerns with poverty and vagrancy, evoked a wide variety of emotions among the settled population in Europe's cities and villages. Yet some descriptions of these bands of 'Egyptians', as well as certain laws and regulations concerning them in the two centuries following their first sightings in western Europe, went far beyond expressions of the 'heterophobia' (to use Zygmunt Bauman's term[62]) aroused by strangers. These reactions were not only based on the assumption that Gypsies were of an incorrigible 'stock', but they also dehumanized them in terms of the utmost virulence by comparing them to vermin – thus expressing both fear and hatred which justified, if not extermination, at least organized manhunts.

The urgent debate over the definition of other peoples, in these early stages of European colonialism and imperialism, was conducted in relation to human civilizations discovered on other continents, so strange and unfamiliar in every respect. Armed with arguments from classical texts – not only those recovered, as Peter Biller shows in his article, in the late Middle Ages, but also those accumulated and reinterpreted during the Renaissance – and enjoying easy access to ideas of past times thanks to the new printing press, learned Europeans in the sixteenth and seventeenth centuries (whether they experienced the 'new worlds' at first hand or only by proxy) continually attempted to understand, categorize and define the different types of human beings and cultures they were encountering – and in some cases conquering and enslaving – around the globe. In fact, the sixteenth century witnessed a veritable 'explosion' in comparative ethnography, unparalleled in the past, and inevitably some participants in this endless debate about hierarchy within the human section in the universal 'chain of being' expressed notions which cannot be defined as anything but racist.

Either very explicitly (as in explorers' reports or in public ideological disputations such as the well-known confrontation between Juan Ginés de Sepúlveda and Bartolomé de Las Casas) or implicitly and obliquely (as in slave traders' matter-of-fact accounts), innumerable extant early-modern documents reflect attitudes to alien peoples. These attitudes ran the entire gamut of possible sentiments: from idealization or admiration for a superior civilization, through relativism or indifference, down to contempt and disgust. Scholarly literature nowadays on the development of ideas and policies towards various 'others' during the sixteenth and seventeenth centuries is simply vast. The question whether any of theses attitudes, prior to the eighteenth century, contained elements which could be

---

[62] Zygmunt Bauman, *Modernity and the Holocaust* (Ithaca, NY: Cornell University Press, 1989).

termed 'racist' has also received a great deal of attention from historians, anthropologists and literary critics in recent decades, particularly in relation to Africans and American Indians.

Thus, in a short conference or in a single volume, which attempted to 'cover' the history of an idea in the West for two millennia, one could not possibly hope to include all the relevant issues, particularly in regards to the post-Gutenberg, post-Columbus era. Consequently the lacunae in this part of our discussion are big and wide: from the often-raised question of cause and effect with regard to racism and the early Atlantic slave trade, through the influence of ancient colour symbolism on attitudes to Africans, or sentiments and stereotypes expressed in popular travel literature, down to the clearly racist representations of the people of the Cape of Good Hope, the so-called 'Hottentots', constructed in early-modern British writings as 'the world's most beastly people'.[63] From the enormous field of reactions to the transatlantic encounters, we offer here only two articles which analyze the complex impact of the early-modern establishment of European colonies and empires on the evolution of racist ideologies. These two, however, present novel interpretations and completely new emphases.

Anthony Pagden in 'The peopling of the New World: ethnos, race and empire' succeeds in showing how muddled was early-modern European thought with regard to the inhabitants of other continents. The confusion arose, he believes, mainly from the conflicting interests of the empire builders. On the one hand they needed to justify conquest, colonization and enslavement, and for that purpose they could usefully rely on Aristotelian concepts of 'natural slavery', on proto-racist theories of environmental determinism, or on the seventeenth-century theories of multiple creations. On the other hand, all these theories not only threatened the idea of a single human kind; they also had the effect of placing those races outside human history, which was supposed to run from a single act of creation until the end of human time. And although such theories would serve the purpose of later exclusionists – true racists, that is – they were deeply inimical to the early European ideologues of empire, since the only ethical and theological justification for the European overseas expansion had been incorporation – i.e. the Christian mission to bring all mankind into the fold. Although not denying that there were virulent racists long before the emergence of 'true physiological racism' in the eighteenth century, Pagden emphasizes that, ultimately, the overriding concern was to maintain a single Christian historical narrative, which – despite the fact that

---

[63] Linda E. Merians, *Envisioning the Worst: Representations of "Hottentots" in Early Modern England* (Newark, DE: University of Delaware Press, 2001), p. 1.

it recognized cultural differences in customs, laws and religion – could not co-exist with conceptions of immutable race distinctions between peoples.

Jorge Cañizares-Esguerra, in 'Demons, stars, and the imagination: the early modern body in the Tropics', also asserts that it was not at the early stages of European colonial rule in Latin America that a racist view of the Indian body had crystallized. He offers a most original argument in claiming that the impediments to racism were the early-modern European views of the body as permeable and easily penetrated by outside forces, including demons. He goes over early-modern views that held that the maternal imagination, diet, constellations and demons were responsible for the constitution of bodies. If so, the idea of the physical constitution as an immutable reality – which, he holds, is a *sine qua non* for any racist theory – could not be fitted into the theories of bodies moulded by external forces. However, it was in the New World that these views slowly gave way to alternative representations of the body as less malleable and thus amenable to a racist presentation. By the eighteenth century the Spaniards, and in particular the Creoles, developed a very rigorous scale of racial types, which was clearly depicted in the *Casta* paintings.

Conflicting ideologies and contradictory conceptions of the essence of human nature vied with each other more than ever before during the period which for the Europeans was defined as the Age of Discovery. Racist attitudes may not have been predominant at its early stages, but once the sons and daughters of Europe rose from the ranks of ignorant, hungry, poor explorers seeking the riches of other civilizations to the level of conquerors, enslavers and carriers of the torch of religious truth and refined culture, restraints and impediments were overcome. Two millennia of debates (albeit neither constant nor continuous) over the question whether certain groups of human beings are defined by immutable attributes provided a huge arsenal of arguments from which to develop 'scientific' racist theories, destined to wreak so much havoc.

*****

Overall it would seem that, despite some disagreement among the contributors, there is sufficient common ground to justify the title of this volume. Racism, understood as an ideology or an attempt to construct a rational, conceptual framework for irrational and emotional forms of group hatred, they all seem to agree, existed in different forms and degrees long before the emergence of the 'scientific' modern variety. And although certain teachings, ideological interests and practices of co-existence often hindered the development of a racist worldview or limited its impact, the seeds or the roots had always been there since the time of the ancient Greeks – to be cultivated into a coherent set of beliefs when the circumstances appeared to demand it.

2 Racism: a rationalization of prejudice in Greece and Rome

Benjamin Isaac

Proto-racism, racism, ethnic prejudice and xenophobia

The existence of early, pre-modern forms of racism originating in the West is the central point of the present book. The introduction set forth the parameters of the discussion as the editors see it. The subject has also been discussed in my own recent work.[1] Numerous reviews and other publications were written which contained various degrees of disagreement and approval, as well as suggestions for correction or reconsideration. This paper has two aims: the first is to clarify the essence of the argument; the second, to respond to some of the comments. The chapter is organized thematically and conceived as a continuation of the introduction to this book, although the latter is the joint responsibility of the three editors while this chapter is my work alone.

Proto-racism

In the Introduction we have attempted to clarify the terminology as we use it, notably the meaning of 'racism'. In my earlier work on the subject I have used the term 'proto-racism' to indicate a form of racism encountered in Greek and Roman literature. It seemed useful to make this sort of distinction between ancient forms of racism and its more recent manifestations. However, it appears to be necessary to clarify what exactly I mean when using the term 'proto-racism', for there has been some disagreement about its proper meaning.[2] In employing it I assumed that 'proto-racism' could be used like the term 'prototype' in the sense in which it appears in the *OED*: 'The first or primary type of anything; the original (thing or

---

[1] Benjamin Isaac, *The Invention of Racism in Classical Antiquity* (Princeton: Princeton University Press, 2004).

[2] Andrew Gillett, 'Review of Isaac, *Invention of Racism in Antiquity*', *Polis* 23(2) (2006), 410–14, at 411, succinctly phrases it: 'a series of interlocking attitudes forming a matrix that not only parallels modern racist attitudes but is in fact their forebear'.

person) of which another is a copy, imitation, representation, or derivative, or to which it conforms or is required to conform; a pattern, model, standard, exemplar.' Similarly the prototype of an aircraft is the model which will later be mass produced, after suitable adaptations, corrections and improvements. Thus it is clear that proto-racism, as the prototype of racism, is not meant to be just a weakened form of racism. It is racism in the full sense, but it is an early form which precedes Darwin, based on pre-modern scientific concepts. It is only fair to note that I am by no means the first to introduce the term. It has been used rather frequently by several historians, among them Roxann Wheeler who remarks that 'most histories of race [sc. racism] have not adequately acknowledged the power of residual proto-racial [sc. proto-racist] ideologies, or older conceptions of national and religious difference that persisted despite the fact that the socioeconomic conditions which gave birth to them changed'. She calls this 'the sedimentation of racial [sc. racist] ideology'.[3]

It has also been argued that Greek and Roman prejudices produced something that might be termed simply racism rather than proto-racism.[4] The term racism itself is appropriate, according to this argument, for Graeco-Roman attitudes, but possibly the religious ideologies of pre-Greek social orders such as the Assyrians might appropriately be termed proto-racist. The written sources from the Near East are never likely to provide evidence that will allow us to reach a conclusion. In any event, I am not competent to pursue this question further. I would happily

---

[3] Roxann Wheeler, *The Complexion of Race: Categories of Difference in Eighteenth-Century British Culture* (Philadelphia: University of Pennsylvania Press, 2000), p. 9. The term is said to have been used by Jean Yoyotte for Egypt according to Léon Poliakov (ed.), *Ni Juif ni Grec: Entretiens sur le racisme* (Paris, New York: Mouton, 1978), preface pp. 7–22, at p. 8, while George Fredrickson, *A Short History of Racism* (Princeton: Princeton University Press, 2003), applies it to the later Middle Ages. Imanuel Geiss, *Geschichte des Rassismus* (Frankfurt am Main: Suhrkamp, 1988), uses it without definition for what he regards as pre-modern forms of racism among which he includes Graeco-Roman antiquity, Egypt and China. See especially p. 49: 'Proto-rassistische Dispositionen ... gingen dem euramerikanischen Rassismus voraus, überall und zu allen Zeiten'; p. 79: 'Die stil- und bewusstseinsprägende Langzeitwirkung des älteren Proto-Rassismus auf den modernen Rassismus ist fast so wichtig wie die Vorgänge in der Antike und im Mittelalter selbst.' It reappears in E. Balibar and I. Wallerstein, *Race, Nation, Classe: Les identités ambiguës* (Paris: La Découverte, 1988; English translation: *Race, Nation, Class: Ambiguous Identities*, London/New York: Verso, 1991). David Graizbord, 'Inquisitorial Ideology at Work in an *Auto Da Fé*, 1680: Religion in the Context of Proto-Racism', *Journal of Early Modern History* 10 (2006), 331–60, at 333, n. 6, writes that he first used the term in 1996, but gives no reference. He uses it in a different context and a rather different sense, namely as 'a way of imagining human differences on the basis of pre-modern (which is to say, non-scientific and/or non-pseudoscientific) notions of "race"'. As should be clear now, I argue that pre-modern racist notions were in fact based upon contemporary (pseudo-)scientific ideas.
[4] Brent D. Shaw, 'Review of B. Isaac, *The Invention of Racism in Classical Antiquity*', *Journal of World History* 16(2) (2005), 231.

concede the point if it could be shown that such a society developed the type of imaginary schema and intellectual construct that, in my view, is typical of pre-modern racism. It may be appropriate here to note that my introduction of the term 'proto-racism' was rather tentative. While I would and will defend the reality of early forms of racism in antiquity, I shall not insist on calling them proto-racism rather than simply racism.

Racism, ethnic prejudice and xenophobia

A few critics attempt to delegitimize the argument by accusing me of racism.[5] A related phenomenon may briefly be indicated here. One review cites vulgar and racist comments on Palestinians made by two notorious American radio personalities.[6] This is followed by the assertion that, according to my definitions, these remarks would not qualify as racist, but as ethnic prejudice. This is untrue for several reasons that are not worth discussing here. It is appropriate, however, to repeat again that the difference between ethnic or religious prejudice and racism does not lie in the crudity or ferocity of the utterance, but in the nature of the ideological framework behind it. There are mild expressions of racism and violent forms of ethnic prejudice. The difference, I repeat, lies in the fact that ethnic and religious prejudice leaves its victims with the presumption of choice or change, while racism does not. Ethnic and religious prejudice ascribe to their target groups common mind-sets and patterns of behaviour; racism assumes the existence of physical and mental qualities that are passed on from one generation to the next and are not subject to individual choice or the possibility of change. In Greek terms, racism is associated with nature (*physis*), ethnic prejudice with culture/custom (*nomos*). *Physis* is stable; *nomos* is determined by free will and is variable.

Similarly we must distinguish between xenophobia as such and racism. Xenophobia may be racist, but not all forms of it are. Juvenal's satire clearly represents both xenophobia and (proto-)racism in combination. Juvenal expresses his hatred (or satirizes other people's hatred) of the foreigners he encounters in Rome. Xenophobia is a form of hostility towards 'the strangers in our midst' and has peculiarities that are different from generalizations concerning distant foreigners and foreign peoples.

---

[5] Shelley P. Haley, *American Journal of Philology* 126 (2005), 451–4.
[6] Jeremy McInerney, 'Review of B. Isaac, *The Invention of Racism in Classical Antiquity*', *Social History* 31 (2006), 83–7, at 83, citing Don Imus and Sid Rosenberg. McInerney must be suspected of attempting to score points by associating an Israeli scholar with anti-Palestinian racism, an association for which there is no basis in the text of my book.

The value of literary sources

Since racism is an ideology,[7] or rather a set of ideas developed in an attempt to rationalize the irrational, it is natural to look for its origins in the intellectual sphere. It may be useful here to emphasize once again that the characteristic feature of Graeco-Roman (proto-)racism is the deployment of presumed evidence and reasoning in defence of irrational ideas of superiority and inferiority.[8] It is this use of allegedly rational arguments in the defence of prejudice and discriminatory attitudes in antiquity as an intellectual exercise, which justifies the title of my recent book, *The Invention of Racism*. The existence of group prejudice, persecution and discrimination in other societies is not the issue here, but a specific manner of handling such prejudices.

Unlike regular stereotypes which may have their basis and origins in all levels of society, racism, as defined above, spreads from top to bottom, even if its simple and crudest forms may appeal to all strata of society. It is then justified to study the writings of upper-class authors to trace its inception. This may look like an opportunistic argument on the part of a Graeco-Roman historian, for we have no other coherent collection of sources. We are involved in a field of historical study which depends almost entirely on the writings of upper-class, male intellectuals. The development of influential ideas is where such a literature can be most instructive and it would therefore be absurd to deny the validity of these writings precisely where they are truly representative. Yet this is what some classicists attempt to do for the present topic. The records concerning popular opinion in the eighteenth and nineteenth centuries are totally different in quality and quantity from those for popular opinion in Athens and Rome. We can try to imagine what ethnic slurs we would meet at a Roman dinner party or in any *caupona*,[9] but that is the stuff of historical novels. None of us knows what really happened at Greek dinner parties or in Roman pubs. It may be difficult to understand what exactly ancient satirists and orators meant when they produced ethnic slurs, but that is no reason to refrain from making the attempt. Indeed, I believe it is possible to understand Lucian's references to himself as a Syrian in the Roman Empire, for at least they are first-hand and direct utterances.

---

[7] See above, Introduction, pp. 1, 2, 12.

[8] Mary Lefkowitz, *The American Historical Review* 110 (2005), 198.

[9] William Harris, 'Phoenician Trash', *TLS* September 10 (2004), 9, apparently thinks we can and he regards it a false position to study the history of racist ideas. Yet numerous twentieth-century scholars have held that the development of racist ideology is a worthwhile topic even where we do have copious information about the popular mood and this has resulted in the publication of a large number of highly influential works for the modern period.

Many modern historians, at any rate, emphatically regard it as relevant to study the history of ideas, even if these have been produced by the intellectual elite. Several works written by historians of various periods of which I was unaware when I wrote my book clearly state the possibility of racism preceding the colonial period.[10] Why then would several classicists insist that we exclude this possibility? Modern history shows that there is a clear connection and interdependence between prejudices emanating from the upper levels of society, of which most politicians are part, and the wider population. In the case of modern racism it is obvious that one needs to study both the intellectual history – the development of the ideas – and what happened in the street. Those who want to understand Nazi racism must recognize the popular mood as well as the writings of Houston Stewart Chamberlain, Gobineau, Alfred Rosenberg and Richard Walther Darré – regarded as important by the Nazis themselves.[11] Or, to phrase it less specifically, there are shelves and shelves of books and journals full of articles written by historians who considered it

[10] Thomas F. Gossett, *Race: the History of an Idea in America* (Dallas: Southern Methodist University Press, 1963; New York: Oxford University Press, 1997), chapter 1, pp. 5–9; Christian Delacampagne, *L'invention du racisme: Antiquité et Moyen Age* (Paris: Fayard, 1983); David Brion Davis, 'Constructing Race: A Reflection', *The William and Mary Quarterly* 3rd Ser., 54(1) (1997), 7–18; William C. Jordan, 'Why "Race"?', *Journal of Medieval and Early Modern Studies* 31(1) (2001), 165–73. David M. Goldenberg, *International Journal of the Classical Tradition* 5(4) (1999), 561–70, points out the relevance of the ancient theory of environmental determinism for the present discussion. More about this in the Introduction to this book. Note also, against Snowden: Cornel West, 'A Genealogy of Modern Racism' in Philomena Essed and David Theo Goldberg (eds), *Race Critical Theories: Text and Context* (Malden, MA: Blackwell Publishers, 2002), pp. 90–112 at 108: 'race did matter in classical antiquity'.

[11] Michael Lambert resists the relevance of the history of ideas in politics, 'Review of B. Isaac, *The Invention of Racism in Classical Antiquity*', *Classical Review* 55 (2005), 658–62, at 660: 'I doubt whether Eichmann or Verwoerd had copies of Aristotle's *Politics* or Tacitus' *Germania* next to their beds.' Whatever Eichmann's bedtime reading, it is no futile exercise to trace the history of Nazi ideology and its racism, as amply demonstrated, for instance, by Léon Poliakov, *Le mythe aryen* (Paris: Calmann-Lévy, 1971), translated as *The Aryan Myth* (New York: Basic Books, 1974) and by the work of George Mosse, for instance his *Toward the Final Solution: A History of European Racism* (New York: H. Fertig, 1978). Or, for a different view on the part of an ancient historian, we may cite Momigliano's suggestion that Tacitus' *Germania*, together with the *Iliad*, should be given high priority among the hundred most dangerous books ever written: 'Some Observations on Causes of War in Ancient Historiography', *Proceedings of the Second International Congress of Classical Studies*, I (Copenhagen: E. Munksgaard, 1958), 199. Ann L. Stoler, 'Racial Histories and their Regimes of Truth', *Political Power and Social Theory* 11 (1997), 183–206, reprinted in Essed and Goldberg, *Race Critical Theories*, pp. 368–91, at 376–7, following Foucault, notes that racism may develop and be instigated at entirely different social and intellectual levels, among both those who rule and those who do not. See now Naomi Zack, *Philosophy and Science and Race* (New York and London: Routledge, 2002), which deals with the modern history of racist ideas and its scientific background.

worthwhile to make the history of racist ideas their subject of research.[12] As regards antiquity, it is a matter for serious consideration and not for easy dismissal to assume that there might have been a connection between the intellectual climate and popular opinion in Greece and Rome. Moses Finley had no doubt in this respect.[13] Classicists who deny the possibility of such a connection in the present case may be suspected of protecting special interests.

Corruption through foreign influence

An essential point in the evaluation of both Greek and Roman imperialism is their long-standing ambivalence about the effect of contact with foreigners and the resulting influences. While it is obvious that there were such contacts – and there should be no need to emphasize that any empire by definition represents ethnic and cultural diversity – it is important to realize that this ambivalence or even hostility was an enduring feature of Greek and Roman social thinking.

It has been argued, in this connection, that besides the Athenians' ideas regarding their own pure lineage (autochthony), one must take into account Athenian ideology as expressed, for instance, in sections of Pericles' funeral oration as represented by Thucydides. These emphasize Athens' receptivity to foreign goods and ideas (Thuc. 2.38f.).[14] This oration, of course, does not purport to be a description of reality; it is probably the most perfect glorification of one's own society and its superiority over others in all of classical literature. In the passage referred to we read that the Athenians enjoy goods imported from all over the world and are not afraid to open up their city to foreign visitors.[15] Whatever the reality, this is the message. However, it is equally significant

---

[12] See above, Introduction, p. 12, n. 33.

[13] Moses I. Finley, *Ancient Slavery and Modern Ideology* (London: Chatto & Windus, 1980), pp. 118–19 'a logical consequence of the slave–outsider equation, is racism, a term I insist on ... The issue is not of a concept of "race" acceptable to modern biologists or of a properly defined and consistently held concept, but of a view commonly taken in ordinary discourse, then as now.'

[14] Craige Champion, 'Review of B. Isaac, *The Invention of Racism in Classical Antiquity*', *Scholia Reviews* n.s. 14 (2005), 10. For Athenian autochthony see now Susan Lape, *Reproducing Athens: Menander's Comedy, Democratic Culture and the Hellenistic City* (Princeton, NJ: Princeton University Press, 2004), pp. 5–8, 73–4. See also Lape, 'Racializing Democracy: The Politics of Sexual Reproduction in Democratic Athens', *Parallax*, 9(4) (2003), 52–63, which argues that 'in classical Athens ... Citizens and non-citizens were distinguished on the basis of a race ideology.' This paper appeared too late for me to take into account when I delivered my book to the Press.

[15] Champion, 'Review of B. Isaac', writes 'foreign goods and ideas'. Classen thinks the 'foreign goods' include intellectual goods, i.e. ideas, but Arnold W. Gomme, *A Historical*

that Pericles fails to say that the visitors would be welcome as a permanent presence in the city. Furthermore, this oration hardly neutralizes the numerous sources in which Athenian autochthony appears as a cherished and powerful part of the Athenian self-perception.

A similar claim has been made for Rome as seen in the writings of Cicero. The view that Roman contact with foreign peoples and customs had been beneficial to Rome is allegedly stated by him at length in *De Republica* 2.30. It is instructive to look at this passage here, for in fact it reinforces the opposite impression: chapter 29 of *De Republica* contains a discussion of the reports that King Numa was a pupil of Pythagoras. Scipio, as cited by Cicero, denies this very firmly. The text then continues: *'Manilius*: "Ye immortal gods! What an error to remain current so long! Yet I am not sorry that we Romans got our culture, not from arts imported from overseas, but from the native excellence of our own people."'[16] In chapter 30 Scipio answers: 'Nay, more you will deem our ancestors' wisdom worthy of praise for the very reason that, as you will learn, even of those institutions that have been borrowed from abroad, many have been improved by us until they are much better than they were in the countries from which we obtained them and where they had their origin.'[17]

This is part of the ongoing argument about the impact of Greek culture. Scipio says that (a) rumours about very early influence are untrue and (b) later influences and borrowings cannot be denied, but Rome always improved what it borrowed. This is grudging, partial admission rather than enthusiastic affirmation. It does not say or imply that Roman contact with foreign peoples and customs had been beneficial to Rome, let alone that the absorption of foreigners into Roman society had been a salutary process.

Constitution and institutions or Nature

Three concepts are crucial in the shaping of Graeco-Roman racist ideas: environmental determinism,[18] the belief in the heritability of acquired

Commentary on Thucydides 2 (Oxford: Oxford University Press, 1962), p. 117, doubts this. For the import of goods Gomme cites Ps.-Xenophon, *Constitution of the Athenians*, 2.7; Hermippos, fr. 43; Isocrates, *Or.* 4.42.45

[16] Di inmortales, inquit Manilius, quantus iste est hominum et quam inveteratus error! Ac tamen facile patior non esse nos transmarinis nec inportatis artibus eruditos, sed genuinis domesticisque virtutibus.

[17] quin hoc ipso sapientiam maiorum statues esse laudandam, quod multa intelleges etiam aliunde sumta meliora apud nos multo esse facta, quam ibi fuissent, unde huc translata essent atque ubi primum extitissent.

[18] The historical importance of these concepts has been emphasized before by Ann Laura Stoler, 'Racial Histories and their Regimes of Truth', in Essed and Goldberg, *Race Critical*

characteristics[19] and the belief in the importance of lineage. That is: first, the conviction that climate and geography shape collective characteristics of peoples; second, the assumption that people pass on from one generation to the next characteristics which they acquired during their lifetimes; and, third, the belief in the negative effect of marriage between foreigners. It is for present purposes not uninteresting that environmental determinism was an essential and even predominant ingredient of racism in the seventeenth century[20] and as late as the twentieth century, for instance in the works of Ratzel and Taylor.[21] An anti-Semitic variety may be recognized in the claim that the Jews always had been, and still were in modern times, a nomadic people: unreliable merchants, parasites, cosmopolitan and restless.[22] It is often claimed, however, that constitution and form of government were regarded as more decisive in their impact on the nature and qualities of a state in Greek literature. Political and social institutions are obviously a central topic in Greek social thought and therefore the subject of extensive discussion. Indeed oriental kingships seemed to the Greeks consistently to produce inferior and slavish humans. However,

---

Theories, p. 382. Cf. Denise K. Buell, *Why This New Race: Ethnic Reasoning in Early Christianity* (New York: Columbia University Press, 2005), pp. 15–17, on the 'mutability of race'. See also her contribution to this volume, below, pp. 114–15.

[19] Biologists use the technical term 'acquired characters' in the sense of 'the distinguishing features of a species or genus', see *OED* second edition s.v. character, n. 8 and s.v. acquired *ppl.a. (c)*, but non-biologists usually assume this to be an error, so it seems easier to use the term 'characteristics'.

[20] Peter Harrison, *'Religion' and the Religions in the English Enlightenment* (Cambridge: Cambridge University Press, 1990), pp. 112–20.

[21] Friedrich Ratzel, *The History of Mankind* (1896–98), translated from the second German edition, 3 vols. (London: Macmillan and Co., Ltd.; New York: The Macmillan Co., 1896–98), vol. 1, p. 23. The most elaborate defence of it may be found in the work of Griffith Taylor, *Environment, Race and Migration*, second (enlarged) edition (Chicago: University of Chicago Press, 1946, first printed 1937, which is an expansion of Taylor, *Environment and Race: A Study of the Evolution, Migration ... of Man* (London: Oxford University Press, 1927)). This work represents a major attempt to combine racist theory typical of this period with environmental determinism. The racist treatment rests heavily on German theories of the time, notably those of Eickstedt, but is combined with speculations from then current endocrinal theories which held that climate affects the functioning of glands and thus influences human evolution (Taylor, 276). Taylor offers a relatively mild and optimistic form of racism: he regards most races as roughly equal in quality, apart from the blacks, whose 'poor achievements in world-history are probably due to their non-stimulating environment. To this also is due their small advance from a primitive stage of racial evolution' (Taylor, 476). This does not worry Taylor unduly, for the blacks will ultimately disappear through intermarriage with more viable races. 'As regards the future, it seems clear that *environment* will be the most potent factor in moulding every race and nation' (Taylor, 477).

[22] The best-known presentation of this image is by the Viennese scholar Adolf Wahrmund, *Das Gesetz des Nomadenthums und die heutige Judenherrschaft* (Karlsruhe and Leipzig: H. Reuther, 1887; second edition, Munich: Deutscher Volks-Verlag, 1919).

the underlying cause of the formation of political systems as seen in Greek literature was climate and geography. It will suffice to cite two essential texts in translation:

As regards the lack of character and of courage among the inhabitants [sc. of Asia], the reason why the Asiatics are less belligerent and gentler in character than the Europeans is mostly the nature of the seasons, which do not change much towards heat or cold, but are equable ... Through these causes, I think the Asiatic race is feeble and also because of its institutions. Kings rule most of Asia. Now where men are not masters of themselves and free, but are ruled by despots, they are not interested in military training but intent on not appearing to be combative.[23]

Hippocrates, *Airs, Waters, Places* 16 (fifth century BC)

This clearly points at the environment as the original cause and the social institutions as a secondary factor: because they are feeble they let themselves be ruled by kings and that reinforces their feebleness. The same source in chapter 24 states: 'Similarly, courage and endurance are not by nature (*physei*) part of their character, but the imposition of law (*nomos*) may produce them artificially.'[24] This again indicates the primacy of nature and environmental determinism and the secondary effect of *nomos*, which can only have an artificial effect, if it contradicts nature. *Airs, Waters, Places* and other Greek and Latin authors, notably Strabo, again and again, also emphasize the effects on the character of peoples of such geographical features as mountainous or low-lying areas.[25]

The primacy of nature and geography is brought out even more emphatically in the text most influential in later periods, Aristotle's *Politics* 1327b (fourth century BC):

The peoples of cold countries generally, and particularly those of Europe, are full of spirit, but deficient in skill and intelligence; and this is why they continue to remain comparatively free, but attain no political development and show no capacity for governing others. The peoples of Asia are endowed with skill and intelligence, but are deficient in spirit; and this is why they continue to be peoples

---

[23] Περὶ δὲ τῆς ἀθυμίης τῶν ἀνθρώπων καὶ τῆς ἀνανδρείης, ὅτι ἀπολεμώτεροί εἰσι τῶν Εὐρωπαίων οἱ Ἀσιηνοί, καὶ ἡμερώτεροι τὰ ἤθεα, αἱ ὧραι αἴτιαι μάλιστα, οὐ μεγάλας τὰς μεταβολὰς ποιεύμεναι, οὔτε ἐπὶ τὸ θερμὸν, οὔτε ἐπὶ τὸ ψυχρὸν, ἀλλὰ παραπλησίως ... Διὰ ταύτας ἐμοὶ δοκέει τὰς προφάσιας ἄναλκες εἶναι τὸ γένος τὸ Ἀσιηνόν· καὶ προσέτι διὰ τοὺς νόμους. Τῆς γὰρ Ἀσίης τὰ πολλὰ βασιλεύεται. Ὅκου δὲ μὴ αὐτοὶ ἑωυτέων εἰσὶ καρτεροὶ ἄνθρωποι μηδὲ αὐτόνομοι, ἀλλὰ δεσπόζονται, οὐ περὶ τουτέου αὐτέοισιν ὁ λόγος ἐσὶν, ὅκως τὰ πολέμια ἀσκήσωσιν, ἀλλ' ὅκως μὴ δόξωσι μάχιμοι εἶναι.
[24] τὸ δὲ ἀνδρεῖον καὶ τὸ ταλαίπωρον ἐν τῇ ψυχῇ, φύσει μὲν οὐκ ἂν ὁμοίως ἐνείη, νόμος δὲ προσγενόμενος ἀπεργάσαιτ' ἄν.
[25] I found these features emphasized to such an extent as to merit a separate chapter in my book (chapter 10).

of subjects and slaves. The Greeks, intermediate in geographical position, unite the qualities of both sets of peoples. They possess both spirit and intelligence: the one quality makes it continue free; the other enables it to attain the heights of political development, and to show a capacity for governing every other people – if only it could once achieve political unity.

(Politics, 1327b, trans. Ernest Barker)

Clearly Aristotle is one of the major Greek thinkers who attached central importance to political institutions and constitutions. He devoted major works to the subject. Yet in this passage he explicitly gives primacy to environmental factors: climate and geographical position.

It is the environment which allows or inhibits the political development of societies. If the latter is the yardstick whereby social achievements are measured, the former is the basic and essential determinant. Both authors are considering different levels here. The environment determines basic qualities: good political institutions are essential, but can exist only when elementary human qualities exist. Greek cities, situated in a roughly similar geography, may have more or less successful constitutions, but Scythians and Asiatics are prevented by nature from equal achievement in this respect. Thus Greek environmental determinism held that there was a basic determinant, beyond human control, which created the conditions for human action in the political and social sphere. It is precisely the lack of human control and choice which, according to the definition proposed in the Introduction, is an essential ingredient of racist thinking. Climate and geography are believed to be decisive in a rather abstract way and the sources therefore do not deal with these factors, apart from the treatise *Airs, Waters, Places* which attempts to give medical reasons. Political institutions are the work of men and therefore a fruitful topic for extensive discussion: Plato's *Republic* and *Laws* and Aristotle's *Politics*. Yet these do not deny the primacy of nature. This is not to say that ancient opinion was monolithic. There were exceptions, such as Cicero, who held that human behaviour is not determined by origin, seed or mechanical factors, but by a combination of environment and society. In mentioning 'mechanical factors' Cicero makes it clear what he thinks of astrology, the movements of the stars and the conditions of the moon as factors influencing or even determining human behaviour.

It is possible that in Graeco-Roman thinking the gods also played an indirect role in this complex interplay, for the goddess Athena was assumed to have picked the site for the city of Athens, a site believed to have placed its citizens in the ideal temperate climatic zone, while Vitruvius, who asserted the same for Rome, claims that this was the result of the activity of a 'divine spirit' which thus made Rome fit to rule the whole world.[26]

Inconsistency

Environmental determinism, I have argued, was often combined with the idea of the heredity of acquired characteristics.[27] There is no doubt that this was the common assumption in antiquity, as is clear, for instance, from several pronouncements of Aristotle:

> From deformed parents come deformed children, lame from lame and blind from blind, and speaking generally, children often inherit anything that is peculiar in their parents and are born with similar marks, such as pimples or scars. Such things have been known to be handed down through three generations.[28]
>
> (Aristotle, *Historia Animalium*, 585b)

On the face of it this is inconsistent, because the notion of the transmission of acquired characteristics does not fit racism as I define it. If the characteristics have been acquired and are then transmitted, they are not constant and stable, it may be claimed. Indeed, this is inconsistent. However, inconsistency is an essential ingredient of racism throughout the ages and this is true for ancient prejudice no less than for its modern manifestations.[29] When analyzing patterns of thought and concepts which are illogical by definition, the result necessarily reflects the lack of consistency of the original ideas. The assumption in the ancient texts is that acquired characteristics are transmitted from one generation to the next and then become stable and permanent. Thus, a people is believed to lose

[26] Athens: Plato, *Timaeus* 24c–d; Rome: Vitruvius 6.1.11; as observed by Denise McCoskey, 'Naming the Fault in Question: Theorizing Racism among the Greeks and Romans', *International Journal of the Classical Tradition* 13(2) (2006), 258–9.

[27] This feature of traditional thinking has long been known. See Conway Zirkle, 'The Early History of the Idea of the Inheritance of Acquired Characteristics and of Pangenesis', *Transactions of the American Philosophical Society*, n.s. 35 (1946), 91–151, at 91: 'What Lamarck really did was to accept the hypothesis that acquired characters were heritable, a notion which had been held almost universally for well over two thousand years and which his contemporaries accepted as a matter of course, and to assume that the results of such inheritance were cumulative from generation to generation, thus producing, in time, new species.' See also Harrison, *'Religion' and the Religions*, pp. 120–1. for its significance in seventeenth-century England where the idea was applied to the concept of original and inherited sin.

[28] Aristotle, *Historia Animalium* 585b (trans. D'Arcy Wentworth Thompson). See also *De Generatione Animalium* 721b on scars and brands that are passed on to the next generation.

[29] Robert J. C. Young, *Colonial Desire: Hybridity in Theory, Culture and Race* (London and New York: Routledge, 1995), p. 94: 'race theory possesses its own oneiric logic that allows it to survive despite its contradictions, to reverse itself at every refutation, to adapt and transform itself at every denial'. The reader might have been spared Young's subsequent comparison of racism with psychoanalysis.

its capacity as a fighting power after having been subjected for a generation or two, as it then becomes and remains servile. In other words, by then it may be called a constant characteristic, unalterable by human will. This is why I call it an ancient form of racism. Denise Kimber Buell, in her contribution to this volume, points out the central role the concept played in the Early Christian self-definition as a people. It is found also in the contributions to this volume by Biller, Nirenberg and Cañizares.

Second, and no less important, both Greek and Roman thinking, as is well known, did not recognize the concept of progress and, instead, assumed that decline was inevitable and irreversible. It could be accelerated or it could be slowed down, but one generation could never improve on the previous one, just as a single individual cannot be healthier at age 85 than at age 15. This was assumed to be a given situation determined by nature, and it may be worth observing that in the early seventeenth century the outlook was no different.[30] The characteristics that could be acquired during one's life and transmitted to posterity were all negative ones. These then became irreversible. Sturdy people who moved from the frigid north to the warm and balmy south, became soft and spineless and that is what they and their descendants continued to be. The reverse was unthinkable and I challenge anyone to show me an ancient text which claims that a people gained strength through a transformation such as moving from south to north.[31] Again, that may not be consistent reasoning by modern standards, but it was the ancient view of the human fate.

Third, there was an essential belief in the inevitability of the decline of peoples, whatever their institutions and constitution, even if they did not move elsewhere. Nations were seen as living organisms which grow into adulthood, decline with age, and die. Polybius famously attended Scipio Africanus as he watched Carthage burning, while he wept and 'reflected on the inevitable fall of cities, nations, and empires, as well as of individuals',[32] a fate which Scipio saw as awaiting also his own Rome. The idea that nations and empires function like living organisms, which originates in Hellenistic literature, had profound influence on eighteenth- and

---

[30] Harrison, 'Religion' and the Religions, 102–12.
[31] Pagden, below, p. 297, claims that 'Aristotle's lethargic Asians, and un-civil northerners, might well become perfectly balanced Greeks were they to take up residence in the Mediterranean.' However, he gives no example from any Greek sources that this was ever regarded as a real possibility. Indeed, it was not, but it was regarded as such in medieval literature; see Robert Bartlett, 'Concepts of Race and Ethnicity', *Journal of Medieval and Early Modern Studies* 31(1) (2001), 39–56, at 47 with note 13, referring to Albertus Magnus, *De natura locorum* 2.2–4; ed. A. Borgnet, *Opera omnia*, 38 vols. (Paris: L. Vivès, 1890–9), 9:56–65.
[32] Polybius, 38.21–2 as quoted by Appian, *Punica* 132.

nineteenth-century thinking.[33] It is best known from the works of Spencer[34] and, above all, Friedrich Ratzel.[35] This then is a deterministic view which is incompatible with a consistent belief in the primacy of institutions or of climate and geography. Also, it leaves no room for any assertion of the autonomy of the individual. It both reduces the individual to the parameters of an imagined collective and represents the collective as if it were a single individual. All these ideas could somehow co-exist in shifting forms of varying inconsistency: the primacy of the environment, the heredity of acquired characteristics, and the merging of individuality and collective. Such observations, I might repeat, do not mean I accuse Greeks or Romans of being proto-Nazis.[36] I claim some of them were proto-racists.

Anachronisms

The words 'race', 'racialism' and 'racism' did not occur with their modern meanings in English until the first decades of the twentieth century.[37] It might be argued that there could not have existed (proto-)racism in antiquity because there were no terms that formed the equivalent of modern 'race' and 'racism'.[38] Even though the words did not exist, however, it is methodologically correct to trace concepts fundamental to these phenomena, provided one avoids using modernizing definitions and

---

[33] See James W. Johnson, *The Formation of English Neo-Classical Thought* (Princeton, NJ: Princeton University Press, 1967), pp. 57–68.

[34] Herbert Spencer, *The Principles of Sociology*, 3 vols. (New York: D. Appleton and Company, 1876–96).

[35] Friedrich Ratzel, *Politische Geographie* (Munich and Leipzig: R. Oldenbourg, 1897); Ellen Churchill Semple, *Influences of Geographic Environment, on the Basis of Ratzel's System of Anthropogeography* (New York: H. Holt and Co., 1911). For the environmental ideas of Spencer and Ratzel: Franklin Thomas, *The Environmental Basis of Society: a Study in the History of Sociological Theory* (New York: Century, 1925), pp. 78–91.

[36] This seems to be the implication of comments by Christopher Jones, *Scripta Classica Israelica* 24 (2005), 289. Citing with approval E. R. Dodds on the indirect influence of Plato through Nietzsche on Nazi ideology, Jones says Dodds thereby 'does not make Plato a "proto-Nazi"'. I have been careful in distinguishing clearly between ancient forms of prejudice and modern forms of persecution, notably Nazi ideology. Indeed I do not link Plato with Nazi ideology, but in fact it is Dodds who does so, explicitly comparing Plato's political ideas with the applied Nazi and Soviet policy: 'We can see why Plato, like the Nazis and the Russians wished to restrict opportunities of foreign travel' (E. R. Dodds, *The Ancient Concept of Progress and other Essays on Greek Literature and Belief* (Oxford: Clarendon Press, 1973), p. 98). All Nazis were racists, but not all racists were, are, or will be Nazis.

[37] *Invention of Racism*, p. 25. For the semantic history of the term 'race' see the paper by Miramon in this volume.

[38] Gillett, 'Review of Isaac's', 410–11 rejects the apparent anachronism: 'This broad definition [sc. of racism] may not be agreeable to every sociologist, but it provides a reasoned platform for discussion.'

keeps a number of differentiated terms in circulation.[39] With these as tools
I claim to have shown that scientific concepts were deployed in antiquity
to lay the foundations for such ideas, even if these never were combined to
formulate the sort of monist and coherent ideology that we encounter in
modern times.[40] By the same token one can speak of an Athenian Empire
in the fifth century, even though there is no precise parallel in fifth-century
Greek for the English term 'empire' or the Roman 'imperium'.

Moral anachronisms are another thing. It could be asserted that it is
intellectually fallacious to analyze ancient authors in terms of our contemporary value system, even if it is conceded that proto-racist concepts
did circulate. Generally speaking this type of argument may be valid, but
this cannot be the case if the ancient norms were disputed at the time. It is
problematic to condemn torture carried out as part of interrogations in a
period when it was standard judicial practice and if there is no evidence
that its moral justification or efficacy were doubted. However, if there
were such doubts and if the matter was a topic of dispute, this means that
one could make an intellectual choice at the time and a modern discussion
of all aspects of the issue is then no anachronism.

Regarding the argument concerning proto-racism one such response
may briefly be discussed because a matter of principle is at stake. At issue
is an extreme form of determinist stereotype found in the astrological work
of Ptolemy, *Tetrabiblos*. He essentially lists the usual stereotypes of his age
for each people in its region, claiming that these are characteristics determined by astrology.[41] Now, astrology, being the study of the movements
and relative positions of celestial bodies interpreted as having an influence
on human affairs and the natural world, is a pseudo-science. It can be used
by its practitioners any way they want without anybody being able to prove
they are wrong. Ptolemy uses it as a scientific method to show that the
prejudices he cherishes regarding various peoples are a reality imposed by
observable facts, analyzed in a scientific manner. This makes it a classic case
of (proto-)racism, for we are faced with a case of pseudo-science employed
to prove the existence of a hierarchy of peoples with unalterable qualities
imposed collectively by external factors in nature. This is not a modern
supposition, for astrology was by no means universally accepted as a system

---

[39] As noted by McCoskey, 'Naming the Fault in Question', 247–8. Christian
Delacampagne, 'Racism in the Ancient World?', *Patterns of Prejudice* 41 (2007), 83,
considers the term 'proto-racism' a useful one, given the absence of any word for 'race'
in the modern sense in ancient Greek. For discussion of this problem see Buell, *Why This
New Race*, 14–15.

[40] As emphasized by Shaw, 'Review of B. Isaac', 229. See also Daniel Richter, 'Review of
Isaac, *Invention*', *Classical Philology* 101 (2006), 290.

[41] Isaac, *Invention of Racism*, 99–101.

among Roman and Hellenistic intellectuals. The stoic philosopher Panaetius is said to have rejected it in the second century BC.[42] Cicero, *De Divinatione* 2.96, rejected it *in toto* more than a century and a half before Ptolemy wrote and, in the second century AD, Sextus Empiricus wrote a treatise against astrology.[43] It follows that intellectuals in the Roman world made an explicit decision as to whether and how they used astrology and this is what Ptolemy did, exploiting science to prove his conventional chauvinist prejudices and xenophobia.

Ptolemy wrote that persons whose 'co-rulers' were Jupiter, Mars and Mercury 'are more gifted in trade and exchange; they are more unscrupulous, despicable cowards, treacherous, servile, and in general fickle on account of the stars mentioned'.[44] This refers to Phoenicians and other peoples in their vicinity. I have cited this as an example of traditional stereotypes expressed in a deterministic framework of astrological pseudoscience. This has been termed a naïve modernist presupposition on my part, criticism which was based on the speculation that 'Ptolemy probably noticed that [these people were] "unscrupulous, despicable cowards [and] treacherous" etc. because those who handled money in those days generally were "servile," as Ptolemy calls them.'[45] The reviewer presumably means that they were of low social status, which is in itself not necessarily true and that they were therefore – in his view – understandably despised. This formulation in fact admits that we are facing not science, but a serious form of group prejudice, reputedly stemming from differences in social class and dressed in a coat of scientific rationalization. At another level it is to be regretted to find this type of argument in a scholarly publication in our times. No clarity is gained by condoning (as distinct from analyzing) collective chauvinism in the past. A traditional defence of historical anti-Semitism in Eastern Europe holds that Jews were moneylenders and traders whose sharp practices lay at the root of understandable or even justifiable hatred on the part of their non-Jewish clients.

Missing topics

There are gaps in my discussion, some of them to be filled by the present book. In the Introduction we mentioned the fact that some scholars felt Turkish, Chinese, Japanese, Hindu and African societies and their

---

[42] Cicero, *De Divinatione* 2.88: 'Panaetius, qui unus e Stoicis astrologorum praedicta reiecit.'
[43] Emidio Spinelli (ed.), *Sesto Empirico. Contro gli Astrologi* (Naples: Bibliopolis, 2000).
[44] Ptolemy, *Tetrabiblos* 2.3.65–6.
[45] John Nordling, 'Review of Isaac, *The Invention of Racism in Classical Antiquity*', *Journal of the American Academy of Religion* 74 (2006), 806–8, at 807.

prejudices should be considered and we have explained why we disagree with this assertion. Furthermore I have not discussed Homer on the Trojans or considered the biblical background. I might have discussed Alexander of Macedon and the Hellenistic period;[46] attitudes towards Jews in Hellenistic authors;[47] early Christian attitudes; laws, constitutions and institutions; Egyptian papyri; Scythians and Blacks in antiquity. The visual evidence could have been discussed more extensively. Some of these missing topics are genuine lacunae. However, it was not my ambition to write a history of racist ideas for all of antiquity. I meant to show that the essence of racism, as a conceptual mechanism serving to rationalize stereotypes and prejudices, has its origin in fifth-century Greece. I then traced the phenomenon through some major Greek and Latin authors who were read widely and exerted influence in later times.

Undoubtedly it will be worth considering the Hellenistic period. It remains to be seen whether this will decidedly affect the impression of patterns encountered in Greece before Alexander and in Rome. It seemed instructive to consider the image of Jews in Roman/Latin literature in order to gain an impression of their status in Rome, unaffected by the more intensive and rather different hatred projected by the Hellenized Alexandrian authors.[48] For instance, there are no accusations of Jewish cannibalism to be found in Latin sources, while these do occur in

---

[46] See now Craige Champion, *Cultural Politics in Polybius's* Histories (Berkeley and Los Angeles: University of California Press, 2004), chapter 2: 'Greeks, Romans, and Barbarians: The Cultural Politics of Hellenism' and chapter 7: 'Practical Contexts and Political Realities'. Chapter 2 contains also a short section on Greek hostility to Rome, a subject not dealt with in my work.

[47] See now René Bloch, *Antike Vorstellungen vom Judentum: Der Judenexkurs des Tacitus im Rahmen der griechisch-römischen Ethnographie* (Stuttgart: Steiner, 2002), which appeared too late for me to take it into account in *Invention of Racism*, chapter 13. See also below, p. 48.

[48] Bloch, *Antike Vorstellungen vom Judentum*, discusses the Hellenistic-Roman, non-Alexandrian treatment of the Jews (Hecataeus of Abdera, Posidonius, Pompeius Trogus and Tacitus) and his work only reinforces my impression that the Alexandrian authors were quite different in their attitudes to the Jews from other Hellenistic and Roman authors. His chapter 4 is especially illuminating, clarifying the topics and stereotypes encountered in many ethnographic texts, particularly in Tacitus, *Germania* and *Agricola*, but absent in his excursus on the Jews. Particularly noteworthy for present purposes is that the Jews are not described in terms of geographic determinism, unlike the Germans and Britons, possibly, says Bloch, because of their dispersion in both Judaea and the diaspora. They are not termed 'barbari'. The Jews live in a contrary world, the opposite of a normal society, but it is one of their own making, not one imposed by external influences. I conclude that we are faced with ethnic stereotyping, rather than proto-racism. Bloch disagrees: see 'Die Anfänge des Rassismus in der Antike', *Tachles: das jüdische Wochenmagazin* 4(49) (2004), 1–3. I would agree, however, that what we know of Alexandrian hatred of the Jews was different in character from the regular fare encountered in Latin literature.

literature of Alexandrian origin.[49] Also, the only straightforward discussion of plans of total extermination of the Jewish people may be found in texts of Hellenistic origin.[50]

It may well be profitable to study legal texts. Two examples must suffice. In 212 Caracalla called for the expulsion from the city of Alexandria of 'all Egyptians who are in Alexandria, and particularly country folk who have fled thither from elsewhere and can be easily identified'.[51] The formulation of the edict is significant. Those fulfilling specific useful professions are excluded from the planned expulsion, but country folk who come to the city in order to avoid farm work should be expelled to 'the countryside where they belong'. An exception is made for those who visit the city out of a desire to see it, or 'those in pursuit of a more cultured existence or on occasional business'. Again, to be expelled are Egyptian weavers who can easily be recognized by their speech, which reveals that they are affecting the appearance and dress of others but by their lifestyle clearly are Egyptian rustics. Second, a constitution dating from the joint reign of Valentinian I and Valens, probably in the 370s, prohibited marriage (*coniugium, copula*) between Romans (*provinciales*) and non-Romans (*gentiles, barbarae*) (*Codex Theodosianus* 3.14.1).[52]

Early Christian attitudes towards the Jews and other non-Christians are different in character from those of pagan Romans and ought to be studied both from the perspective of Christian attitudes towards non-Christians in general and as part of the history of anti-Semitism.[53] I have therefore

---

[49] Josephus, *Contra Apionem* 2.89. Cassius Dio reports Jewish cannibalism during the revolt in the diaspora under Trajan (Dio 68.32.1), but this is very likely based on an Alexandrian source, for Dio relates no such stories in his (abbreviated) passage on the Bar Kokhba revolt: 69.12.1–14.3.

[50] Diodorus 34–35.1.5 and Jos., *Ant.* 13.8.2 (245): advice given Antiochus Sidetes by his advisors.

[51] *P. Giss.* 40.2, trans. Naphtali Lewis, *Life in Egypt under Roman Rule* (Oxford: Clarendon Press, 1983), pp. 202–3. For present purposes, see the analysis by Buell, *Why This New Race*, 38–9.

[52] Hagith S. Sivan, 'Why Not Marry a Barbarian?: Marital Frontiers in Late Antiquity (The Example of *CTh* 3.14.1)', in Ralph W. Mathisen and Hagith S. Sivan (eds), *Shifting Frontiers in Late Antiquity* (Aldershot, Hants and Brookfield, VT: Variorum, 1996), pp. 135–45; Alain Chauvot, *Opinions romaines face aux barbares au IVe siècle ap. J.-C.* (Paris: De Boccard, 1998), pp. 131–44 with further references on p. 132). See now Jason Moralee, 'Maximinus Thrax and the Politics of Race in Late Antiquity', *Greece & Rome* 55 (2008), 55–82. Moralee shows that a powerful movement against the marriage of Roman citizens with non-Romans developed in the fourth century.

[53] For this topic see Buell, *Why This New Race* and her contribution to this volume, chapter 5. For early Christian attitudes towards blacks: Gay L. Byron, *Symbolic Blackness and Ethnic Difference in Early Christian Literature* (London/New York: Routledge, 2002) which contains ample references to blacks, Ethiopians and Egyptians in the sources, but does not

restricted myself to the writings of mainstream classical Greek and Latin authors.

I admit, however, that attitudes towards Blacks in antiquity should have been discussed because it is a major topic of current interest and I should have anticipated that my failure to do so would frustrate readers who expect serious treatment of the subject in a book about the history of racism, independently of any strictly logical arguments I may have had for their exclusion.[54] The difficulties standing in the way of serious discussion of the subject are clear.[55]

Apart from the sensitivity of the subject, it is hard to deal satisfactorily with the significance of skin colour through various periods and cultures, because the contents of the terms and their emotional impact vary strongly and are often difficult to grasp. Skin colour could operate in a remarkably elastic way also in English texts of the eighteenth century: 'The assurance that skin colour was the primary signifier of human difference was not a dominant conception until the last quarter of the eighteenth century, and even then individuals responded variously to nonwhite skin colour.'[56] 'Even today ... *black* and *white* are simplifying, though powerful, cover stories for a dense matrix of ideas as closely associated with cultural differences as with the body's surface.'[57] It is probably impossible to say what feelings the ancient images of Blacks would convey to the public for which they were produced, for the emotional responses to physical differences vary a good deal over time and between cultures. In this connection it may be noted that Shapiro's contribution to this volume shows the message concerning the Persians conveyed by Greek vase painting to have been radically different from that found in the contemporary

specifically discuss issues of prejudice and racism as such. Note also Aaron P. Johnson, *Ethnicity and Argument in Eusebius'* Praeparatio Evangelica (Oxford/New York: Oxford University Press, 2006) which is less concerned with the themes of the present volume.

[54] According to Harris, 'Phoenician Trash', 9, 'the paradigm case of racism for most people now is discriminatory behaviour by a person with a more or less pale skin towards a person of darker colour or different physiognomy'. First, racism is not just behaviour of one person to another, as observed by J. L. A. Garcia, 'Three Sites for Racism: Social Structures, Valuings, and Vice' in M. P. Levine and T. Pataki (eds.), *Racism in Mind* (Ithaca, NY: Cornell University Press, 2004), pp. 35–55, at p. 43: 'We ordinarily think the person who feels racial hostility, contempt, or indifference is already marked with racism whether or not she "display[s]" it.' Second, racism as an ideology and set of attitudes is only restricted to conflict between peoples of different skin colour in some parts of the world in some periods. It is not the case in other parts and there should be no need to repeat that it is incorrect for periods in the past, some rather recent or not past at all, as Bosnian Muslims and Rwandan Tutsis will confirm.

[55] See now David Goldenberg, *The Curse of Ham: Race and Slavery in Early Judaism, Christianity, and Islam* (Princeton, NJ: Princeton University Press, 2003) and his chapter in this volume.

[56] Wheeler, *Complexion of Race*, pp. 3–4.   [57] Ibid., p. 2.

literature, the former representing objects used at home, and the latter public ideology. Similarly, as Bartlett points out below, 'the two most consistent traditions of representing black Africans physiologically, with not only black skin but also full lips, broad nose and curly hair, originated in parts of Europe where Europeans were least likely to meet actual black Africans, namely in Germany and central Europe.' They were depicted not to register a social reality but to make a theological point, about the universal mission of the Church. We may assume that the Athenians and Romans in antiquity felt themselves to be quite superior to Blacks, for they regarded themselves as superior to all foreigners. In Athens black slaves were a favourite expensive commodity as follows quite clearly from a passage in Theophrastus' *Characters*:

> The man of Petty Ambition is one who, when asked to dinner, will be anxious to be placed next to the host at table. He will take his son away to Delphi to have his hair cut. He will be careful, too, that his attendant shall be an Aethiopian.
>
> (Theophrastus, *Char.* 21, trans. Jebb)[58]

Attic vase paintings seem to reinforce this impression that black slaves were fashionable property in Athens, apparently because they were rare and regarded as exotic.[59]

It is difficult to measure the numerical impact Blacks had in Graeco-Roman society in general[60] and even more problematic to judge how the numerical impact was connected with attitudes towards Blacks. In Late

---

[58] Theophrastus, *Char.* 21 Ἡ δὲ μικροφιλοτιμία δόξει εἶναι ὄρεξις τιμῆς ἀνελεύθερος, ὁ δὲ μικροφιλότιμος τοιοῦτός τις, οἷος σπουδάσαι ἐπὶ δεῖπνον κληθεὶς παρ' αὐτὸν τὸν καλέσαντα κατακείμενος δειπνῆσαι. καὶ τὸν υἱὸν ἀποκεῖραι ἀπαγαγὼν εἰς Δελφούς, καὶ ἐπιμεληθῆναι δέ, ὅπως αὐτῷ ὁ ἀκόλουθος Αἰθίοψ ἔσται.

[59] Wulf Raeck, *Zum Barbarenbild in der Kunst Athens im 6. und 5. Jahrhunderts v. Chr.* (Bonn: R. Habelt, 1981), pp. 179–82. Yvon Garlan, *Slavery in Ancient Greece* (Ithaca, NY: Cornell University Press, 1988), pp. 60–1: in the Hellenistic period the number of black slaves increased, but it remained always limited and more a form of curiosity than a common appearance; Frederick Hugh Thompson, *The Archaeology of Greek and Roman Slavery* (London: Duckworth, 2003), pp. 19–20. The majority of Greek slaves came from Thrace and the Black Sea and from Asia Minor. This does not contradict the supposition that black slaves were regarded as a valuable commodity because they were unusual.

[60] Frank M. Snowden, Jr., *Before Color Prejudice: The Ancient View of Blacks* (Cambridge, MA: Harvard University Press, 1983), p. 27: 'The popularity of Negroes in the art of the fifth century and of Ethiopian themes in the theater was probably a reflection of an interest stimulated both by the experience of Greek residents in Egypt and contemporary reports of Ethiopian soldiers.' Snowden, pp. 65–7, discusses the size of the black population in ancient Mediterranean societies and expresses doubts that there is a clear correlation between numbers and colour prejudice. He further asserts (p. 88): 'Enslaved prisoners of war undoubtedly accounted for a substantial portion of the black population in countries beyond Nubia.' See also the earlier work of Jean Vercoutter, Jean Leclant, Frank M. Snowden, Jr., and Jehan Desanges, *The Image of the Black in Western Art*, 1: *From the Pharaohs to the Fall of the Roman Empire* (Cambridge, MA: Harvard University Press, 1976), pp. 148–67 at pp. 164–5 and figs. 194–8, on the blacks appearing on several vases who, he assumes, are slaves.

Antiquity, but not before, we hear about trade in Ethiopian children.[61] There is certainly no correlation between the number of references in the sources and demographic reality, as may be illustrated by the great interest in Blacks seen in the sources analyzed by Peter Biller and Valentin Groebner in their chapters below. A further point also to be taken into account is that there seems to have been a rather vague notion of the heritability of skin colour, as is clear from Aristotle's assertion that a Greek woman in Elis and a black man had a white daughter and a black grand-daughter.[62] This indicates at least some confusion about the physiological basis and acquisition of skin colour, a confusion that also existed in Latin America in the eighteenth century, as shown by Cañizares in his chapter, below.

Another serious omission was proper consideration of the Middle Ages.[63] The assumption maintained throughout my book was that the Greek and Latin literature contained ideas taken up, after a long gap, by intellectuals of the sixteenth and seventeenth centuries, who then began applying and expanding them into what was to become modern racism. As already indicated, it would have been illuminating to consider more of the late antique sources.[64] It further appears that there is much to say about the intervening centuries.[65] The present book therefore contains six chapters that deal with these periods.

There is still one intriguing subject that might have been included and was not, namely Judah Halevi's much discussed assertions regarding the essential difference between born Jews and converts,[66] notably the

[61] Cosmas Indicopleustès, *Topographie chrétienne*, ed. Wanda Wolska-Conus (Paris: Éditions du Cerf, 1968–70) II, pp. 43–64. A papyrus from the sixth century indicated the selling of a 6-year-old black girl by Ethiopian traders for 4 *nomismata*. P. Str., 1404, edited and commented by Friedrich Preisigke, 'Ein Sklavenkauf des 6. Jahrhunderts. (P. gr. Str. Inv. Nr. 1404)', *Archiv für Papyrusforschung* 3 (1906), 415–24. I owe these references to Youval Rotman.

[62] Aristotle, *Historia Animalium* 586a; cf. Antigonus, *Mirabilia* 112b; Aristotle, *De Generatione Animalium* 722a. See the similar case cited by Pliny, *Naturalis Historia* 7.51.

[63] I should have been aware of the special issue of *The Journal of Medieval and Early Modern Studies* 31(1) (2001) on 'Race and Ethnicity in the Middle Ages', edited by Thomas Hahn.

[64] See Moralee's paper, cited above, n. 52.

[65] See now Steven A. Epstein, *Purity Lost: Transgressing Boundaries in the Eastern Mediterranean, 1000–1400* (Baltimore, MD: Johns Hopkins University Press, 2007), p. 11: 'Fredrickson, and Goldenberg and Isaac, by coming at the problem of racism from two chronologically opposed perspectives, have in effect challenged mediaevalists to fill in the middle of the story and resolve inconsistencies in the grand narrative of western racism.' I would not have been capable of treating the Middle Ages, but I ought to have made the challenge explicit.

[66] Lippman Bodoff, 'Was Yehudah Halevi Racist?', *Judaism* 38(2) (1989), 174–84; Daniel J. Lasker, 'Proselyte Judaism, Christianity, and Islam in the Thought of Judah Halevi', *The Jewish Quarterly Review*, n.s., 81(1/2) (1990), 75–91.

passage from the Kuzari (*c.* 1130–40) which seems to leave no doubt that he was familiar with Aristotle's theory of natural slavery: 'Those, however, who become Jews do not take equal rank with born Israelites, who are specially privileged to attain to prophecy, whilst the former can only achieve something by learning from them, and can only become pious and learned but never prophets.'[67] It is, of course, not surprising to find such influence in an author who read Greek texts in Arabic, including Plato, Aristotle and Galen, and who appears to be familiar with geographic determinism.[68]

At another level it might be useful to contribute more of a comparative analysis of the link between ancient and modern ideas.[69] This would have reinforced the argument if reception processes had been traced in depth rather than noted as a possibly significant phenomenon.

To conclude these observations on the missing topics, it can be said that there clearly is room for more work in future.

East–West: Greeks and Persians

Herodotus, I have argued, describes the Greeks who resisted Persia as fighting for political independence, not for personal liberty or other moral ideals. Herodotus, moreover, did not see the war between Greece and Persia as a struggle between East and West and he does not disparage Persia, but describes it as a formidable enemy defeated at great peril. Greek victory was achieved in spite of the immense power of the enemy. The image of the Persians as soft, servile, arrogant and corrupt belongs to a later stage, the end of the fifth and beginning of the fourth centuries. The opposition between western Greeks and eastern Persians, I claim, is not found in Herodotus. The importance of the matter goes far beyond a question of chronology, for it concerns the issue of the ideological context of a particularly chauvinist attitude on the part of the Greeks towards the eastern major power. Did it develop immediately following the victories over Persia in the first quarter of the fifth century in what had been a defensive war for the Greeks? Was it an almost instantaneous response on the part of those who had been under threat and managed to defend themselves against attack? Or was it the result of a gradual shift in spirit of those who had been successful defenders and then became attackers and

---

[67] Judah Halevi, *Kuzari* 1.115, trans. Hartwig Hirschfeld; cf. 1.27: 'any Gentile who joins us unconditionally shares our good fortune, without, however, being quite equal to us.'

[68] *Kuzari* 2.10–12, explaining why the inhabitants of Palestine were better than other people; 2.20, Palestine, the centre of the world.

[69] Emma Bridges, *Journal of Hellenic Studies* 125 (2005), 180–1.

conquerors? In my opinion the latter is the right answer. This view has been accepted by quite a few scholars,[70] but it has also been called both 'neither new nor controversial'[71] and 'the most controversial' of my claims and 'unconvincing'.[72] The subject is considered by Alan Shapiro through the perspective of the visual arts in another chapter of this volume. This strongly confirms that fifth-century Greeks had quite a different view of the Persians than the one conveyed by Isocrates. As Shapiro puts it: 'The image of the Persians presented by Classical Athenian art is an invented one, in which an attitude of extreme ambivalence – condescension and admiration, attraction and repulsion – is continually played out.'

One reviewer offers discussion of two passages from Herodotus' *Histories* and one from Aeschylus' *Persae* in order to refute my interpretation:

(a) 7.135 where a Spartan ambassador explains to a satrap why the Spartans refuse to submit to the Persian king. They refuse to be enslaved and decide to fight for freedom. The point of my book is not that, in Herodotus' view, the Greeks thought freedom irrelevant. It is that he represents them as fighting for independence from foreign rule, not for individual liberty. It is true that Herodotus regards monarchy and tyranny always as a form of enslavement. Tyranny and monarchy are forms of rule which, in Herodotus' view, deny the state its proper ruling institutions. Still, that does not mean he thinks the Greeks were fighting for individual liberty. Furthermore it is my point that Herodotus did not think in terms of a freedom-loving West versus a slavish East.[73]

(b) 7.96, where Herodotus says of non-Persian officers serving in the fleet: 'In any case these native officers were not really commanders; like the rest of the troops, they merely served as slaves.' The reviewer cites this to refute my claim that Herodotus regarded the Persian army as a formidable fighting force and not as an army of slaves, i.e. an army that could not function in battle because its component troops were slavish. It is true that Herodotus here describes the troops provided by the subject nations and their commanders as *douloi*, slaves. However, the point is that the word 'slaves' is used here as the common term for

---

[70] Maurice Sartre, *L'histoire* 291 (October 2004) 30–1; Joseph Geiger, *Zion* 70 (2005), 553–8 (Heb.), at 555; Johannes Engels, *Sehepunkte* 5 (2005), Nr. 5 [15.05.2005]; Paula Fredriksen, *The New Republic* March 21 (2005), 25–9, at 26. Note, independently, Champion, *Cultural Politics in Polybius'* Histories (2004), pp. 36–9, who observes that Herodotus and Aeschylus give the Persians a sympathetic hearing and concludes: 'Aeschylus' *Persians* and Herodotus's historical writing undermine the idea of an impenetrable fifth-century Athenian evaluative boundary between Greek and non-Greek.'

[71] Daniel Richter, *Classical Philology* 101 (2006), 287–90, at 289.

[72] McInerney, 'Review of B. Isaac', 85–6.   [73] Isaac, *Invention of Racism*, p. 266.

subject peoples without any possibility of independent action. They were subject peoples, but this did not make the Persian army weak in Herodotus' eyes.[74]

(c) The third and rather different point concerns a brief reference to Queen Atossa's dream in Aeschylus' *Persae* 181–7.[75] The point here is just that two women, one Persian, the other Greek, are both described in equally superlative terms. One allows herself to be subjugated, the other rebels. The essence of my argument is that the Persian woman is not depicted as inferior, while Aeschylus' public knew, as we do, that the *Persae* celebrates a Greek victory that actually took place.

Generally speaking I do not deny the value of poetry written for the stage as has been claimed, but I do assert that the material is hard to interpret. Edith Hall, an author who has made such an attempt, has reached conclusions different from mine, different also from those of other scholars who analyzed Aeschylus' poetic treatment of the struggle between Greece and Persia.[76] Rather than arguing with Hall's work, I have based my work mostly on explicit statements in prose, as distinct from implicit allusions in dramatic poetry.

A step farther?

Besides sceptics who deny the existence of racism in antiquity, there are critics who argue that I have not gone far enough.[77] Racism, they say, was there, and it should not be called proto-racism. After some consideration I now tend to agree with them. However, it remains a fact that in antiquity

---

[74] Ibid., p. 267.   [75] Ibid., pp. 275–6.

[76] Edith Hall, *Inventing the Barbarian: Greek Self-Definition through Tragedy* (Oxford: Clarendon Press, 1989). See the earlier work of Helen Bacon, *Barbarians in Greek Tragedy* (New Haven, CT: Yale University Press, 1961) and see Thomas Harrison, *The Emptiness of Asia: Aeschylus' Persians and the History of the Fifth Century* (London: Duckworth, 2000). Bacon is concerned primarily with realia and factual information concerning non-Greeks in Greek tragedy. For Aeschylus, discussed on pp. 15–63, he concludes that his work is relatively accurate in its differentiation and representation of foreigners which, he says, takes the emphasis off foreignness as such, and the related idea of the superiority of Greeks to all foreigners. Harrison's book has quite a different focus from that of Hall; see pp. 113–4 for some interesting observations regarding the assumption of Greek superiority and Persian inferiority in recent scholarship. See now Ema Bridges, Edith Hall and Peter J. Rhodes (eds.), *Cultural Responses to the Persian Wars: Antiquity to the Third Millennium* (Oxford: Oxford University Press), 2007.

[77] Lefkowitz, 198: 'As Isaac might have brought out even more forcefully, it is not the fact that Greco-Roman proto-racism was unique in the history of the ancient world that made it more influential and destructive than that of other peoples. Rather, it was their ability to deploy "evidence" and "reasoning" in defense of their questionable theories'; Shaw, 'Review of B. Isaac'.

racism never developed into the unified, general ideology which formed the motor for a uniform mental and social system, such as developed in recent times.[78] There are several essential elements in ancient society that may have influenced racist ideology, but in a somewhat different direction from the one we have known in recent centuries: (1) Religion: monotheist or polytheist. (2) Connected with this, the development of secular science. (3) Concepts of liberty, equality and the justification of slavery or, conversely, the desire to deny the right to liberty and equality and to justify slavery.

(1) and (2), religion and the development of secular science: it is worth noting that the ideas of environmental determinism and the heredity of acquired characteristics are most explicitly formulated in works of Greek and Latin literature that are devoid of any religious content: medical treatises (Hippocrates and Galen); political philosophy (Plato, Aristotle); architecture and geography (Vitruvius, Strabo); a handbook of military science (Vegetius); astrology (Ptolemy of Alexandria). It is worth considering to what extent this fact played a role in the development of racism in various periods. Ancient pagan civilization never really distanced itself from religion, but monotheistic religions far more committed their cultures ideologically and intellectually than Greek and Roman paganism ever did. I have not traced the position of Early Christian authors on the present subject, but it is central in a recently published work.[79] It is, in any event, possible that the popularized conclusions of scientific analysis were at some stage combined with the developing monotheistic religions.[80]

Finally (3), there are the concepts of liberty and slavery. In spite of Aristotle's unique attempt to develop the idea of natural slavery, antiquity never saw a need to justify the existence of servitude. Individual and

[78] See on these matters Shaw, 'Review of Isaac'.
[79] Richard H. Popkin, 'The Philosophical Basis of Eighteenth-Century Racism', in Harold E. Pagliaro, *Studies in Eighteenth-Century Culture: Racism in the Eighteenth Century* (Cleveland, OH: Press of Case Western Reserve University, 1973), pp. 245–62 at 245–6. Popkin argues that the root theory in the various forms of eighteenth-century racist thinking was universalistic, benign, and neutral, but that each went through a transformation so that it became a basis for a racist ideology. In this connection may be mentioned Henri Grégoire's attack on eighteenth-century racism in his *De la littérature des Nègres* (Paris: Maradan, 1808). He argues that all this happened because people had given up biblical humanism and with it the conviction that everyone, no matter what he looked like, was an image of god. See also: Henri Grégoire, *Enquiry concerning the Intellectual and Moral Faculties and Literature of Negroes*, English trans. (Brooklyn, NY: Printed by T. Kirk, 1810), p. 39, and on this Ruth F. Necheles, 'Grégoire and the Egalitarian Movement' in Pagliaro, *Studies*, pp. 355–68. Grégoire denied that racial mixture produced an inferior population and favoured intermarriage.
[80] See above, n. 53.

collective bondage were a matter of course, because there was no assumption that a person had a natural or moral right to freedom, just as the subjection of one people by another was not in itself morally condemned. Genocide occurred in antiquity as it has occurred in modern history. While it is in our times regarded as the ultimate crime, that was not the case in antiquity. 'The foreign nations which could with safety be pardoned I preferred to save rather than destroy',[81] claims Augustus in his report on his achievements. The implications are clear: another general might have destroyed them even if they could with safety be pardoned, and it was natural to destroy those regarded as unsafe. The difference in moral considerations may have meant that the urge to build a systematic and consistent theory proving that one set of human beings was inferior to another was less strong than in modern times.

These ideas are seductive although difficult to prove or disprove, but they are worth following up.

To conclude this chapter, I tend to say that it is not very significant whether we speak of proto-racism or racism in the classical world, as long as we recognize the phenomenon for what it is: a pattern of recurring efforts to ascribe to groups of human beings common characteristics on seemingly logical and presumed scientific grounds from the late fifth century BC to late antiquity.

---

[81] Augustus, *Res Gestae Divi Augusti* 3: 'Externas gentes quibus tuto ignosci potuit, conservare quam excidere malui.'

3   The invention of Persia in Classical Athens*

H. A. Shapiro

The late Edward Said considered Aeschylus's play *Persians*, produced in
472 BCE, to be the earliest instance of what he famously termed orientalism, a process in which "Asia speaks through and by virtue of the
European imagination."[1] The play, set in a Persian court that neither
Aeschylus nor any other Athenian of his time had ever seen or knew
anything reliable about, nevertheless invents an entire community –
from the Queen Mother Atossa and her son Xerxes down to the ordinary
Persian elders who form the chorus – that is both familiar (i.e. Greek)
enough for the Athenian audience to recognize, and indeed to sympathize
with, and yet foreign and exotic enough to fire its imagination.[2] In this
paper, I will suggest that Athenian visual artists, over a period of almost a
century and a half, did precisely this: they invented an imaginary world
called Persia that fired the imagination of customers both at home and
abroad and, in a few instances, they were even clever enough to sell this
vision to customers in the Persian Empire, who would hardly have recognized themselves.

As regards the issue of racism, I agree with the conclusions of Ben
Isaac's definitive study, that there is nothing in fifth-century Greek

* I wish to thank the organizers of the Tel Aviv conference for the invitation to participate
  and for their extraordinary hospitality during my entire stay in Israel. In re-working this
  paper for publication I have benefited from discussion with colleagues and audiences at the
  University of Arizona; the Columbia University Society of Fellows in the Humanities; and
  Washington University in St. Louis. I also thank my hosts on these occasions: Eleni
  Hasaki, Andrew Lear, and Johanna Hobratschk and Susan Rotroff, respectively. I partic-
  ularly thank Ralph Rosen of the University of Pennsylvania and my former student
  Gregory Jones for helpful discussion of the Eurymedon oinochoe (Figs. 7–8).

[1] Edward W. Said, *Orientalism* (New York, 1979), 56. For more detailed discussions of the
  "orientalism" of the play see Edith Hall, *Inventing the Barbarian* (Oxford, 1989); Thomas
  Harrison, *The Emptiness of Asia. Aeschylus' Persians and the History of the Fifth Century*
  (London, 2000).
[2] See, among recent discussions of the play, Pericles Georges, *Barbarian Asia and the Greek
  Experience* (Baltimore, 1994), 96–102.

attitudes toward Persia that can be termed even "proto-racism."[3] And I would go further, to argue that this is true not only for all the reasons that Isaac gleans from the literary sources (especially Herodotos),[4] but because, in the case of the visual imagery, the construct called "Persians" is in most instances no more "real" or historical than the Amazons or the Trojans to whom the Persians are most often likened. The image of the Persians presented by Classical Athenian art is an invented one, in which an attitude of extreme ambivalence – condescension and admiration, attraction and repulsion – is continually played out.

The earliest Persians: before and after the Persian Wars

It is unlikely that many Athenians had ever seen a Persian up close before the battle of Marathon in 490.[5] There are only a handful of possible depictions of Persians on Attic vases in the few decades before that fateful year, and none of them is certain. Perhaps the earliest is a curious individual on a black-figured amphora in Florence that can be dated to the 520s (Fig. 3.1).[6] Seated upon a simple stool, this gentlemen is dressed in an outfit that has only a vague resemblance to the "real" Persians in Achaemenid art but is close enough to later Greek depictions to suggest that he is indeed intended as a Persian: a snug, sleeveless jacket and patterned trousers (both accented by white stripes), white socks, and a turban-like hat that is flatter than the high-crowned style usually called Persian. The short kilt decorated with flowers is a unique feature, while the thin battle-axe anticipates later Persian iconography.[7] Though the figure has sometimes been called a Scythian, it is quite clear that he is not, since the man standing before him *is* a typical Scythian archer, known

---

[3] Benjamin Isaac, *The Invention of Racism in Classical Antiquity* (Princeton, 2004), 1–2 and *passim*. For a recent assessment of scholarly approaches to the study of Athenian attitudes toward the Persians – itself a subject fraught with ambivalence – see Thomas Harrison's introduction, in Thomas Harrison (ed.), *Greeks and Barbarians* (New York, 2002), 6–21.

[4] On the issue of "orientalism" and "anti-orientalism" in Herodotos, especially in his use of Persian and Greek terms, see now Rosaria V. Munson, *Black Doves Speak: Herodotus and the Languages of Barbarians* (Washington, 2005), 56–63.

[5] On relations between Greeks and Persians before the Persian Wars see Arnaldo Momigliano, *Alien Wisdom: the Limits of Hellenization* (Cambridge, 1975), 123–129. Herodotos 5.73 notes a short-lived treaty between Athens and Persia in *c.* 508.

[6] Florence, Museo Archeologico 3845; J. D. Beazley, *Attic Black-Figure Vase-Painters* (Oxford University Press, 1956) (hereafter *ABV*) 287, 1; J. D. Beazley, *Paralipomena. Additions to Attic Black-Figure Vase-Painters and Attic Red-Figure Vase-Painters*, Oxford, 1971 (hereafter Para) 125, 7*bis*; Konrad Schauenburg, "Eurumedon eimi," *Mitteilungen des Deutschen Archäologischen Instituts, Athenische Abteilung* 90 (1975), 112; Maria Frederika Vos, *Scythian Archers in Archaic Attic Vase-Painting* (Groningen, 1963), 13–14.

[7] See Wulf Raeck, *Zur Barbarenbild in der Kunst Athens im 6. und 5. Jahrhundert v. Chr* (Bonn, 1981), 101–103 for a summary of Persian dress and attributes on vases.

Fig. 3.1 Persian King or satrap with attendants. Florence, Museo
Archeologico 3845. Attic black-figure neck-amphora, *c.* 520 BCE.

from scores of Attic vases from the middle of the sixth century, in a short
kilt without trousers and a pointed cap.[8] Note also that the beard of the
Persian is considerable longer and fuller than that of the Scythian, a trait
that remains consistent in Attic iconography and does seem to reflect
observed reality.

Why the sudden appearance of a Persian three decades before Marathon?
In the context of this particular vase, the point seems to turn on the role of
the Scythians as mediators between Greece and the Persian Empire.[9] On
the reverse side of the amphora (Fig. 3.2), a Greek hoplite warrior takes
leave of his mother and father as his Scythian companion waits quietly at the
side. On the front side (Fig. 3.1), the Persian – perhaps a satrap – gives

---

[8] For the iconography of Scythian archers see the fundamental study of Vos, *Scythian
Archers*, and, of recent discussions, Balbina Bäbler, *Fleissige Thrakerinnen und Wehrhafte
Skythen. Nichtgriechen im klassischen Athen und ihre archäologische Hinterlassenschaft*
(Stuttgart and Leipzig, 1998), 163–181 and Askol'd I. Ivanchik, "Who were the
'Scythian' Archers on Archaic Attic Vases?" in: David Braund (ed.), *Scythians and
Greeks* (Exeter, 2005), 100–113.

[9] Cf. François Lissarrague, *L'autre guerrier. Archers, peltastes, cavaliers dans l'imagerie attique*
(Paris, 1990), 112.

Fig. 3.2 Departure of a Greek hoplite. Side B of the amphora in Fig. 3.1.

orders to his Scythian attendant and the hoplites take the subsidiary positions. There is no particular event, either real or mythological, just a snapshot of the increasingly cosmopolitan world of the later sixth century.

The Persian Empire probably first impinged on the Athenian imagination in the 540s, with the fall of Lydian Sardis and the death of Croesus, who was well known to the Greeks for his fabled wealth and extravagant dedications in the sanctuary at Delphi (Herodotos 1.50–51). Within a few decades, Croesus would become a quasi-mythical figure for the Greeks, the story of his spectacular and heroic end a subject not just for the poet Bacchylides,[10] but also for one of the greatest painters of the turn of the

[10] Ode 3; Herwig Maehler, *Bacchylides. A Selection* (Cambridge, 2004), 80–83. See Walter Burkert, "Das Ende des Kroisos: Vorstufen einer herodoteischen Geschichtserzählung," in *Catalepton. Festschrift Bernard Wyss*, ed. Christoph Schäublin (Basel, 1985), 4–15 on the different versions of the death of Croesus.

Fig. 3.3 Croesus on the pyre. Louvre G 197. Attic red-figure
amphora attributed to Myson, 500–490 BCE.

sixth to fifth centuries (Fig. 3.3).[11] It is likely that Croesus's conqueror
Cyrus acquired a similarly mythical status for the Greeks.

With Darius (522–486), the Persians start to become more "real" in
Greek eyes. A few images that can be dated earlier than 490 suggest that
stories may have circulated that seemed to prefigure the Persian threat to

---

[11] Amphora by Myson in the Louvre, G 197; J. D. Beazley, *Attic Red-Figure Vase-Painters*,
second edition (Oxford, 1963) (hereafter *ARV²*), 238, 1; Erika Simon and Max Hirmer,
Die griechischen Vasen (Munich, 1981), pls. 132–133; Tonio Hölscher, *Griechische
Historienbilder des 5. und 4. Jahrhunderts v. Chr.* (Würzburg, 1973), 30–31.

Fig. 3.4 Greek hoplite fighting a Persian archer. Basel, Antikenmuseum + Sammlung Ludwig BS 488. Attic red-figure cup, *c.* 520 BCE.

Greece. A remarkable red-figure cup of about 520 (Fig. 3.4),[12] for example, shows a Persian archer in the characteristic high-crowned headgear overwhelmed by a Greek warrior. The Persian is even given an exotic name – Seraguê – that occurs on a second Attic vase but is otherwise unattested.[13]

The vases also suggest that, even before the first Persian invasion of Greece, the process of assimilating them to other quasi-mythical, or entirely mythical, Eastern barbarians, such as Black Ethiopians, Scythians, and Amazons, had already begun. Thus, a single workshop in Athens around 500 produced several dozen alabastra in the so-called white-ground technique, that is, silhouette figures on a thin white slip that simulates ivory or marble or stone.[14] In this case the shape, and the name, derive from the alabaster from which this distinctive type of perfume vessel was made in Egypt and the Near East. Typically, these Athenian alabastra show a woolly-haired Black African in an imaginary costume probably never seen below the Sahara (hence the archaeological

---

[12] Basel, Antikenmuseum + Sammlung Ludwig BS 488; ARV² 172, 4; 1631; *Corpus Vasorum Antiquorum* (hereafter *CVA*) (Basel 2) pl. 9, 2.

[13] Amphora, British Museum E 253; *ARV²* 35, 2. Cf. Schauenburg, "Eurumedon eimi," 104 and 116 for another possible depiction of a Persian before 490.

[14] Group of the Negro Alabastra: *ARV²* 267–269. On the iconography of the group see Jenifer Neils, "The Group of the Negro Alabastra: Study of Motif Transferal," *Antike Kunst* 23 (1980), 13–23.

nickname "Negro alabastra"), combined with an Amazon or Scythian archer. One shows what could be a pair of young Persians with the characteristic curved sword and bow.[15] The figures on these vessels have been taken to be a kind of "logo," advertising the exotic sources of the precious, imported scents that they contained.[16] These examples should warn us that any attempt to bring the evidence of vase-paintings into the discussion must take account of the shape, function, provenance, and archaeological context of the vessels on which the image appears.

The development of Persian imagery on Athenian vases between Xerxes' invasion of 480 and the beginning of the fourth century has been sketched out by several scholars, most notably Wulf Raeck and Tonio Hölscher.[17] I would like here both to modify the picture somewhat and to make the argument that to measure the scenes in each succeeding generation by their supposed fidelity to actual events, manners, and styles is to miss the bigger picture. Although I, too, take a diachronic approach in this paper and, like Hölscher, try to trace subtle shifts in Athenian *mentalité*, I would argue that, to some degree, *all* of these scenes are fantasies. They are fictions that reflect the often self-contradictory interests and preoccupations, first of the Athenians themselves, then of their clients in various parts of the Mediterranean world and beyond.

There is no doubt that one historical event to which the vase-painters immediately responded is the Persian invasion of Greece in 480–479. Not that they ever attempt to depict any recognizable battle, such as the naval victory at Salamis or the land battle at Plataea; rather that a small series of drinking cups in the decade 480–470 depicts Greek warriors defeating Persians in scenes that embody, rather than represent, the recently won victories (Fig. 3.5).[18] At first sight, these vases seem to violate the

---

[15] Louvre CA 1682; Anne Bovon, "La representation des guerriers perses et la notion de barbare dans la première moitié du Ve siècle," *Bulletin de Correspondance Hellénique* 87 (1963), 583.

[16] Neils, "The Group of the Negro Alabastra; a Study of Motif Transferal," 14.

[17] Raeck, *Zur Barbarenbild*, 101–163; Hölscher, *Griechische Historienbilder*, 38–49; Tonio Hölscher, "Ein Kelchkrater mit Perserkampf," *Antike Kunst* 17 (1974), 78–85; Tonio Hölscher, "Feindwelten–Glückswelten: Perser, Kentauren und Amazonen," in Tonio Hölscher (ed.), *Gegenwelten: zu den Kulturen Griechenlands und Roms in der Antike* (Munich, 2000), 300–308. Cf. Bovon, "La representation," and the brief comments of Brian A. Sparkes, "Some Greek Images of Others," in Brian L. Molyneaux (ed.), *The Cultural Life of Images* (London, 1997) pp. 130–158.

[18] Oxford, Ashmolean Museum 1911.615; *ARV*^2 399; *Corpus Vasorum Antiquorum* (*CVA*) (Oxford 1) pl. 6, 3–4. On these vases see Raeck, *Zur Barbarenbild*, 109–116; Konrad Schauenburg, "Siegreiche Barbaren," *Mitteilungen des Deutschen Archäologischen Instituts, Athenische Abteilung* 92 (1977), 91–95. Not all are drinking cups: cf. the calyx-krater published by Hölscher, "Ein Kelchkrater," though he observes that the depiction on the krater, dated *c.* 460, is already less concerned with "historical accuracy" than the cups dated to the decade 480–470.

Fig. 3.5 Greek fighting Persian. Oxford, Ashmolean Museum
1911.615. Attic red-figure cup, *c.* 480–470 BCE.

principle that Archaic and Classical Greek art never depicts historical
people and events, whether directly or indirectly, but at most only alludes
to them in mythological guise.[19] The point here is that the historical
victory over the Persians instantly acquired the status of a legendary
event, and the response in all art forms – from drama and epinician poetry
to frescoes and vase-paintings – treated it in the same way as legends like
the Greek victory at Troy. It is no accident that the only extant tragedy on
a historical subject is the *Persians* of Aeschylus, which focuses on the Battle
of Salamis and its aftermath. Likewise, the Croesus amphora by Myson
(Fig. 3.3) can violate the taboo on depicting historical individuals
because, by the time it was made, Croesus himself was a legend. And
the same could be said of the well-known depiction of the murder of
Hipparchos, painted about 470 – a "real" event in the year 514, but one
that quickly took on the status of legend because it gave rise to the charter
myth of the Athenian democracy.[20]

Unlike Raeck and Hölscher, I would argue that the Persians in these
battle scenes are portrayed as worthy opponents, only they always lose.[21]
It is surely significant that all these scenes are on cups used at symposia,

[19] See Hölscher, *Griechische Historienbilder des 5. Und 4. Jahrhunderts v. Chr.*, 11–17.
[20] Red-figure stamnos by the Copenhagen Painter, Würzburg 515; *ARV²* 256, 5; Hölscher,
Griechische Historienbilder, 87–88; pl. 7.
[21] Raeck, *Zur Barbarenbild*, 132; Tonio Hölscher, *Die unheimliche Klassik der Griechen*
(Bamberg, 1989), 19 (elsewhere, however, Hölscher ["Ein Kelchkrater," 83] notes that

elite male drinking parties at which those very victories would have been celebrated in poetry and song. These scenes of combat are only one of several ways of alluding to the defeat of Xerxes. Another is the creation of the animal-head rhyton in clay, an elaborate sympotic vessel inspired by Persian examples in gold and silver left behind by the Great King in his hasty retreat.[22] On a few of these vases, one of the (undoubtedly Athenian) symposiasts wears the Persian headdress, or *kidaris*, either because it was by now a kind of fashion statement, or because it was a way of rubbing in the defeat of Persia by appropriating the attribute along with the shape of the vessel.[23]

By appropriating this quintessentially Persian form of the rhyton for use in the quintessentially Athenian setting of the symposium, the potters and painters reveal for the first time a profound ambivalence toward the Eastern enemy: pride in resisting the Persian attempt to enslave the Greeks (as they would have put it), combined with unabashed admiration for the wealth, refinement, and taste of Persian material culture. Nothing could capture this duality better than a spectacular ram's head rhyton made just after 480 and featuring a symposium of legendary Athenian kings, from Kekrops, the earliest of them all and the embodiment of the chauvinistic notion of Athenian autochthony, to Theseus, the symbol of the young democracy that proved its mettle by beating back the vastly superior army of Xerxes.[24]

Kimon and Athenian triumph

Some time between 470 and 465, the Athenian general Kimon led a Greek force to its greatest victory over the Persians, in fact a double victory on land and sea, on the south coast of Asia Minor beside the River

the Persian on the Basel krater is a worthy opponent). Cf. Isaac, *Invention*, 276–283 for the more general point that the Persians were almost never seen as an inferior people in fifth-century Greece.

[22] On animal-head vases and their relation to Persian prototypes see Margaret C. Miller, "Foreigners at the Greek Symposium?," in William J. Slater (ed.), *Dining in a Classical Context* (Ann Arbor, 1991), 69–71; Margaret C. Miller, *Athens and Persia in the Fifth Century B.C.: a study in Cultural Receptivity* (Cambridge, 1997), 141–144; Herbert Hoffmann, *Sotades* (Oxford, 1997), 5–9; M. True in Beth Cohen, *The Colors of Clay. Special Techniques in Athenian Vase Painting* (Malibu, 2006), 243–247.

[23] See Miller, "Foreigners." These figures are not to be confused with those on two fragmentary cups that do seem to show actual Persians, in full Persian dress, as symposiasts: Miller, *Athens and Persia*, figs. 49, 80. These scenes would be comparable to the contemporary *Persians* of Aeschylus: imagined glimpses into the private life of the Persian court.

[24] Richmond, Virginia Museum of Fine Arts 79.100; J. Robert Guy, "A Ram's Head Rhyton in Richmond Signed by Charinos," *Arts in Virginia* 21.2 (1981), 2–15 (1981); *Lexicon Iconographicum Mythologiae Classicae* (Zurich/Stuttgart, 1981–1997) (hereafter *LIMC*) IV 942, s.v. Erechtheus no. 78.

Eurymedon.[25] As Plutarch explains, the wildly excited response to these events in Athens was based on the feeling that, whereas the victories of 490 and 480–479 were all in defense of Greece from foreign invasion, Kimon's campaign had for the first time prosecuted the war deep into the enemy's territory (*Life of Kimon* 8.2). The new tone of supreme Athenian self-confidence is expressed on a variety of vases of the 460s. One small group allegorizes the victory in traditional Athenian fashion (Fig. 3.6): the city's patron goddess, Athena, holds the prow ornament, in the form of a bird's beak, from a captured Phoenician ship in the Persian fleet.[26] The mood is calm and dignified, the role of the gods in assuring Greek victory quietly acknowledged.

A very different group of contemporary vases poke gentle fun at the humiliated Persian Empire in ways that anticipate the comic stereotyping of Aristophanes. On a skyphos – another type of drinking vessel – one hapless Persian, perhaps a deserter, has stopped to rest on a free-form rock and set aside his wicker shield, while another comes running to chastise or urge him on.[27] In a similar vein, an oinochoe (a small wine jug) shows one Persian stalled on a recalcitrant mule and a second coming to the rescue.[28] These humorous vignettes can hardly be called racism or even ethnic prejudice. Their closest parallels may be the antics of feckless satyrs, especially popular in this period.[29]

The most notorious member of this group of vases is the much-discussed Eurymedon oinochoe (Figs. 3.7–3.8),[30] another jug of the same

[25] For the much-debated date of the battle see Ernst Badian, *From Plataea to Potidaea* (Baltimore, 1993), 4.
[26] Lekythos, New York, Metropolitan Museum of Art 25.189.1; *ARV*² 284, 211. On the motif see Ulrich Hausmann, "Akropolisscherben und Eurymendonkämpfe," in Konrad Schauenburg (ed.), *Charites. Festschrift E. Langlotz* (Bonn, 1957); Marion Meyer, "Bilder und Vorbilder. Zu Sinn und Zweck von Siegesmonumenten Athens in klassischer Zeit," *Jahreshefte des Oesterreichischen Archaeologischen Instituts* 74 (2005), 284–286.
[27] Berlin inv. 3156; *ARV*² 804, 65; Bovon, "La representation," 390, fig. 14; Miller, *Athens and Persia*, 77; figs. 24–25.
[28] British Museum 1912.7–9.1; *ARV*² 775, 1; Raeck, *Zur Barbarenbild*, 109; figs. 47–48; Isaac, *Invention*, figs. 4a–b.
[29] Cf. Ralf Krumeich, in Ralf Krumeich, Nikolaus Pechstein, and Bernd Seidensticker, *Das griechische Satyrspiel* (Darmstadt, 1999), 65–69.
[30] Hamburg, Museum für Kunst und Gewerbe 1981.173; first published by Schauenburg, "Eurumedon eimi"; recently discussed in detail, with full references, by Detlev Wannagat, "Eurymedon Eimi. Zeichen ethnischer, sozialer und physischer Differenz in der Vasenmalerei des 5. Jahrhunderts v. Chr.," in Ralf von den Hoff and Stefan Schmidt (eds.), *Konstruktionen von Wirklichkeit* (Stuttgart, 2001). For other recent discussions of the vase see the contributions of Karim W. Arafat, "State of the Art – Art of the State. Sexual Violence and Politics in Late Archaic and Early Classical Vase-Painting," in Susan Deacy and Karen F. Pierce (eds.), *Rape in Antiquity* (London, 2002), 101–104 and Martin Kilmer, "'Rape' in Early Red-Figure Pottery," in Deacy and Pierce (eds.), *Rape in Antiquity*, 135–138.

Fig. 3.6 Athena holding prow ornament of Persian ship (*Aphlaston*).
New York, Metropolitan Museum of Art 25.189.1, Purchase,
1925. Attic red-figure lekythos, *c*. 470–460 BCE.

type as the one with the mule-rider. Here, a Greek, grasping his penis as a
weapon, prepares for a sexual assault on a terrified Persian. In a clear
reference to the recent battles, the inscriptions read: EURUMEDON
EIMI KUBAD' HESTEKA ("I am Eurymedon. I stand bent over"). This
has sometimes been construed as a dialogue – Greek: "I am Eurymedon";
Persian: "I stand bent over" – at other times with the Persian speaking both
lines. I would agree with those who read it as a snatch of dialogue.[31] If the
Greek represents himself as the site of the great victory, the image could be a
kind of travesty of the dignified depictions of personified rivers on vases of
this period.[32]

The comically upraised hands and frontal face of the Persian are a
caricature of the cowardice of the Oriental, as on a slightly later calyx-
krater with the frightened Persian on one side and, on the other, a second

---

[31] Gloria F. Pinney, "For the Heroes are at Hand," *Journal of Hellenic Studies* 104 (1984);
Amy C. Smith, "Eurymedon and the Evolution of Political Personifications in the Early
Classical Period," *Journal of Hellenic Studies* 119 (1999), 135, who makes a strong argument on the basis of the placement of the inscription EURUMEDON EIMI, just to the
right of the Greek's head; Tonio Hölscher, "Feindwelten–Glückswelten," 302.

[32] E.g. the red-figure pointed amphora in a German private collection: Carina Weiss,
"Spitzamphora des Syriskos," in *Mythen und Menschen*, Exh. Cat. Würzburg (Stuttgart
1997), 106. Nile, Maeander, and Strymon are all labeled, as well as their father Okeanos.
Cf. Smith, "Eurymedon," 135–136 for discussion of Eurymedon as a personification,
though she thinks more likely of the battle than the river.

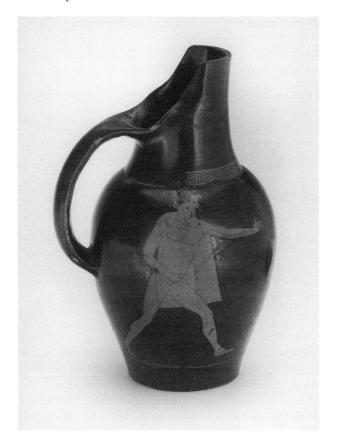

Figs. 3.7–3.8 Greek preparing a sexual attack on a Persian. Hamburg, Museum für Kunst und Gewerbe 1981.173. Attic red-figure oinochoe, *c.* 460 BCE.

Persian being overcome by a Greek (this one more conventionally armed, with a spear).[33] The visual formula of the hands in alarm is ultimately derived from mythological foreigners, such as the terrified Egyptian attendants of King Busiris, as they are overwhelmed by the rampaging Herakles.[34] Much has been made of the notion of feminizing the Asian

[33] Hölscher, "Ein Kelchkrater."
[34] E.g. Margaret C. Miller, "The Myth of Busiris: Ethnicity and Art," in Beth Cohen (ed.), *Not the Classical Ideal: Athens and the Construction of the Other in Greek Art* (Leiden, 2000), 418, Fig. 16.1; 423, Fig. 16.3; 427, Fig. 16.5; 431, Fig. 16.7.

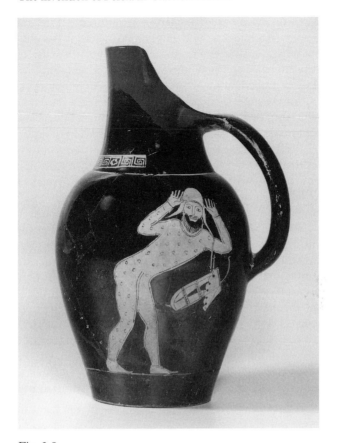

Fig. 3.8

barbarian in this sexual metaphor of the Eurymedon vase.[35] While that may be true, I would rather point out that this kind of sexual invective is widespread in Athens, well before Aristophanes and in contexts that have nothing to do with Persians. Inscriptions scratched on vases found in Athens, from the seventh century to the late fifth, insult an enemy as *katapugón*, a word that describes literally what is happening to the Persian here, but seems to have become a generalized term of abuse.[36]

---

[35] James Davidson, *Courtesans and Fishcakes: the Consuming Passions of Classical Athens* (New York, 1998), 169–171, 180–182; David Castriota, "Feminizing the Barbarian and Barbarizing the Feminine," in Judith M. Barringer and Jeffrey M. Hurwit (eds.), *Periklean Athens and its Legacy: Problems and Perspectives* (Austin, 2005), 99–100.

[36] See Ann Steiner, "Private and Public: Links Between *Symposion* and *Syssition* in Fifth-Century Athens," *Classical Antiquity* 21 (2002), 359–361, with earlier references.

The rare word for "bent over" – *kubda* – is attested before this only in invective poetry (Archilochus and Hipponax) where it has the obscene connotation illustrated here, but usually in a heterosexual context.[37] Similarly, the motif of the phallus wielded like a weapon,[38] unique to this vase, finds a precedent in Archaic invective. Archilochus uses *sideros* (iron sword) for the male member by means of which a particularly voracious pathic wishes to be penetrated.[39] If the humor of the sexual assault has an Aristophanic flavor (a half-century *avant la lettre*), it is perhaps not surprising to find a similar joke in the playwright's *Wasps* (1087–1088): the leader of the wasp chorus, an old man who fondly recalls doing battle with the Persians in his youth, boasts of "pricking" (*kentoumenoi*) the baggy pants of the barbarian with his stinger.[40]

Hölscher describes the scene on the Eurymedon oinochoe as "the most disgusting" of those showing Greek superiority over the Persians,[41] but surely disgusting is not the right word for a kind of sexual humor that was pervasive in Athenian culture, nor for an image that is rather mild compared with much of the erotic violence seen on vases of this period.[42] As Hölscher himself acknowledges, vase-painting, as a private medium, might adopt a coarser tone than such expressions of "high art" in the public sphere as a tragedy like Aeschylus's *Persians* or the Marathon Painting in the Stoa Poikile.[43] We might compare, in this regard, another well-known vase of the same years: the fragmentary pelike in the Louvre depicting three herms (Fig. 3.9).[44] It is generally agreed that this vase, made only a few years after Kimon set up a monument commemorating

---

[37] Cf. *A Greek-English Lexicon*, compiled by Henry George Liddell and Robert Scott, rev. and augm. throughout by Henry Stuart Jones (Oxford). s.v. *kubda*. Archilochos 32; Douglas E. Gerber, *Greek Iambic Poetry: From the Seventh to the Fifth Centuries* (Cambridge, MA, 1999), 113, no. 42; Hipponax fr. 17; Gerber, *Greek Iambic Poetry*, 366–367 uses a participial form, *kupsasa* ("having stooped over").

[38] Tonio Hölscher, "Images and Political Identity: the Case of Athens," in Deborah Boedeker and Kurt A. Raaflaub (eds.), *Democracy, Empire and the Arts in Fifth-Century Athens* (Cambridge, MA, 1998), 178 aptly writes of the "erect penis, held in his hand like a pistol."

[39] Fr. 327; Gerber, *Greek Iambic Poetry*, 288–289.

[40] See Jeffrey Henderson, *The Maculate Muse: Obscene Language in Attic Comedy* (New Haven, 1975), 179, on the verb *kentein* ("pierce") with a sexual connotation.

[41] Hölscher, "Images and Political Identity," 178.

[42] Although I cannot agree with Ferrari's attempt (Gloria Ferrari, "For the Heroes are at Hand," *Journal of Hellenic Studies* 104 [1984]) to disassociate the scene entirely from the Battle of the Eurymedon, I do agree that the sexual humor is the key element in the scene. She, too, finds parallels in Aristophanes. Cf. Sparkes, "Some Greek Images," 144. Martin Kilmer, *Greek Erotica on Attic Red-Figure Vases* (London, 1993), 128–129 suggests that the Athenian symposiast viewing the scene would have experienced sexual arousal as well as a feeling of triumph.

[43] Hölscher, "Feindwelten–Glückswelten," 302–303.

[44] Louvre 10793; Juliette de la Genière, "Une pélikè inedité du Peintre de Pan au Musée du Louvre," *Revue des Études Anciennes* 62 (1960) 249–253.

Fig. 3.9 Three herms. Louvre 10793. Attic red-figure pelike, *c*. 460 BCE.

his capture of Eion on the River Strymnon in Thrace, in the form of three
marble herms, must refer to that victory monument.[45] But whereas the
actual herms were best known for their high-minded inscribed epigrams
that celebrated the valor of the Athenians and compared them to the men
who fought at Troy, the painter's cheeky humor once again frames the
victory in sexual terms.

The neat Greek–Persian polarity on the Eurymedon vase is complicated
by the strange appearance of the Greek, with his scruffy goatee and side-
burns and strange cloak, none of which describes the Athenian *kalos-
k'agathos* we would expect him to look like if this were a serious contrast
of noble Greek and humiliated Persian. Through a careful analysis of every

---

[45] For the Kimonian monument see Plutarch, *Life of Kimon*, ch. 7 (who also records the
epigrams on the herms); Alec Blamire, *Plutarch: Life of Kimon* (London, 1989), 112–114;
Robin Osborne, "The Erection and Mutilation of the Hermai," *Proceedings of the
Cambridge Philological Society* 31 (1986); Meyer, "Bilder und Vorbilder," 294–296.

72   *H. A. Shapiro*

detail, Detlev Wannagat has recently shown that the figure is most likely a caricature of an East Greek mercenary fighting in Kimon's army.[46] The point of the joke for the Athenian symposiasts who used this little jug is irrevocably lost to us. But the assortment of unique features on this oinochoe, from the remarkable inscription to the metaphor of military victory as sexual penetration, makes it almost certain that the vase was a special commission for a particular symposium. And it is as sympotic humor that the sexual joke must be understood. Plutarch conjures up just such an occasion, in his *Life of Kimon* (9.2), when he pictures the great general as a symposium guest at the home of one Laomedon, singing and recounting war stories late into the night. Plutarch's source for this is Ion of Chios, the poet who came to Athens as a young man in the glory days of Kimon and could well have been an eyewitness to such a gathering.[47]

Periklean Athens and the Persians

In the middle years of the fifth century, with Perikles now presiding over the expansion of the Athenian Empire in the Aegean of which Kimon can be said to be the principal architect, Persian iconography moves off in several different directions. One is a reminiscence of earlier victories, now heroized through the improbable nudity of the Greek warrior and turned into an essentially rhetorical trope symbolizing Greek superiority over the Barbarian.[48] The closest parallels are depictions of Theseus's defeat of the Amazons, who look remarkably like Persians minus the beard.[49] This is the visual equivalent of funeral orations for the war dead (*epitaphioi logoi*) in which it became a commonplace to catalogue earlier Athenian victories over the barbarian, whether Amazons or Persians or even centaurs.[50] With the Peace of Kallias in 449,[51] the Persian Wars were officially history, and on the way to becoming myth.

Nothing could be more eloquent proof of how far the Persian Wars had receded into memory than an astonishing pair of vases made in a single

---

[46] Wannagat, "Eurymedon Eimi," 55–63; cf. Hölscher, *Die unheimliche Klassik*, 42, n. 40.
[47] On Ion see Martin L. West, "Ion of Chios," *Bulletin of the Institute of Classical Studies* 32 (1985).
[48] Raeck, *Zur Barbarenbild*, 110.
[49] Dietrich von Bothmer, *Amazons in Greek Art* (Oxford, 1957), 184–192. Raeck, *Zur Barbarenbild*, 110 calls the new style with a nude Greek fighting a Persian a "Mythisierung des Historischen."
[50] See Nicole Loraux, *The Invention of Athens. The Funeral Oration in the Classical City*, trans. Alan Sheridan (Cambridge, MA, 1986), 145–150.
[51] For the dating (still controversial) see Badian, *From Plataea*, 1–72, who believes there was an initial peace treaty right after the Battle of the Eurymedon, which was renewed in 449.

Fig. 3.10 Amazon on horseback; on the cup, mounted Persian killing a Greek warrior. Boston, Museum of Fine Arts 21.2286. Attic red-figure rhyton, *c.* 450 BCE. Harvard University – Boston Museum of Fine Arts Expedition.

Athenian workshop for clients living in Persian-ruled Egypt. Both are spectacular examples of the potter's craft, combining a modeled figure with a drinking vessel decorated in red-figure. One, found at Meroë in what is now Sudan, depicts an Amazon on horseback (Fig. 3.10).[52] The other, now in fragments from Memphis, was apparently in the shape of a camel led by a

---

[52] Boston, Museum of Fine Arts 21.2286; Beth Cohen, *The Colors of Clay*, 284–287, with earlier bibliography.

Figs. 3.11–3.12 Persians battling Greeks. Louvre CA 3825.
Fragmentary Attic red-figure rhyton, *c.* 450 BCE.

Persian (Figs. 3.11–3.12).[53] Such unique objects could only be special commissions. The painted scenes on both objects have a common theme: a battle of Greeks against Persians, with the Persians winning! The conclusion, first voiced by Lilly Kahil, is inescapable: the fantasy of Persian victory was intended to appeal to the Egyptian buyer.[54] Athenian potters and painters were businessmen, not ideologues, and they knew their market.

A much larger group of vases of the Periklean period purports to offer intimate glimpses into the private lives of the Persian elite, local satraps or even the Great King himself (Fig. 3.13).[55] They are scenes of quiet conversation, offerings, sometimes a libation. In one sense, they are descendants of the *Persians* of Aeschylus, with its imagined scenes of life at the Persian court, based on no first-hand knowledge. Among these Classical vases is one that even labels the Persian king (*basileus*) and queen

[53] Louvre CA 3825; Lilly Kahil, "Un nouveau vase plastique du potier Sotades au Musée du Louvre," *Revue Archéologique* (1972) 271–284. On both plastic vases see also Raeck, *Zur Barbarenbild*, 124–126; Hoffmann, *Sotades*, 89–96.

[54] Kahil, "Un nouveau vase plastique," 281–282. I am reminded of another monument I once saw in Egypt, this one in a public square in Cairo, celebrating the glorious victory over Israel in the 1973 War.

[55] Pelike, Louvre, Campana 11164; Schauenburg, "Eurumedon eimi," pl. 40, 1. See Raeck, *Zur Barbarenbild*, 137–146.

Fig. 3.13 Persian king with attendants. Louvre, Campana collection 11164. Attic red-figure pelike, *c.* 440 BCE.

(*basilis*), who reaches out to him an offering from a funnel-shaped vase.[56] This is one of the few instances in which the woman has been given Oriental dress, but, ironically, the royal status of both king and queen is indicated by putting a Greek-style himation over their Persian dress! Because of the inscriptions, Ernst Buschor took the scene for an illustration of Aeschylus's *Persians*: Atossa conjuring the spirit of her dead husband Darius.[57] We now know that this very scene did make a huge impression on the audience and is probably indeed depicted on Attic vases, but in a way that looks nothing like this.[58]

[56] Vatican 16536; *ARV*² 1065, 8; Raeck, *Zur Barbarenbild*, 137, 143; Fig. 58. The shape is an oinochoe type 7, similar to the one in London (above n. 28) and the Eurymedon oinochoe.

[57] Ernst Buschor, "Kanne im Vatikan. Der Perserkönig," in Adolf Furtwängler and Karl Reichhold, *Griechische Vasenmalerei*, vol. III (Munich, 1932).

[58] E.g. the red-figure column-krater Basel, Antikenmuseum BS 415; Erika Simon, *Festivals of Attica: An Archeological Commentary* (Madison, 1983), pl. 32, 3. Cf. the fragments of a hydria found at Corinth that may have shown Darius rising from his tomb: Nicholas G. L. Hammond and Warren G. Moon, "Illustrations of Early Tragedy at Athens," *American Journal of Archaeology* 82 (1978), 374, fig. 2.

Figs. 3.14–3.15 Persian king with attendants. Stockholm, Historical
Museum V294. Attic red-figure squat lekythos from Cyprus, 440–430 BCE.

Indeed, one indication that there is nothing "realistic" about the scenes
that appear to have a Persian setting is that, in general, no attempt is ever
made to orientalize the women: they wear purely Greek dress, and the focus
is solely on the male: truly a Persian peacock (cf. Fig. 3.13).[59] A few of these
could once again be specially made for the Eastern market, such as a squat
lekythos found on Cyprus (Figs. 3.14–3.15),[60] or a pelike from near
Bodrum in Turkey.[61] One sub-group of vases showing this type of scene
that has troubled commentators is the white-ground lekythoi, oil containers
that were made almost exclusively as a funerary offering in Athenian tombs
(Figs. 3.16–3.17).[62] They were rarely exported. If you were an Athenian
citizen in the 440s, why put a Persian on, or in, your loved one's tomb?
Various unlikely scenarios have been proposed: a grave offering for an
Athenian who had served as an ambassador to the Persian court, or one

[59] For other examples cf. two red-figure lekythoi: Frankfurt, University: Gerhard Kleiner,
"Eine rotfigurige Lekythos klassischer Zeit in der Sammlung des Frankfurter
Archäologischen Seminars," in *Mélanges Mansel* II (Ankara, 1973), 933–938; and
Athens, National Museum 1295; Schauenburg, "Eurumedon eimi," pl. 37, 1.
[60] Stockholm, Historical Museum V294; *ARV*² 1150, 27; Einar Gjerstad *et al.*, *Swedish
Cyprus Expedition*, vol. III (Stockholm, 1937), pl. 85, 1–2; Raeck, *Zur Barbarenbild*, 146.
[61] Istanbul Archaeological Museum 7501; *Anatolian Civilizations* (exh. Cat. Istanbul 1983)
vol. II, no. B.151. Keith deVries, "Attic Pottery in the Achaemenid Empire," *American
Journal of Archaeology* 81 (1977) discusses the phenomenon of subjects specially chosen
for clients in the Persian Empire.
[62] Tübingen, Archäologisches Institut S./10 1365; *ARV*² 850, 270; CVA (Tübingen 5) pl.
28, 4–8.

Figs. 3.16–3.17 Persian and attendant. Tübingen University S./10
1365. Attic white-ground lekythos, c. 440 BCE.

for a Persian official who died during a visit to Athens.[63] I think all we can
say is, we don't always know why certain images appealed to the Athenians
in certain contexts, any more than we know why wealthy Romans buried
their loved ones in marble sarcophagi showing Medea murdering her
children or the lovesick Phaedra. We might speculate that the Persians on
white lekythoi are a fantasy of faraway wealth and happiness that the
deceased and his family hoped lay in store.

[63] Schauenburg, "Eurumedon eimi," 115; cf. John H. Oakley, *Picturing Death in Classical
Athens* (Cambridge, 2004), 187–188; John H. Oakley, "Barbarians on White Lekythoi,"
in Filippo Giudice and Rosalba Panvini (eds.), *Il greco, il barbaro e la ceramica attica I*
(Catania, forthcoming).

Imagining Persia in wartime Athens

In the last third of the fifth century – essentially the period of the Peloponnesian War – two interrelated iconographical developments complete the process of turning the Persians into a mythological race inhabiting a fantasy world of luxury and sensuous pleasure. One is a new set of scenes, still set in an imagined Persia, but instead of the quiet decorum of the Periklean Age, we find lively entertainment for the ruler in the form of music and a wild dance usually identified as the *oklasma*.[64] On a well-known squat lekythos – a perfume jug – the ruler (whether a satrap or the Great King himself) observes the festivities from his mount on a camel,[65] while on a much larger krater, the King sits within a shrine-like enclosure, attended by a fan-bearer, and watches the adjacent performers (Fig. 3.18).[66] The camel lekythos illustrates, according to Isaac, the stereotype that "Oriental courts were seen as a hotbed of orgiastic dissipation."[67] But I would suggest that something rather different is going on.

In the second half of the fifth century, a number of Oriental cults reached Athens, often by way of the port city of Piraeus, and attracted considerable followings.[68] The turmoil of the Peloponnesian War years, together with a questioning of the old Olympian gods that we find reflected in Euripides' plays, contributed to the popular appeal of these cults. They included Bendis (Fig. 3.19),[69] whose home was in Thrace, and several whose place of origin was not always clear, but certainly far to the East and certainly in areas at that time under the sway of the Persian King, like Adonis (from Syria via Cyprus),[70] Cybele, the Phrygian Great Mother, and her consort Sabazios.[71] The belief in Dionysos' Eastern

---

[64] On this dance see Thomas Schäfer, *Andres Agathoi* (Munich, 1997), 92–93, with references. Pausanias 10.31.8 observes that Paris was depicted performing the oklasma in Polygnotus's painting of the Nekyia at Delphi. For Paris as the archetype of the decadent Eastern barbarian see below 80–83.

[65] British Museum E 695; *ARV²*; Schäfer, *Andres Agathoi*, pl. 55; Isaac, *Invention*, Fig. 3; Raeck, *Zur Barbarenbild*, 151–152.

[66] Vienna, Kunsthistorisches Museum 158; *ARV²* 1409, 1; Francesca Curti, *La bottega del pittore di Meleagro* (Rome, 2001) pl. 1. Cf. Raeck, *Zur Barbarenbild*, 152–153.

[67] Isaac, *Invention*, caption to Fig. 3.

[68] For general discussions of this phenomenon, see Ronda R. Simms, 'Foreign Religious Cults in Athens in the Fifth and Fourth centuries B.C.' (Ph. D. thesis, University of Virginia, 1985); Robert Garland, *Introducing New Gods: the Politics of Athenian Religion* (Ithaca, NY, 1992).

[69] Skyphos, Tübingen S./10 1347; *CVA* (Tübingen 5) pl. 21. For the cult of Bendis see Simms, *Foreign Religious Cults*, 7–58; *LIMC* III 95–96, s.v. Bendis.

[70] For the cult of Adonis in Athens see Gina Salapata, "*Triphiletos Adonis*: An Exceptional Pair of Terra-cotta Arulae from South Italy," in *Studia Varia from the J. Paul Getty Museum* 2 (2001), 25–50; Joseph D. Reed, "The Sexuality of Adonis," *Classical Antiquity* 14 (1995), 319–347.

[71] The most spectacular image of these two in Athenian art is that on a red-figure volute-krater from Spina: Ferrara 2897; *ARV²* 1052, 25; *LIMC* VIII 756, s.v. Kybele no. 66. Cf. Thomas H. Carpenter, *Dionysian Imagery in Fifth-Century Athens* (Oxford, 1997), 70–78.

Fig. 3.18 Entertainment for the Persian king. Vienna, Kunsthistorisches
Museum 158. Attic red-figure bell-krater, *c.* 400 BCE.

roots may also have originated in this period. Once again, vase iconography is our best guide to the often orgiastic rituals associated with these
cults as they established themselves in Greece. The images of such rituals
in their Oriental homeland (as in Fig. 3.18) can thus no longer be seen as
representing a dissipated, degenerate, and un-Greek world, but rather as
the source of beliefs and practices that were now *au courant* in Athens.
Indeed, the *oklasma* dance was enthusiastically adopted at symposia and
banquets in Athens and elsewhere in Greece, as attested by several vase-
paintings of the end of the fifth century and beginning of the fourth
(Fig. 3.20).[72] As in so many other ways, the negative stereotyping of the
Eastern Barbarian that permeates official Athenian ideology is constantly
undermined by an avid receptivity toward everything from dress and
drinking vessels to music, dance, and religious ritual.

The second development is a gradual convergence of Persians and
Trojans until, by the late fifth century, they are virtually indistinguishable

and pls. 28–29, who discusses at length Erika Simon's interpretation of the principal
divinities as Cybele and Sabazios enthroned, but concludes that it is not possible to
identify them with certainty.
[72] E.g. the calyx-krater Athens NM 12683; see Schäfer, *Andres Agatho*i, 93.

Fig. 3.19 Bendis and Themis. Tübingen University S./10 1347. Attic red-figure skyphos, 430–420 BCE.

in the visual record. When we first encounter the Trojans, in the *Iliad*, they are no different from the Greeks in their language, dress, weapons, cults, and so on. In a sense, Homer has anticipated Aeschylus's technique in the *Persians* of co-opting the Other and making him Greek. It was only after the Persian invasions of Greece that the analogy was first drawn between Trojans and Persians as Eastern enemies of the Greeks, both ruled by kings of unimaginable wealth.[73] After the middle of the fifth century, King Priam begins to be shown in Oriental dress on red-figure vases,[74] but the quintessential representative of the Trojan-as-Eastern-Prince is his son Alexandros, or Paris.

Already in the *Iliad*, Paris is portrayed as the cowardly and womanish weakling that will later define the stereotype of the Persian male. The visual image of Paris, in the favorite scene of the Judgment on Mount Ida, traces an astonishing evolution over two centuries: from the long-robed, bearded male of Archaic art to the young, rustic shepherd of Early Classical red-figure, and finally to the languid, ornately dressed, Persian-style prince of the last third of the fifth century and beginning of

---

[73] See Andrew Erskine, *Troy Between Greece and Rome: Local Tradition and Imperial Power* (Oxford, 2001), 61–92. A striking example is the famous carpet scene in Aeschylus's *Agamemnon*, when Klytemnestra imagines Priam as an Oriental potentate, clearly modeled on the Great King of Persia (935–936).

[74] Margaret C. Miller, "Priam, King of Troy," in Jane B. Carter and Sarah P. Morris (eds.), *The Ages of Homer* (Austin, 1995), esp. 458, Fig. 28.15.

Fig. 3.20 Dancer performing the "oklasma." Athens, National Archaeological Museum 12683. Boeotian red-figure calyx-krater, c. 400 BCE.

the fourth (Fig. 3.21).[75] It is usually argued that this costume is influenced
by the Athenian stage, because other non-Greek mythological figures who
were the subjects of popular tragedies, such as Andromeda and Medea,

---

[75] Calyx-krater, St. Petersburg, Hermitage 1807; *ARV*² 1185, 7; *LIMC* VII 180, s.v. Paridis
Iudicium, no. 48. For an overview of the iconography of Paris in the Judgment see
Christoph W. Clairmont, *Das Parisurteil in der antiken Kunst* (Zurich, 1951); *LIMC* VII
177–182, s.v. Paridis Iudicium.

Fig. 3.21 The Judgment of Paris. St. Petersburg, Hermitage O.28
(St. 1807). Attic red-figure calyx-krater, *c.* 400 BCE.

are now also shown in orientalizing dress.[76] In the case of Paris, no extant
play features him as a character. We can only guess at how he might have

[76] On these figures, and scenes inspired by the theatre, see John R. Green, *Theatre in Ancient
Greek Society* (London, 1994), 19–26; Jocelyn Penny Small, *The Parallel Worlds of Classical Art
and Text* (Cambridge, 2003), 40–52; and on the depiction of actual Persians in theatre scenes,
Margaret C. Miller, "In Strange Company: Persians in Early Attic Theatre Imagery,"
Mediterranean Archaeology 17 [Festschrift in Honour of J. Richard Green] (2004), 165–172.

appeared, for example, in Euripides' lost Trojan trilogy, one play of which was called after him, *Alexandros*.[77] The earliest orientalized Paris is on a vase of about 440 BCE, where he not only wears an elaborate oriental helmet, but also strikes an especially languid pose that could easily be mistaken for that of a woman.[78] The association between Paris and a Persian ruler goes beyond the conventions of costume. His reckless adventure in Greece, in pursuit of a beautiful – and married – woman could be likened to the *hubris* of the young Xerxes in 480. Herodotos (1.1–4) famously summarized the entire history of adversarial relations between Greece and the East, of which the Persian Wars were the culmination, as one of reciprocal woman-stealing.

Epilogue: the fourth century

Isocrates' great oration, *Panathenaikos*, of 380 has sometimes been cited as a turning point in the portrayal of the Oriental in Greek rhetoric in terms of all the negative stereotypes that will persist down to modern times: "lack of discipline, softness, servility combined with arrogance, luxury and corruption."[79] It is at this point in time that our visual sources start to desert us, since by the early fourth century, the figured style in Attic red-figure is approaching its end. I very much doubt, however, that even if we had more red-figure contemporary with Isocrates, it would ever portray Persians in this light. Among the last great examples of the classical Athenian ceramic tradition, already experimenting with a new technique of polychrome relief decoration, is a pair of vases depicting members of the Persian court hunting in a *paradeisos*, or paradise garden.[80] This motif is no doubt inspired by actual accounts of the Persian royal hunt, but depicted as a Greek fantasy world inhabited by Persians.

---

[77] On the trilogy see Ruth Scodel, *The Trojan Trilogy of Euripides* (Göttingen, 1980). The "barbarism" of the Trojans is thematized in tragedy, e.g. in the *Andromache* of Euripides (168–177); cf. Erskine, *Troy Between Greece and Rome*, 61; 73–4.

[78] Skyphos, Syracuse 2406; *ARV²* 1076, 16; Bonna D. Wescoat, *Syracuse, the Fairest Greek City*, Exh. cat. Emory University (Rome, 1989), 82–83 and color pl. 1. I discuss this vase in more detail in H. A. Shapiro, "Alcibiades. The Politics of personal style," in Olga Palagia (ed.), *The Timeless and the Temporal. The Impact of the Peloponnesian War on Athenian Art* (Cambridge, 2009), 251–255.

[79] Isaac, *Invention*, 285–286; cf. Erskine, *Troy Between Greece and Rome*, 51, 88f. on Isocrates as anti-Persian propagandist.

[80] The best known is the lekythos signed by Xenophantos: St. Petersburg P 1837.2 (St. 1790); *ARV²* 1407, 1; Cohen, *The Colors of Clay*, 140–142. For the interpretation of the imagery see Michales A. Tiverios, "Die von Xenophantos signierte grosse Lekythos aus Pantikapaion: alte Funde neu betrachtet," in William D. E. Coulson, John H. Oakley, and Olga Palagia (eds.), *Athenian Potters and Painters* (Oxford, 1997) 473–490; Margaret C. Miller, "Art, Myth and Reality: Xenophantos' Lekythos Re-examined," in Eric Csapo and Margaret C. Miller (eds.), *Poetry, Theory, Praxis: the Social Life of Myth, Word and Image in Ancient Greece. Essays in Honor*

From this point to the end of red-figure, the mythologizing of the Persians is complete, since the only remaining reference to them is in the semi-comical scene of griffins battling Arimasps, who are, as Margaret Miller puts it, "the Persians' mythological cognates."[81]

I have been arguing that the conventions of Greek public oratory, about the negative qualities of the Persians and the irrevocable differences between the Hellene and the barbarian Other, are largely foreign to the world of Athenian vase-painting made for the private sphere. The point may be driven home by one final image from a vase that does in fact approximate the discourse of Greek rhetoric, but comes from a later period still – the age of Alexander the Great – and a different artistic tradition, far from Athens. The famous Darius krater, made in a Greek workshop in Taranto about 340 BCE, presents a complex allegory of the first Persian invasion of Greece (Fig. 3.22).[82] The scene is even given a title – *Persai* – inscribed on a pedestal, that suggests the inspiration of a now-lost play: not Aeschylus's *Persai*, but another, perhaps by Phrynichos.[83] The Great King listens calmly to a worried-looking messenger, probably recently returned from Greece with grave misgivings about the wisdom of the planned expedition. The five councilors who flank the King also look perturbed and uncertain. Below, an official receives the tribute from subject states of the Persian Empire that will fund the invasion of Greece. So far, a straightforward, if highly imaginative rendition of a moment in time at the Persian court in the year 490.

But the celestial plane, in the upper register, frames the momentous occasion in cosmic terms. This is the "clash of civilizations" (to borrow a highly charged, recent turn of phrase): Asia and Hellas, depicted in female form. They make manifest the two personifications first envisioned by Aeschylus, in Atossa's dream (*Persians* 181 ff.). Asia is regal and confident, like the King himself, but it is a confidence that is misplaced, as the next figure makes clear: Apatê. She represents the deception, the delusion, that fires, with her blazing torches, the ambition of Darius.[84] Hellas

of William J. Slater (Oxford, 2003), 19–43. The second, related vase is the lekythos St. Petersburg 108K; see Tiverios, "Die von Xenophantos signierte grosse Lekythos," 279, fig. 10; Miller, "Art, Myth and Reality", 19.

[81] Miller, *Athens and Persia*, fig. 18. Cf. *LIMC* VIII 609–611, s.v. Gryps.

[82] Naples, Museo Nazionale H 3253 (inv. 81947). For detailed discussions of the scene see Margot Schmidt, *Der Dareiosmaler und sein Umkreis* (Münster, 1960); Christian Aellen, *A la recherche de l'ordre cosmique: forme et fonction des personnifications dans la céramique italiote* (Kilchberg, 1994), 109–117.

[83] Arthur D. Trendall and T. B. L Webster, *Illustrations of Greek Drama* (London, 1971), 112 suggest a fourth-century version of Phrynichos's *Persai*.

[84] For the personifications here see especially Margot Schmidt, "Asia und Apate," in Luigi Beschi *et al.* (eds.), *APARCHAI. Festschrift P. E. Arias* (Pisa, 1982); Aellen, *A la recherche de l'ordre cosmique*, 115–116.

Fig. 3.22 The Darius Vase. Naples, Museo Nazionale Archeologico inv. 81947 (H 3253). Apulian red-figure volute-krater, *c.* 340–330 BCE.

is less confident – an accurate reflection of the mood in Greece on the eve of Marathon – but is assured of divine favor from both Athena and Zeus, further to the left. Nike, the embodiment of Greek victory to come, and the divine twins and avengers of impiety, Apollo and Artemis, fill out the Olympian company. The whole ensemble has an epic, Homeric flavor about it. The fate of nations is in the hands of the gods; the Justice of Zeus protects the Hellenes. Men are led to destruction by Atê (blindness, recklessness) – the word favored by Homer and Aeschylus – or, as here, by Atê's close associate, Apatê. Like the Athenian orators, who developed themes already adumbrated in Aeschylus's play, the painter presents the Persian Wars as a violation of the divinely sanctioned order, of the immutable separation of Europe and Asia. This is not to denigrate the character of the noble Darius, any more than Agamemnon's Atê in the *Iliad* (9.18) diminishes his nobility of purpose. The pitiful, servile subjects of the Great King in the lower frieze, drained of their resources to feed his folly, hint at a theme found throughout the orators, the inherent weakness of an empire based on absolute rule.

The Apulian artist has attempted something no Athenian vase-painter ever did, to envision a specific moment in the history of the confrontation between Persia and Greece. His manner of doing so recalls an earlier Athenian work of a very different genre: the monumental fresco of the Battle of Marathon made by the painter Polygnotos of Thasos about 460 for the Stoa Poikile (or Painted Stoa) in the Athenian Agora.[85] In this, perhaps the most famous and admired painting of Antiquity, the battle was depicted with reasonable fidelity to the event, but its significance was brought home by the inclusion (probably in the upper register) of those heroes and gods who assured success to the outnumbered Athenians: Athena, Herakles, Theseus, Echetlos (a minor Attic hero), and the local hero Marathon (Pausanias 1.15.3.)

In analyzing the evolution of Greek attitudes toward the Persians, we must inevitably stress the role of Athens' growth as an imperial power from the second quarter of the fifth century. The greater Athens' power, the more arrogant her treatment of her own subject cities, the more strident becomes the Athenian rhetoric of superiority over the weak, effeminate Persians.[86] In the early fourth century, with Athenian imperial ambitions shattered and the warring Greek city-states reduced to the humiliation of a peace treaty dictated by the Persian king (387 BCE), the

---

[85] For the stoa see T. Leslie Shear, Jr., "The Athenian Agora: Excavations of 1980–1982," *Hesperia* 53 (1984) 5–19. On the Marathon painting see most recently Mark D. Stansbury-O'Donnell, "The Painting Program in the Stoa Poikile," in Judith M. Barringer and Jeffrey M. Hurwit (eds.), *Periklean Athens and its Legacy* (Austin, 2005), 73–87, with earlier references to the vast bibliography on this painting.

[86] See, e.g., Castriota, "Feminizing the Barbarian," 89–102; Isaac, *Invention*, 255, 296–297.

increasingly strident rhetoric that we find in Isocrates takes on a delusional air of unreality. For those of us steeped in this material, it is hard to escape a queasy sense of recognition when listening to the rhetoric of freedom and tyranny, democracy and oppression, that shapes the official American attitude toward the descendants of Darius in Iran and, even more so, Iraq. An imperial power itself, the United States nevertheless defines itself as the champion of freedom for those oppressed by tyrants like Saddam Hussein. As the Athenian Empire used its enormous military might to install democracies in many of the subject cities – whether they wanted one or not – so the United States' express policy is to plant democracy in foreign soil that may not be so receptive to it. Looking at the fate of Athens and her Empire does not inspire confidence in this policy.

4   Racism, color symbolism, and color prejudice

David Goldenberg

One of the many benefits for me of Ben Isaac's new book, *The Invention of Racism in Classical Antiquity* (Princeton, 2004), was that it spurred me to do some fundamental rethinking about the definition of racism. It is not only Isaac's extensive introduction on the definition of terms, or his distinction of and preference for the term proto-racism, or even his delineation of (to use his terminology) the hostile thinking against others found in Greek and Roman writers. It is also what is not in the book that has spurred my thinking.

For Isaac does not discuss black Africans, the one group with which, in our time, the term racism is most closely associated. Isaac gives his reasons for this exclusion (pp. 49–50), but as I thought about it, I began to realize that anti-Black racism is of an entirely different sort than the racism that is discussed in the book. I can do no better in illustrating this than by quoting David Wiesen's 1970 article on "Juvenal and the Blacks." There is no doubt, says Wiesen, that Juvenal was strongly biased against the outsider. But there is a difference. Greeks, Orientals, Egyptians – they are all hated for their foreign ways and their potential to corrupt Roman culture. Blacks, on the other hand, are hated not for what they do, but for what they are; "it is their physical being that Juvenal despises."[1] Now, of course, we must ask to what extent Juvenal represents general attitudes, but Wiesen is convincing in arguing that a satirist would not expect his work to be accepted were he not echoing general attitudes among his readers.

It seems to me that the distinction between Blacks (or Ethiopians, as they are known in Greco-Roman sources) and others that Wiesen makes is important. Yes, the environmental theory held that Blacks were innately cowards, but generally speaking, it is the Blacks' physical being, and in particular their skin color, that is found objectionable, not their customs or what was believed to be their innate characteristics. Syrians and Asians are born for slavery; they are effeminate and servile. Phoenicians are

---

[1]   David Wiesen, "Juvenal and the Blacks," *Classica et Mediaevalia* 31 (1970) 132–50, quote on 149.

cheats and faithless. Greeks are soft, degenerate, and morally inferior; they are not virile or courageous. And so on, for other foreigners. All these characteristics are non-physical characteristics, whereas the objections to the Blacks are, for the most part, based on physical characteristics of the body, their hair, lips, nose, but especially their skin color.[2]

James Jones in his book *Prejudice and Racism* makes a telling point, made by others as well, and although he, as a sociologist, is speaking of con-temporary times, what he says is, I believe, applicable to the ancient world. Speaking of the situation in America, he says, "We talk about blacks as a group. However, needless to say, the variability in skin color, eye color, hair texture, and cultural background is enormous."[3] And yet we talk about them as a group. Why? Because what is most distinguishing among them all is that combination of physical features – to a greater or lesser extent – that they all hold in common. It is precisely their physical appearance that so marked off these people from others. And we call them "Blacks" because among their distinctive features, their skin color is the most prominent and most remarkable.

One is struck by how often and in how many different contexts a derogation of Africans turns on their color. Stephen J. Gould quotes Benjamin Franklin's hope that America would be a land of white people unspoilt by less pleasing colors: "Why should we … darken its people?" ask Franklin. "Why increase the Sons of Africa, by planting them in America, where we have so fair an opportunity, by excluding all blacks and tawneys, of increasing the lovely white and red?" To this and similar remarks Gould comments: "I have been struck by the frequency of such aesthetic claims as a basis of racial preference. Although J. F. Blumenbach,

---

[2] See also Lloyd Thompson, "Roman Perceptions of Blacks," *Scholia* 2 (1993) 27: "Several Roman texts clearly attest a quite widespread upper class perception of the *Aethiops* phenotype as a combination of certain somatic 'defects' or 'flaws' (*vitia*): colour, hair, facial morphology, and (in black women) over-large breasts (Juv. 13.162–66; Sen. *De Ira* 3.26.3; Mart. 6.39.6–9, 7.89.2; Pet. *Sat.* 102; *Anth. Lat.* 182f.; Moretum 13–35; Claud. *Bell. Gild.* 193; Luxorius 43, 71, 78)." This article is a good summary of Thompson's main points in his book published three years earlier, *Romans and Blacks* (Norman, Okla.: University of Oklahoma Press, 1989). Similar to Wiesen and Thompson in this regard is P. R. Helm, who, speaking of the negative references to Blacks in Juvenal, says that "the physical appearance of blacks was regarded by proper Romans as at best unfortunate, and at worst a perversion of nature" (P. R. Helm, "Races and Physical Types in the Classical World" in Michael Grant and Rachel Kitzinger (eds.), *Civilization of the Ancient Mediterranean: Greece and Rome* [New York: Scribner's, 1988], vol. 1, pp. 152–3).

[3] James Jones, *Prejudice and Racism*, 2nd edn (New York: McGraw-Hill, 1997), p. 341. Similarly Winston James writing about Caribbean immigrants in England ("The Making of Black Identities," in John Hutchinson and Anthony Smith [eds.], *Ethnicity* [Oxford: Oxford University Press, 1996], pp. 155–61; originally in R. Samuel [ed.], *Patriotism: The Making and Unmaking of British National Identity* [London: Routledge, 1989], vol. 2, pp. 234–41, 243–4).

the founder of anthropology, had stated that toads must view other toads
as paragons of beauty, many astute intellectuals never doubted the equation of whiteness with perfection."[4]

Studying Caribbean race relations, the sociologist H. Hoetink showed
that a preference for the "somatic norm image" – the toad's beauty – is a
universal phenomenon.[5] Neither the Greeks nor the Romans saw very
dark skin or very light skin as aesthetically pleasing. Expressions of distaste
for the darker or lighter complexion are commonly found in Greco-Roman
sources and have been thoroughly documented by Frank Snowden and
Lloyd Thompson.[6] Both of these scholars furthermore found that a
preference for the Mediterranean somatic norm of light brown skin was
largely responsible for any expressions of anti-Black sentiment in the
classical world, which was explained as an ethnocentric manifestation of
conformism to dominant aesthetic tastes.[7] It should be noted that the
Greek environmental theory for anthropological differences also favored
the somatic norm and was not as devoid of racist or proto-racist sentiment
as Snowden claims. Implicit in the theory is its ethnocentric character,
which viewed others' skin color as an aberrant result of extreme environmental conditions on the normal complexion. The Greeks and Romans
were not unusual in this regard. As I have shown elsewhere, Rabbinic
etiologies of dark-skinned people similarly express a late-antique Jewish
preference for the somatic norm, as do also black African etiologies of
light-skinned people. Only, in Africa the colors are reversed.[8]

The Greco-Roman distaste for the Ethiopian skin color is clear.[9] In an
effort to better understand the roots of racism, the question I would like to

---

[4] *Mismeasure of Man* (New York: Norton, 1981), p. 32; see also the quotation from Charles
White (1799) showing how "White's criteria of [racial] ranking tended toward the aesthetic" (p. 42).
[5] H. Hoetink, *The Two Variants in Caribbean Race Relations* (London: Oxford University
Press, 1967), pp. 120–1 (originally published in Dutch in 1962).
[6] Frank Snowden, *Before Color Prejudice* (Cambridge, Mass.: Harvard University Press,
1983), pp. 75–9, and *Blacks in Antiquity* (Cambridge, Mass.: Belknap Press of Harvard
University Press, 1970), pp. 171–9; Lloyd Thompson in *Romans and Blacks, passim*; see
index, "somatic norm image."
[7] Similarly Jean-Jacques Aubert, "Du noir en noir et blanc: éloge de la dispersion," *Museum
Helveticum* 56 (1999) 159–82, especially 176.
[8] David Goldenberg, *The Curse of Ham: Race and Slavery in Early Judaism, Christianity, and
Islam* (Princeton, N. J.: Princeton University Press, 2003), pp. 95–112.
[9] Snowden's claims for counterbalancing expressions of a preference for dark skin are problematic, as many have noted. Often these citations prove just the opposite, for in many cases
these favorable expressions are voiced by their ancient authors precisely in an attempt to
counter the prevailing contemporaneous view of society. See, e.g., Dieter Metzler and
Herbert Hoffmann, "Zur Theorie und Methode der Erforschung von Rassismus in der
Antike," *Kritische Berichte* 5.1 (1977) 6, or François de Medeiros, *L'occident et l'Afrique
(XIII*^e*–XV*^e *siècle)* (Paris: Editions Karthala; Centre de recherches africaines, 1985), p. 159.

pose is whether this distaste constitutes racism, or even proto-racism. I add proto-racism because the two major studies on this issue, those by Snowden and Thompson, concluded that there was no racism against Blacks in classical antiquity. Their conclusions hinged on their definition of racism as a socially defined creation. Racism exists where we find discriminatory social structures based on and justified by an ideology of a biologically determined hierarchy. If we accept this definition then we must agree that racism against Blacks did not exist in the Greco-Roman world, or, at least, we have no evidence for it. But did proto-racism exist? According to Ben Isaac's definition it did, for he defines proto-racism as patterns of "hostile thinking" about others, and this definitely applied to the black African. There is considerable negative sentiment, in the form of sensory aversion, toward the Ethiopian that qualifies, to my mind, as hostile patterns of thinking.

But Isaac has a further definition that is important. Racism is "an attitude toward individuals and groups of people which posits a direct and linear connection between physical and mental qualities" (p. 23). Indeed a crucial component of racist thinking is that link between physical and nonphysical characteristics, such as temperament, character, and culture, aspects of which (e.g. courage, cowardice, intelligence, stupidity, morality) are explicitly or implicitly considered as inferior or superior.[10] Toynbee made the same point and Lloyd Thompson, as Ben Isaac, noted the influence of this kind of thinking on later racist theories.[11] This definition is, of course, the definition of a stereotype, that is, the belief that all people belonging to a certain group share certain nonphysical characteristics. The Greek environmental theory falls into this category for it links physical and nonphysical characteristics. In the case of Blacks, it joins together with their skin color the traits of cowardice and intelligence. But, and this is the point, the hostility exhibited toward Blacks in the ancient world is primarily, almost exclusively, focused on their physical characteristics, especially their skin color. The link to the nonphysical negative trait of their presumed cowardice is not at all prominent in the patterns of hostile thinking toward them. The crucial component,

---

[10] "Physical" is used here in the sense of biological physicality, i.e. belonging to a biological (real or imagined) group, that is, ethnicity or race. It need not mean strictly phenotype, for some ethnic groups are not noticeably marked off physically from the group attributing the stereotype (e.g. Jews in the Hellenistic and Roman worlds). Further, to the extent that distinct phenotype is present, it is but a marker of the biologically distinct group. By "biologically distinct group" I mean a group that shares (real or imagined) common ancestry.

[11] For references, see David Goldenberg, "The Development of the Idea of Race: Classical Paradigms and Medieval Elaborations," *International Journal of the Classical Tradition* 5 (1999) 561–70.

therefore, in a definition of racism or proto-racism, that is stereotype or the physical–nonphysical link, is absent.

I would like now to look more closely at the nature of this hostile thinking toward the Black. Isaac quoted with approval George Fredrickson's definition of racism, which "originates from a mindset that regards 'them' as different from 'us' in ways that are permanent and unbridgeable" (Isaac, p. 23). According to Fredrickson, this mindset must be used for advantages of power and the differences must be permanent and unbridgeable, but the fundamental element is the perception that there is a difference between "them" and "us." Now, what can be a greater, more persistent exhibition of difference than the physical body? And what can be a greater exhibition of difference in the body than skin color? A crucial element, therefore, in hostile thinking toward Blacks is that they are so very visibly not "us," that they are glaringly the Other. This element is not present in the hostile thinking directed towards other Others, such as the Greeks or the Asians or the Jews.[12] The only other groups whose natural physical appearance seems to evoke reaction are the Scythians and others from the extreme north, the counterparts to the Ethiopians in the extreme south. Their skin color was found to be too light and their bodies too large.[13] And it was really only their size and not their complexion that evoked negative reaction.[14] For references to the northern, light skin color are usually found in descriptions of the environmental theory as an explanation for somatic distance, but not in other contexts. In short, as opposed to all others, the Black is expressly

---

[12] For the lack of distinguishing characteristics between slaves of different ethnicities and Roman citizens, see David Brion Davis, *The Problem of Slavery in Western Culture* (Ithaca, N.Y.: Cornell University Press, 1966), pp. 48–9, 70–2, but see David Goldenberg, *The Curse of Ham*, pp. 118–22, 127–8. For the Jews, see my review of Abraham Melamed's *The Image of the Black in Jewish Culture* in *Jewish Quarterly Review* 93 (2003) 561 n. 7. Two Rabbinic texts indicating a lack of physical difference between Roman and Jew, except for circumcision, are found in *GenR* 82.8 (ed. Theodor-Albeck, p. 985) and *bTaʿan* 22a. In the first it is reported that during the Hadrianic persecutions, two students of R. Joshua disguised themselves in non-Jewish clothing, so as not to be recognized as Jews; i.e. physical appearance alone would not have indicated their Jewishness to the Roman authorities. A similar situation obtains in the second text where the clothing is specified: a Jewish jailer is reported as saying to a R. Beroqaʾ Hozʾa that he did not wear *ṣiṣit* and he wore black shoes (?) so that the non-Jews among whom he worked would not know that he was a Jew.

[13] See John P. V. D. Balsdon, *Romans and Aliens* (Chapel Hill, N. C.: University of North Carolina Press, 1979), p. 215.

[14] Adrian N. Sherwin-White, *Racial Prejudice in Imperial Rome* (Cambridge: Cambridge University Press, 1970), pp. 57–8, citing Caesar, Livy, Strabo, and Tacitus. Even their size, according to Wiesen (p. 137), wasn't considered an object of contempt. It was rather admired and feared by the Romans.

denigrated for his color. His somatic distance, and his alone, became an object of derision and contempt.

But derision and contempt were not due only to an ethnocentric-driven manifestation of aesthetic tastes, of conformism to the somatic norm. When we look at expressions of negative sentiment, aside from those evocative of somatic distance and sensory aversion, we find that they reflect the values of color symbolism, in particular the negative value associated with the color black. Many studies have shown how deeply embedded, and how widespread, are the negative associations of blackness and the positive associations of whiteness. I need not rehearse here the findings from various disciplines showing that these associations with black and white are apparently universal, including even black African cultures. That is why, in discussing the origins of American racism, the historian Winthrop Jordan assigned such importance to the meaning of blackness. It was, he said, "loaded with intense meaning."[15] That is why, in discussing early English attitudes toward the black African, Elliot Tokson said about blackness, "It was not likely that the black man could escape the consequences of inevitable associations."[16]

Greece and Rome were no different. Black was associated with death and the underworld, the realm of the dead.[17] The color thus took on ominous symbolism. One of the signs portending the death of the emperor Septimius Severus (reigned 193–211) was that black-skinned animals were presented to him for sacrifice to the gods, and that although he rejected them in disgust, the animals refused to leave him.[18] In Terence, the second-century BCE Roman playwright, a black dog

[15] Winthrop Jordan, *White over Black: American Attitudes toward the Negro, 1550–1812* (Chapel Hill: University of North Carolina Press, 1968), p. 97.
[16] Elliot H. Tokson, *The Popular Image of the Black Man in English Drama, 1550–1688* (Boston, Mass.: G. K. Hall, 1982), p. 43.
[17] See Christopher Rowe, "Conceptions of Colour and Colour Symbolism", in *The Realms of Colour*, ed. Adolf Portman and Rudolf Ritsema, Eranos Jahrbuch, 1972 (Leiden, 1974); *Theological Dictionary of the New Testament*, ed. Gerhard Kittel; Eng. edn (Grand Rapids, Mich.: Eerdmans, 1964), s.vv. σκότος (7:424–425; Conzelmann), μέλας (4:549; Michaelis); E. Irwin, *Colour Terms in Greek Poetry* (Toronto: Hakkert, 1974), pp. 173–87. See the sources collected in Alan E. Bernstein, *The Formation of Hell: Death and Retribution in the Ancient and Early Christian Worlds* (Ithaca, N.Y.: Cornell University Press, 1993), Index s.v. Darkness. See also G. Radke, "Die Bedeutung der weissen und schwarzen Farbe in Kult und Brauch der Griechen und Römer" (Ph.D. diss., Berlin, 1936), and Thompson, "Roman Perceptions of Blacks," *Scholia* 2 (1993) 27. Note, as well, Richard Seaford's study of the "black Zeus" found in papyrus fragments of Sophocles' *Inachos*: "Black Zeus in Sophocles' *Inachos*," *Classical Quarterly* 30 (1980) 23–9. As Apollonius of Tyana is supposed to have said, "All whiteness is life, all blackness death" (quoted from the MS by Peter Dronke, "Tradition and Innovation in Medieval Western Color-Imagery," *The Realms of Colour*, p. 76).
[18] *Scriptores Historia Augusta*, Severus 22.6–7.

appears as an ominous warning.[19] This color of ill omen applied as well to people's complexion. There are three reports of the Roman soldiers under Brutus killing an Ethiopian whom they met on the way to the battle of Philippi, believing that the encounter portended a disaster.[20] Septimius Severus's encounter with an Ethiopian is said to have been one of the portents of Severus's impending death. At least Severus didn't have the man killed; he only had him removed from his sight, "troubled as he was by the man's ominous color."[21] Suetonius reports that one of the portents of Caligula's impending death was a nocturnal performance of some play in which "scenes from the lower world were represented by Egyptians and Ethiopians."[22] And a poem in the *Anthologia* says that Troy fell because Priam accepted "ill-omened assistance from [the Ethiopian king] Memnon and his black troops [*nigrum auxilium*]."[23]

Black and white serve as metaphorical representations for good and evil, life and death, etc. also in biblical literature although, interestingly, sin is red, not black, in the Hebrew Bible.[24] Biblical literature, however, does not include the dark-skinned person in its repertoire of metaphors representing evil. That begins in the postbiblical period. Philo, the first-century Hellenistic-Jewish philosopher, allegorizes the blackness of the Ethiopians as evil. In a passage dealing with Kush and his son Nimrod, who rebelled against God, Philo says that Nimrod's evil nature is hinted at in his father's blackness; "because pure evil has no participation in light, but follows night and darkness."[25]

The application of the metaphor to dark-skinned people was also made in rabbinic and patristic exegesis. One midrashic (amoraic) interpretation of Amos 9:7 ("Are you not like Kushites to me, O Israelites?") explains: "When Israel sins against God, He calls them Kushites."[26] Underlying

[19] Terence, *Phormio* 705–6.
[20] Appian, *The Civil Wars* 4.17.134; Florus 2.17.7–8; Plutarch, *Brutus* 48.5.
[21] *Historiae Augustae*, Severus 22.4–5   [22] Suetonius, *Caligula* 57.4.
[23] *Anthologia Latina*, ed. David R. Shackleton Bailey (Stuttgart: Teubner, 1982), pp. 124–5, no. 179. The translation is Snowden's (*Blacks in Antiquity*, p. 180).
[24] See the *Theological Dictionary of the Old Testament*, ed. G. Johannes Botterweck and Helmer Ringgren, trans. David E. Green (Grand Rapids, Mich.: Eerdmans, 1990) s.vv. אור (1:147–67; Aalen); חשׁך (5:245–59; Mitchel, Lutzmann, Ringgren, Geraty); *Theological Dictionary of the New Testament*, s.vv. λευκός (4:241–50; Michaelis), μέλας (4:549–551; Michaelis), σκότος (7:423–445; Conzelmann) and φῶς (9:310–58; Conzelmann). For sin being represented as red, not black, see the literature in David Goldenberg, *The Curse of Ham*, p. 249 n. 50.
[25] *Quaestiones in Genesim* 2.82. Contrary to Marcus (see his note in the LCL edition), Philo is not confused here; see Lester Grabbe, *Etymology in Early Jewish Interpretation: The Hebrew Names in Philo* (Atlanta, Ga.: Scholars Press, 1988), p. 191.
[26] *Midrash Psalms* 7.14, ed. S. Buber, *Midrash Tehilim* (Vilna: Romm, 1891), p. 70. On this work, see the Glossary in Goldenberg, *The Curse of Ham*.

this explanation is the idea of blackness as a metaphor for sin (moral evil). We can see this even more clearly in another midrash (also amoraic) which interprets the verse in Song of Songs (1:5) "I am black but beautiful," as referring to Israel when she sins, and then cites as prooftext the Amos verse, *"Are you not like Kushites to Me, O Israelites* (Amos 9:7)."[27] In other words, the blackness of the maiden in Song 1:5, which is a metaphor for sin, is identified with the Kushites. So here, as in Philo, we have the application of the metaphor to the black African.

The most extensive use of the metaphor of darkness as sin as applied to dark-skinned people was made by the church fathers in their allegorical interpretations of the Bible. The most ramified of such interpretations, as well as the one with the greatest influence, was that of Origen (d. *c.* 253). Using the metaphor of blackness as sin, he identified various biblical references to Ethiopia or Ethiopian(s), as well as the black maiden in Song 1:5 as symbols ("types") for the gentiles, who, not having known God, as had the Israelites, were born and lived in sin. Thus Moses' marriage to the Kushite (Num. 12:1) represents God's embrace of the gentiles; "Ethiopia shall stretch out her hands to God" (Ps. 68:32/31) means that the gentiles outstrip the Jews in their approach to God; God's words to the prophet Zephaniah, "From beyond the rivers of Ethiopia will I receive the dispersed ones" (Zeph. 3:10), means that although the Ethiopian "has been stained with the inky dye of wickedness [and] has been rendered black and dark," he will nevertheless be accepted by God; Ebed-melech, the Ethiopian eunuch (Jer. 38:7–13), because he is "a man of a dark and ignoble race," represents therefore the gentiles; and when Matthew (12:42) speaks of "the Queen of the South … who condemns the men of this generation," he means the Queen of Sheba who, being identified by Origen as an Ethiopian, represents the gentiles who will condemn the Jews.[28]

---

[27] *Song of Songs Rabba* 1:5.1 (ed. Warsaw 1.35). On this work, see the Glossary in Goldenberg, *The Curse of Ham.*

[28] Origen, *Homilies to Song* 1.6, *Commentary to Song* 2.1, 2.2, *Die griechischen christlichen Schriftsteller der ersten drei Jahrhunderte* (hereafter *GCS*) (Leipzig: Hinrichs, 1901–) 33 [Origen 8] 35–8, 113–26; English translation in *Ancient Christian Writers* (Westminster, Md.: Paulist Press, 1946–) 26:91–107, 276–7 (R. P. Lawson, 1957). Similarly, Origen writes in his *Homilies on Jeremiah* 11.5, "We are black when we begin to believe. Therefore it is said at the beginning of Song 'I am black and beautiful.' At first our soul is compared to an Ethiopian. Then we are cleansed and become all white (bright), as it says 'Who is she who comes up having been made white?'" (*GCS* 6 [Origen 3] 84–5; *Sources Chrétiennes* 232:428–31; German translation, Erwin Schadel, *Origenes: Die griechisch erhaltenen Jeremiahomilien,* Bibliothek der griechischen Literatur 10 [Stuttgart: Hiersemann, 1980], 11.6, p. 130). In his *Homilies on Numbers* 6.4, and similarly in 7.2, Origen again equates the Ethiopian wife of Moses with the gentile church (and Miriam, Moses' sister, with the synagogue, the Jews); *GCS* 30 (Origen 7) 36, 39; *SC* 415:156–9, 172–3. For an

Describing the gentiles metaphorically as being in darkness or even being dark did not begin with Origen. Paul is particularly fond of the metaphor. He refers to the gentiles as those who are in the dark (Rom. 2:19), or dark in their understanding (Eph. 4:18), or who are darkness, such as in Ephesians 5:8, "you were once darkness, but now you are light in the Lord" (cf. Isa. 9:2), and he explains that he preaches to the gentiles so that they might "turn from darkness to light" (Acts 26:18; cf. Isa. 42:16).[29] But Origen took this a big step further in identifying those in the dark with the Ethiopian. And even that was not entirely new, for the germ of the idea appears in Irenaeus in the second century.[30] Origen's innovation was to apply this idea systematically throughout the Bible in a sustained exegetical enterprise, and it was this hermeneutical superstructure that influenced those who followed.[31]

Origen's biblical exegesis, in general, and particularly his works on Song, in which this exegesis is laid out, were enormously influential on the church fathers who followed.[32] It is not surprising therefore that his

analysis of this theme in Origen's commentary to Song, see Jacques Chênevert, *L'église dans le commentaire d'Origène sur le Cantique des Cantiques* (Montreal: Bellarmin, 1969), pp. 127–9. See also Buell's chapter in this volume.

[29] Beverly Gaventa, *From Darkness to Light: Aspects of Conversion in the New Testament* (Philadelphia, Pa.: Fortress Press, 1986), pp. 86–7, notes that such lightness–darkness imagery is common in descriptions of conversion. She cites 1 Peter 2:9; Philo, *On Virtue* 179, *Joseph and Asenath* 8.10, 15.13; *Odes of Solomon* 14.18–19; cf. 2 Cor. 4:6.

[30] Irenaeus interprets the Kushite in Numbers 12:1 as referring to the gentile church, and Moses' marriage to the Kushite as symbolizing the acceptance of the gentiles into the Christian faith (Irénée de Lyon, *Contre les Hérésies* 4.20.12, SC 100/2:672–3). See also Tertullian, *De Spectaculis* 3.8, *Corpus scriptorum ecclesiasticorum Latinorum* 1/1: 231, SC 332: 112–15: "When He threatens destruction to Egypt and Ethiopia, assuredly He warns every sinful nation of judgment to come. Thus the single case stands for the general class; every sinful race is Egypt and Ethiopia (Sic omnis gens peccatrix Aegyptus et Aethiopia a specie ad genus)" (trans. T. R. Glover, *LCL*).

[31] Cf. the comments of Manlio Simonetti, *Biblical Interpretation in the Early Church: An Historical Introduction to Patristic Exegesis*, trans. John Hughes (Edinburgh: T.&T. Clark, 1994; original Italian, 1981), p. 39:

If they are taken one by one, almost all the characteristics of Origen's exegesis ... can be found in exegetes who preceded him ... But compared to his predecessors, Origen organized and systematized these more or less traditional features .... He not only widened and deepened all that he received, but he ordered it, for the first time on precise methodological criteria, into a total synthesis which would in many ways remain definitive. In short, Origen made biblical hermeneutics into a real science, and, in that sense, he conditioned decisively all subsequent patristic exegesis.

[32] Dennis Brown, *Vir Trilinguis: A Study in the Biblical Exegesis of Saint Jerome* (Kampen, The Netherlands: Kok Pharos, 1992), pp. 17, 141, 153–5; Joseph W. Trigg, *Biblical Interpretation* (Wilmington, Del.: M. Glazier, 1988), pp. 23, 26; Manlio Simonetti, *Biblical Interpretation in the Early Church*, p. 39; Jean Daniélou, *Origen*, trans. W. Mitchell (New York: Sheed and Ward, 1955), p. 304; Bertrand de Margerie, *An Introduction to the History of Exegesis. I: The Greek Fathers*, trans. L. Maluf (Petersham, Mass.: St. Bede's, 1993), pp. 112–13; original French, 1980, p. 132; and for even later influence, see G. R. Evans, "Origen in the Twelfth Century," in Richard Hanson and

interpretation of the biblical Ethiopian as a metaphor for those in sin became widespread in later patristic literature. It "set the tone of all later exegesis," as one scholar put it.[33] I have identified seventeen church fathers from Origen's time through the sixth century who incorporated this theme in their writings.[34] In sum, the patristic hermeneutic tradition saw the biblical Ethiopian as a metaphor signifying any person who, not having received a Christian baptism, is black in spirit and without divine light. In a similar way "Ethiopia" came to symbolize, in Thompson's words, the "as yet unevangelized, and spiritually unregenerated world of sin."[35] Speaking of the negative metaphorical meaning of words for "black" in Greek and Latin, Thompson remarks that the fact that the Latin verb *denigrare* meaning not just "to blacken" but "to denigrate" is "not attested to until the fourth century AD is perhaps significant of a more pronounced tendency towards this sort of metaphorical usage in Christian times."[36]

Henri Crouzel (eds.), *Origeniana Tertia: The Third International Colloquium for Origen Studies* (Rome: Edizioni dell'Ateneo, 1985), pp. 279–81; Jean Daniélou, *The Bible and the Liturgy* (Notre Dame, Ind.: University of Notre Dame Press, 1956), pp. 198ff.; Helmut Riedlinger, *Die Makellosigkeit der Kirche in den lateinischen Hoheliedkommentaren des Mittelalters* (Münster: Aschendorff, 1958), pp. 7, 19, 26, 78–9, 126, 155, 400.

[33] François de Medeiros, *L'occident et l'Afrique*, p. 47 n. 45; see also Paul H. D. Kaplan, "Ruler, Saint and Servant: Blacks in European Art to 1520" (Ph.D. thesis, Boston University, 1983), p. 81. Note that Origen's exegesis, which, as we shall see, played a key role in the development of anti-Black racism, is based, at least partly, on a biblical text that is not found in the Hebrew. Origen's exegesis of the Ethiopian proceeds from his interpretation of the "black but beautiful" passage in Song of Songs 1:5, which is contrasted with Song 8:5:

This person who is now called black is mentioned toward the end of this Song as *coming up, having been made white, and leaning on her kinsman/beloved.* She became black, then, because she went down [in sin]; but once she begins to come up and to lean on her kinsman/beloved [i.e. Christ], to cleave to Him, then she will be made white and fair.

Again, from his First Homily on Song:

In what way is she black and how, if she lacks whiteness, is she fair? She has repented of her sins ... that is the reason she is hymned as beautiful. She is called black however, because she has not yet been purged of every stain of sin, she has not yet been washed unto salvation; nevertheless she does not stay dark-hued, she is becoming white ... [and] they say concerning her: *Who is this that cometh up having been washed white?*

We see, then, that crucial for Origen's interpretation is the line from 8:5, "who is that coming up having been made white?" This line, which is the reading of the LXX, allowed him to construct his exegetical edifice. Without the verse, the structure would have been only half-built and would have collapsed. The Hebrew text of 8:5, however, does not say "having been made white," but "who is that coming up from the desert [מי זאת עולה מן המדבר]?"

[34] Goldenberg, *The Curse of Ham*, p. 49.

[35] Thompson, *Romans and Blacks*, pp. 40, 112. For early Christian attitudes to Blacks, see also Buell, chapter 5, below.

[36] *Romans and Blacks*, p. 211 n. 97.

Does this indicate a nascent racism in early Christianity? Snowden feels that the Christian texts merely reflect an aesthetic for the somatic norm, continuing the same lack of prejudice that he sees in the classical world.[37] Although Snowden's position has been severely criticized by others,[38] in essence I believe that he is right: Christian color symbolism, i.e. the negative value of black as applied to Black people, is no different from what we find in the classical sources or in Philo and the rabbinic texts. The Greek and Roman sources may indicate bad luck, ill omen, and an association with death and the underworld while the Christian and Jewish sources metaphorically associate blackness with sin, but both interpretations stem from the same negative color symbolism of blackness. The innovation of Christianity was not in the essential nature of the association of black and evil. It was, rather, in the degree of application of this association. In the church fathers the theme of Ethiopian blackness became a crucial component of the Christian focus on the battle between good and evil, which pervades patristic writing.

It is true, of course, that we have the same dichotomy in the dualistic theology of Qumran, which depicts the two ways that a person may live his life as the ways of lightness and darkness, with the members of the sect being the Children of Light and those outside the sect the Children of Darkness.[39] But this usage is still in the realm of abstract metaphor, whereas in patristic

[37] See his "Asclepiades' Didyme," *Greek, Roman, and Byzantine Studies* 32 (1991) 251–2 n. 30. Snowden's position was stated earlier in his *Blacks in Antiquity* and his *Before Color Prejudice* and has been accepted by some.

[38] In his chapter in *The Image of the Black in Western Art*, for example, Jean Devisse says, "We find that the said Christians displayed none of the optimistic open-mindedness that Snowden attributes to the man of antiquity," and: "The element that does not seem to have been present in antiquity, but which developed in later civilizations, is a marked antipathy toward blackness itself, and, as a consequence, toward black people" ("From the Demonic Threat to the Incarnation of Sainthood," in Ladislas Bugner [ed.], *The Image of the Black in Western Art*, trans. William G. Ryan [Fribourg: Office du livre; Cambridge, Mass.: distributed by Harvard University Press, 1976] vol. 2, pt. 1, pp. 50, 51; see also p. 58). So too Philip Mayerson: "The evidence, as I see it, runs contrary to the conclusions put forward by Professor Frank M. Snowden, Jr., who maintains that the early Christians continued the Greco-Roman tradition of considering no race superior or inferior to the other" ("Anti-Black Sentiment in the *Vitae Patrum*," *Harvard Theological Review* 71 [1978] 304). Similarly, Wout van den Boer, in a review of Snowden's *Blacks in Antiquity*, agrees with the book's conclusion of a lack of racism in the Greco-Roman pagan world but takes exception to the similar conclusion in early Christianity (*Mnemosyne* 24 [1971] 437–9). See also B. H. Warmington in his review in *African Historical Studies* 4 (1971) 385. For Thompson's critique of Snowden's position, see below and *Romans and Blacks*, p. 41.

[39] See, e.g., the *Manual of Discipline* (1QS 3.20–21): "In the hand of the Prince of Lights [שר אורים] [is] the dominion of all the Sons of Righteousness; in the ways of light they walk. But in the hand of the Angel of Darkness [מלאך חושך] [is] the dominion of the Sons of Deceit; and in the ways of darkness they walk" (translation by E. Qimron and J. Charlesworth in James H. Charlesworth [ed.], *The Dead Sea Scrolls* [Tübingen:

literature the notion of evil or sin is attached to a real person who is really black, i.e. the Ethiopian, even if that person existed only in Scripture.[40] Not only this, but the Ethiopian theme is related to another phenomenon in Christianity: the identification of the devil and demons as Ethiopians. This phenomenon is commonly found from the third century onward, especially in the writings of the desert fathers between the third and fifth centuries.[41] As I noted before, the idea of the underworld and its inhabitants as without light, and therefore black, is found in classical sources, and accounts for the depiction of the god of the underworld, as black (*niger*) and the sometimes theatrical casting of those from the underworld as dark-skinned Ethiopians and Egyptians.[42] Snowden and, before him, Dölger, believe that the Christian depiction of the devil as black in color is related to this Greco-Roman association of blackness with the underworld and with evil.[43] And it is not just the Greco-Roman world that paints the

J. C. B. Mohr (P. Siebeck); Louisville : Westminster/John Knox Press, 1994], pp. 14–15). See also 1QS 1.9–10. On the development of the Two Ways tradition, see George Nickelsburg, "Seeking the Origins of the Two-Ways Tradition in Jewish and Christian Ethical Texts," in *A Multiform Heritage*. Festschrift Robert Kraft (Atlanta, Ga.: Scholars Press, 1999), pp. 95–108.

[40] See Appendix.

[41] The sayings and stories of the desert fathers (250–500) were transmitted by the monks of the Egyptian desert and were eventually compiled into various collections. An overview of the history of these collections and publications of sayings, with literature, is given by D. Burton-Christie, *The Word in the Desert: Scripture and the Quest for Holiness in Early Christian Monasticism* (New York and Oxford publisher, 1993), pp. 76–103, with a bibliography of primary sources, including translations, pp. 305–8. The best introduction to the desert fathers literature that I've seen is that of Jean-Claude Guy, *Les Apophtegmes des Pères: Collection Systématique ch. I–IX. SC* 387 (Paris, 1993), pp. 13–87.

[42] Seneca, *Hercules Oetaeus* 1705 and Statius, *Thebaid* 2.49 (*nigri Iovis*); Statius, *Thebaid* 4.291 and Ovid, *Metamorphoses* 4.438 (*niger Dis*); Virgil, *Aeneid* 6.128 (*atri Ditis*), 134–5 (*nigra Tartara*). For Ethiopians and Egyptians representing the underworld, see Suetonius, *Caligula* 57.4. Sources are cited in Frank Snowden, *Before Color Prejudice*, pp. 84, 139 nn. 100–2. See also Jennifer Hall, "A Black Note in Juvenal: Satire V 52–55," *The Proceedings of the African Classical Associations* 17 (1983) 110–11.

[43] Frank Snowden, "Greeks and Ethiopians" in J. E. Coleman and C. A. Walz (eds.), *Greeks and Barbarians* (Bethesda, Md.: CDL Press, 1997), p. 117. Franz Dölger, *Die Sonne der Gerechtigkeit und die Schwarze* (Münster/Westf.: Aschendorff, 1918; reprint Munich, 1971), pp. 49–52, 57, 71. For the association of the devil with the underworld and hell in early Christian sources, see, e.g., Rev. 9:11, 20:10–15, cf. Matth. 25:41. For later sources, see, e.g., the Acts of Thomas 55 (Sixth Act), a third-century work, in which Satan, the tour guide of hell, is described as "an ugly looking man, entirely black." See J. K. Elliott (ed.), *The Apocryphal New Testament* (Oxford: Clarendon Press, 1993), p. 470; Wilhelm Schneemelcher (ed.), *New Testament Apocrypha*, revised edition, English translation, ed. R. McL. Wilson (Cambridge: Cambridge University Press, 1991–2), vol. 2, p. 473 (ed. 1965, G. Bornkamm); A. F. J. Klijn, *The Acts of Thomas* (Leiden: Brill, 1962), p. 94; *New Testament Apocrypha* vol. 2, p. 362 (ed. 1991–2, Han J. W. Drijvers): "hateful of countenance, entirely black."

Depictions of the devil as black in color are very common in Christian literature and art. The literature on this is extensive. See Jean Devisse, "Christians and Blacks," in *Image of the Black in Western Art*, vol. 2, pt. 1, pp. 64–80 and p. 225 n. 269; J. M. Courtès, "The

underworld black. In the ancient Near East, as well, the underworld and, by
extension, its inhabitants, the chthonic deities, are dark or black.[44]

Theme of 'Ethiopia' and 'Ethiopians' in Patristic Literature", ibid., vol. 2, pt. 1,
pp. 19–21; Lellia Cracco Ruggini, "Il negro buono e il negro malvagio nel mondo
classico," in M. Sordi (ed.), *Conoscenze etniche e rapporti di convivenza nell'antichità*
(Milan: Vita e pensiero, 1979), pp. 126ff.; Carmelina Naselli, "Diavoli bianchi e diavoli
neri nei leggendari medievali," *Volkstum und Kultur der Romanen: Sprache, Dichtung, Sitte*
15 (1942–3) 244ff. Also see the indexes in Jeffrey Russell, *The Prince of Darkness* (Ithaca,
N. Y.: Cornell University Press, 1988), s.v. "blackness," and idem, *Lucifer: The Devil in the
Middle Ages* (Ithaca, N. Y.: Cornell University Press, 1984), s.v. "blackness of devil";
G. W. H. Lampe, *A Patristic Greek Lexicon* (Oxford: Clarendon Press, 1961), s. v. Αἰθίοψ;
Snowden, *Before Color Prejudice*, pp. 146–7 nn. 203, 205–6; Peter Frost, "Attitudes toward
Blacks in the Early Christian Era," *The Second Century* 8 (1991) 4–11; Philip Mayerson,
"Anti-Black Sentiment," *Harvard Theological Review* 71 (1978) 307–11; O. Chadwick,
ed. and trans., *Western Asceticism* (Philadelphia: Westminster Press, 1958) pp. 33, 61, 66,
191, 211 and 217; Dölger, *Die Sonne*, pp. 49–57, 159–61; P. Basilius Steidle, "Der
'schwarze kleine Knabe' in der alten Mönchserzählung," *Benediktinische Monatschrift
zur Pflege religiösen und geistigen Lebens* 34 (1958) 339–50. See also G. R. Dunstan and
R. F. Hobson, "A Note on an Early Ingredient of Racial Prejudice in Western Europe,"
Race 6 (London, 1965) 334–7. J. J. Winkler, "Lollianos and the Desperados," *Journal of
Hellenic Studies* 100 (1980) 161, cites several Christian and classical sources. The Council
of Toledo in 447 formally defined the devil as having, among other characteristics, black
skin, fiery eyes, a huge phallus, and a sulfurous smell (Russell, *Lucifer*, p. 69 n. 13).
Descriptions of the devil as black or as Ethiopian are very common in Coptic monastic
accounts of the desert fathers (M. Blanc-Ortolan, "Art, Coptic Influence on European,"
in Aziz S. Atiya [ed.], *The Coptic Encyclopedia* [New York: Macmillan; Toronto: Collier
Macmillan, 1991] vol. 1, pp. 248–9).

[44] *Theological Dictionary of the Old Testament* 5:247 (Lutzmann); *Theological Dictionary of the
New Testament* 4:549 (Michaelis); 7:426; A. Heidel, *The Gilgamesh Epic and Old Testament
Parallels* (Chicago: University of Chicago Press, 1946), pp. 121, 178–9, 192; see also
pp. 180–1 and Bernstein, *The Formation of Hell: Death and Retribution in the Ancient and
Early Christian Worlds* (Ithaca, N. Y.: Cornell University Press, 1993), pp. 4 and 8. In
Mesopotamian texts, two names for the underworld are "Darkness" and "House of
Darkness." Those who enter "see no light, in darkness they dw[ell]" (Wayne Horowitz,
Mesopotamian Cosmic Geography [Winona Lake, Ind.: Eisenbraun date], pp. 349, 352–3.
See W. Heimpel, "The Sun at Night and the Doors of Heaven in Babylonian Texts,"
Journal of Cuneiform Studies 38 [1986] 127–51 on the question whether the sun ceases to
shine when it passes through the underworld). In another text a prince has a vision of the
underworld where he encounters "a man, his body black as pitch" (A. Livingstone, *Court
Poetry and Literary Miscellanea*. SAA 3 [Helsinki: Helsinki University Press, 1989] p. 72,
line 10). The Egyptian netherworld is also (less often, for the sun shines there) described
as a place of darkness, and the damned, who are in the "outer darkness," are depicted as
dark or black. See Conzelmann in *TDNT* 7:426; E. Hornung, *The Ancient Egyptian Books
of the Afterlife*, trans. David Lorton (Ithaca, N. Y.: Cornell University Press, 1999), p. 27;
and H. Kees, *Farbensymbolik in ägyptischen religiösen Texten*. Nachrichten von der
Akademie der Wissenschaften in Göttingen: Philologisch-Historische Klasse 11
(Göttingen, 1943), p. 416. The Egyptian god Osiris, "being none other than he whom
the Greeks call Hades and Pluto" (*Isis and Osiris* 19 [358B], 78 [382E], ed. and trans.
J. Gwyn Griffiths, *Plutarch's De Iside et Osiride* [Cardiff: University of Wales Press, 1970],
pp. 242–3), who rules the underworld, is often painted black, "recalling his dark realm of
death" (Erik Hornung, *The Valley of the Kings*, trans. D. Warburton [New York: Timken
Publishers, 1990; original German 1982], p. 118; see also p. 134, pl. 93 and p. 164, pl.
125). On Osiris's black color, see further Alessandra Nibbi, "The Hieroglyph Signs *gs* and
km and their Relationship," *Göttingen Miszellen* 52 (1981) 47. In Hittite the term for the

It is thus not surprising to find that as early as the end of the first or beginning of the second century, the devil, whose association with the underworld and hell in early Christian sources was noted above (n. 43), is called "the Black One" (ὁ μέλας).[45] For the same reason Osiris, the Egyptian god of the underworld, is similarly called "the Black One."[46] But soon enough, "the Black One," and demons in general, gain an ethnic identity. Beginning apparently in the second century, they become identified with the black African, the Ethiopian. In two second-century apocrypha, the *Acts of Andrew* and the *Acts of Peter*, devils or demons appear as Ethiopians.[47] A third-century apocryphon, the *Acts of*

---

underworld is "Dark/Gloomy Earth" (V. Haas, "Death and Afterlife in Hittite Thought," *Civilizations of the Ancient Near East*, ed. J. Sasson *et al.* [New York: Scribners, 1995], p. 2021). Finally, see the references to the Mountain(s) of Darkness at the entranceway to the underworld in Mesopotamian, Ugaritic, Jewish, and Mandaic literature cited in Goldenberg, *The Curse of Ham*, p. 63.

[45] *Epistle of Barnabas* 4.9 and 20.1: "The way of the Black One is crooked and full of cursing." (On the difficulty of determining whether Barnabas was a Jew, see the discussion in James C. Paget, *The Epistle of Barnabas* [Tübingen: J. C. B. Mohr], 1994, pp. 7–9.) In *The Life of St. Melania* (fourth–fifth centuries) the devil appears as a young black man who is called "the Black One" ("Of Fornication" 579, *Apophthegmata Patrum*, trans. E. A. W. Budge, *The Paradise, or Garden, of the Holy Fathers* [London: Chatto and Windus, 1907], vol. 2, p. 131). Similarly in Athanasius's *Life of Antony* 4 (R. T. Meyer, *St. Athanasius: The Life of Saint Antony*, ACW 10 [Westminster, Md.: Newman Press, 1950, pp. 23–4]). On the author, traditionally considered to be Rufinus, see the Introduction, pp. 6–7. The "Black One" is also found in a Greek–Egyptian Christian papyrus; see R. Reitzenstein, *Poimandres: Studien zur Griechisch–ägyptischen und früchristlichen Literatur* (Leipzig: B. G. Teubner, 1904), p. 293 n. 1. On the name and symbolism of the devil as black, see S. Vernon McCasland, "'The Black One,'" in Allen Wikgren (ed.), *Early Christian Origins* (Chicago: Quadrangle Books, 1961), pp. 77–80. In Jewish sources, we find a demon or spirit referred to as *ṭlnyth*, which was translated by André Dupont-Sommer as "la Ténébreuse" i.e. "the Dark One." This Aramaic word is presumably derived from *ṭll* "to cover" (Michael Sokoloff, *A Dictionary of Jewish Palestinian Aramaic of the Byzantine Period* [Ramat Gan: Bar Ilan University Press, 1990], s. v. *ṭlnyth*), the root also of *ṭl* (Heb. *ṣl*) "shadow, shade." Thus Gershom Scholem translates "shade" and Naveh–Shaked "shadow-spirit." See Joseph Naveh and Shaul Shaked, *Amulets and Magic Bowls: Aramaic Incantations of Late Antiquity*, 2nd edn (Jerusalem: Magnes Press, Hebrew University, 1987), pp. 58–60, 69–71, with earlier literature cited. Francis X. Gokey believes that the Two Ways doctrine found at Qumran was the immediate cause for the description of the devil as black in early Christianity; see his *The Terminology for the Devil and Evil Spirits in the Apostolic Fathers* (Washington: Catholic University of America Press, 1961), pp. 101–13, 121–74.

[46] Gay Robins in Donald Redford (ed.), *The Oxford Encyclopedia of Ancient Egypt* (Oxford: Oxford University Press), 1:291b, s.v. colour symbolism; see also 292b–293a and Mitchel in *TDOT* 5:246. See also the sources cited by Franz Dölger, *Antike und Christentum* (Munich: Aschendorff, 1932) vol. 3, p. 282 ("'Der Schwarze' als Benennung des Teufels"), especially Varro.

[47] *Acts of Andrew* 22 (James, *Apocryphal New Testament*, p. 345; Elliott, *Apocryphal New Testament*, p. 279). Literature in Elliott and Schneemelcher, *New Testament Apocrypha*, vol. 2, pp. 101–51, see esp. 108 and 115 (dating). See also the discussion of Dennis R. MacDonald, *The Acts of Andrew and The Acts of Andrew and Matthias in the City of the*

Xanthippa and Polyxena, has the devil appearing as the King of Ethiopia.[48]
The church father Ambrose (fourth century) reports meeting an
Ethiopian demon sitting on the scales of a fraudulent merchant.[49]
Macarius (fourth century), one of the desert fathers, encounters tiny,
repulsive Ethiopian boys who torment people in church.[50] Another desert
father, Palladius (fifth century), transmits a report of two demons who
appeared as Ethiopian women and committed indecent acts with a
monk.[51] And so on and so on.[52] So just as in the case of blackness as a
metaphor for evil and sin, so too in the case of the devil and demons, the

Cannibals (Atlanta, Ga.: Scholars Press, 1990), pp. 55–9, and Jean-Marc Prieur in *The
Anchor Bible Dictionary* (New York: Doubleday, 1992), vol. 1, p. 246 who conclude that
the date should be no later than 200 CE. In the *Acts of Peter* 22 (Schneemelcher, *New
Testament Apocrypha*, vol. 2, p. 305; Elliott, *Apocryphal New Testament*, p. 415), a demon
appears as "a most evil looking woman, who looked like an Ethiopian, not an Egyptian,
but was all black." On this work and its dating, see also Robert Stoops in *The Anchor Bible
Dictionary*, 5:267.

48 *Acts of Xanthippa and Polyxena* 17. Greek text: M. R. James, *Apocrypha Anecdota*. Series:
Texts and Studies, Contributions to Biblical and Patristic Literature, ed. J. A. Robinson, vol. 2,
no. 3 (Cambridge: Cambridge University Press, 1893), p. 70. English trans.: *The Ante-
Nicene Fathers* 9:210, ed. A. Roberts and J. Donaldson; rev. A. Cleveland Coxe, 1885–7,
1896 ("American edition"), repr. Peabody, Mass.: Hendrickson Publishers 1994.
Literature: Elliott, *Apocryphal New Testament*, pp. 524–5.

49 J. Amat, *Songes et visions: L'au-delà dans la littérature latine tardive* (Paris: Etudes augustiniennes, 1985), p. 333. Epiphanius and Nemesius of Emesa report that Origen was forced
to choose between apostasy and sodomy with an Ethiopian. *Adv. Haer* 64.2.1, now in *The
Panarion of Epiphanius of Salamis*, trans. F. Williams (Leiden: Brill, 1994) 2:132. *Némésius
d'Émèse: De Natura Hominis* 29, ed. G. Verbeke and J. R. Moncho (Leiden: Brill, 1975),
p. 121. For our purposes, it is irrelevant whether Origen believed that this occurred or
whether the story is folklore, as claimed by Jon F. Dechow and others; see Dechow's *Dogma
and Mysticism in Early Christianity: Epiphanius of Cyprus and the Legacy of Origen* (Macon,
Ga.: Mercer University Press, 1988), pp. 135–7. To those who recounted and heard the
report, the point of the choice is that the only thing that might be more detestable to Origen
than apostasy, would be sodomy with an Ethiopian.

50 Rufinus, *Historia Monachorum in Aegypto* 29, *PL* 21. 454B. N. Russell (trans.) and
B. Ward (introduction), *The Lives of the Desert Fathers: The Historia Monachorum in
Aegypto* (London: Mowbray, 1980), p. 153.

51 Lucien Regnault, *Les sentences des pères du desert: nouveau recueil; apophtegmes inedits ou peu
connus*, 2nd edn (Solesmes: Abbaye Saint-Pierre-de Solesmes, 1977), p. 184, from Paul
Evergetinos, *Recueil de paroles et d'enseignements des Pères* (Athens, 1957–66) vol. 3, p. 16.
English translation of Palladius: R. T. Meyer, *The Lausiac History*, ACW 34 (London:
Longmans, Green & Co., 1965). Palladius also tells that Pachon saw the devil as a young
Ethiopian girl. When he hit her to drive her away, the smell remained on his hand for two
years (*Historia Lausiaca* 23.5, trans. Meyer, *The Lausiac History*, p. 82; so too in the Syriac
version, E. A. W. Budge, *The Paradise, or Garden, of the Holy Fathers*, translated out of the
Syriac, with notes and introduction by Ernest A. Wallis Budge, 2 vols. (London: Chatto &
Windus, 1907) vol. 2, 131; see also p. 341.

52 Some examples: Origen, *On Prayer* 27.12, *GCS* 3 (Origen 2) 370, trans. J. J. O'Meara,
ACW 19. Didymus the Blind (fourth cent. Alexandria), *In Zachariam* 4.312, *SC*
85.964– 65. Cassian (fourth–fifth century), *Collationes* 1.21, *Corpus scriptorum ecclesiasti-
corum Latinorum*, 13:32–3; *SC* 42.105, trans. in C. Luibheid, *John Cassian: Conferences*
(New York: Paulist Press, 1985), p. 56, and E. C. S. Gibson in Philip Schaff and Henry
Wace (eds), *Nicene and Post-Nicene Fathers*, Second Series, 1890–9 ["American edition"],

abstract became real in the form of an identifiable human being, the black African.

This is not to say that early Christianity was racist. But we must ask whether these depictions of the Black man are nevertheless responsible for a later anti-Black development. Jean-Marie Courtès pointed out that although Christian patristic literature refers to Blacks only as metaphors, as he puts it "a mark of identity ... in the diptychs of darkness and light," nonetheless, he admits that these themes were destined for a long life.[53] And Carolyn Prager, speaking of a later period, during the Renaissance in England, points to the impact of such long-lived themes. However much, she says, the church fathers may have interpreted the biblical Ethiopian meta-phorically, the very fact that these interpretations "associate Ethiopianism with fallen man bonded by sin, reinforces a habit of mind that has chosen already between the ecumenical and diabolical African. Although the theo-logical intent is to gloss sacred text, the result ... is to encourage attention to ... the blackness of Ethiopians ... overlaid with the metaphoric associa-tions of contemporary divines linking the African to sin and slavery."[54]

repr. Peabody, Mass.: Hendrickson Publishers, 1994, 11:306. Jerome, *The Homilies of Saint Jerome*, trans. M. L. Ewald, Homily 3, on Psalm 7, FC 48, (Washington, D.C: Catholic University of America Press, 1964), vol. 1, p. 29. Augustine (d. 430), *City of God* 22.8. Pope Celestinus (d. 432), "A Homily on the Archangel Gabriel" in W. H. Worrell, *The Coptic Manuscripts in the Freer Collection* (New York: The Macmillan Company, 1923), pp. 354–5. Father Apollo in the *Historia Monachorum* 7 (8 in the Greek version), in Russell's translation, *The Lives of the Desert Fathers*, p. 70; Budge, *Paradise of the Holy Fathers*, vol. 1, p. 341; in the Syriac version of the *Apophthegmata*, E. A. W. Budge, *The Paradise of the Holy Fathers* 579, vol. 2, p. 130. (Another Syriac source is found in R. Payne Smith, *Thesaurus Syriacus* [Oxford: Clarendon Press, 1879–1901], 1:183.) Theodoret of Cyrrhus (d. 466), *Théodoret de Cyr: Histoire des moines de Syrie* 21.23, SC 234, 257; 1977–9, ed. P. Canivet and A. Leroy-Molinghen, 2:106–7. (Strangely, in the English translation, which is based on the *SC* text, which shows no variant here, the translator has "Egyptian" instead of "Ethiopian"; see Theodoret of Cyrrhus, *A History of the Monks of Syria*, trans. R. M. Price, Cistercian Studies 88 [Kalamazoo: Cistercian Publications, 1985], p. 142.) E. Amélineau, ed., "Vie de Paul de Tamoueh," *Mémoires publiés par les membres de la mission archéologique française au Caire* 4.2 (Paris: Ernest Leroux, 1895), p. 766. John Moschus (d. 619), *Patrum spirituale*. Cyril of Alexandria, *Homiliae diversae* 14, and *De exitu animi* (PG 77:1076C). *Lives of the Fathers of Merida* (9.7–8), a hagiography from Visigothic Spain, trans. and ed. A. T. Fear, *Lives of the Visigothic Fathers* (Liverpool: Liverpool University Press, 1997), p. 70. *Pistis Sophia* 140, ed. C. Schmidt, trans. V. Macdermot, in Douglas M. Parrott et al., *Nag Hammadi codices V, 2–5 and VI: with Papyrus Berolinensis 8502, 1 and 4*, Coptic Gnostic Library (Leiden: Brill, 1978), pp. 724–7. See also Amélineau's translation of `abd aswad` as "nègre abyssinien" in *The Arabic Life of Shenoute (Schnoudi)* (fourth–fifth century desert father) in reference to the devil in *Mémoires publiés par les membres de la mission archéologique française au Caire*, 4.1 (1888), p. 444.
[53] Jean-Marie Courtès, "The Theme of 'Ethiopia' and 'Ethiopians' in Patristic Literature," *Image of the Black in Western Art*, vol. 2, pt. 1, pp. 9–32, esp. 19–21.
[54] Carolyn Prager, "'If I Be Devil': English Renaissance Response to the Proverbial and Ecumenical Ethiopian," *Journal of Medieval and Renaissance Studies* 17 (1987) 264.

Such effects over time were compounded by iconographic representations. Jean Devisse asks rhetorically, "How many generations of Christians have been conditioned by looking at a grimacing black man torturing Christ or his saints? ... A whole mental structure, unconscious for the most part, was erected to the detriment of the blacks."[55] Similarly Ladislas Bugner writes of the artistic image of the Black that it is "beyond question that this pejorative extension of the symbolism of black color reflected unfavorably on the person of the African."[56] It had to be so because once evil is represented by a human image, we are one step removed from abstract metaphor and one step closer to reality, the black African person.

When we see a full-blown anti-Black attitude in Christian England beginning with the voyages of discovery, it is reasonable to suppose that the, by then, almost 1,300-year-old Christian exegetical tradition may have been a contributing cause. When, with the discovery of Africa, the Ethiopian was encountered in reality, scriptural metaphor was easily translated onto a live human being.

So, in considering the origins of racism in regard to the black African, I find that color symbolism played a key role. The very dark skin color of the African was interpreted negatively in the classical world (as a color of ill omen and death), in Philo (as evil), and in Rabbinic literature (as sin). Christian interpretation then adopted this symbolism, greatly expanding its application for its own exegetical and theological purposes. From here, it influenced the West's developing racism against black Africans. As Devisse wrote:

> From the simplistic but readily accepted idea that black is the sign of death and therefore of sin, it was easy to go on to the more dangerous idea that the man whose color was black was a menace, a temptation, a creature of the Devil. A whole imagery, conscious or unconscious, grew up in the minds of Western Europeans during the centuries of their physical and cultural isolation from the African world ... This imagery ... had become consubstantial with the cultural life of the Christian West.[57]
>
> (*Image of the Black in Western Art*, 2[1]: 38)

Let me now recapitulate my main points. Anti-black sentiment seems to be different from the hostile thinking encountered against other peoples.

---

[55] *Image of the Black in Western Art*, vol. 2, pt. 1, p. 80.
[56] *Image of the Black in Western Art*, vol. 1, p. 14.
[57] Devisse's continuation is noteworthy: "The marvel is that no one [i.e. of Christian theologians and exegetes] thought to explore the grave consequences of this prejudice, which had come down through the centuries without occasioning discussion or criticism, nor even a second look. It fastened itself upon the popular unconscious without ever becoming a subject of theological discussion – or doing so very late indeed" (ibid., p. 60).

Against others it is for what they do; against Blacks it is for what they are. And what they are, that is their blackness, is found to be objectionable because (a) it most visibly indicates their otherness, their somatic dissonance, and (b) its symbolic value connotes a host of negative notions. In short, anti-Black sentiment is truly color prejudice. The disparagement of black skin color began in classical antiquity, reached a height in Christian literature and in the literature of Christian societies.

It is of no small interest to note that the African-American novelist Toni Morrison recognized the crucial importance of the two fundamental elements of anti-Black sentiment that I have outlined here, that is, visibility and color symbolism. Speaking of the slaves in antebellum America, she says:

The distinguishing features of the not-Americans were their slave status, their social status – and their color. It is conceivable that the first would have self-destructed in a variety of ways had it not been for the last. These slaves, unlike many others in the world's history, were visible to a fault. And they had inherited, among other things, a long history on the meaning of color; it was that this color "meant" something.[58]

In conclusion, I return to the question of defining racism. If it is the case that the meaning of color is so crucial to a definition of anti-Black racism; if, then, as Wiesen said, it is what Blacks are that is objectionable and that led to racism, how then do we define that hostile feeling toward others that is not based on what one is, but on how one acts? Are we to lump together these two different sources of negative sentiment under the umbrella of "hostile feeling"? Even if our defining qualifications are heredity and unalterability, nevertheless there is still a difference between Blacks and others. For others stereotype is crucial, that is the belief that all who belong to a certain group have certain inherent character flaws. In the case of Blacks in antiquity, for the most part that crucial link between physical and nonphysical characteristics is absent. Hostile thinking toward Blacks was primarily based on their physical being and the otherness this indicates, and, most importantly, on the ideas associated with color symbolism. There is no connection between what they are and how they act. Is, then, hostility toward Blacks in Greece and Rome not to be considered racism since stereotype is absent? Or, if we agree intuitively, and with a disquieting glance at subsequent history, that it is to be considered racism or proto-racism, then do we have two different types of racism, one focused on physical characteristics (Blacks) and the other

---

[58] Toni Morrison, *Playing in the Dark: Whiteness and the Literary Imagination* (Cambridge, Mass.: Harvard University Press, 1992), pp. 48–9.

on the nonphysical (Jews, Greeks, Asians, etc.)? How exactly are we to define racism?

These questions essentially constitute the methodological underpinnings of Thompson's critique of Snowden and others who explored the issue of racism in Greco-Roman antiquity. Thompson argues that one should not apply the term racism, even in formulating the enquiry, to a Roman negative reaction to Blacks. For racism defines a social structure which "renders pigmentation and other physical traits a repository of messages about personal beliefs, cultural habits, and social status."[59] In other words, racism requires a link between the physical and the nonphysical, which then ranks the nonphysical in a hierarchy of social status. The Greco-Roman reaction to the Black, however, does not carry any such repository of messages about the innate character and behavior of the black African. This qualitative difference in type of hostile thinking may explain why racism against Blacks seems harder to eradicate in our time when the ancient stereotypes of the Egyptian, the Asian, the Jew, etc. have diminished (or, in some cases, have at least mutated) if not outright disappeared. Stereotype disappears with familiarity but skin color does not.

Appendix

The patristic exegesis of the black African as a metaphor for sin does not lie behind Christian interpretations of Numbers 12 concerning Moses' Ethiopian wife, despite the fact that the passage has commonly been understood as turning on anti-Black racism.[60] When the Bible says, "Miriam and Aaron spoke against Moses because of the Kushite woman whom he had married, for he had indeed married a Kushite woman" (Num. 12:1), abolitionist writers in antebellum America commonly understood that Miriam and Aaron's complaint was motivated by racist sentiments. The basis for this interpretation is the biblical description of Miriam's punishment as "leprosy as white as snow" (12:10). It is thought that a white disease is apt punishment for a racial anti-Black slur. Since, however, the original Hebrew text (והנה מרים מצרעת כשלג) does not say "white," the analogy to snow being rather to its flaky texture and not its

---

[59] Thompson, *Romans and Blacks*, p. 8.
[60] For the following discussion, see Goldenberg, *Curse of Ham*, pp. 26–9, and Rodney Sadler, "Representing the Cushite Other: The Use of Cushite Phenotypes in Numbers 12 and Jeremiah 13:23," in Douglas R. Edwards and C. Thomas McCollough (eds.), *The Archaeology of Difference: Gender, Ethnicity, Class and the "Other" in Antiquity* (Boston: American Schools of Oriental Research, 2007), pp. 127–37.

color, it might be concluded that the insertion of "white," which appears in the Vulgate, derived from the early Christian negative image of the scriptural black African.

This conclusion, however, is not warranted. For while it is true that "white" is not found in the Hebrew Bible (nor in the LXX or the Vetus Latina) but does appear in the Vulgate, *ecce Maria apparuit candens lepra quasi nix*, it can be attributed to the more mundane motive of an explanatory elaboration, such as is also found in the Vulgate translation of Ps. 68:14, where the Hebrew "it snowed in Salmon" became *nive dealbatur Selmon*.[61]

It is true that in other, non-Kushite, passages in the Bible where "leprosy" is compared to snow, the Greek and Latin translations do not add "white" to the analogy. Thus in Exodus 4:6, where Moses' hand is turned "*ṣara'at* like snow" according to the Masoretic text, the Vulgate, as the Vetus Latina and the Greek (with the exception of one manuscript), present literal translations of the Hebrew, and in 2 Kgs. 5:27 and 15:5, 2 Sam. 3:29, and 2 Chr. 26:19–23, where *ṣara'at* afflicts various people, the Greek and Latin translations do not add "white" to the Hebrew. These literal translations, however, do not provide proof that the patristic interpretation of Num. 12:10 was the cause for the Vulgate's addition of "white" there, for in his *Contra Ioannem Hierosolymitanum* 33, Jerome does add "white" when quoting Ex. 4:6, as does Augustine, *Sermon* 6.6.[62] So also *Targum Ongelos* and *Targum Pseudo-Jonathan* to Ex. 4:6 have "white like snow" (*Targum Neofiti* does not). On the other hand, in Num. 12:10, in addition to the Vulgate, the explanation "white" is found in the non-Christian tannaitic midrash and Targums to the verse.[63] Snow naturally suggests color. Indeed, in the Bible itself snow is used elsewhere to illustrate the color white (Isa. 1:18, Ps. 51:9/7, Dan. 7:9; see also Lam. 4:7). It is also thus used in Latin diction.[64] It would therefore

---

[61] For the passage in Numbers, see Pierre Sabatier's edition, *Bibliorum sacrorum latinae versiones antiquae seu vetis italica et ceterae quaecunque in codicibus manuscriptis et antiquorum libris reperiri potuerunt* (1739–49), ad loc., 1:288 in the three-volume Turnhout, 1976 reprint. The new edition of the Vetus Latina by the Beuron Institute has not yet produced Numbers. In addition to the Vulgate, Sabatier quotes Ambrose and Augustine with the reading "white," and the files of the Vetus Latina, which are now available online (at the Brepols website, www.brepols.net), refer also to Ps.-Augustine and Salvianus, Presbyter in Marseilles (d. after 470). See also Lam. 4:7 and my comments in *Curse of Ham*, p. 93.

[62] Sabatier, ad loc. (Exodus is also not yet available in the new edition).

[63] *Sifre Num* 104, ed. H. Horovitz, 2nd edn (Jerusalem: Wahrmann, 1966), p. 103, *Sifre Zuṭa* 12:10 (ibid., p. 276), *Targum Onqelos*, and *Targum Ps-Jonathan*, ed. pr. (1591).

[64] For Latin diction, see the following cases, for which I am indebted to Adam Kamesar: Homer, *Iliad* 10.437; Theocritus 11.20; Virgil, *Aeniad* 12.84; Catullus 80.2; Ovid, *Amores* 3.5.11, 3.7.8; *Metamorphoses* 8.373; *Ex ponto* 2.5.38; *Heroides* 16.251–255. On Jerome's use of the diction of classical writers, especially Ovid, in translating the Bible, see

not surprise us to find that the Vulgate, the Rabbis, and the Targums paraphrase or translate Num. 12:10 as "leprosy as white as snow." Thus, despite the fact that the addition of color is not found in the Vulgate to Ex. 4:6, we cannot attribute its addition in Num. 12:10 to racist sentiment born of the patristic exegesis of the black African as a metaphor for sin.[65]

Catherine Brown Tkacz, "*Quid Facit cum Psalterio Horatius?* Seeking Classical Allusions in the Vulgate," in Douglas Kries and Catherine Brown Tkacz (eds.), *Nova Doctrina Vetusque* (New York: P. Lang, 1999), pp. 93–104, and Tkacz, "Ovid, Jerome and the Vulgate," *Studia Patristica* 33 (1997) 378–82. On Jerome's translation techniques in general, see Benjamin Kedar-Kopfstein, "The Vulgate as a Translation: Some Semantic and Syntactical Aspect of Jerome's Version of the Hebrew Bible" (Ph.D. diss., Hebrew University, 1968), and Brown, *Vir Trilinguis*, pp. 104–20.

[65] Even if "Jerome's comments regarding them [the Ethiopians] are generally harsh" (Devisse in *Image of the Black in Western Art*, 2[1]:61).

5   Early Christian universalism and modern forms of racism

Denise Kimber Buell

> There is neither Jew nor Greek, there is neither slave nor free, there is no male and female, for you are all one in Christ Jesus. And if you are Christ's, then you are Abraham's offspring, heirs according to the promise.   (Galatians 3:28–9)

> Unless one is born of water and the spirit, one cannot enter the kingdom of heaven.   (Gospel of John 3:5)

Universalism is a well-known feature of early Christian rhetoric, associated especially with three ideas: that membership is available to people of all backgrounds; that Christians actively sought to win over all humans as members; and that Christians sought to be a unified whole from early on. Universalizing claims in early Christian writings are also frequently invoked by Christians as evidence that Christianity is – and always has been – antithetical to racism, even by many who point to racist Christian practices in the histories of colonialism, Atlantic world slavery, historical relations between Christians and Jews, and the ongoing organization of Christian communities largely along ethnic and racial lines. When Christianity has been implicated in racist practices and ideologies, interpreters often contrast Christian racism with perceived original inclusive and universal Christian ideals.[1]

---

[1] This essay consists primarily of a revision of the paper I delivered in the Howard Gilman International Conference, "Racism in Western Civilization before 1700" held at Tel-Aviv University, Israel, in December 2005. Parts of the essay also draw from my unpublished papers, "Ethnicity and the Book of Acts," delivered in the "Race, Place and the Book of Acts" symposium held at Furman University, USA, in April 2006; and "Spilled Blood and Ink: Modern Racism Meets Early Christian Collective Self-Definition" delivered in the "Ink and Blood: Textuality and the Human in Judaism, Christianity, and Islam" Conference, held at Dartmouth College, USA, July 2006. My thanks to the organizers of these conferences, Miriam Eliav-Feldon, Benjamin Isaac, and Joseph Ziegler as well as Shelly Matthews and Susannah Heschel, for the opportunities to present my work in stimulating interdisciplinary contexts. My thanks also to Melanie Johnson-DeBaufre and Laura Nasrallah for their ongoing critical support for this work.

After all, is it not a gross distortion of early Christian ideals, such as those found in Galatians 3:28–39, for the white supremacist minister Jarah Crawford to declare that Jews and nonwhites may become Christians "not as heirs in the family of God but as servants" because "they are not from the seed of Abraham. They will not share the inheritance of Israel"?[2] Certainly, there is no precise first–third-century CE counterpart to Crawford's toxic position. Crawford presumes that there are essences that individuals have that cannot be changed by conversion to Christianity, resulting in an internal hierarchy among Christians, with whites as the only "real" members of God's family and Abraham's lineage. While early Christians do tend to claim that only those who believe in Jesus as the Christ are Abraham's true descendants and the heirs of God's promises to Abraham, they generally depict this ancestry and inheritance as one that any human can acquire through conversion, a position seen as first documented in Paul's letters. Nonetheless, early Christians articulated what it would mean to become and be Christian in a context of struggle, both in local and imperial contexts and in relation to rival Jews and Christians, with the result that early Christian texts also contain discursive traces of arguments about who actually embodies salvation and authentic "Christianness" that have a noncausal but uneasy relationship to modern racist ideologies.

The surviving textual and material evidence by and about early Christians supports neither a purely utopian nor purely dystopian vision of Christian origins, including early Christian universalizing claims: they have both racist and antiracist potential. We can see this mixed legacy in the ways that markers of cultural difference, including *ethnos*, gender, slave/free status, and color remain salient within early Christian universalizing arguments and their subsequent adaptations.

All of these forms of difference could be used to emphasize the universal character of Christianness – that it can embrace all these differences. For example, the Acts of the Apostles, part of Christian scriptures, emphasizes the universal scope of its version of earliest Christianity in two major ways: first, by portraying its founding members – the apostles – as part of a movement with global spread when they receive the ability to speak all the languages of the Jewish diaspora (Acts 2:5–11); second, by defining Israel's destiny as global when an Ethiopian court official is one of the first named men to be baptized (Acts 8:26–38), Ethiopia being the

[2] Jarah Crawford, *Last Battle Cry* (Middlebury, VT: Jann, 1984), 67; cited and analyzed in James A. Aho, *The Politics of Righteousness: Idaho Christian Patriotism* (Seattle and London: University of Washington Press, 1990), 99.

equivalent of the ends of the earth from a Roman perspective.[3] This position could certainly have a positive valence, foregrounding inclusivity. Furthermore, these categories of cultural difference could serve to emphasize the counter-hegemonic values of the community – that all members should view themselves as slaves of God, regardless of status; that all should position themselves as passive and feminine in relation to the divine even as all should cultivate *andreia* as a Christian virtue, regardless of sex; and that all should view themselves as citizens of heaven and *xenoi* in this world, regardless of their civic status.

The positive side of Christian universalism does not constitute the whole picture, however. While not functioning as simply racist or proto-racist, early Christian forms of universalism adapt ancient discriminatory logics and can sustain modern racist interpretations. This negative legacy is perhaps most readily apparent in the ways that color and other kinds of somatic and cultural differences remain salient as a way for Christians to negotiate intra-Christian difference – such that deviance is illustrated by means of "marked" forms of difference, notably including Jewishess, blackness, and Ethiopianness.[4]

In this essay I focus on a less well-recognized factor contributing to the racist potential in early Christian universalizing claims, a discursive practice I call "ethnic reasoning." Ethnic reasoning refers to rhetorical strategies that employ ideas of peoplehood to communicate what it means to become and be Christian.[5]

Contrary to popular and scholarly opinion, early Christian writings regularly describe membership as belonging to an *ethnos*, *genos*, or *laos*.[6] That is, many Christian texts from the late first through early third centuries do not instruct readers to understand themselves as simply members of a new "religion," a voluntary cult that entails rejection of ancestral customs (for gentiles) or a radical reinterpretation of them (for Jews). Instead, many Christian texts explicitly guide readers to understand their entrance into these emerging communities as a transformation from one descent

---

[3] See Gay L. Byron, *Symbolic Blackness and Ethnic Difference in Early Christian Literature* (New York: Routledge 2002), 109–15.

[4] See, e.g., Vincent L. Wimbush, "Ascetic Behavior and Color-ful Language: Stories about Ethiopian Moses," *Semeia* 58 (1992): 81–92; Robert E. Hood, *Begrimed and Black: Christian Traditions on Blacks and Blackness* (Minneapolis: Fortress, 1994); Shaye J. D. Cohen, *The Beginnings of Jewishness: Boundaries, Varieties, Uncertainties* (Berkeley and Los Angeles: University of California Press, 1999), 175–97; Byron, *Symbolic Blackness*.

[5] See Denise K. Buell, *Why This New Race: Ethnic Reasoning in Early Christianity* (New York: Columbia University Press, 2005); Judith M. Lieu, *Christian Identity in the Jewish and Graeco-Roman World* (Oxford: Oxford University Press, 2004), 239–68.

[6] I shall focus on early Christian writings in Greek, but comparable terms occur in other languages: e.g., *gens* and *natio* (Latin): *genea* and *rēte* (Coptic).

group, tribe, people, or citizenship to a new and better one. In this respect early Christians are more like than unlike their ancient contemporaries, despite the fact that both early Christian texts and modern scholarly interpretations observe the persistent motif of breaking one's familial, civic, and ethnic social obligations in the process of becoming Christian.[7]

Neither conversion nor universalism precluded early Christian self-definition as membership in a people. And the fact that early Christians never gained recognition as an *ethnos* or *genos* did not prevent them from defining themselves in these terms. Rather than dismissing this collective self-definition, we need to ask what rhetorical and social functions it might have served and how it relates to Christian universalizing arguments.[8]

Early Christians understood the process of becoming Christian as one that transforms or activates one's very being. This change is often figured in relation to essences such as *pneuma* (spirit), *pistis* (faith), or Jesus' blood. As the opening quotes from Paul's letter to the Galatians and the Gospel of John illustrate, *pistis* and *pneuma* are often presented in imagery of altered kinship and rebirth. In other texts, Jesus' blood not only makes it possible to become Christian but is explicitly interpreted as begetting or birthing a people linked by faith *and* ancestry – an understanding pro-duced and reinforced through communal rituals, especially the eucharist. For example, in the late second century, Clement of Alexandria writes that the Lord has conceived and given birth to the "new people" (*Paidagogos* 1.42.2), interpreting the blood Christ shed at the passion as the pain and blood of childbirth.[9] This rhetoric blurs distinctions between

---

[7] See discussion in Buell, *Why This New Race*, 35–62.

[8] The perception that Christians did not form a people (despite what Tertullian claims for Carthage; see *Ad Nationes* 1.8; *Scorpiace* 10) may indeed have been widespread, and may explain its prohibition, as Benjamin Isaac claims:

> the difference between legitimacy and prohibition of a religion was determined by birth and descent. Religion, like citizenship, was inherited – not acquired – apart from Roman citizenship and state-cult ... Roman views of other peoples practicing their ancestral religion, such as the Jews, varied from admiration to highly critical and contain elements of prejudice and proto-racism. There was, however, no doubt as regards their legitimacy, while Christianity was definitely regarded as an illegitimate religion without proper histor-ical roots.
>
> (Isaac, *The Invention of Racism in Classical Antiquity*, 491)

This may have been the perspective of many, but it does not explain why a number of Christian texts do insist on defining membership in terms of *genos, ethnos, laos*, etc. Perhaps even more importantly, when we have established that race and ethnicity are "not real" in any case, we need to ask why scholars reinforce interpretations of early Christians as not a people.

[9] For an extended discussion of this portion of Clement's writings, see Denise K. Buell, *Making Christians: Clement of Alexandria and the Rhetoric of Legitimacy* (Princeton: Princeton University Press 1999), 107–79. See also Gal. 3:26–4:7; Rom. 8:12–17.

"religious" and "ethnic" or "racial" belonging and suggests a way of thinking about collective belonging that attributes essences to the members of a group while accommodating (indeed requiring) change.

Early Christian materials construct Christianness in ways disturbingly compatible with Ann Stoler's characterization of (modern) racial discourse: namely, that "the force of racial discourse is precisely in the double-vision it allows, in the fact that it combines notions of fixity and fluidity in ways that are basic to its dynamic."[10] Understanding attributions of fixity as the *sine qua non* of race and racism is insufficient since it omits both the slippery mutability of racial discourse and the contexts in which race has been characterized by both fixity and fluidity. Modern biologizing discourses have so naturalized the idea of race as "fixed" that they occlude recognition of competing *modern* racial discourses and resonances with other modern and premodern discourses of human difference, including ethnic and theological ones, that posit essences in a framework of mutability.[11]

The racist potential of early Christian universalism inheres in claims that Christian belonging is both membership in God's people and the full expression of humanness. This combination of claims raises the specter of *compulsory mutability* (if one can change, one must). We have failed to see this because of models of race and racism that focus exclusively on fixity. Instead of simply looking for the (pre)history of fixity, we need also to explore how exhortations or coercion to change constitute a vital facet of the history of racist rhetoric and social arrangements.

My basic argument is that early Christian universalizing arguments constitute an unstable legacy for later discourses of human difference, including racialized and racist ones. This essay challenges two common perceptions: that early Christianity has no relationship to later discourses about human difference widely recognized as racialized and racist, and that race and racism necessarily exclude ideas about mutability. These challenges require attention to how the concepts of race and racism are defined and how they are plotted historically.

---

[10] Ann Laura Stoler, "Racial Histories and their Regimes of Truth," *Political Power and Social Theory* 11 (1997), 198.

[11] E.g., as Stoler's work on the nineteenth- and early twentieth-century colonial context of the Dutch East Indies demonstrates, we cannot presume that assertions of "fixity" remain constant. The Dutch racialized colonists and colonized according to a cluster of criteria, including religious affiliation, education, color, marital arrangements – race in this modern colonial context was a moving target (see Stoler "Racial Histories"; ibid., *Carnal Knowledge and Imperial Power: Race and the Intimate in Colonial Rule* [Berkeley and Los Angeles: University of California Press, 2002]).

Proceeding in three major sections, this essay first tackles the relationship of definitions of racism and race to ideas about change. The second
section demonstrates some of the ways in which early Christian universalizing arguments, framed in contexts that define Christians as members of
God's people, contain racist potential. The final section takes up the
question of anachronism in speaking about race or racism for early
Christianity.

Defining "race": accounting for change

The question of change is, of course, the other side of the question of identity.
    (Bynum, *Metamorphosis and Identity*, p. 19)

There are distinctly modern forms of racism and racial discourse – I am
not asserting that these are transhistorical or ahistorical practices. But I do
not think we are best served by approaching race or racism from their
constraints within a biologized discursive framework, which characterizes
race in terms of fixed traits, transmitted intergenerationally through sexual reproduction. Today, we usually subvert this assertion of fixity by
defining race as a social construct. To expose race as a construct and
document that the characteristics used to classify someone as a member of
a racial group may differ according to time and place is to expose the
fluidity of race. Yet even when race is agreed to be a construct that
"matters," its hallmark is generally seen to be an assertion of fixity.

According to this approach, any group classification viewed as arising
from changeable traits – including membership in a Christian community –
would not be racial. That is, conversion and universalizing aspirations
might seem to preclude Christianity from being a race. Early Christian
universalizing rhetoric and aspirations are generally taken to mean that
early Christians formed something other than an *ethnos*, *genos*, or *laos* – all
Greek terms that relate to collective identity and have histories of translation into English terms such as "ethnicity" or "nation" (especially
ethnos), "race" (for *genos*), and "people" (*laos*).[12]

I am not convinced that "fixity" necessarily distinguishes race from
ethnicity or other discourses of human difference. I have found Ann
Stoler's work particularly valuable in coming to see racial discourse as

---

[12] Of course, just because the modern English term "ethnicity" has a philological relation to
ethnos does not mean that ethnicity best translates the term. Translating *genos* is even more
vexed, in that this term signifies very differently according to the context. See Jonathan
Hall, *Ethnic Identity in Greek Antiquity* (Cambridge: Cambridge University Press, 1997),
35–7. It would make a fascinating study to track the history of the translation of these
terms to note how different modern translations reflect, contribute to, or resist modern
projects of racialized ideologies.

characterized by both fixity and fluidity.[13] Racial discourses are pluriform and do not remain constant over time; in some historical contexts factors including custom, education, and religious affiliation have been part of the ethnography of race. To be sure, some fundamental essence such as blood, flesh, or seed is often asserted as the basis for reckoning membership in a group classified as a race. But ideas about race, like ethnic, religious, and national claims, "gain persuasive power by being subject to revision while purporting to speak about fundamental essences."[14] I emphasize this double-sided character of racial discourse, in part to indicate its resonances with other discourses, notably theological and ethnic ones, that similarly modulate between an insistence on essences while accommodating change.

What we mean by change is not, however, always obvious. Caroline Walker Bynum distinguishes between two major conceptualizations of change, what she calls "replacement-change" and "evolution-change." She convincingly points out that "whether we think of change as, at one end of the spectrum, replacement or, at the other, the unfolding of an essence or core forever present, our conception of change is intrinsically tied to our conception of entity or identity."[15] As she further notes, with its emphasis on core continuity, evolution-change makes it difficult to speak about "difference over time," whereas a replacement notion of change makes it difficult to account for change at all: "unless there is some connection, or nexus, between what was and what comes after, we tend to think we have not change but merely two things."[16]

Modern discourses of race tend to favor evolution-change metaphors and images, emphasizing continuity of identity. Early Christian discourses of conversion share with modern discourses about race an abundance of metaphors for evolution-change, where Christian belonging is understood as a perfection, distillation, fulfillment of individual human and collective human potential. When Justin Martyr declares that all humans have been implanted with the *logos spermatikos* but need to activate it through faith in Christ as the incarnated Logos and participation in Christian cult and ethics (see *Second Apology* 8.1), he foregrounds an understanding of conversion to Christianity as a development of an

---

[13] See Ann Laura Stoler, *Race and the Education of Desire: Foucault's History of Sexuality and the Colonial Order of Things* (Durham: Duke University Press, 1995); ibid., "Racial Histories"; ibid., *Carnal Knowledge*; ibid., "Reflections on 'Racial Histories and Their Regimes of Truth' (A. Stoler)," in Philomena Essed and David Theo Goldberg (eds.), *Race Critical Theory: Text and Context* (Oxford/Malden, MA: Blackwell, 2002) 417–21.

[14] Buell, *Why This New Race*, 7.

[15] Caroline Walker Bynum, *Metamorphosis and Identity* (New York: Zone, 2001), 20.

[16] Bynum, *Metamorphosis and Identity*, 20.

essence all humans already contain, rather than an apparently revolutionary change entailing the replacement of one identity with another. Similarly, early Christian supersessionist arguments, which interpret Jesus' significance and Christian belonging as the fulfillment of God's promises to Israel, as contained in scriptures, portray Christianity as the realization, maturation, and in some cases restoration of Israel and Judaism rather than as an entirely new entity.

On the other hand, early Christian texts differ from most modern discourses about race by also employing replacement-change imagery. Death and rebirth imagery abounds for baptism, the signal ritual that confers full membership in most early Christian communities. As the Gospel of John has it, rebirth is necessary for salvation; one must replace birth from flesh with birth from the spirit (John 3:6). In addition, the idea that conversion to Christianity makes one a descendant of Christ, Abraham, or other individuals and thus eligible to inherit salvation can suggest replacement-change: that the convert receives some essence (such as divine *pneuma* at the moment of baptism) that alters one's kin relations in a fundamental way.

In practice, early Christian texts often employ both evolution-change and replacement-change imagery, negotiating between claims to be in continuity with the past (as "true" Israel, as the heirs and correct interpreters of especially Jewish scriptures and sometimes other traditions, including the Greek texts that formed the core of classical *paideia*) and proclamations of novelty (the significance of the recent historical life and death of Jesus, emphasis on the importance of conversion).

In both ancient and modern contexts, these two notions of change are combined in the idea that one can acquire characteristics which one can then transmit to others; acquisition comes through environmental influences, proximity to those culturally different from oneself, habituation (e.g., through education, ritual, language use). The idea of acquiring permanent characteristics may support either an understanding of change as either evolutionary (one's essence being fully revealed or distorted by certain habits or external factors) or substitution (that certain factors fundamentally alter one's identity).

The notion of acquirable characteristics that transform or activate one's fundamental essence is central to early Christian self-definition as a people. It also makes possible universalizing claims that Christians are a people that all can, and thus all *ought to*, join. I shall briefly explore selected early Christian texts to show how they construe the transformation one undergoes to become a Christian, considering first replacement-type imagery and then processual-type imagery; ethnic reasoning can be configured to both ends.

New ancestors, new way of life: change as novelty

For many Christians, becoming Christian is explicitly interpreted as a transformation that creates not simply a new relationship to divine power but also new geneaological ties. Many ancient Christians very explicitly tie what might seem like their religious belonging – affiliation to God – to the histories of specific peoples and kin groups, notably "Israel" and "Israelites" in contrast to Egyptians and Canaanites, or more specifically as descendants of Abraham, Isaac, Jacob, and Japheth *not* of Ishmael, Shem, or Ham.[17] Paul, for example, envisions a way to bring gentiles into relation with the God of Israel by making them descendants of Abraham and siblings of Christ. Both faith and baptism are central to Paul's view: "For in Christ Jesus you are all sons of God, through faith. For as many of you as were baptized into Christ have put on Christ. There is neither Jew nor Greek, there is neither slave nor free, there is no male and female, for you are all one in Christ Jesus. And if you are Christ's, then you are Abraham's offspring, heirs according to the promise" (Gal. 3:26–9).[18]

We see this imagery not only in Paul's assertion that those in Christ are now descendants and heirs of Abraham but also in a range of second-century Christian writings. The plot of the Acts of the Apostles relies on the image of the holy spirit entering into both Jewish and gentile men to demonstrate not only the scope of God's power but also the means by which this new "way" indexes membership in Israel throughout the known world (see especially Acts 10:34–48; 15:8). Also in the early second century, the Christian Aristides writes that, while Jesus was "born of the *genos* of the Hebrews ... the Christians reckon the beginning of their *genos* to Christ" (*Apology* 2.4). According to this text, Christians imagine themselves as a descent group whose belief in teachings about

---

[17] We tend to forget that modern Christians did this too, especially before the biological sciences became the primary authority for producing knowledge about race in the latter part of the nineteenth century. In the US:

> race discourse concerned narrations that associated God with a people. Some people were people of God. Others were not; they were heathens. The heathen as a social construct, furthermore, was symbolically associated with Native Americans and Negroes. And this confluence of the religious and the racial definitively shaped American religious experience ... American religious themes were founded upon the biblical story, and explanations of race identities were a subset of that worldview.
> (Sylvester Johnson, *The Myth of Ham in Nineteenth-Century American Christianity* [New York: Palgrave, 2004], 12)

[18] For further discussion, see Denise K. Buell and Caroline Johnson Hodge, "The Politics of Interpretation: The Rhetoric of Race and Ethnicity in Paul," *Journal of Biblical Literature* 123 (2004), 235–52 and Caroline Johnson Hodge, *If Sons, Then Heirs* (Oxford: Oxford University Press, 2007).

Jesus and righteousness in religious worship has produced and now indexes their membership in a *genos*.[19]

In the mid-second century, Justin Martyr also insists that Jesus started a new *genos*, one that is at the same time the "true" Israel: "we who have been led to God through this crucified Christ are the true spiritual Israel, and the descendants [*genos*] of Judah, Jacob, Isaac, and Abraham" (*Dialogue with Trypho* 11.5). In this passage, Justin suggests that crucifixion is the key to a belonging that is religious, genealogical, and possibly ethnic or racial. It is both Jesus' death and Christian belief in and commemoration of it that serve as the hinge between God and those who count as God's people. Justin frames his argument about Christians being the true heirs of Abraham and other key biblical figures by distinguishing between descent from the flesh and descent from the spirit; the latter is not metaphorical for Justin but rather the result of a transformation that he views all humans as capable of but needing to undergo through ritually and ethically embodied faith.

Slightly later in this text, Justin makes vivid the causal connection between Jesus' shed blood and the formation of a new people: "After that righteous one [Christ] was slain, we sprouted up afresh as another people (*laos heteros*) ... but we are not only a people but also a holy people" (*Dial.* 119.3). "For Christ, being firstborn of every creature, has also become again the head of another race (*allo genos*), which was begotten anew of him by water and faith and wood, which held the mystery of the cross" (*Dial.* 138.2). This last passage is especially interesting because it shows that Justin gives Christ a pre-incarnational role at the creation of humanity but also an incarnated role as the progenitor of a historical people. Casting Christ in these two roles allows Justin to claim that all humans are related to Christ but nonetheless need to transform themselves – through faith, ritual, ethics, and education – in order to become a member of the Christian *genos*.[20]

When early Christians explain the acquisition of faith (*pistis*) and spirit (*pneuma*), as well as blood (notably Jesus' blood), as producing kinship and descent, the imagery leans towards the replacement-change end of the spectrum. Nonetheless, this imagery is tempered by claims that the descent groups produced through conversion to Christianity constitute an evolution (or restoration) of an intrinsic historical or primordial connection between humans and the divine.

[19] See Buell, *Why This New Race*, 35–6, 46.
[20] For further analysis of Justin's *Dialogue with Trypho*, see Buell, *Why This New Race*, 94–115.

Change as restoration or fulfillment

When Justin proclaims the salvific and generative power of Jesus' blood, I take this to mean that he views the implications of faith as having embodied social consequences. Justin has "faith" do the kind of work of an acquirable yet fixed essence that we are more used to seeing accomplished by "blood" or "flesh." Justin's definition of descent suggests replacement-change, even as his arguments about the implications of this change include "evolution," since genealogical connection functions to authorize Christians as the fulfillment of God's promises to biblical patriarchs and through biblical prophets. Christian supersessionism can be understood as partly enabled by Christian claims to be the *people* of God.

Positioning Christians as forming a distinctive *ethnos* that both restores the ideals of an earlier *ethnos* (notably, the Hebrews or *Ioudaioi*) and fulfills pan-human potential is a common motif in early Christian writings. The second-century Pseudo-Clementine *Recognitions*, for example, depicts Jesus as the emissary of God sent to remove the obligation upon the Hebrew people to offer sacrifices to God. The institution of sacrifice is explained as God's response to the bad habits that the Hebrew people had acquired through years of living in proximity to Egyptians. Ritual practices thus function to reestablish Hebrew distinctiveness and correct for the change brought on by cultural proximity with Egyptians. In the *Recognitions*, the moment has come to "restore" what it means to be Hebrew, through the cessation of sacrifices. Crucially, though, this restoration entails a change – namely, faith in Jesus as God's prophet. Moreover, this new form of being Hebrew is open to those who have not formerly been counted as Hebrew. While Hebrew remains the collective category of self-understanding, both the borders and the "fixed content" are redefined even as the change is framed in terms of restoration.[21]

While the author of the *Recognitions* clearly foregrounds restoration when explaining the significance of Jesus, other early Christian authors prefer to balance novelty with appropriation of Israel's history through arguments about prophetic fulfillment. We have already seen that Paul and Justin Martyr, for example, link the followers of Christ to biblical prophecy about Abraham's descendants, defining descent from Abraham as acquirable through faith and practice in relation to Christ.

Writing on the brink of Christianity's legalization in the early fourth century, the bishop Eusebius offers a particularly vivid example of ethnic reasoning employed to support an understanding of Christians as a people who are both new yet in continuity with God's plans and hopes for

---

[21] See Buell, *Why This New Race*, 71–3.

humanity, earlier embodied in the Hebrew people. Eusebius defends Christians as an "admittedly new *ethnos*" (*Ecclesiastical History* 1.4.2) through a combination of appropriation of Jewish history and ancestors and theological arguments about the pre-existence of Christ as the logos of God who assisted in creation (1.4.1). He asserts, "it must clearly be held that the announcement to all the gentiles (*ethnē*), recently made through the teaching of Christ, is the very first and most ancient religion (*theosebeia*) discovered by Abraham and those beloved of God who came after him" (1.4.10). Of course, this argument is made possible through Eusebius' use of the texts and ancestors linked to another *ethnos*.

Eusebius claims that "the children of the Hebrews boast" Abraham "as their originator and ancestor" (1.4.5), but that in fact "at the present moment it is only among the Christians throughout the whole world that the manner of religion that was Abraham's can actually be found in practice" (1.4.14). Here Eusebius implies that Christians are the true successors to Abraham. But Eusebius makes an even more sweeping claim: "if the line be traced from Abraham to the first man, anyone who should describe those who have obtained ... righteousness as Christians, in fact, if not in name, would not shoot wide of the truth" (1.4.6). By claiming that the historical Jesus is just the recent manifestation of the Logos of God, Eusebius can give the Christian *ethnos* historical roots, stretching back "even to the first human," while acknowledging its novelty in relation to the name "Christian."[22] Eusebius locates piety squarely within the ancient conventions of viewing it as tied to one's *ethnos* or *genos*, especially by appeal to ancestral traditions. Christians are not just the successors of the Hebrews but in fact members of the new *ethnos* that preserves the most original and true religion which corresponds to the true form of humanness.[23]

Early Christian universalism and compulsory mutability

And [God] made from one every race of humans to live on the face of the earth, having determined allotted periods and the boundaries of their habitation, that they should seek God, in the hope that they may feel after [God] and find [God]. (Acts 17:26–27)

And there is salvation in no one else. (Acts 4:12)

[22] "Even if we are clearly new, and this really new name of 'Christian' is recently known among all peoples, nevertheless we have not recently invented our life and the mode of conduct that corresponds to our religion's (*eusebeia*) teachings" (*Eccl. Hist.* 1.4.4).
[23] See Buell, *Why This New Race*, 76–7. For further analysis of Eusebius, see now Aaron P. Johnson, *Ethnicity and Argument in Eusebius'* Preparatio Evangelica (Oxford: Oxford University Press, 2006).

Christian universalism, with its emphasis on fluidity, may seem to be the "other" to modern racism – when it is defined as all about fixity. But ideas about change may also sustain racist ways of imagining and enacting human difference. That is, racist potential lies both in discourses and practices that attribute fixity to others and in those that exhort a specific kind of transformation for all.[24] Universalizing Christian arguments can be employed in service of *compulsory mutability*: if one can change, one ought to or must change – to ensure that one will not only be saved but even count as fully human.

Writing about modern theoretical racism, Etienne Balibar argues that it consists of an "ideal synthesis of transformation and fixity, or repetition and destiny," a synthesis that always invokes the instability of the borders between the human and the less-than-human such that what is at stake are claims to police the very boundaries of humanness.[25] Balibar notes that, in the discourse of nationalism, theoretical racism produces both universalism and nationalism:

[T]here is actually a racist "internationalism" or "supranationalism" which tends to idealize timeless or transhistorical communities such as the "indo-Europeans," "the West," "Judeo-Christian civilization," and therefore communities which are at the same time both closed and open, which have no frontiers or whose frontiers are only ... "internal" ones, inseparable from the individual individuals themselves or ... from their "essence." In fact these are the frontiers of an ideal humanity. Here the excess of racism over nationalism ... stretches out to the dimensions of an infinite totality.[26]

That is, it is not only the insistence on fixity that characterizes racism, but also the insistence on idealized universals. While early Christian universal claims are not identical with the modern forms of racism with which Balibar is concerned, they share the pattern of formulating a synthesis of transformation and fixity.

Balibar reminds us that racism flourishes in contexts of totalizing, imperializing cultural politics, which rely on universalizing knowledge claims. The Roman imperial period was also one in which universalizing

---

[24] Here I am thinking of discursive and material practices that include the "whitening" of Irish, Jews, and other European (largely Catholic) "ethnic groups" in North America (see, e.g., Karen Brodkin, *How Jews Became White and What That Says about Race in America* [New Brunswick, NJ: Rutgers University Press, 1998]) as well as the aggregative formation of "blacks" and "Asians" as categories of collective identity constituted by individuals from a range of backgrounds (see, e.g., Michael Gomez, *Exchanging Our Country Marks: The Transformation of African Identities in the Colonial and Antebellum South* [Chapel Hill: University of North Carolina Press, 1998]).

[25] Etienne Balibar, in Balibar and Immanuel Wallerstein, *Race, Nation, Class: Ambiguous Identities*, English translation of Balibar by Chris Turner (London: Verso 1991), 57.

[26] Balibar, *Race, Nation, Class*, 61–2.

discourses proliferated. That is, folks were not just interested in delineat-
ing and ranking differences among humans but also in speaking about
humans collectively. Of course, universalizing claims are always particular
insofar as they privilege as universal ideals and concepts that emerge from
a specific time, place, and vantage point: culturally dominant universals
generally privilege those who already hold social power.

In the Roman imperial period of the first three centuries CE, Romanness
or Greekness, depending on the context, could be claimed as the
"unmarked," that is, as the culturally particular site from which to make
universalizing claims – even as Romanness and Greekness themselves
were never static and always under negotiation. As Jeremy Schott puts
it, "in the Roman world, difference was polarized and hierarchical, with
Greco-Roman cultural formations privileged as universally authentic and
other provincial (or barbaric) literatures, religions, and philosophies considered ethnically specific, contextually bound by geography and history
in a way that Greco-Roman culture was not."[27] While overstating the
unity of Greco-Roman culture, Schott usefully illuminates what was at
stake for Christians and others to make claims to offer universal philosophies or collective identities against the backdrop of an empire seeking to
make totalizing claims and policies affecting all.

Of course, early Christians were members of groups with no legal
standing. But emerging Christian groups were forged in the context of
empire – mostly the Roman one, but also Persian and Ethiopian ones. It is
not surprising that early Christian authors adapted universal frameworks
(historical and political) to locate and authorize themselves. Early
Christians take a page out of the book of other regional and/or subordinated groups in asserting their greater antiquity and claiming to be a
source of wisdom for other peoples. Christians also borrow from hegemonic groups such as the Romans by claiming both to be the superior
descendants of a once glorious people and to be a people potentially open
to all.[28]

For some early Christian texts, becoming Christian makes one the
descendant and heir not only to Israel but, in some cases, also to Greek
and Roman patrimony. In his *Apologies,* putatively addressed to Roman
emperors, Justin Martyr uses the idea that all humans have the *Logos*
implanted in them, but that few were able to access it before the arrival
of the incarnated Logos in the world. This universal framing allows Justin
to argue that Greek and Jewish texts and traditions contain truth but that

[27] Jeremy Schott, "Porphyry on Christians and Others: 'Barbarian Wisdom,' Identity
Politics, and Anti-Christian Polemics," *Journal of Early Christian Studies* 13/3 (2005), 279.
[28] See Buell, *Why This New Race,* 63–93.

Christians uniquely embody correct access to this truth. In the late second century, Clement of Alexandria uses both biblical and Homeric prooftexts to position Christians as the sole heirs to these cultural heritages with their attendant claims to truth.[29]

Early Christian universalizing claims were sometimes deployed both to make assertions about ontological essences and to authorize hierarchical classification of human groups that simultaneously linked them while privileging some (notably certain kinds of Christians) over others. Those who did not convert to Christianity could be rhetorically (and later politically) condemned and marginalized as those who had failed (in different ways) to activate the potential available to all humans. Such marginalization and condemnation is frequently coded in theological categories: Jews, gentiles, heretics. At the same time that Christians aim to formulate competing universalizing visions of Christianness, they participate in the dynamics Schott notes by continuing to treat as "marked" the more marginalized and contested ones of Greek and Roman antiquity, including Egyptian, Ethiopian, Syrian, Jew, as well as "magician," "woman," and the color label of "black."

To develop these ideas further I will explore in turn the two facets of universalizing Christian arguments that I view as related to later racist ideologies and practices: (1) defining the "other" as particular or defining the "other" as one who ascribes fixed characteristics to themselves and their others; (2) exhorting a single collective identity and path for transformation as normative for all humans. The Acts of the Apostles, which became canonical for Christians, serves as a basis for illustrating these two points.

The other as fixed and particular

When universalism is presented as a signal characteristic of early forms of Christianness, it is often explicitly contrasted with ethnicity or race. That is, the dominant narratives, theological and academic, about the history of early Christianity, implicitly and explicitly define universalism not simply in contrast to "particularism" but especially in contrast to ethnic or racial affiliation. This is most clear in claims about how the Jesus movement differed from other forms of Jewishness.

When reconstructing a vision of a multiethnic, multiracial, inclusive early Christianity, many scholars and Christians portray it as a startling contrast to what was already available. While all acknowledge that Jesus

[29] See, e.g., Clement of Alexandria *Protreptikos* (*passim*) as well as *Paidagogos* 1.50.1.

and his first followers were Jews, Christians look to explain both what made their form of Jewishness distinctive and then what made the movement "Christian," not simply a form of Jewishness. The most common explanations foreground universalism: for example, some argue that Jesus and his followers distinguished themselves by offering "a universalistic Judaism, which was open to outsiders,"[30] and that this universalism led to the formation of a distinctive "Christian" identity which is "a social not an ethnic group."[31] These scholars characterize being an ethnic group as belonging that entails exclusivity or requires "unnecessarily drastic" changes (read: circumcision) for potential converts.

One of the favored texts for making such arguments about Christian origins is the canonical Acts of the Apostles. For this text, the identification of the true God with the God historically affiliated with the people of Israel means the people of Israel have to accept the claim that their God has sent Jesus into the world, resurrected him after his death, made him Lord and Christ (2:22–35), and is now calling for them to repent of their sins to receive the gift of the Holy Spirit (2:38). They must also accept that Jesus is the only means by which all humans can gain salvation from this God: "there is salvation in no one else, for there is no other name under heaven given among humans by which we can be saved" (4:12). Acts clearly situates the origins of Christianity within the history and scriptures of Israel, and it also carves out a space for the group it is promoting by depicting many Jews as willfully resistant to the new revelation of their God, with the result that later Christians have felt justified in seeing themselves as the only true followers of the God historically allied with Jews.

What most Christians have missed is how Acts' use of the scriptures and history of Israel presumes that Christians constitute the real Israel, the true people of God. Acts clearly argues that it is through the apostles that God will restore the rule of Israel – not simply in the earlier geographical territory, but over the entire world. This is an argument about Christianness that understands belonging as membership in a specific people, even when the claim is that all humans should belong.

Moreover, Acts makes it easy for Christians to racialize differences *among* Christians since it characterizes opposing *insider* views in terms attributed also to Jewish unbelievers, such as circumcision for gentile male

---

[30] DeYoung et al., *United by Faith: The Multiracial Congregation as an Answer to the Problem of Race* (Oxford: Oxford University Press, 2003), 26, citing Gerd Theissen, *The Sociology of Early Palestinian Christianity* (Philadelphia: Fortress, 1978), 17.

[31] DeYoung et al., *United By Faith*, 29, citing Ben Witherington III, *The Acts of the Apostles: A Socio-Rhetorical Commentary* (Grand Rapids, MI: Eerdmans, 1998), 371.

converts or social segregation based on dietary practices. For example, Acts 15 describes a meeting in Jerusalem of apostles and elders to resolve differences of opinion about the status of gentiles in the community. Acts presents the debate as two-sided: one side, identified with "believers of the Pharisees' group" (Acts 15:5), supposedly argued that gentile men must be circumcised to be full members of the Jesus movement; the other side, represented also by Jewish believers such as Paul and Peter but presented as distinctive from apparently partisan views (as epitomized here by "Pharisees"), argues that God's gift of the holy spirit to uncircumcised gentiles demonstrates that this is not necessary.

The author of Acts sets up two positions which modern Christians have regularly used to define true Christianity as an open, inclusive movement in contrast to a "Jewish" vision – either a Jewish vision within Christianity or a non-Christian vision: "The idea that Gentiles and Jews could or should worship and socialize together in the same congregation was foreign to the worldviews of most people … Some early church leaders did not grasp what developed at Antioch and other congregations."[32] This statement, ironically, comes from a multi-authored recent work striving to end racism in North American Christian churches. While the goal is laudable, the argument relies unfortunately on depicting as "Jewish" modern Christians who, consciously or not, promote racist policies inside Christianity.

Racist potential also appears in internal Christian polemics of the later second and early third centuries. Writers such as Irenaeus, Clement of Alexandria, and Origen condemn Christian rivals for allegedly holding the view that some humans are saved by nature (*physis*) or birth (usually *genos*, in the sense of descent). We also find a related accusation about Jews posed by Justin Martyr, who claims that at least some Jews claim to be saved by birth, because they are the descendants of Abraham and Jacob "by flesh" (*kata sarka*). These Christian polemicists imply that some Christians and some Jews view salvation as a fixed attribute, which makes those endowed with salvation superior to other humans.

If these charges could be sustained, it would appear that some early Christians and Jews were racist in a recognizably modern sense – when racism is defined as discriminatory practices justified by appeal to alleg-edly immutable features. Yet it appears that we have little evidence to support these charges. Of the scanty evidence that has survived from the perspective of those on the receiving end of this polemic, there is little to support strongly deterministic views. In the case of rival Christians

---

[32] De Young *et al.*, *United By Faith*, 33.

(usually so-called Gnostic Christians and the followers of the mid-second-century teachers Basilides, Valentinus, and Marcion), while some excerpts and texts linked to these Christians classify humans into different groups, including different kinds of Christians, movement from one kind to another is often explicitly imagined.[33] In the case of Jewish rivals, it is very difficult to interpret Talmudic and midrashic evidence in relation to early Christian texts because of both provenance and difficulties in dating. If we consider the rhetoric of Christian texts themselves, a more complex picture emerges than one of particularism or soteriological determinism linked to physical descent – Justin's *Dialogue with Trypho* clearly portrays his imagined Jewish interlocutor (Trypho) as favoring an understanding of Jewish belonging and salvation as open to all, and defined by ritual practices and beliefs not descent by birth.[34]

In fact, as I have argued elsewhere, because we expect racism to take the form of claims of fixity, we have too often missed how early Christian polemicists such as Irenaeus, Justin, Clement – retrospectively viewed as purveyors of proto-orthodoxy – rely on the idea that salvation requires having a specific kind of essence. They each define this essence as acquirable through their preferred interpretations of Christianity.[35]

One God: compulsory mutability

Early Christian universalizing claims have generally been viewed as benign or even a resource to combat modern racism. For example, Acts 17:26 has been one of the most frequently cited New Testament verses in African-American struggles for racial equality. In 1963, civil rights activist Fannie Lou Hamer was arrested after having demanded to be served at a segregated lunch counter in Winona, Mississippi. In prison, she was beaten. After her beating, the white wife of the jailer showed kindness to Mrs. Hamer. According to one biographer, "Mrs. Hamer thanked her and remarked that she must be 'Christian people.' The jailer's wife … [told] her that she really tried her best to live right and to please God … Mrs. Hamer … told the jailer's wife to get out her Bible and read the verses in Proverbs 26:26 and Acts 17:26."[36] After this, the jailer's wife did not return. What did she read in these passages that might have disturbed

---

[33] See especially Michael Williams, *The Immovable Race: A Gnostic Designation and the Theme of Stability in Late Antiquity* (Leiden: Brill, 1985), 158–85 and references in Buell, *Why This New Race*, 212 nn. 7–12.

[34] See Buell, *Why This New Race*, 109–12.

[35] See Buell, *Why This New Race*, 116–37 and 166–9.

[36] Charles Marsh, *God's Long Summer* (Princeton, NJ: Princeton University Press, 1997), 20–1; cited in Cheryl J. Sanders, "African Americans, the Bible, and Spiritual

her? The passage from Proverbs refers to God's punishment for those "whose hatred is covered by deceit." Acts 17:26, taken from a speech attributed to Paul, affirms that "God has made from one every race of humans who live on the earth."[37]

Hamer might have hoped that this speech would lead the jailer's Christian wife to repent of her racism and, ideally, to work for racial justice as God's will. Indeed, for many Christians, this verse continues to be a powerful prooftext for arguing that racial distinctions are antithetical to being Christian and that God is not only the creator of all humans from a common source, but has a plan that encompasses humanity in all its differences in such a way that followers of God should be brought together in their diversity. This way of thinking about the relationship between race, ethnicity, and Christianity means that ethnically and racially exclusive forms of Christianity are viewed as corruptions of true Christianity.

Those who engage Acts in this way are most often themselves Christians. They rarely question the implications of this universalizing claim about the power and scope of the Christian God for non-Christians. Acts defines those unaffiliated with the Christian God as lacking (unsaved, ignorant) and exhorts submission to the authority of this God and its human representatives.

Acts 17:26 is embedded in a speech that communicates a message that the God proclaimed by the apostles trumps the gods of the gentiles and that joining with the God of the apostles means relinquishing membership in one *ethnos* for another people (*laos*).

So, Paul, standing in the middle of the Areopagus said, "Men of Athens, I perceive that in every way you are very religious. For as I passed along, and observed the objects of your worship, I found an altar with this inscription, 'To an unknown God.' What you worship as unknown, this I proclaim to you. The God who made the world and everything in it, being Lord of heaven and earth, does not live in shrines made by humans, nor is God served by human hands, as though he needed anything, since he gives everyone life and breath and everything. And he made from one every race of human to live on all the face of the earth, having determined allotted periods and the boundaries of their habitation, that they should seek God, in the hope that they might feel after him and find him. Yet he is not far from each one of us, for 'in him we live and move and have our being,' as even some of your

Formation," in Vincent L. Wimbush (ed.) with the assistance of Rosamond C. Rodman, *African Americans and the Bible: Sacred Texts and Social Textures* (New York: Continuum, 2000), 599.

[37] The King James version follows the ancient manuscript tradition to read "God has made from one blood every race of humans who live on the earth." This manuscript tradition, and the wide circulation of this translation in English, was especially useful for modern Christians who sought to challenge polygenetic accounts of human creation.

poets have said, 'we are indeed his offspring.' Being God's offspring, we ought not to think that God is like gold, or silver, a representation by the art of imagination of humans. The times of ignorance God overlooked, but now God commands all humans everywhere to repent, because he has a fixed day on which he will judge the world in righteousness by a man whom he has appointed, and of this he has given assurance to all by raising him from the dead."

(Acts 17:22–31)

In this speech set in Athens, Paul first links the God he proclaims to one familiar to his gentile audience as an "unknown" god. But then he asserts that this unknown god is in fact the creator of the universe, including all humanity. His remark about gold and silver images indirectly condemns his listeners for honoring false gods. At the end of the speech, Paul leaves no doubt that nothing less than full commitment to his God is required.

The insistence on God's role as creator of all humanity, and responsibility for the diversity of human groups and polities undergirds the argument that conversion to Christianity is not a fundamental alteration of oneself so much as a necessary acknowledgment and expression of what makes one truly human.

This passage from Acts offers a mixed legacy as both a site for intra-Christian attempts to combat racism and more troubling totalizing claims. As Sylvester Johnson puts it,

New Testament texts only reinforce the assumption that some folk are people and others are not; it is only through becoming one with the people of God, their deity, and their narrations that any Others may enter into the body of folk affirmed by and affiliated with divinity. In fact, one might argue that the Christian tradition presents a more difficult problem because it assumes a more explicitly universal scope and has acted upon that scope of sight through zealously missionary strategies.[38]

Christian claims about the possibility of conversion to Christianity for all humans can be used to authorize compulsory mutability: if one can change, one ought to or must change – to ensure that one will not only be saved but even count as fully human. Such a claim seems to fly in the face of familiar definitions of racism as based on claims that members of certain groups have immutable traits. But compulsory mutability needs to be understood as a strategy legible also as racist in producing and authorizing hierarchical, discriminatory power arrangements legible on the body.

---

[38] Johnson, *The Myth of Ham*, 23.

Thinking beyond anachronism

Strictly speaking, there are no periods in history, only in historians.
(E. R. Dodds, *Pagans and Christians in an Age of Anxiety*, 3)

In addition to viewing race and racist practices as characterized by assertions of fixity, most analyses of racism and race propose that both come into being in a specific historical period – "the modern" – and are, along with European imperial colonization and the slave trade, the negative legacies of a Western era otherwise viewed as being the positive successor to prior centuries of theologically centered medieval backwardness. As the very existence of this volume suggests, scholars remain divided not only about how to define racism and race but also about when and where to locate its historical origins. I am not interested in trying to pinpoint a singular origin, historically or culturally, for racism and "race." Indeed, I think this effort is doomed to failure. More useful, I think, are historiographical approaches that do not reproduce methodologically the essentializing and deterministic content often asserted to be the hallmark of racism. Speaking about the periodization of race, Lisa Lampert sagely cautions that "using nineteenth- and twentieth-century biological models as the standard for determining whether one can make connections between ideological formations ... hinders investigations into how [premodern] concepts, particularly theological ones, may have shaped later ones in ways about which we are still unaware."[39]

The relationship between ancient discourses of human difference and modern forms of racism cannot simply be charted in any causal or linear fashion. While it is worthwhile to identify and analyze historical precedents for features associated with modern forms of racism, including color symbolism, obsession with sexual reproduction, and claims about environmental determinism, it is equally important to attend to indirect and unstable resonances and echoes. Early Christian universalizing claims to be a people whom all can and ought to join in order to count as fully human allow for arguments that those who do not become Christian (or even the correct kind of Christian) should be signified as only potentially human/Christian or less than fully human. Internal controversies among

---

[39] Lisa Lampert, "Race, Periodicity, and the (Neo-)Middle Ages," *Modern Language Quarterly* 65:3 (2004), 396. Medieval texts differ from modern notions of racial essence because they "point to the possibility of change, although this change requires conversion and is based on a fixed belief in Christianity as the only true religion" (409). Medievalists have been arguing that European Christian theological renderings of human difference enable and undergird those expressions of race identified as distinctly modern, even as religious difference *qua* religion gets rendered as "fluid" and thus nonracial. I am suggesting that we ought to ask how this might affect our interpretation of early Christian materials and their legacies.

early Christians provide further fodder for later racist arguments, to the extent that polemic among Christians includes designation of one's Christian rivals as Judaizing or Jewish[40] and the use of ethnic and color labels to designate proximity to or distance from a Christian ideal.[41]

I take it for granted that each historical and cultural moment is distinctive and internally variegated, requiring careful attention to context. But I am suspicious of overstating either sameness or difference across time or place. The "modern" is often defined in terms of a rupture between the theological past and the rational, scientific modern. We know the break was not clean. Most periodizations of racism and definitions of race assert sharp discontinuity from rather than unpredictable continuities with other discourses about human difference.

Benjamin Isaac's important recent work destabilizes such neat periodizations, persuasively arguing that those who articulated modern forms of racism knew and drew from ancient Greek texts.[42] Nevertheless, Isaac leans heavily on modern articulations of racial difference as his key for distinguishing "ethnicity" from "race" and ethnocentrism from proto-racism in classical sources, defining racism as prejudice linked to assertions of immutable, inherited characteristics.[43] He finds both proto-racism and ethnocentrism present in classical sources. His own examples from ancient texts suggest, however, that ancient authors did not neatly differentiate between classifying human groups in terms of characteristics viewed as fixed (Isaac's necessary criteria for "race") and those viewed as potentially mutable (which Isaac defines as "ethnic"). The ancient notion that individuals may acquire characteristics from their environment, characteristics which may then be transmitted to their descendants, offers one instance of such blurring. As I have suggested, conversion to Christianity offers another kind of example – where conversion could be interpreted as the acquisition of substance that alters one's lineage, the way in which one could be classified in relation to other humans, and one's ontological status (as "saved").

Isaac's astonishing range of examples demonstrates that ancient authors thought in terms of classifying human difference in ways that informed modern constructions of racial thought. But Isaac does not consider the significance of Jewish and Christian writings for the transmission of discriminatory logics. Given that the modern framers of racialized and racist ideologies lived in Christian majority contexts and that many of the classical sources were preserved and interpreted through

[40] See Cohen, *The Beginnings of Jewishness*, 175–97.
[41] See especially Robert Hood, *Begrimed and Black* and Gay Byron, *Symbolic Blackness*.
[42] Isaac, *The Invention of Racism*.   [43] See, for example, Isaac, *Invention*, 36–7.

Christian lenses, Christianity must minimally be viewed as a vector for transmitting ideas that informed the construction of modern racisms, even if in indirect and refracted ways. As James Perkinson succinctly puts: "in early modernity, racial discourse emerged as a species of theological evaluation."[44]

Although Perkinson explicitly limits race to the modern period, as an idea arising sometime around the sixteenth century, his observation invites exploration of how premodern inheritances have been recuperated and transformed to accommodate and shape the racialized visions of specific modern contexts. Medievalists such as Robert Bartlett and Geraldine Heng have broken important ground in demonstrating ways that premodern theological discourses, including claims about *change* as well as fixed essences, anticipate and inform some modern forms of racism.[45] My work suggests that Roman-period and late antique Christian ideological formations about human difference also resonate with medieval and modern ones.

---

[44] James Perkinson, *White Theology: Outing Supremacy in Modernity* (New York: Palgrave, 2004), 53. For detailed studies see, e.g., Peter Harrison, *'Religion' and the Religions in the English Enlightenment* (Cambridge: Cambridge University Press, 1990); Matthew Jacobson Frye, *Whiteness of a Different Color: European Immigration and the Alchemy of Race* (Cambridge: Harvard University Press, 1998); Peter van der Veer, *Imperial Encounters: Religion and Modernity in India and Britain* (Princeton, NJ: Princeton University Press, 2001); Irene Silverblatt, *Modern Inquisitions: Peru and the Colonial Origins of the Civilized World* (Durham, NC: Duke University Press, 2004).

[45] Robert Bartlett, "Medieval and Modern Concepts of Race and Ethnicity," *Journal of Medieval and Early Modern Studies* 31 (2001), 39–56; Geraldine Heng, *Empire of Magic: Medieval Romance and the Politics of Cultural Fantasy* (New York: Columbia University Press, 2003); see also Lampert, "Race, Periodicity," 408–9.

Robert Bartlett

We are all familiar with the construction of ethnicity through vivid visual stereotyping. Anyone who has seen a vintage Hollywood film knows how 'Chinamen', 'Arabs' or 'Mexicans' can be summoned up by a hat, a moustache or a hint of swarthy skin. This paper takes a preliminary look at this issue for the pre-cinematic, indeed pre-print, era of the Middle Ages, asking whether and how ethnic difference was represented pictorially in medieval illustration.

It is possible to distinguish three ways ethnicity is handled in medieval illustrated texts.

In one type of text–image relationship, the reader/viewer 'knows' from the text that the group depicted is ethnically distinct but the image contains no visible signs of this difference. For example, the picture of the battle between Charlemagne's Franks and the Saracens in the fourteenth-century *Grandes chroniques de France* in London, British Library (BL), MS Royal 16 G. VI, folio 171v (Fig 6.1), shows the Frankish and Muslim soldiers with exactly the same arms and armour; nor (although the visible parts of their bodies are limited by the armour) is any physiological difference apparent. We know from the text that the two sides are distinguished by ethnicity and religion but the picture alone would not tell us that.

The ethnic 'invisibility' in this type of depiction can be paralleled by the well attested ahistoricism of much historical illustration in the medieval period. More often than not, figures of the distant past are shown in contemporary costume and surroundings. In fifteenth-century depictions of the armies of Alexander the Great the soldiers wear fifteenth-century armour. The image in BL Royal 16 G. VI itself provides an example. Just as there is no sharp visual difference between the Franks and the Saracens, so there is no sense of incongruity in having these eighth-century warriors depicted in fourteenth-century armour. The image gives no sense either of ethnic differentiation or of historical distance.

A second type of ethnic illustration to be found in the Middle Ages does rely on physiological differentiation, and this obviously requires distinctive bodily features to be present. An important point, however, is that,

Fig. 6.1 Franks and Muslims. *Grandes chroniques de France*. London, British Library, MS Royal 16 G. VI, fol. 171v.

in comparison with modern colonial experience, which brought together people of radically differing body types, the medieval situation generated few encounters which could be clearly marked by the common genetic indicators, such as skin colour, morphology of eyes and lips, and so on. There seem to be only two important instances in the Middle Ages of ethnic depictions with a strong physiological component: one is the so-called Jewish nose, given to some, but by no means all, Jews portrayed by Christians, and the other is the general physiology of some depictions of black Africans.

The most notorious Jewish caricature from medieval England is that on the Exchequer Roll for 1233 (Fig. 6.2), which shows not only Jews with distinctive hooked noses but also a devil pointing them out.[1] Other examples of the 'Jewish nose' are not hard to find.[2] Jews are not always depicted with this distinctive physiological feature and are as often

[1] Kew, National Archives, E 401/1565 (Receipt Roll for 1233); reproduced in Cecil Roth, *A Short History of the Jewish People*, rev. edn (London: East and West Library, 1953), plate 79, opp. p. 209 (and many other places).

[2] E.g. Bernhard Blumenkranz, *Le juif médiévale au miroir de l'art chrétien* (Paris: Etudes augustiniennes, 1966); Ruth Mellinkoff, *Outcasts: Signs of Otherness in Northern European Art of the Late Middle Ages*, 2 vols. (Berkeley: University of California Press, 1993); Debra Higgs Strickland, *Saracens, Demons, and Jews: Making Monsters in Medieval Art* (Princeton, N.J.: Princeton University Press, 2003).

Fig. 6.2 Anti-semitic caricatures. Exchequer Roll for 1233. Kew,
National Archives, E 401/1565 (Receipt Roll for 1233).

marked out by the so-called 'Jewish hat', which is tall, pointed, often
conical (Fig. 6.3). There is discussion amongst scholars about whether
such depictions of the Jewish hat are representational or symbolic in
nature – 'a faithful documentation of historical reality' or 'a pejorative
identifier'[3] – neither position giving a complete answer, but legislation
from thirteenth-century Silesia (and elsewhere) shows that such hats
were, at least in certain times and places, real distinguishing marks.[4]

While anti-Jewish caricature arose in an environment where real Jews
could be met in everyday situations, it is worthy of comment that the
two most consistent traditions of representing black Africans physiologically, with not only black skin but also full lips, broad nose and curly hair,
originated in parts of Europe where Europeans were least likely to meet
actual black Africans, namely in Germany and central Europe. Those two
traditions are the Black Maurice and the Black Magus.[5] The idea that
St Maurice was black may well stem from simple word-play – 'Mauritius'

[3] Sara Lipton, *Images of Intolerance: The Representation of Jews and Judaism in the Bible
moralisée* (Berkeley: University of California Press, 1999), p. 16. One of the best-known
of all medieval Hebrew illuminated manuscripts, the Leipzig Mahzor (Leipzig,
Universitätsbibiliothek, MS Vollers 1102), contains numerous illustrations depicting
Jews wearing pointed hats. This suggests that the hat was not a pejorative identifier for
the Jews who used this liturgical text around 1310 in southern Germany.

[4] 'We decree and ordain that the Jews should resume the pointed hat (*cornutum pileum*)
which they once used to wear in these parts and have presumed in their temerity to cease
wearing, so that they may be visibly distinguished from Christians, as was formerly decided
in the general council.' Council of Wroclaw/Breslau, 1267, cited in Guido Kisch, 'The
Yellow Badge in History', *Historia Judaica* 19 (1957), 89–146, at 107 n. 16.

[5] On these themes, and the representation of black Africans in general, see Jean Devisse, *The
Image of the Black in Western Art*, vol. 2, *From the Early Christian Era to the "Age of*

Fig. 6.3 The Jewish poet Susskind. "Manesse codex". Heidelberg, Universitätsbibliothek, Cod. Pal. germ. 848, fol. 355.

sounds rather like 'Maurus', which means both 'dark' and 'inhabitant of North Africa' – as also from the fact that St Maurice is described as a member of the Theban Legion, from Thebes in Upper Egypt. The earliest representation of the saint as a black man is the striking sculpture of

Discovery". *Part 1: From the Demonic Threat to the Incarnation of Sainthood*, Eng. trans. (Cambridge, Mass.: Menil Foundation, 1979); Jean Devisse and Michel Mollat, *The Image of the Black in Western Art, Part 2: From the Early Christian Era to the "Age of Discovery": Africans in the Christian Ordinance of the World (Fourteenth to the Sixteenth Century)*, Eng. trans. (Cambridge, Mass.: Menil Foundation, 1979); Paul H. D. Kaplan, *The Rise of the Black Magus in Western Art* (Ann Arbor, Mich.: UMI Research Press, 1985); Gude Suckale-Redlefsen, *Mauritius: Der heilige Mohr/The Black Saint Maurice* (Houston, Munich and Zürich: Menil Foundation/Schnell & Steiner, 1987) (Foreword and Introduction in German and English).

Fig. 6.4 Maurice, the black saint, Magdeburg cathedral.

St Maurice from Magdeburg cathedral, dating to the middle of the thirteenth century (Fig. 6.4). The Black Magus emerges rather later. The main impulse here is presumably the association of the three kings with the three continents (they were also of course frequently identified with the three Ages of Man).

The purpose of illustrating black Africans naturalistically was not to register a social reality but to make a theological point, about the universal mission of the Church. The saints included *even* a black man; the three kings, the first gentiles to seek Christ, represent the whole of humanity. A good instance is Hans Memling's *Last Judgment*, now in Gdansk. It shows one black man amongst the saved and one amongst the damned (Fig. 6.5). The implication must be that God is colour-blind: even a kind of humanity as alien to Bruges, where Memling worked, as the black African, could be saved – or could be damned.

But the visual is not limited to the physiological markers of skin colour, size and shape of nose, etc. Crucial visual cues are also provided by hair-style and clothes. Although hair grows from the body, it should be grouped with clothes rather than with the body, because, in its malleability and responsiveness to fashion, hair is in fact more like clothes than like body.[6] As we shall see, treatment of hair and choice of clothing were extremely important ways of indicating ethnic identity.

A starting point could thus be the simple taxonomy of (a) ethnic differ-ence identifiable in the text but not in the illustration; (b) ethnic difference conveyed physiologically, through such bodily features as skin colour, hair type (as distinct from style), shape of eyes, nose, lips, etc.; (c) ethnic difference conveyed non-physiologically, primarily through hair-style and clothing. Longer-term research might be able to identify when, where and why choices were made between the three types.

Ethnicity is particularly neatly conveyed through hair and dress codes in a picture in the *Liber ad honorem Augusti*, an illustrated poem by Peter of Eboli. Peter's work has a quite specific political context. In the early 1190s the Holy Roman Emperor, Henry VI, undertook the conquest of the Kingdom of Sicily. Peter was one of his supporters and wrote a eulogistic account of these events in verse. His work survives in the author's own copy, in which each page of text is faced with a full page of illustra-tions.[7] Some of these attempt ethnic differentiation. A quite well-known example occurs on folio 101, where three groups of Sicilian notaries are depicted. There are two Greek notaries, with uncovered heads and full black hair and beards; two 'Saracen' notaries, with turbans and beards; and two Latin notaries, clean-shaven and with uncovered heads (Fig. 6.6). The visual differentiation here is accomplished by two simple signs: head-dress and hair. Sicily was a region where the three languages and the three religions met. The image could serve as an illustration of a line in Peter's

---

[6] For further discussion see the present writer's 'Symbolic Meanings of Hair in the Middle Ages', *Transactions of the Royal Historical Society*, 6th series, 4 (1994), 43–60.

[7] Bern, Burgerbibliothek, Codex 120 II; facsimile edition, Petrus de Ebulo, *Liber ad honorem Augusti sive de rebus Siculis. Eine Bilderchronik der Stauferzeit aus der Burgerbibliothek Bern*, ed. Theo Kölzer and Marlis Stähli (Sigmaringen: Thorbecke, 1994).

Fig. 6.5 Black men amongst the saved and the damned. Hans Memling, *Last Judgment*. The National Museum, Gdańsk. Photographer: Ryszard Petrajtis.

Fig. 6.5 (cont.)

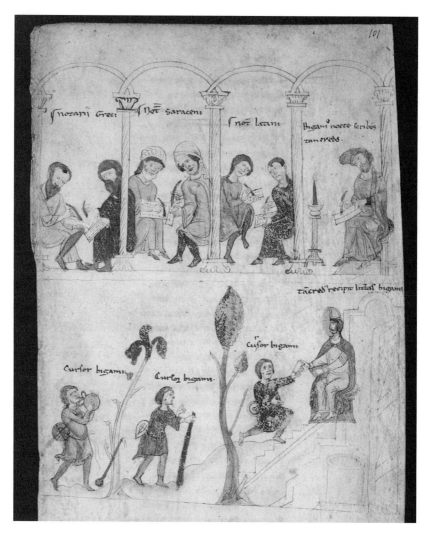

Fig. 6.6 "Greek, Saracen and Latin notaries" in the Kingdom of Sicily. *Liber ad honorem Augusti*, Peter of Eboli. Burgerbibliothek, Bern, MS 120. II, fol. 101r.

texts. Palermo, he writes, is 'endowed with a population speaking three languages (*populo dotata trilingui*)'.[8] Trilingualism might be difficult to portray, but the image of three groups of notaries makes the point.

[8] Fol. 97v, line 56, facs., pp. 44–5.

It is worth noting that the three groups in this picture are not only distinguished by simple visual cues but are also labelled – *notarii Greci*, etc. Peter of Eboli uses this device elsewhere in his text in a rather different way. In the illustrations of the imperial siege of Naples in 1191, two groups are singled out amongst the besieging troops and labelled 'the Bohemians' and the 'men of Cologne'.[9] Nothing else in their depiction differentiates them. A label is a recognition that purely visual means of differentiation would in this case prove inadequate.

Of course, a central issue is not simply whether or how ethnic difference is represented but why it is represented. In what circumstances is it important to ascribe ethnic identity? The general point that ethnicity is 'situational', i.e. that it can be used tactically, that its claims vary with circumstances, that it is not essential or given, etc., etc., has been made often enough. It is the specific reasons for ethnic identification that need to be examined.

Political motives are often important and an example of ethnic illustration which can be located in a clearly identifiable political situation is the Bayeux Tapestry, the famous embroidery, 70 metres in length, which tells the story of the Norman Conquest of England in 1066.[10] The Tapestry systematically shows the English as long-haired and with moustaches (but no beard, except in the case of the aged King Edward),[11] while the Normans are clean-shaven and have their hair cut very high at the back. Although there are running captions, identifying the actors and the action ('here a messenger comes to duke William', 'here a house is burned', etc.), this hair code is communicated by visual means alone. While the captions do contain ethnic terms ('dux Anglorum', 'Normannorum dux', 'Anglica terra', 'rex Anglorum', 'navis Anglica', 'Anglorum exercitus', 'Angli', 'Franci'), they never mention the contrasted hair-styles. Nevertheless, it is hair that makes ethnic identity visible at every point in the Tapestry.

The Norman style, with no beard or moustache and the extremely high hair-line at the back of the head, apparently came to them from the south, for the Burgundian chronicler Rodulfus Glaber attributes the introduction of this affected style among the French to the dandies from Aquitaine who accompanied Queen Constance on her marriage to Robert, king of France, around 1004.[12] It is ironic that this foppish piece of effeminacy became, over the course of time, the mark of that *Herrenvolk*, the Normans.

---

[9] Fol. 109, facs., p. 91.

[10] There are numerous facsimile editions, e.g. London, 1985; Munich, 1994.

[11] The only other bearded figures are one of the diners at bishop Odo's improvised field kitchen and one of the English retreating at the very end of the tapestry.

[12] 'a medio capitis comis nudati, histrionum more barbis rasi'. Rodulfus Glaber, *Historiarum libri quinque* 3.40, ed. John France, *Opera* (Oxford: Clarendon Press, 1989), p. 166.

Fig. 6.7 Anglo-Saxon and Norman hairstyles. Detail of the Bayeux Tapestry – 11th century. With special permission of the city of Bayeux.

Amongst the English of the eleventh century men wore moustaches, and the absence of a moustache signified, for them, not ethnicity but ecclesiastical status – priests did not wear them. This explains the astonished (or outraged?) comment of the Anglo-Saxon Chronicle on Leofgar, bishop of Hereford (1056) – 'he wore his moustaches during his priesthood' – this was, at any rate, noteworthy.[13] The assumption that 'clean-shaven' means 'priests' also lies behind the surely apocryphal story that the English scouts sent out to spy on the Norman army in 1066 reported back that 'almost everyone in that army appeared to be priests'.[14]

This stark ethnic contrast embodied in a rigid hair-code gives extra meaning to the incidents shown in the Tapestry. The central scene of the Bayeux Tapestry, in which the English strongman Harold swears (falsely) on the relics of the saints, in the presence of duke William of Normandy, therefore shows not just a man perjuring himself, but a man with a moustache perjuring himself before a clean-shaven man (Fig. 6.7).

[13] 'se werede his kenepas on his preosthade'; 'on his preosthade he hæfde his nepas'. Anglo-Saxon Chronicle (C and D) s.a., in Charles Plummer and John Earle (eds.), *Two of the Saxon Chronicles Parallel*, 2 vols. (Oxford: Clarendon Press, 1892–9), vol. 1, pp. 186–7.

[14] William of Malmesbury, *Gesta regum Anglorum* 3.329, ed. Roger Aubrey Baskerville Mynors, Rodney M. Thomson and Michael Winterbottom, 2 vols. (Oxford: Clarendon Press, 1998–9) 1, p. 450.

The Bayeux Tapestry records a claim and a conquest. It was the political situation that made it essential to distinguish the two sides. Another situation which stimulated ethnic categorization was the inter-action of laws. In many periods of the Middle Ages and in many parts of Europe, law was conceived of as 'personal', that is, the procedures and substantive law to be applied in a given case varied according to the group status of the individual concerned. One law applied to clerics, another to lay people; one law applied to the free, another to the unfree. Amongst the different kinds of group membership that might have legal consequences were ethnic and religious identity.

Such legal distinctions based on ethnic identity are to be found in the thirteenth-century German law-book, the *Sachsenspiegel*.[15] The text was composed in the 1220s or early 1230s and contains a guide to Saxon law. In the following century illustrated versions were made, four of which survive, with related iconography. They are known as the Heidelberg, Oldenburg, Dresden and Wolfenbüttel manuscripts (Heidelberg is the oldest and the one used for reference here).[16]

The illustrations are carefully keyed into the text by large coloured capital letters. Thus, if the relevant passage of text begins with a large capital 'S' in red, a similar letter is placed in the picture field. These illustrated copies of the *Sachsenspiegel* are also distinguished by a curiously – almost surreally – literal iconography. A discussion of the inheritance rights of full-brothers and half-brothers solves the problem of illustrating a half-brother by the radical device of representing the full-brother as possessing a double-torso; the half-brother can then be simply portrayed as a figure with one torso.[17] If a discussion of rent mentions rent due on St Bartholomew's day, then the illustrator depicts a man carrying his flayed skin on a stick over his shoulder (with reference to the method of St Bartholomew's martyrdom).[18]

This same literalism is applied to the depictions of ethnic interaction that illustrate the text of *Landrecht* 3. 70 (Fig. 6.8).[19] This rules that, in courts not held under royal *Bann*, every man must give judgment or bear witness, except Wend against Saxon or Saxon against Wend – 'Wend' was the common German name for the West Slavs who lived on Germany's

[15] *Sachsenspiegel: Landrecht and Lehnrecht*, ed. Karl August Eckhardt, Monumenta Germaniae historica, Fontes iuris Germanici antiqui, n.s. 1, 2 vols. (Göttingen: Musterschmidt, 1955–6).
[16] Heidelberg, Universitätsbibliothek, MS. Pal. germ. 164; on-line at http://digi.ub.uni-heidelberg.de/diglit/cpg164.
[17] MS Pal. germ. 164, fol. 7; *Sachsenspiegel, Landrecht* 2. 20. ed. Eckhardt, pp. 148–9.
[18] MS Pal. germ. 164, fol. 9; *Sachsenspiegel, Landrecht* 2. 58. ed. Eckhardt, p. 176.
[19] MS Pal. germ. 164, fol. 24; ed. Eckhardt, pp. 256–7.

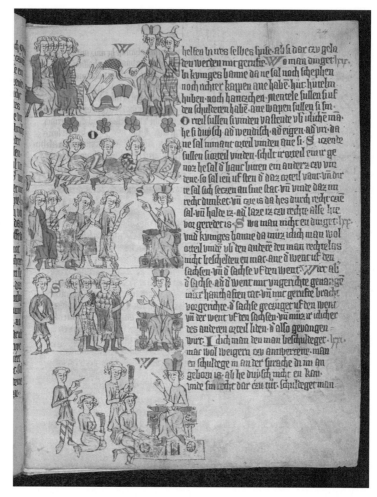

Fig. 6.8 Slavs ("Wends") and Saxons. Heidelberg, Universitätsbibliothek, Cod. Pal. germ. 164 (Sachsenspiegel), fol. 24.

eastern borders, usually, by this time, under the rule of German dynasties and intermingled with German populations. The only exception to this rule about Wends and Saxons was if the offender was caught red-handed – then they *could* bear witness against each other, 'Saxon against Wend and Wend against Saxon'.

The pictures illustrating this passage seize the opportunity it offers to depict an assortment of ethnic types. The fourth drawing down shows the case of the exclusion of Wends and Saxons from judging or bearing witness against each other. Standing before the count are a Saxon, a Frank, a Jew (identified by his hat) and an unidentifiable man. Standing behind them and apart is a Wend, to whom the Saxon turns in a gesture of rejection. The Wend is identified by his short hair, which is cut to the top of the ears, rather than flowing over them, as with the other figures depicted. Below this is an illustration of the exceptional circumstance of an offender caught red-handed. Here a Saxon stands above a kneeling (short-haired) Wend, while next to them a Wend stands above a kneeling Saxon, all in the presence of the count. The iconic nature of the image is clear from the fact that both the Saxon accuser and the Saxon prisoner bear the identifying weapon of the Saxon, the *Sachse*, or hooked knife – clearly not a likely courtroom situation for a suspect caught red-handed. The text emphasizes the point that legal procedures here are governed by the ethnic identity of the individuals in question and the illustrator uses hair and clothing to give these identities a visual reality.

The short hair of the Wends is attested in other sources. In the early twelfth century Germans told vivid atrocity stories of the pagan Slavs to their east. One such tale was that the Slavs scalped their German Christian victims and then, 'taking off the skin of their heads, they break into Christian territory disguised in this way and, pretending to be Christians, they plunder with impunity'.[20] Whether this story of disguise by scalp is true or not, it only makes sense if a difference in hair treatment was a real ethnic marker on this frontier. Later in the twelfth century the Danish chronicler Saxo Grammaticus, describing the idols of the pagan Rani, a West Slav people inhabiting the Baltic island of Rügen, noticed that their gods had shaven beards and trimmed hair, 'so you would think that the craftsman who had made them had imitated the custom of the Rani in treatment of the head'. He also notices that the priests of the Rani have long beard and hair, 'contrary to the common custom of the country'.[21]

* * *

An important development which stimulated ethnographic illustration was the movement of western friars and merchants into Asia in the thirteenth and fourteenth centuries, reaching places that Europeans had not previously visited. Some of these missionaries and traders left written accounts of their journeys, and in them, naturally enough, descriptions of foreign peoples are very prominent. The most famous of these accounts

---

[20] Herbert Helbig and Lorenz Weinrich (eds.), *Urkunden und erzählende Quellen zur deutschen Ostsiedlung im Mittelalter (Ausgewählte Quellen zur deutschen Geschichte des Mittelalters)*, XXVI, 2 vols. (Darmstadt: Wissenschaftliche Buchgesellschaft, 1968–70), I, no. 19, p. 98.

[21] Saxo Grammaticus, *Gesta Danorum* XIV. xxxix. 4, ed. Jørgen Olrik and Hans Raeder, 2 vols. (Copenhagen: Levin & Munksgaard, 1931–57), I, 465.

of Asia is that of Marco Polo and several manuscripts of his work are illustrated. The earliest seems to be London, BL, MS Royal 19 D. I, produced in France in the mid-fourteenth century,[22] while the most elaborate is Paris, Bibliothèque nationale de France (BnF), MS fr. 2810, made for the Duke of Burgundy *c.* 1410, which has 84 illustrations of Polo's text.[23]

Of course, Marco Polo and the other European travellers in Asia did not take artists with them to sketch out what they saw, in the manner of later explorers and colonists – although one Franciscan friar, William of Rubruck, did remark wistfully, 'I would illustrate everything for you, if I knew how to draw'.[24] Because of this gap between the observer, recording his impressions in words, and the illustrator, perhaps a hundred years later, attempting to turn those words into pictures, imagination and preconception play a bigger part in these illustrations than in Peter of Eboli, the Bayeux Tapestry or the *Sachsenspiegel*, where depiction could be based on life-models.

One result was, unsurprisingly, that the illustrators often relied on 'conventional traits' to evoke 'a fabulous Orient'.[25] A particular aspect of this was a process of 'Saracenization'. Since the best known eastern 'Others' were the Muslims of the Mediterranean, it was simple to export their conventional identifying attributes, such as the exotic head-dress and curved sword, to the Mongols and other Asian peoples. In London, BL, MS Royal 19 D. I, the depiction of Mongols on folio 78v is indistinguishable from that of the Muslims on folio 65 (Figs. 6.9–6.10). Both are characterized by dark skin, bare feet and turbans. The Mongols of Paris, BnF, MS fr. 2810, wield curved scimitars and have elaborate head-dresses. The template for such images was clearly the Saracen as illustrated in western chronicle literature.[26]

---

[22] See David John Athole Ross, 'Methods of Book-Production in a XIVth Century French Miscellany (London, B. M., MS. Royal 19. D. I)', *Scriptorium* 6 (1952), 63–75.

[23] There is a facsimile edition with commentary of Paris, BnF, MS fr. 2810 (Luzern: Faksimile Verlag, 1994). Other examples of illustrated Marco Polo texts are Oxford, Bodleian Library, MS Bodley 264, fols. 218–71v, with 2v (early fifteenth-century England) and New York, Pierpont Morgan Library, MS M. 723, of *c.* 1400.

[24] 'omnia depinxissem vobis si scivissem pingere'. William of Rubruck, *Itinerarium* 2, ed. Anastasius van den Wyngaert, in *Sinica Franciscana I: Itinera et Relationes fratrum minorum saec. XIII et XIV* (Quaracchi: Apud collegium S. Bonaventurae, 1929), pp. 164–332, at p. 173.

[25] Philippe Ménard, 'L'illustration du *Devisement du Monde* de Marco Polo. Etude d'iconographie comparée', in François Moureau (ed.), *Métamorphoses du récit de voyage* (Paris and Geneva: Champion, 1986), pp. 17–31, at pp. 26 and 28. Cf. ibid., 'Réflexions sur l'illustration du texte de Marco Polo dans le manuscrit fr. 2810 de la Bibliothèque nationale de Paris', in *Mélanges in Memoriam Takeshi Shimmura* (Tokyo: Comité de Publication, 1998), pp. 81–92.

[26] 'An Kreuzzugsgeschichten gewöhnt verwandelt der Künstler die Nicht-Christen in diesem Zyklus oft in Mauren': 1994 facsimile commentary, p. 89 (Gousset).

Fig. 6.9 Depiction of Mongols.   Fig. 6.10 Depiction of Muslims.
London, British Library, MS Royal 19   London, British Library, MS Royal 19
D. I (Marco Polo), fol. 78v.   D. I (Marco Polo), fol. 65.

Just as crusade literature offered 'Saracenic' models for illustration, so
there was also already a rich repertoire of 'eastern' iconography at hand in
the Alexander texts. Alexander the Great's exploits in Asia, as recorded in
a complex and ever expanding body of legend and literature, were often
illustrated in the later Middle Ages and several manuscripts contain both
Alexander literature and the accounts of Marco Polo and other travellers
(MS Royal 19 D. I is an example). Their iconographic traditions cross-
fertilized each other.[27]

Another of the preconceived notions influencing the ethnic illustrations
in Polo's text concerns the so-called 'Plinian races', those improbable
semi-human people known to the Middle Ages from the list in Pliny's
Natural History. They were frequently illustrated in works with such titles
as 'The Marvels of the East'.[28] Naturally, therefore, one would expect to
find these peculiar creatures in the East and, since Polo's text concerns the
East, they could be assumed to be there, whether he described them or
not. Hence a fairly bland passage of Marco Polo's, describing the wild
races of central Asia, is taken by the illustrator of BnF, MS fr. 2810 (or

[27] David John Athole Ross, *Alexander Historiatus: A Guide to Medieval Illustrated Alexander
Literature*, Warburg Institute Surveys 1 (London: Warburg Institute, 1963).
[28] See Rudolf Wittkower, 'Marvels of the East: A Study in the History of Monsters', in
Allegory and the Migration of Symbols (London: Thames and Hudson, 1977), pp. 45–74;
John B. Friedman, *The Monstrous Races in Medieval Art and Thought* (Cambridge, Mass.:
Harvard University Press, 1981, reprint Syracuse: Syracuse University Press, 2000).

Fig. 6.11 "Plinian" (monstrous) races. Paris, Bibliothèque nationale de France, MS fr. 2810 ("Livre des merveilles"), fol. 29v.

whoever instructed the illustrator) as a cue for introducing the 'Plinian races': we see one of the Blemmyae with his head in his chest, a monopod protecting himself from the sun with his giant single foot and a Cyclops (Fig. 6.11). Here cultural expectation, not the text, drives the illustration; as Wittkower commented, 'somewhere among the 84 illustrations of the text such a picture had to appear'.[29]

But very often too, the illustrators of Marco Polo's texts made no effort at all to create an exotic sense of Otherness. In MS Royal 19 D. I the image of the Great Khan and his wives at table on fol. 86 could be any western king at a feast, while those same wives depicted in BnF, MS fr. 2810, folio 36, have been described as 'de blondes dames vêtues à la mode française'.[30] The mingling of exoticized and unexoticized depictions in the same cycle refutes any simple interpretation based on theories of Otherness.

★ ★ ★

As a final example of the vivid depiction of ethnic difference in medieval illustration, we can take the case of the Irish works of Gerald of Wales (*c.* 1146–1223). Gerald was closely related to the first Anglo-Norman conquerors in Ireland and he wrote both a detailed narrative account of the conquest (the *Expugnatio Hibernica*) and a description of Ireland's

---

[29] Paris, BnF, MS fr. 2810, fol. 29v; Rudolf Wittkower, 'Marco Polo and the Pictorial Tradition of the Marvels of the East', in *Allegory and the Migration of Symbols*, pp. 75–92, at p. 85 (illustration on p. 84). Oxford, Bodleian Library, MS Bodley 264, fol. 260, also shows the 'Plinian races'.

[30] 1994 facsimile commentary, p. 478.

Fig. 6.12 The Irish king Dermot MacMurrough. Dublin, National Library of Ireland, MS 700, fol. 56.

landscape, fauna, marvels and inhabitants (the *Topographia Hibernica*), a tendentious but invaluable picture of an early Celtic society.[31]

There are few illustrations in surviving copies of the *Expugnatio*, but those few depict the difference between the native Irish and the invading Anglo-Normans in an instantly recognizable way. The marginal illustrations of the Irish king Dermot MacMurrough (Fig. 6.12) and the Anglo-Norman barons Robert fitzStephen and Richard fitzGilbert (Fig. 6.13) in Dublin, National Library of Ireland (NLI) MS 700, show the first with a long-flowing beard, a short tunic and a large axe, while the two invaders are clean-shaven, have long surcoats and carry the longsword. The long beard is clearly one of the distinguishing ethnic markers of the Irish. Gerald in fact makes a great deal of this in his other work about Ireland, the *Topography of Ireland*, enjoying the Latin word-play *barba*, 'beard' and *barbarus*, 'barbarian'.[32]

---

[31] *Expugnatio Hibernica: The Conquest of Ireland*, ed. A. Brian Scott and Francis X. Martin (Dublin: Royal Irish Academy, 1978); *Topographia hibernica*, ed. James Dimock, in *Giraldi Cambrensis Opera*, 8 vols. (London: Rolls Series, 1861–91), vol. 5, pp. 1–204.

[32] 'barbarus tamen barbarum quam vestium necnon et mentium cultus'. *Topographia* 3. 10, p. 150; 'Gens igitur haec barbara et vere barbara. Quia non tantum barbaro vestium ritu verum etiam comis et barbis luxuriantibus ... incultissima'. *Ibid.*, p. 153.

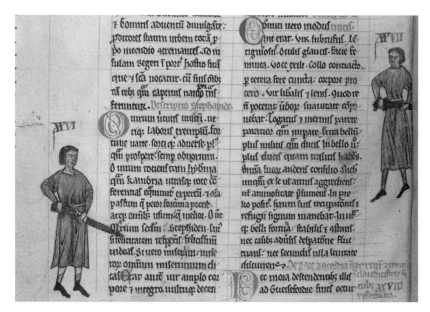

Fig. 6.13 Robert fitzStephen and Richard fitzGilbert. Dublin, National Library of Ireland, MS 700, fol. 64v.

The two ethnic groups are thus identified by hair-style (as in the Bayeux Tapestry), and by weapons. Such marks of distinction were to have a long history. The illustrations to the *History of Richard II* attributed to Jean Creton, produced *c.* 1405, and thus 200 years after the Dublin manuscript of Gerald's works, include one depicting an encounter between the English and Anglo-Irish army, in full armour, and Irish chiefs, with long beards, scanty if any armour, spears and bare feet (Fig. 6.14). The passage it illustrates describes the Irish king Art McMurrough: 'He had a horse without saddle or saddle-bow … in his right hand he carried a dart, big and long, which he threw very well. His likeness, exactly as he was, see portrayed here.'[33]

Gerald's *Topography of Ireland* was a popular work. There are 25 medieval manuscripts, plus fourteenth-century excerpts, an abbreviated version (which was translated into Provençal) and early modern transcripts,

---

[33] 'Ung cheval ot sans sele ne arçon … En sa main dextre une darde portoit/Grant et longue, de quoy moult bien gettoit:/Sa semblance, tout ainsi qu'il estoit,/Vée pourtraite/Icy endroit'. London, BL, MS Harley 1319, fol. 8v (text), 9 (illustration); ed. J. A. Buchon, Jean Creton, 'Poëme sur la deposition de Richard II', *Collection des chroniques nationales françaises* 23 (1826), pp. 323–466, at p. 335.

Fig. 6.14 Irish and English warriors in the 1390s. London, British Library, MS Harley 1319 ("Creton"), fol. 9.

not to mention its influence on later writers. Gerald gave a public reading of the work at Oxford in 1187 or 1188, entertaining the members of the nascent university as well as both the rich and the poor of the town.[34]

There are four surviving illustrated copies of the *Topography*:

- London, BL, MS Royal 13 B. VIII, produced *c.* 1200; the manuscript was at St Augustine's, Canterbury, by the fifteenth century.
- Dublin, NLI, MS 700, also produced *c.* 1200; it belonged to the vicars choral of Hereford Cathedral by the fifteenth century.
- Oxford, Bodleian Library, MS Laud misc. 720, produced *c.* 1260, probably a copy of NLI 700; it was in Durham by the early seventeenth century.
- Cambridge, University Library, MS Ff. 1. 27, produced at Bury St Edmunds *c.* 1320, a copy of the Royal manuscript.

The illustrations in each of the four manuscripts are closely related. There are forty or so individual images (although many of those in the Oxford manuscript have been cut out), carefully placed in the margins – it

[34] Gerald of Wales (Giraldus Cambrensis), *De rebus a se gestis*, ed. J. S. Brewer, in *Giraldi Cambrensis Opera*, vol. 1, pp. 1–122, at pp. 72–3.

Fig. 6.15 Inauguration of an Irish king. London, British Library, MS Royal 13 B. VIII, fol. 28v.

has in fact been argued that the illustrations in the *Topography* had an important role in the development of free-standing marginal illustration.[35] They depict the birds and animals of Ireland, some of the marvels and monstrosities described in the text and – what is of interest here – the native Irish and their customs.

An especially arresting scene is the inauguration rite of an Irish king in Ulster. Gerald describes how, after the people have assembled, the king-elect copulates with a mare, which is then killed and made into a vast horse stew. The king then bathes in this stew and both he and the people eat it.[36] The illustrations in the *Topography* do not depict the actual copulation (although other stories of bestiality in the text are illustrated) but both the killing of the mare and the bathing in the stew are the subjects of marginal paintings (Fig. 6.15). The long hair, long beards and dress make it clear at a glance that it is Irishmen who are engaging in this barbarous rite.

Hair as an ethnic marker also figures in another illustrated episode in the *Topography*, when sailors driven by a storm to an island off the Atlantic coast of Ireland encounter 'a little boat being rowed towards them'.[37] Gerald's description makes it clear that this is a coracle, a small boat made of wickerwork covered with hides, used in Wales and Ireland: 'It was narrow and roughly rectangular and woven and sewn together with wicker and animal hides.' Its occupants were equally distinctive: 'In it were two

[35] See Michelle Brown's comments on the illustrations of Gerald of Wales' *Topography of Ireland* (discussed below): 'he deserves to be recognised as a key figure in the perception and development of marginal space as a vehicle for new programmes of illustration: a major contribution to Gothic art'. Michelle Brown, 'Marvels of the West: Giraldus Cambrensis and the Role of the Author in the Development of Marginal Illustration', *English Manuscript Studies 1100–1700* 10 (2002), 34–59, at 35.

[36] *Topographia* 3. 25, p. 169.   [37] *Topographia* 3. 26, pp. 170–1.

moderata· in omnes affectus uehementissima.

Fig. 6.16 Two Irishmen in a coracle. London, British Library, MS Royal 13 B. VIII, fol. 29.

men, their bodies completely naked except for wide belts of untanned animal hide with which they were bound. They had, in the Irish way, very long hair, hanging down over their shoulders and covering a large part of their bodies.' Nakedness is of course one of the great tropes of savagery (Fig. 6.16).

Gerald elaborates this image of the primitive. When the Irishmen were invited into the ship,

they began to marvel at everything they saw, as if they were quite unfamiliar. For, as they claimed, they had never before seen a ship so big and made of wood, or even human clothing. When they offered them bread and cheese to eat, they declined, not knowing what either of them was. They said they were accustomed to eat only meat, fish and milk. Nor did they make use of clothing, except occasionally animal hides when in great need.

Big European ships, clothes, processed foods – all are amazing novelties for this prehistoric pair.

Nor is their religious education anywhere near civilized standards. When the Irishmen ask the sailors for meat, they are told it is Lent, when Christians forgo meat. The two natives turn out to know nothing of Lent – nor about the year, the month or the week or the names of the days of the week.

When asked whether they were Christians and had been baptized, they answered that until now they had heard nothing of Christ and knew nothing about him. And thus they returned, taking with them a loaf of bread and some cheese, in order that they might show to their own people as an object of wonder the kind of food that foreigners ate.

The story is of course incredible. The Irish were converted to Christianity before the English and indeed had had an important role in converting their pagan neighbours. The point of the story is to create a powerful image of nakedness, rawness and religious ignorance. The Irish are 'backward' in a technical sense, maintaining, as Gerald points out elsewhere in the *Topography*, the original pastoral way of life (*gens a primo pastoralis vitae vivendi modo non recedens*).[38] The same association of pastoralism and the earliest way of life, along with an interesting comparison between the Mongols and the Irish, is made by the Franciscan William Woodford, writing in 1373–4. His fellow friars, journeying in Asia, had informed him that the Mongols do not eat bread. 'And the diet of some of the pure Irish, our neighbours,' comments William, 'is the same. Therefore it is clear that this was the first way of living (*primus modus vivendi*), without material bread.'[39]

The evocation of Irish backwardness had an obvious political context, the English invasion and partial conquest that began in the late twelfth century. Gerald's contemporary, Gervase of Tilbury, makes the link explicit. Henry II of England, he writes, was

the first who, having expelled the filthy nations of the Irish, divided up the land to be held by the English as knights' fees (*feodis militaribus*) … Hence it came to pass that a land that had despised religion from most ancient times, living from the milk of flocks, spurning the Lenten fast, taking its meat raw and given up to filthiness, is esteemed by the new religion of its inhabitants.[40]

This cocktail of milk, raw meat, ignorance of Lent and moral turpitude is exactly that found in the *Topography*. An opening such as folios 28v–29 in the Royal manuscript, with a series of images across the bottom margins – killing of the mare, inaugural bath, naked men in a coracle, a woman riding astride – is a window into the imagery of the colonial mind (Figs. 6.15–6.17).

---

[38] *Topographia* 3. 10, p. 151.
[39] Cambridge, University Library, MS Add. 3571, fol. 108, cited by Jeremy I. Catto, 'Guillaume de Pré and the Tartars', *Archivum Franciscanum Historicum* 60 (1967), 210–13, at 211.
[40] Gervase of Tilbury, *Otia Imperialia* 2. 10, ed. S. E. Banks and J. W. Binns (Oxford: Clarendon, 2002), p. 308.

Fig. 6.17 Colonialist imagery. London, British Library, MS Royal 13 B. VIII, fols. 28v–29.

A long-standing defence of English imperialism in Ireland has been the argument that the Irish are incapable of ruling themselves because they are always at each other's throats. The great medievalist, controversialist and die-hard Tory, J. H. Round, writing at the end of the nineteenth century, neatly brought together this argument with the belief that the Irish were still at an earlier stage of development. Between the English and the Irish, he wrote, lay

a gulf impassable because dividing two wholly different stages of civilization … We went to Ireland because her people were engaged in cutting one another's throats; we are there now because, if we left, they would all be breaking one another's heads.[41]

Nor did the creation of a separate Irish state in 1922 dispel this way of thinking. In 1938 the Marchioness of Londonderry could reflect, 'democracy as the British know it … is not for southern Ireland. They are of different race. They want firm, wise but powerful control, to prevent them from trying to eat each other up.'[42]

Amongst the illustrations of Gerald's *Topography* is one depicting an Irishman splitting open the head of another Irishman with an axe (Fig. 6.18). It stands in the margin of a page where Gerald explains that

[41] John Horace Round, *Commune of London* (Westminster: A. Constable, 1899), pp. 168–9.
[42] Marchioness of Londonderry, *Retrospect* (London: F. Muller, 1938), p. 189.

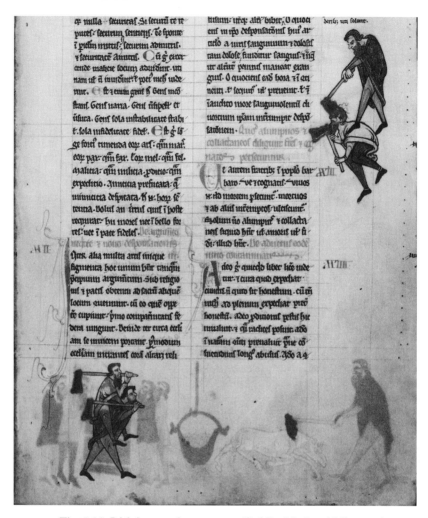

Fig. 6.18 Irish internecine savagery. Dublin, National Library of
Ireland, MS 700, fol. 39.

the Irish always have an axe ready in their hands and that brothers and
relatives pursue each other to the death.[43] This powerful combination of
image and text stands at the head of a direct line of descent reaching to
Round and the Marchioness of Londonderry.

If one is looking for 'the origins of racism in the West', such visual
imagery must surely have a part to play.

---

[43] *Topographia* 3. 21–3, pp. 165–8.

7   Proto-racial thought in medieval science[1]

Peter Biller

In his *The Invention of Racism in Classical Antiquity* Benjamin Isaac discusses definitions of proto-racist thought and then proceeds to survey the classical texts,[2] giving pride of place to the Hippocratic *Airs, Waters and Places*. The *Airs, Waters and Places* looks first at the effects on peoples of winds, waters and seasons, then at the contrast between the peoples of Asia and Europe, and finally at the effects of such geographical features as mountainous or low-lying areas. These external conditions affect groups or peoples in regions, bringing about certain physiques, ways of digesting, illnesses, length of life, and, among the women, distinctive patterns of menstruation, conception, childbirth and lactation. Colours of hair and skin are also there. There are polarities of causal factors and their effects, and the most striking of these is the contrasting of Asians and Europeans. Asian peoples are more homogeneous, they are of finer physique, but they lack courage and spirit and they are politically subject. Europeans are more varied. Though the nomadic Scythians are treated at greatest length, it is the 'other' Europeans who provide the clearest contrast with Asians, living in climactic extremes, wild, unsociable, spirited, courageous, and not in political subjection. Inserted is a chapter on the long-headed people, where the custom of shaping heads, pursued over a long time, eventually made long-heads a matter of nature.

Isaac moves on to Aristotle's *Politics*, which reworked and modified the *Airs, Waters and Places* into a succinct contrast of peoples of cold countries, especially Europe, and those of Asia. The former are spirited, not skilful and intelligent, relatively free, but not politically developed or capable of ruling others; the latter lack spirit, and are skilled, intelligent and politically subject; the Greeks on the other hand are in the middle, spirited, intelligent, free, politically developed and capable of ruling

---

[1] I am grateful to Mark Jenner for comment on an earlier draft.
[2] Benjamin Isaac, *The Invention of Racism in Classical Antiquity* (Princeton and Oxford: Princeton University Press, 2004). Reference should be made to Isaac's analyses of all the classical texts whose medieval reception is discussed below.

others. Isaac then turns to the Pseudo-Aristotelean *Problems*. One book in this was devoted to variations by region, and the *Problems'* literary form – a series of short questions and answers – helped to engender the almost aphoristic polarities of what was produced by hot and cold regions, such as lack of spirit (versus courage) and intelligence (versus stupidity).

This reminder of what is in these classical texts is suspended at this point – the reader who wants more should go back and read the rest of Isaac's survey of a much wider range of classical texts. Since its publication in 2004 his remarkable book has set the agenda for the investigation of the history of proto-racist thought, but when looking at the later influence of classical environmental thought, the book goes straight from the classical period to the sixteenth century. The middle ages do not feature. Like the dog that did not bark in the Sherlock Holmes story, they are silent.

Isaac's book prompts the question: how far were these texts known in the middle ages, and what was their impact? Put more generally, what role is played by the medieval period in the after-history of classical environmental thought and proto-racial outlook? It is not easy to point to useful modern scholarship on this theme. The one general history of the tradition of environmental thought that tackles the middle ages is valuable, but it is not bent towards our topic, it was not written by a medievalist and it is now very outdated.[3] The classical texts analysed by Isaac are predominantly scientific, and this points to a problem. There are orthodoxies about the nature of the medieval outlook, which encourage us to underplay or ignore science. In the study of the stereotypes and hostilities of groups and peoples in the middle ages, nearly all modern work concentrates on faith and, when it moves beyond faith, on the analysis of monstrous races in art and literature and popular mentality. The continuing reign in modern minds of ancient stereotypes of the medieval outlook – sunk in faith and superstition and given over to everything bizarre and fantastic – has its consequences in this particular area. Science usually has little place. Little attention is paid to the investigation of what might seem to clash with received ideas about the medieval: scientific views of peoples or, in medieval terminology, views of peoples according to natural philosophy and medicine.

The combination of this historiography and Isaac's silence has suggested the topic of this chapter, the role of the medieval period in the history of (largely) scientific proto-racial thought. Although this mainly means the reception of environmental thought, the chapter includes some

---

[3] Clarence J. Glacken, *Traces on the Rhodian Shore: Nature and Culture in Western Thought from Ancient Times to the End of the Eighteenth Century* (Berkeley, Los Angeles and London: University of California Press, 1967), part 2.

thought coming from another part of science, namely humoral medicine. There are deliberate limitations, both of theme and of mood (in a grammatical sense). This survey only looks at the later life of a selection of the earlier texts; one important exclusion is the physiognomic texts studied by Joseph Ziegler.[4] It is largely a map of texts being transmitted and received. There is little on the subtle twists and turns in ideas and the new emphases detectable in the way ideas are selected and presented, which a longer study could include. Its few allusions to the content of treatises and commentaries are thematically confined to the simple ascriptions to groups of physical and moral characteristics. The focus is on the reception of texts hitherto unavailable in Latin, translated in the high middle ages from Greek and Arabic; the chapter does not attempt to compare them to the unbroken but thinner tradition of texts in Latin containing classical environmental thought that have been analysed in Robert Bartlett's magisterial account of twelfth-century ethnographic thought.[5] The fundamental research on the topic presented here has not yet been done. Consequently, what follows is a prospectus, a brief account of what that work might show. Most of this chapter should be in the subjunctive mood – 'a fuller account *would* show'. To avoid irritating the reader, the chapter uses the indicative mood, but the reader should bear in mind its broad-brush and provisional character.

The two most significant intellectual events of the high and later middle ages were the translation into Latin of an enormous quantity of learned Greek and Arabic texts, and the coming into existence of universities. It is necessary to bring these to bear on the most important texts, the Hippocratic *Airs, Waters and Places*, Aristotle's *Politics*, the pseudo-Aristotelian *Problems*, Galen's *On Complexions*, and, from later Arabic medicine, two medical encyclopaedias, the *Pantegni* and Avicenna's *Canon*, alongside the brief medical 'introduction', the *Isagoge* of Johannitius.

The major translation campaigns constitute the first theme: medical texts translated from Arabic to Latin, but also from Greek, in the milieu of Monte Cassino (and Salerno) in the eleventh to early twelfth centuries; the translations done in Spain from Arabic in the second half of the twelfth century and the early thirteenth century; a miscellany of Greco-Latin translations in the Italian peninsula from the early twelfth to the mid-thirteenth centuries; and the large number of Greco-Latin translations carried out by William of Moerbeke in the third quarter of the thirteenth century. The

---

[4] For example: Joseph Ziegler, 'Médecine et physiognomie du XIVe au début du XVe siècle', *Médiévales: Langue, Textes, Histoire* 46 (2004), 89–107 and his article in the present collection.

[5] Robert Bartlett, *Gerald of Wales 1146–1223* (Oxford: Clarendon Press, 1982), chapter 7.

second theme is the rise of universities, beginning with Bologna and Paris in the twelfth century, continuing with their spread in the thirteenth and fourteenth centuries, and concluding with the filling in of the map of northern and central Europe with the foundation of more regional universities in the later middle ages, beginning with Prague in 1348.

The spotlight is not on the faculties of Theology and Law, but Arts – which came to cover much that is now called natural science – and Medicine. What can be said about the entry of our texts into these faculties? Which texts became known at the level of, say, difficult research monographs, that hovered in the background but were not read by the ordinary student? Which texts, by contrast, became common currency? Here what is crucial is whether a text became a standard text for regular timetabled lectures, dinned into the minds of students. One clue here is the simple copying of books, attested by the number of still extant copies or the occasional survival of university statutes about the copying of books. Two such statutes survive from Paris, listing the numbers of 'pieces' into which particular books were divided for copying and their prices: hard evidence that a text had wide diffusion in this university.[6] An impression of the statistics of a complementary late medieval fact is provided by the biographical registers of medieval graduates compiled by modern scholars. The fact: tens of thousands of graduates going out into the courts and towns of later medieval Europe, with some of the science-based vocabulary and commonplaces of the characteristics of peoples in their heads.

The catalogue of transmitted texts begins with *the* fundamental text, the *Airs, Waters and Places*.[7] This is a 'near miss' story. Its first translation from Greek into Latin was probably in sixth-century Ravenna.[8] While the

---

[6] Dating from 1272–6 and 1304, the two lists are in Heinrich Denifle and Emile Chatelain (eds.), *Chartularium universitatis parisiensis*, 4 vols (Paris: Ex typis fratrum Delalain, 1889– 97), I 644–9 no. 530 and II 107–12 no. 642. See on them Louis-Jacques Bataillon, 'Les textes théologiques et philosophiques diffusés à Paris par exempla et pecia', in Louis-Jacque Bataillon, Bertrand G. Guyot and Richard H. Rouse (eds.), *La production du livre universitaire au Moyen Age: exemplar et pecia* (Paris: Éditions du CNRS, 1991), pp. 155–63.

[7] The account of the Latin tradition provided here is based on the introduction to Hippocrates, *Airs, Eaux, Lieux*, ed. and trans. Jacques Jouanna (Paris: Les Belles Lettres, 1996) and the editions of Diller and Grensemann cited below. The section in Pearl Kibre, *Hippocrates Latinus: Repertorium of Hippocratic Writings in the Latin Middle Ages* (New York: Fordham University Press, 1985), pp. 25–8, is more useful for listing more manuscripts than for clarification of the sequence of translations. On the text's contents, see Jacques Jouanna, *Hippocrates*, trans. M. B. DeBevoise (Baltimore and London: Johns Hopkins University Press, 1999), pp. 210–32, and Isaac, *Invention*, pp. 61–9.

[8] The complete text, extant in two of the manuscripts, is given in Hippocrates, *De aeribus aquis locis: Interlineare Ausgabe der spätlateinischen Übersetzung und des Fragments einer hochmittelalterlichen Übersetzung*, ed. Hermann Grensemann (Bonn: Habelt, 1996), pp. 104–57, and the incomplete text, extant in the third manuscript, pp. 160–72. On the translation, see Jouanna (ed.) *Airs*, pp. 110–14, and ed. Grensemann (ed.) *De aeribus*, pp. 32–7.

survival of this version in two of its three manuscripts alongside other Hippocratic texts may be a trace of an ancient canon that was once read and studied, its confinement to only these ninth-century copies suggests that it was not being actively copied and read in the high middle ages.[9] There was a second Greco-Latin translation. Its lexical characteristics bring it into the translating circle of Alfanus of Salerno in the eleventh century.[10] This indicates self-evidently knowledge and also some interest, found in what was to be Latin Christendom's first important factory of learned medical texts. The little anthology of short medical texts, the *Art of Medicine*, that emerged from translations and medical activity at Monte Cassino in this period, had become a faculty text at Paris by the late twelfth century, and it was to become *the* fundamental student text.[11] Most important is the fact that while the *Art of Medicine* contained some Hippocratic texts, it did not contain the *Airs, Waters and Places*. We are left with a tantalizing glimpse of interest in the text, at a crucial location and period in the formation of the canon of university medical education. But only some interest: there is only one manuscript, and this contains only a fragment.

At a not precisely ascertainable date – perhaps the late twelfth century – there was another translation into Latin of the *Airs, Waters and Places*. The number of its extant manuscripts – perhaps around twenty – indicates quite wide currency.[12] Made on the basis of an Arabic version (itself in part a clever expansion of the headings contained in Galen's commentary), the text needs careful comparison with the Greek original. The majority of the text and its ideas – the fundamental notions of the effect of region and

[9] Augusto Beccaria, *I codici di medicina del periodo presalernitano (secoli IX, X e XI)* (Rome: Edizioni di storia e letteratura, 1956), nos 28 (no. 3) and 92 (no. 3), pp. 151 and 289; Augusto Beccaria, 'Sulle trace di un antico canone latino di Ippocrate e di Galeno', *Italia medioevale e umanistica* 4 (1961), 1–75 (at 73–4).

[10] The text is given in Grensemann (ed.), *De aeribus aquis locis*, pp. 271–5. See pp. 252–4 on the suggested link with Alfanus, and Jouanna (ed.), *Airs*, pp. 114–19.

[11] Cornelius O'Boyle, *Thirteenth- and Fourteenth-Century Copies of the Ars Medicine: A Checklist and Contents Description of the Manuscripts*, Articella Studies 1 (Cambridge: Cambridge Wellcome Unit for the History of Medicine 1998) lists 197 manuscripts; Cornelius O'Boyle, *The Art of Medicine: Medical Teaching at the University of Paris, 1250–1400*, Education and Society in the Middle Ages and Renaissance 9 (Leiden, Boston and Cologne: Brill, 1998).

[12] The text is edited in Hans Diller, *Die Überlieferung der Hippokratischen Schrift ΠΕΡΙ ΑΕΡΩΝ ΥΔΑΤΩΝ ΤΟΠΩΝ*, *Philologus*, Supplementband 23, Heft 3 (Leipzig: Dieterich, 1932), pp. 83–104, on the basis of ten manuscripts and the incunabular edition, listed pp. 57–9. In her *Hippocrates Latinus*, pp. 26–8, Kibre distributes twenty-one manuscripts between *two* suggested translations. The second of these is described as 'Greek (?)-Latin', but where she provides the incipit it is always the incipit of the Arabo-Latin version edited by Diller. On one copy made by a Paris master in 1334, see Danielle Jacquart, *La médecine médiévale dans le cadre Parisien: xive–xve siècle* (Paris: Fayard, 1998), p. 176.

place on the characteristics of peoples; the idea of a contrast between two large parts of the world, Europe and Asia; and the mixture of nature and nurture in the production of the long-headed people – are transmitted. But a few propositions are mangled. The Scythians are now 'Turks', and a lot is missing from their description.

In university circles there are some glimpses of direct knowledge. Arnau de Vilanova referred to Galenic comments on it,[13] and one of the learned medical men of Bologna University, Mondino dei Liuzzi, included it in a list of Hippocratic works he drew up. This list may suggest a sort of canon of reading and study.[14] The words of the Arabo-Latin version can be picked up in lectures on astrology delivered in Bologna by Cecco d'Ascoli.[15] But the *Airs, Waters and Places* never became a faculty text, and it attracted no formal commentaries.

There was, however, a much larger though indirect channel of transmission into university medicine. The *Airs, Waters and Places* was very well known in the Arab world,[16] and some of it (along with other classical climatic-determining material) was absorbed into medical treatises that were later translated into Latin. Primarily at issue are two massive medical encyclopaedias, Haly Abbas's *Liber Pantegni* and Avicenna's *Canon*. The *Liber Pantegni* was translated twice into Latin, in the later eleventh century by Constantine the African and in 1127

---

[13] Arnau de Vilanova, *Tractatus de consideracionibus operis medicine sive de flebotomia*, I.iii.2, ed. Luke Demaitre, *Opera Medica Omnia* 4 (Barcelona: Seminarium Historiae Scientiae Barchinonense, 1988), p. 198. See Luis García-Ballester, 'Arnau de Vilanova (*c.* 1240–1311) y la reforma de los estudios médicos en Montpellier (1309): El Hipócrates latino y la introducción del nuevo Galeno', *Dynamis* 2 (1982), 97–158 (at 116–17). Ballester takes this to be a reference to the Arabo-Latin translation, in which, however, it is not easy to find the material Arnau seems to be citing.

[14] Edited in Nancy Siraisi, *Taddeo Alderotti and his Pupils: Two Generations of Italian Medical Learning* (Princeton, NJ: Princeton University Press, 1981), p. 411.

[15] Cecco d'Ascoli, *In Spheram mundi*, in Lynn Thorndike (ed.), *The Sphere of Sacrobosco and its Commentators* (Chicago: University of Chicago Press, 1949), p. 345. For general comment, see Siraisi, *Taddeo*, p. 143. Cecco's *non esse minimam partem scientie medicine* echoes the Arabo-Latin *medicine non minimam partem esse* (ed. Diller, p. 85), not the Greco-Latin earlier translation (ed. Grensemann, p. 107) *non parva pars … medicinae* nor the Greco-Latin later translation (ed. Grensemann, p. 272) *non minimam porcionem … in medicinam.*

[16] *Galen's Commentary on the Hippocratic Treatise Airs, Waters, Places in the Hebrew Translation of Solomon ha-Me'ati*, ed. Abraham Wasserstein, The Israel Academy of Sciences and Humanities, Proceedings 6/3 (Jerusalem: Israel Academy of Sciences and Humanities, 1982), p. 6; Gotthard Strohmaier, 'La question de l'influence de climat dans la pensée arabe et le nouveau commentaire de Galien sur le traité hippocratique des *Airs, Eaux et Lieux*', in *Perspectives arabes et médiévales sur la tradition scientifique et philosophique grecque*, ed. Ahmad Hasnawi, Abdelali Elamrani-Jamal and Maroun Aouad, Orientalia Lovaniensia Analecta 79 (Louvain and Paris: Peeters and Institut de monde arabe, 1997), pp. 209–16.

(probably) by Stephen of Pisa.[17] Early chapters on 'change of complexion on account of region' and 'change of air on account of region' transmitted most of the fundamental ideas, dominant among which were the contrasts between south and north, and the blackness, crinkly hair, short lives and lack of spirit of the Ethiopians. In one chapter the proposition 'long-lived custom turns into nature' (*consuetudo diuturna mutatur in naturam*) preserves the point, though not the descriptive material, of the account of long-headed people in the *Airs, Waters and Places*.[18] The *Liber Pantegni* did not become a text listed for formal lectures, but it achieved wide circulation. Around a hundred manuscripts are still extant.[19] In the later thirteenth century – perhaps the 1270s – a Paris master, James of Douai, was citing it as his source on the topic of regions determining life-span, and specifically for the idea that people lived long in the cities of Saxony.[20]

Though Avicenna did not name Hippocrates at the relevant point, close study of his *Canon* has shown that he copied parts of the Arabic version of the *Airs, Waters and Places*.[21] In the theoretical parts of book 1, the chapters on seasons, airs and winds are followed by a chapter on 'those things that arise from habitation'.[22] Avicenna inserts the material into clear and easily graspable sections: hot places, cold, damp, dry, high, low lying, rocky and exposed, mountainous and snowy, near the sea, northern, southern, eastern and western. Hot places bring about black and curly hair, old age at thirty and light bodies, while cold places encourage great strength and boldness and propensity to specific illnesses. The series of polarities overlap with or are expanded in the contrasts of north and

---

[17] On the *Liber Pantegni* in general, see Charles Burnett and Danielle Jacquart (eds.), *Constantine the African and 'Alī ibn Al-'Abbas Al-Maǧūsī: the "Pantegni" and Related Texts*, Studies in Ancient and Medieval Medicine 10 (Leiden, New York and Cologne: Brill, 1994); see p. viii, n. 1 on the date of Stephen's translation.

[18] Constantine's version: *Theorica*, Liber primus; particula 20 De mutatione complexionis propter regionem; particula 23 De mutatione complexionis propter consuetudinem; Liber quintus, cap. 9 De mutatione aeris propter regiones; cap. 10 De mutatione aeris propter loca, in *Omnia opera Ysaac* (Lyon, 1515), fols 3vb–4ra, 4rb, 19vb–20ra, 20ra. Stephen's: *Theorica*, Liber primus, cap. 20 De mutatione complexionis corporis propter regiones; cap. 23 De complexionis mutatione propter consetudinem; Liber quintus, cap. 9 De aeris propter regiones mutatione, in Haly Abbas, *Liber totius medicine necessaria continens* (Lyon, 1523), fols 15vb, 16vb–17ra, 54ra–55ra.

[19] Mark D. Jordan, 'The Fortune of Constantine's *Pantegni*', in Burnett and Jacquart, *Constantine the African*, pp. 286–302.

[20] Cited in Peter Biller, *Measure of Multitude: Population in Medieval Thought*, corrected edition (Oxford: Oxford University Press, 2003), where there is a general account of the theme of region, the characteristics of peoples and length of life, pp. 283–5.

[21] Diller, *Überlieferung*, pp. 106–10.

[22] Avicenna, *Liber canonis*, I.ii.2.11 (Venice, 1507; facsimile reprint, Hildesheim, 1964), fols 32ra–33ra.

south. For example, the north encourages long life and fierceness, 'wolfish customs'. To some extent these polarities are also parallelled in those of high and rocky places and their opposites. Thus high and rocky places induce hardiness, sturdiness, vigilance, fortitude in war and disobedience. Cold and northern places constrict menstruation and miscarriage is rare, testifying to the strength of those living there, while hot and southern places encourage easy menstruation and much miscarriage.

Translated before 1187, the *Canon* was being cited by about 1220.[23] Unlike the *Pantegni*, it did become a text specified for formal lectures in the medical faculties of Bologna and Montpellier. Extant commentaries show that the first book of Avicenna's *Canon* was already standard in teaching in Bologna by the later thirteenth century. However, we must not leap to the conclusion that the chapter on habitable places was automatically included in this. The first book was very long, and the commentaries from around 1300 do not cover this chapter. But the statutes of 1405, laying down the first book of the *Canon* for lectures in the first, second and fourth year of a student's studies, suggest later development. There are very precise exclusions from book 1, but *not* of the 'habitable places' chapter, suggesting that by that date medical students did have to master it.[24]

A possible sign that the section on habitable places was being studied in Montpellier by the late thirteenth century is the fact that the two most important medical authors from Montpellier around this time produced powerful passages on the regional characteristics of peoples, while it is not easy to find contemporary parallels in writings from Bologna. One of them, Arnau himself, is discussed later. The other was Bernard de Gordon, whose *Tractatus de prognosticis* recycled and developed Avicenna's account of the effects of habitable places.[25] The 1309 Montpellier statutes only specify the *Canon* as one of several possible texts, apparently as a result of

---

[23] For the following, see Danielle Jacquart, 'La réception du *Canon* d'Avicenne: comparaison entre Montpellier et Paris au XIIIe et XIVe siècles', *Histoire de l'École Médicale de Montpellier: Colloque: histoire des sciences et des techniques*, 2 vols (Paris: Ministère de l'éducation nationale, Comité des travaux historiques et scientifiques, 1985), vol. 1, pp. 69–77.

[24] Carlo Malagola (ed.), *Statuti delle Università dei Collegi dello Studio Bolognese* (Bologna: N. Zanichelli, 1888), pp. 275–6, where the formula is repeated for each of the three years in question: 'legatur primus Avicenne, excepta Anathomia, et exceptis capitulis de naturis temporum annj secunde fen, et excepta ...'

[25] *De prognosticis*, ii.7 De prognosticacione secundum naturam regionum, in Bernard de Gordon, *Lilium medicine*, 2 vols (Frankfurt, 1617), vol. 2, pp. 927–30. Where (pp. 927–8) this has 'versus Aphricam, homines sunt ut plurimum cholerici, mobiles, veloces in motu, cum faucibus oblongis, sicut melancholi', London, British Library, MS Sloane 334, fol. 189va, has 'ut versus aufricam homines sunt ut plurimum colerici mobiles veloces in motu cum faciebus oblongis ut viella'. Where it has (p. 928) 'In Iudaea autem in terra nigrorum, homines sunt senes in tertio anno', London, BL, MS Sloane 334, fol. 189vb,

the hostility to Avicenna evinced by the statutes' principal architect, Arnau de Vilanova.[26] Arnau's hostility could be seen as reaction – and, as reaction, evidence in itself of the popularity already being enjoyed by Avicenna at Montpellier, before 1309. The *Canon* was certainly firmly established in 1340, when the chapters 'On habitable places' were brought back into the lecture hall, along with much else, by statutes emphasizing the necessity of lectures on the 'whole' of book 1.[27]

University statutes also specified the reading of Johannitius, *Isagoge* – this abridgement in Latin of an Arabic work may have been carried out by Constantine the African in the second half of the eleventh century – and Galen's *On complexions*, translated by Burgundio of Pisa (d. 1193). The *Isagoge* is our lowest common denominator, the text known best and by most medical students.[28] Always copied first in manuscripts of the *Art of Medicine* because it was a general 'introduction', which is the meaning of its name, its shortness and reduction of medical principles to numbers – four of this and nine of that – made its propositions easy to memorize. Let us take the example of colour. Where the *Isagoge* dealt with the inner causes of colours of the skin, it mentioned a range (white, red, black, yellow and blue-grey). It then moved on to external causes: cold, producing men like the Scots, and heat, producing men like the Ethiopians. This reduced the range to two opposits, clearly white and black, and it named two representative peoples. This aphoristic statement – further emphasized by lecturers' questions on it[29] – will have slipped into the minds of medical students, meaning that they spent the rest of their lives *thinking* this elementary division of peoples of the world according to white and black skin colour.[30]

---

has 'In India autem et in terra nigrorum homines sunt senes in 30 anno'. More of Bernard's comments on peoples' regional characteristics can be found in Luke E. Demaitre, *Doctor Bernard de Gordon: Professor and Practitioner* (Toronto: Pontifical Institute of Medieval Studies, 1980), pp. 4–8, where they are used as negative evidence about Bernard's place of origin.

[26] Alexandre C. Germain (ed.), *Cartulaire de l'Université de Montpellier* (Montpellier: La maison Ricard frères, 1890), no. 25, p. 220.

[27] Germain, *Cartulaire*, no. 68, p. 347: 'Primus Canonis totus sit pro uno cursu'.

[28] Francis Newton, 'Constantine the African and Monte Cassino: New Elements and the Text of the *Isagoge*', in Burnett and Jacquart, *Constantine the African*, pp. 16–47; O'Boyle, *The Art of Medicine*, pp. 83–6.

[29] For example, Peter of Spain's twentieth topic on the *Isagoge* contained six questions *de coloribus cutis*, with two on blackness of skin; Fernando Salmón, *Medical Classroom Practice: Petrus Hispanus' Questions on Isagoge, Tegni, Regimen Acutorum and Prognostica (c.1245–50) (MS Madrid B.N. 1877, fols 24rb–141vb)*, Articella Studies 4 (Cambridge and Barcelona: Cambridge Wellcome Unit for the History of Medicine, 1998), p. 108.

[30] Johannitius, *Isagoge ad Techne Galieni*, xx, ed. G. Maurach, *Sudhofs Archiv* 62 (1978), 156: 'Ab exterioribus nempe colores adveniunt sicut ex frigore Scotis, ex calore Aethiopibus.'

Then later on, when hearing lectures on Galen's *On complexions*,[31] they will have heard contrasts of hair and skin colour set within more sophisticated discussion of complexions and hot and cold regions, and attached to the names of Ethiopians, Egyptians, Arabs, Indians, Celts, Germans, Thracians and Scythians. In an early fourteenth-century commentary, Turisanus recycled some of this material. As a representative figure – he had been a medical student in Bologna and became a medical teacher in Paris – he may provide us with a glimpse of the simplifying classification of peoples' physical characteristics that was in the air of the medical classrooms of the time. 'As Galen himself says in the book *On complexions*', wrote Turisanus,

the hair of Egyptians, Arabs and Indians and all those inhabiting hot and dry regions is – virtually without difference – black, slow to grow, hard, coarse, curly, dry, quickly cuttable. The hair of the inhabitants of contrasting regions, that is to say hot and humid ones, such as those of the Turks, Scythians, Slavs and Germans, is – virtually without difference – blonde, quick to grow, fine, straight and soft.[32]

The Pseudo-Aristotelian *Problems* added to the number and richness of the channels transmitting classical thought. It was translated by Bartholomew of Messina between 1258 and 1266,[33] and the commentaries of Pietro d'Abano and Walter Burley contain questions that illustrate the more specific role the *Problems* had in ventilating and further disseminating this material. Burley's, for example, included 'Why Ethiopians and Egyptians are contorted', 'Why those inhabiting high places are long-lived', 'Why northerners are naturally bolder, stronger and more long-lived than southerners', and 'Why southerners are timorous and weak'.[34]

[31] *De complexionibus*, ii.5 and ii.6, in *Burgundio of Pisa's Translation of Galen's ΠΕΡΙ ΚΡΑΣΕΩΝ "De complexionibus"*, ii.5 and ii.6, ed. Richard J. Durling, Galenus Latinus 1 (Berlin and New York: Walter De Gruyter, 1976), pp. 79, 80, 86.
[32] 'Sicut enim dicit ipse Gale<nus> in libro *de complexionibus*, capilli egyptiorum, arabum et indorum et omnium calidas et siccas regiones inhabitantium fere indifferenter sunt nigri, tardi augmenti, duri, grossi, crispi, aridi, velociter scissibilis. Inabitantium vero regiones oppositas, scilicet frigidas et humidas ut turcorum, scytarum, et sclavorum germanicorum, indifferenter fere omnium capilli sunt flavi, velocis augmenti, subtiles, recti et molles.' Turisanus, *Plusquam commentum in Microtegni Galieni*, xi.19 (Venice, 1512), fol. 39va. I am conjecturing that 'et sclavorum germanicorum' is a mistake for 'sclavorum et germanorum'. On Turisanus, see Siraisi, *Taddeo*, pp. 64–6.
[33] See Maaike Van der Lugt, 'Aristotle's *Problems* in the West: A Contribution to the Study of the Medieval Latin Tradition', in Pieter De Leemans and Michele Goyens (eds.), *Aristotle's* Problemata *in Different Times and Tongues*, Mediaevalia Lovaniensia, Series 1, Studia 39 (Leuven: Leuven University Press, 2006), pp. 71–111.
[34] London, British Library, MS Royal 12.E.XVI, fols 130r, 130v, 132r: 'Quare ethiopes et egipcii sunt contorti; Quare habitantes in altis locis sunt longevi; Quare boriales sunt audaciores, forciores et longeviores naturaliter quam australes; Quare australes sunt timidi <et> debiles'.

The *Problems* was not a formally prescribed faculty text. But its wide currency in university arts and medicine is shown by the large number of still extant manuscripts (around sixty), and the specification of costs of its 'pieces' for Paris university stationers (where books were copied by students, piece by piece).[35] In 1344 sixty students were listening to lectures on it by a Paris master, Jean de Beerblenghem, who had also made his own copy of *Airs, Waters and Places*.[36]

Arts faculty texts included Aristotle's *On Animals*, whose constituent parts, especially the *Generation* and *History of Animals*, contained much miscellaneous material bearing on our theme, such as the effect of regions and the characteristics of Ethiopians. There were two translations, Arabo-Latin (before 1220) and Greco-Latin (after 1260), still extant in 115 manuscripts – and the *History of Animals* was also specified for copying in pieces.[37] These treatises were also transmitted through the Arabo-Latin translation of Avicenna's summary of them, Albertus Magnus's commentary (which was itself specified for copying in pieces),[38] and the copies of the lectures Albertus delivered in Cologne in 1258, *Questions on On animals*.[39] Another Arts faculty text was the *Politics*, which was translated in the 1260s by William of Moerbeke.[40] There are today 108 manuscripts from the thirteenth to the fifteenth centuries (and, once again, a text specified for piece-copying), the extant commentaries and questions on this and some university statutes provide the raw material for an investigation of its reception.[41] The history of its reception is in part the story of western intellectuals' reactions to its idealization of the Greeks, as attested in the questions raised by masters and the treatises that adapted and recycled the *Politics*. There is no space to outline this here.[42] But we shall dwell for a moment on the other part of the history of reception. This material was being drummed incessantly into the minds of university graduates of the

---

[35] *Chartularium universitatis parisiensis*, II 107.
[36] Jacquart, *Médecine médiévale dans le cadre Parisien*, p. 176.
[37] *Chartularium universitatis parisiensis*, II 107.
[38] *Chartularium universitatis parisiensis*, II 111.
[39] On the reception of these works, see Biller, *Measure of Multitude*, chapter 10.
[40] See Isaac, *Invention*, pp. 70–2. Moerbeke's Latin version: *Aristotelis Politicorum Libri Octo, cum vetusta translatione Guilelmi de Moerbeka*, ed. Franz Susemihl (Leipzig: Leipzig, 1872), pp. 268–70.
[41] See Christoph Flüeler, *Rezeption und Interpretation der Aristotelischen Politica im späten Mittelalter*, Bochumer Studien zur Philosophie 19, 2 vols (Amsterdam and Philadelphia: B. R. Grüner, 1992), and Biller, *Measure of Multitude*, chapter 11.
[42] I am preparing a study of this.

later middle ages, so that it became part of the language and the commonplaces of the educated and the literate.[43]

Let us get a taste of this, taking Albertus Magnus's commentary as the counterpart, in text, to what an Arts master would do in the lecture hall. The master would introduce a passage, elicit and restate the intention of the author, explain words and phrases, and raise formal questions. So, Albertus introduces the theme. It concerns those who politicize well or badly according to the nature of their complexion, to be considered from the situation of the cities of the Greeks and peoples throughout the world. He refers to two works, his own treatise *On the nature of places and those that are placed* and also to Ptolemy (meaning his *Tetrabiblos*), thereby establishing the topic as part of a larger body of systematic knowledge and discussion about regions and peoples. After summarizing this knowledge insofar as it bears on its most conventional themes, spiritedness and boldness, he shows its particular application to intellectual capacity. External cold intensifies inner heat, clouding and obscuring the spirit which carries forms to the intellect and to that part of the brain which is called 'logistic', rendering men deficient in intellect and skill and subtlety, even though full of spiritedness.

The literalness and brevity of Moerbeke's Latin translation made it often quite difficult for all but the best of Latinists. Helpful here to students and later readers of the commentary was what Albertus now did, going through Moerbeke's Latin word by word, in order to make it easily intelligible. At the most elementary level, Albertus even adds verbs which Moerbeke assumed the reader could supply. Repeating *Quae quidem enim in frigidis locis gentes*, Albertus writes, 'supple *habitant*', meaning, 'add at this point the verb "they inhabit"'. Thus he turns 'The people of cold countries generally' into 'Generally, those people who inhabit cold countries'.[44] And he does this throughout, making tiny additions that make the passage very easy to follow. Through Albertus's commentary, written probably in the late 1260s, we can approach a mental event in the individual histories of thousands of students at many points in time in the later middle ages. This event took place at the moment when each student was struggling to comprehend the text at an elementary level, and was being enlightened by additions and paraphrases provided by the master lecturing on the

[43] Compare O'Boyle, *Art of Medicine*, chapter 7, where a longer account is given of the way the *Art of Medicine*, beginning with the *Isagoge*, was hammered into students' minds in the classroom, and Jacquart's account of teaching and memoration, *La médecine médiévale*, chapter 2.

[44] Albertus Magnus, *Commentarii in octo libros Politicorum Aristotelis*, vii.5, in *Opera omnia*, ed. Auguste Borgnet, 38 vols (Paris: apud Ludovicum Vivès, 1890–99), vol. 8, pp. 663–4.

text – and then suddenly grasped it. This example from Albertus and the *Politics* can stand for one general point in our chapter.

There was earlier allusion to the university map of Latin Christendom in the thirteenth and the first half of the fourteenth centuries, with universities in England, France, Spain and Italy, and large blank spaces in the kingdoms of northern, central and eastern Europe. These 'blank spaces' can be misleading. This is not only because Germans and Poles were also among those crowding into the lecture halls of the 'international' universities of Paris and Bologna, but also because the major cities of these regions had the convents of the mendicant Orders, Dominican, Franciscan and Augustinian friars. These Orders' convents had centres of studies, ranked in a hierarchy at the top of which were those designated *studia generalia* (a widespread term for 'universities'), where philosophical texts, including 'natural' (scientific) ones, were also studied. So, for example, in conventional histories of medieval universities, Cologne had no 'university' until 1388. But part of a realistic picture of formal higher teaching, defined in medieval terms, has to include Dominican students listening to Albertus's lectures on *On Animals* at the Dominican *studium generale* in Cologne in 1258 (these are discussed below).

Bartholomew the Englishman[45] and the Dominicans Thomas de Cantimpré[46] and Vincent de Beauvais,[47] compiled encyclopaedias. These had many sectors of readership, including university masters and students – Bartholomew's was yet another to figure in pieces in the Paris stationers' statutes[48] – but they were fundamentally large resource-books for preachers. And they included a great deal of science, because for the mendicant friars knowledge of the natural world in the light of the best science available was not only a route towards knowledge of God but also an

---

[45] A new critical edition was launched by Brepols in 2007, but until it reaches book 15 recourse must be had to the chapters on German regions in Anton Emanuel Schönbach, 'Des Bartholomaeus Anglicus Beschreibung Deutschlands gegen 1240', *Mitteilungen des Instituts für österreichische Geschichtsforschung* 27 (1906), 54–90, and early printed editions such as the version used here, Bartholomew the Englishman, *De rerum proprietatibus* (Frankfurt, 1601; facsimile reprint, Frankfurt, 1964). For reception, see Heinz Meyer, *Die Enzyklopädie des Bartholomaeus Anglicus: Untersuchungen zur Überlieferungs- und Rezeptionsgeschichte von 'De proprietatibus rerum'* (Munich: W. Fink, 2000).

[46] Thomas de Cantimpré, *Liber de natura rerum*, ed. H. Boese (Berlin and New York: Walter De Gruyter, 1973). 158 Latin manuscripts are listed in Thomas Kaeppeli and Emilio Panella (eds.), *Scriptores Ordinis Praedicatorum Medii Aevi*, 4 vols (Rome: Istituto storico domenicano, 1970–93), vol. 4, pp. 347–50.

[47] Vincent of Beauvais, *Speculum quadruplex, sive Speculum maius*, 4 vols (Douai, 1624, facsimile reprint, Graz, 1965). Forty-nine manuscripts of the *Speculum naturale* and twenty of the *Speculum doctrinale* are listed in Panella and Kaeppeli, *Scriptores*, vol. 4, pp. 437–9.

[48] *Chartularium universitatis parisiensis*, I 644.

important aid in preaching, supplying raw material for use in sermons. Not only was God seen in all that he created, but the natural world supplied countless similitudes for doctrinal truths and moral lessons. Later mendicants also produced smaller compendia of scientific data, as well as specialized collections of natural scientific similitudes for preaching.[49] The encyclopaedias and compendia are the textual–archaeological survivals of a second channel of diffusion, that needs to be set alongside the dinning of commonplaces into the minds of Arts and Medicine students. For these resource books included much of the tradition we have been surveying.

The shortest encyclopaedia, Thomas de Cantimpré's, did not transmit much – at least, quantitatively speaking. Among his authorities was Johannitius's *Isagoge*. Although Thomas did not at this point quote the *Isagoge*, he directed attention to division by skin colour. The colours are spelled out, two of them – white skin and the dusky skin of those who become black – and there is the addition that what was 'natural' was white, and that it was also the most widespread colour in the world.[50] Thomas also repeated a statement from Aristotle about the superiority of the milk of black women.[51] The largest encyclopaedia, Vincent's three-part work, transmitted much more, in a selection of texts which appeared, sometimes twice, in the *Natural* and the *Doctrinal Mirror*. It quoted the *Isagoge* on cold and heat producing the colours of those like the Scots and the Ethiopians.[52] It repeated Thomas de Cantimpré on the naturalness and wide spread in the world of white skin, and the blackness of Ethiopians.[53] It repeated Thomas on black women's milk.[54] And it copied large sections of both the *Liber Pantegni*[55] and Avicenna's *Canon* on regionally determined characteristics.[56] It omitted the last sections of

---

[49] On the latter, see Joseph Ziegler, *Medicine and Religion c.1300: The Case of Arnau de Vilanova* (Oxford: Clarendon Press, 1998), chapter 4.

[50] Thomas de Cantimpré, *Liber de natura rerum*, i.42, ed. Boese, p. 47: 'Cutis alba est naturaliter in hominibus in omnibus fere partibus orbis ... In hiis igitur partibus Ethiopes sunt, qui fusca cute nigrescunt.'

[51] Thomas of Cantimpré, *Liber de natura rerum*, i.46, ed. Boese, p. 48. See on this Peter Biller, 'Black Women in Medieval Scientific Thought', *La Pelle Umana, Micrologus* 13 (2005), 477–92 (at 479–84).

[52] *Speculum doctrinale*, xiii.50, col. 1203; *Speculum naturale*, xxxi.111, col. 2382.

[53] *Speculum naturale*, xxviii.30, col. 2012. Thomas's 'in omnibus fere partibus mundi' is omitted.

[54] Twice: *Speculum naturale*, xxii.54 and xxviii.84, cols. 1639 and 2052.

[55] *Speculum doctrinale*, xiii.13, cols. 1176–7 transmits much of *Liber Pantegni, Theorica*, i.20 and 23. The (unsure) evidence of printed editions suggests that Vincent used Constantine's rather than Stephen's version of the *Liber Pantegni*.

[56] *Speculum doctrinale*, xiii.59–60, cols. 1208–9; *Speculum naturale*, vi.18, cols. 380–1 and iv.110–11 (col. 303) transmits *Liber Pantegni, Theorica*, v.9 (De mutatione aeris propter regiones), with much on peoples' characteristics.

the *Canon*'s treatment of habitable places, on northern, southern, western and eastern regions.

From one point of view, Bartholomew's account of the regional variation of peoples is similar: it retails earlier authorities, not all of which have yet been identified. But otherwise it presents strong contrasts. Whereas Thomas and Vincent dealt in general principles, Bartholomew dealt with specifics. He presented variation within a highly detailed account of different continents, regions and provinces, given in 175 chapters. While much of the material is ancient (with a lot from the Latin tradition), it has pasted on top of it material that is new.[57]

In the entry for Europe, and after quoting Isidore, Orosius and Pliny, Bartholomew crisply inserts a statement of the superiority of European bodies.[58] Europe feeds people that are larger in body, stronger in their force, bolder in spirit, and more beautiful in form and appearance than the peoples that Asia and Africa feeds. There follows a long account of the debilitating effects of heat on the *Affri* – Africans now, not Ethiopians. There are only a few words on Asia, rooted in earlier thought but formulated anew. Then, the major parts of virtually all the description of the provinces of *Germania* and neighbouring connected provinces – Iceland, the Baltic, Scandinavia, the Low Countries and Picardy – are again original, rooted either in Bartholomew himself or in a very recent and now lost source that Bartholomew calls 'Erodatus'. The name's proximity to Herodotus suggests that Bartholomew may have invented the source, in an exercise of wit that is lost on modern readers. Prominent in these pasted-in sections are words about the bodies of the inhabitants, variations on a few stock phrases: elegant in stature, strong or robust in body, with smooth or fair hair, and beauty of form and face. There are a few oddities. For example, the words are left out in the description of Franconia; they appear in two remote southern provinces, Asturia and Dalmatia; and the entry for Iceland hints at logical manipulation of the idea of north–south gradation of skin-colour: people that far to the north are *very* white. But what is most striking is the core of a long list of Germanic provinces, from the Baltic to the Alps, with strong and beautiful bodies. Bartholomew has starkly highlighted the European/African hierarchy of bodies, and has worked older material into a detailed regional map of northern physical strength and beauty.

---

[57] Compare the following with the analysis of Bartholomew's treatment of regionally varying populousness in Biller, *Measure of Multitude*, pp. 219–27.

[58] All of the following appears in Bartholomew, *De rerum proprietatibus*, xv, pp. 624–714, with regions ordered alphabetically according to their initial letters, though for later letters ordered randomly.

There were smaller compendia which drew upon the texts discussed here, often arranged in short question and answer form. One example is the (probably) early-fourteenth-century anonymous *Omnes homines*. This selected two old and commonplace topics: the comparison of the milk of black women (adapted to 'dark' women) and white women, taken from Aristotle's *History of Animals*, perhaps indirectly, and the crinkly hair of Ethiopians, taken probably from the *Problems*. But it also took two newer topics, the bleeding of Jews and the comparison of women's love of black men and white men, possibly under the influence of the ventilation of these topics in quodlibetal discussions in Paris around 1300, discussed below.[59] One of the fourteenth-century Dominican Conrads of Halberstadt – it is not clear which one – was the author of the *Responsorium curiosorum*. Also organized in questions and answers, this parades for explanation many contrasts between people in hot and cold regions (timidity, size of body, length of life, vigour of sex), alongside the crinkly hair of Ethiopians, and the anomaly of their white teeth but dark nails, nearly always citing the *Problems*. Conrad also threw in a question of no obvious source – why Neapolitans have large noses and coarse voices.[60] These two texts, from a larger number of later medieval compendia, form a rich and complex body of material, whose role in diffusing ideas about peoples' characteristics has not yet been investigated.

So far this chapter has been providing a prospectus for an account of the transmission of texts, their reception in university teaching, and their ideas becoming part of the mental furniture of arts and medicine graduates and the alert lay audiences of later medieval mendicant friars. The novelty that is detectable in Bartholomew's text is a reminder that an account would also need to look higher, and ask about writings and discussions which show development or even originality. Here again the account would have to begin with a catalogue of texts. Prominent among these are: Albertus Magnus's treatise *On the Nature of Places*, and his

[59] Biller, 'Black Women', 479, 483–5; Peter Biller, 'A "scientific" view of Jews from Paris around 1300', *Gli Ebrei e le scienze, Micrologus* 9 (2001), 137–68 (at 148–50, 163–4). On *Omnes homines*, see now Iolanda Ventura, 'Aristoteles fuit causa efficiens huius libri: On the reception of Pseudo-Aristotle's Problemata in Late Medieval Encyclopaedic Culture', in De Leemens and Goyens, *Aristotle's Problemata*, pp. 113–44 (at 120–2).
[60] Conrad of Halberstadt, *Responsorium Curiosorum* (Lübeck, 1476): 'Quare sunt homines ferini secundum mores et visum qui sunt in terris excellentis frigoris vel caloris' (fol. 30v); '<P>ropter quid habitantes in terris calidis sunt timidi qui autem in frigidis viriles' (fol. 30v); 'Quare in calidis terris sunt sapientiores quam in frigidis' (fol. 30v); 'Quare in regionibus calidis sunt homines minores cum oppositum inveniatur in plantis et animalibus' (fol. 68v); 'Utrum in regione calida vel frigida magis vigeat coitus' (fol. 73v); 86v 'Quare capilli crispantur' (fol. 86v); 'Quare homines neopolitani habent magnum nasum et grossam vocem' (fol. 93r); 'Quare dentes ethiopum sunt albi et ungues non' (fol. 97v).

lectures *Questions on On Animals*;[61] a manuscript containing quodlibetic discussions from the arts faculty in Paris around 1300;[62] Pietro d'Abano's commentary on the *Problems* (completed 1310) and *Conciliator* (after 1310);[63] and Nicole Oresme's commentary on the *Politics* (*c.* 1371).[64] The high erudition of the authors is immediately striking, narrow at an earlier date with Albertus (he cited Ptolemy's *Tetrabiblos* and Vitruvius in his *On the nature of places*[65] and Avicenna's *Canon* in one relevant *Question*),[66] and extraordinarily wide with Oresme. The latter's impressive parade of classical texts in his long disquisition on the comparison of Asians, Europeans and Greeks in Aristotle's *Politics* – illustrated with a map of the world – drives the reader back to Benjamin Isaac's monograph on classical proto-racial thought. The reader needs a long modern list, to use in answering the question, what did Oresme *not* know?[67]

A few examples of development are given here. In his *On the nature of places*, Albertus takes existing materials on the black man, putting them together into a long and remarkable word-picture. There are blackened bodies, the whiteness of teeth, the particular colour of tongues and throats when open, the prominence of mouths and eyes, the porosity and dryness of bodies, coldness and timidity of hearts, fast aging because of defect of natural *virtus*, the abundance of specific humours, light bodies, fatuous minds, and dryness and heat as the cause of the curliness and paucity of their peppercorn-like hair. Sources can be suggested for individual parts. But as a *whole*, this is a new picture, one of extraordinary power (and to modern minds terrifying).[68] In Albertus's *Questions*, various regional contrasts of peoples are highlighted by their being raised as questions, the scholastic parading of pro and con arguments and provision of a determination of each question, and the careful bringing to bear of Aristotle and Avicenna. An example is the underlining of the continuum from physical to mental or psychological characteristics in the question, why men in hot regions are of smaller size, courage and

---

[61] Albertus Magnus, *De natura loci*, in *Opera omnia*, ed. Bernhard Geyer *et al.*, 50 vols (Aschendorff: Monasterii Westfalorum, 1951–), vol. 5, part 2; *Quaestiones super De animalibus*, ed. Ephrem Filthaut, in *Opera omnia*, ed. Geyer, vol. 12.

[62] Paris, Bibliothèque nationale de France, MS lat. 16089.

[63] *Expositio Problematum Aristotelis in Problemata Aristotelis cum duplici translatione* (Venice, 1501); *Conciliator controversiarum quae inter philosophos et medicos versantur* (Venice, 1565, facsimile reprint, Padua, 1985).

[64] *Le livre de Politiques d'Aristote*, ed. Albert Douglas Menut, Transactions of the American Philosophical Society, n.s. 60, part 6 (Philadelphia: American Philosophical Society, 1970).

[65] *De natura loci*, i.5 and ii.3, pp. 9 and 27.

[66] *Quaestiones de animalibus*, vii.27 – the reference is to the *Canon*, i.2.2.11, fol. 32ra, on the brevity of Ethiopian life.

[67] *Livre de Politiques*, vii.13, pp. 297–9.   [68] *De natura loci*, ii.3, pp. 26–7.

boldness than men in cold regions. The characteristics are now extended to include sexual activity, whether it is more vigorous in hotter colder regions.[69] Albertus was perhaps influenced in introducing this topic by his reading of the sexual map of the world in Ptolemy's *Tetrabiblos*. This concern extends to the greater hotness of black women.[70] Albertus introduces, into the topic of the characteristics of the Jews, science that is rooted in humoral medicine: the dominance in their bodies of *melancholia*.[71] This is of course utterly distinct from the science that has been at issue so far – the elementary qualities of hot/cold and dry/damp, within medical climatic-regional theory. But it should not be excluded from our discussion. In his attention to *both* the sexual heat of black women and the dominance of melancholia in Jewish bodies, Albertus was developing the scientific element in the proto-racial thought of this particular period. He was also making it seem a matter of wider contemporary opinion, as we shall see later.

These texts, these topics and these developments were to continue in the quodlibetic questions of the Arts faculty in Paris. Although some of the questions were commonplace and one or two might have been partly rooted in non-proto-racial concerns, the dense clustering of these questions is significant in itself. Topics raised and answered included whether white men are bold, the causes of (Ethiopian) curly hair, whether a white or black woman desires a man more, whether men in cold regions are bolder than those in hot, whether women in hot regions are more inclined to sex, and whether the milk of a white nurse is better than that of a black.[72] And they further developed the medical-scientific account of the physical and moral characteristics of Jews. This is parallelled in medical writing from Montpellier, in Bernard de Gordon's *Lilium medicine*.

---

[69] *Quaestiones de animalibus*, vii.28, pp. 183–4: 'Quare homines in locis calidis sunt minoris quantitatis et minoris fortitudinis et audaciae quam in frigidis'; v.8, p. 158: 'Utrum operatio coitus magis vigeat in regione calida vel frigida'.

[70] *Quaestiones de animalibus*, xv.19, p. 271: 'Et tale sperma magis invenitur in feminis nigros, quae se prae omnibus aliis magis supponunt, quam albis; quia nigrae sunt calidiores, et maxime fuscae, quae sunt dulcissimae ad supponendum, ut dicunt leccatores, et quia temperatum habent os vulvae, quod suaviter amplectitur virgam'. This is discussed further in Biller, 'Black Women'.

[71] See discussion in Biller, '"Scientific" view of Jews', 143–4; the relevant texts are reproduced at 159–60.

[72] Paris, BnF, MS lat. 16089, fol. 57vb: 'Consequenter queritur utrum homines albi sint audaces'; fol. 60ra: 'Utrum capud crispitudo generatur a calido'; fol. 63ra: 'Alia questio fuit utrum mulier alba magis appetit uirum quam nigra'; fol. 63vb: 'Alia fuit utrum homines in regionibus frigidis sint audaciores quam in calidis'; fols 63vb–64ra: 'Alia fuit utrum mulieres regionibus calidis sint magis coitiue'; fol. 74vb: 'Consequenter queritur utrum lac nutricis albe sit melius quam lac nutricis nigre'.

The predominance of *melancholia* in their bodies is connected with several physical causes (specific diet, lack of bodily movement and laziness) and effects (lechery, withdrawal from society and timorousness).[73]

In the section on regions in his *Speculum introductionum medicinalium*, another Montpellier author, Arnau de Vilanova, produced a quite long account of black men. Like Albertus, he painted a new picture out of older materials. These people are short, shaped like monkeys and black. They are quick to anger, slow to calm down, uncivilized in their mores, quickly apprehensive, precipitous in judgement and impetuous. Frightened of wounds and bloodshed, they are therefore inclined to resist enemies by trickery rather than war. Though they eat sparingly, they engage in lust frequently, bestially engaging in sex with anyone or anything, regardless of gender, age or species. Though physically weak, they are agile in jumping and running.[74]

To recapitulate: whereas the backcloth is the reception and diffusion of ancient ideas, we see in the foreground some new emphases, such as the naturalness of whiteness, and two new conceptions, the hot black woman and the scientific account of Jewish characteristics. 'Advanced' texts such as Arnau's and the cluster of Paris Arts quodlibetic questions point to a marked increase in the 'scientization' of proto-racial thought, and also to a perceptibly darker note being struck in the images of Jews and black people.

The Paris quodlibet on Jews had a clear resonance in the realities of the contemporary world. Its pejorative view of Jews was raised and debated in a Paris which contained Jews and a climate of discussion and politics that was leading up to their expulsion in 1306. However, the context of the ever more degraded view of black people is elusive. Most of the inhabitants of Latin Christendom had never seen black Africans and the broad association of the latter with slavery lay in the future. This problem introduces the final part of the account whose prospectus is offered in this chapter. Prodigious efforts have been made in the last forty years to drag medieval academic thought away from the ancient

---

[73] This is discussed and analysed in Biller, '"Scientific" view of Jews', and the texts are reproduced at 160–3.

[74] Arnau de Vilanova, *Speculum introductionum medicinalium*, c. 87: De regionibus, in *Opera nuperrime revisa* (Lyon, 1532), fol. 26ra–b: 'Meridionales ut plurimum parvi sunt in statura et in forma symi et in colore nigri, veloces ad iram et tarde placabiles, inciviles moribus, facillime apprehensiores, precipites in iudicio et habentes impetuosam audaciam; vulnera tamen et effusionem sanguinis valde timent, natura sibi conscia paucitatis imprimente timorem illum propter quod ingeniis plus quam bello student resistere suis hostibus. Sunt etiam in cibo parcissimi, modicum valde comedentes, licet frequenter luxuriam vero bestialiter exercent, nec sexum nec etatem nec speciem attendentes. Et fragiles quidem sunt viribus sed agiles proinde ad cursum et saltum promptissimi.'

stereotype of its abstraction from the realities of the contemporary world. In this spirit, the account would ask, finally, how we can try to concretize medieval scientific thought about peoples. Our account has constructed a model, one that resembles a past body of thought as far as the evidence and a scholar's wit allow. But what can be done with this model? If we wind up its clockwork engine, where will it go? What can we suggest about its movements among – or relations to – the minds of later medieval people?

'Influence on minds': this chapter has already outlined one line of influence. Through the expanding university system of the high and later middle ages, this range of vocabulary and topics became the commonplaces of the minds of Arts and Medicine students, alongside the vocabulary and concepts of the humours and elementary qualities. Our earlier survey of resource-books used by mendicant friars introduced another line of influence. Much of a modern scholarly account of these encyclopaedias has to deal with what is immediately tangible: the large number of extant manuscripts, their locations in medieval libraries and signs of their use, and their further dissemination later on through vernacular translations and printing. We must not forget, however, the larger past reality which is not so directly attested, namely the countless occasions of friars preaching (and using the science contained in these compendia) to the alert lay people of later medieval towns and cities. In the early fourteenth century there were about 40,000 Dominican and Franciscan friars, many of them preachers. Recently David d'Avray has presented the large number of mendicant friars and their countless sermon books as constituting a means of 'mass communication before print'. He compares their relentless hammering home of messages to newspapers incessantly dwelling on immigration. He argues powerfully that they affected the minds of the many.[75]

D'Avray is concerned with the friars delivering a message about marriage symbolism. It would of course be absurd to suggest that the friars were just as focussed on the material we have been surveying, that their deliberate objective was to get these scientific views across. No: science was a means, not an end. Encyclopaedias and compendia were treasuries, resource-books, used to provide the material of images and similitudes in sermons whose objective was the mass communication of doctrines and moral lessons. It is reasonable to conjecture that a large amount of the material used in this subordinate fashion also got into the minds of the many.

---

[75] David L. d'Avray, *Medieval Marriage: Symbolism and Society* (Oxford: Oxford University Press, 2005), chapter 1.

The model held up so far is one of influence going in one direction. It is easy to *think* of another model – were the minds of ordinary people so passive? What ideas were in some ways already there, and therefore not to be seen as conjured into existence by preaching friars, or the radiation of vocabulary and ideas from Arts and Medicine graduates?

It is obvious that lack of evidence makes it *almost* impossible to do anything. Still, let us try two ploys. First of all, what we do know comes in the writings of the literate religious, monks and friars. If we turn to a different range of texts produced by them – sermons, didactic treatises, chronicles – what material on the physical characteristics of peoples can we find that is *not* religious? Let us take Jews in the thirteenth century in England, Germany and France. The exercise resembles looking for needles in haystacks, simply because our authors were 'religious'. But there *are* some needles to be found. The St Albans monk Matthew Paris (d. 1259) on one occasion referred to the *facies Judaica*, 'Jewish face'.[76] Around 1270 sermons were being delivered in Paris in which Jews were described as having physical weakness in their hands, preventing them from doing proper work; they were also cowards.[77] In a work of spiritual instruction compiled around 1219–23, the German Cistercian monk Caesarius of Heisterbach referred to *foetor judaicus*, while a little later one of the sermons of the German Franciscan Berthold of Regensburg (d. 1272) contained the vernacular phrase *ein stinkender Jude*.[78] While we can at least suggest that the notion of a 'Jewish face' was more widely shared in thirteenth-century England, because of the survival of carica-tures doodled by Chancery clerks,[79] we can do no more than ask a question about smell in Germany and weak hands in France. Was the culture of the literate religious in France and Germany in advance of or correlating with or under the influence of the vocabulary of ordinary French and German people?

[76] *Chronica Majora*, ed. Henry Richard Luard, 7 vols, Rolls Series 57 (London, 1873–85), vol. 2, p. 562. See another example in Arnoul of Lisieux, *De schismate*, iii, *Patrologia Latina* 201, col 180.

[77] Nicole Bériou, *L'avènement des maîtres de la Parole: La prédication à Paris au XIIIe siècle*, 2 vols, Collection des Études Augustiniennes, Série Moyen Âge et Temps Modernes 31 (Paris: Institut d'études augustiniennes, 1998), vol. 1, pp. 378–80, and vol. 2, pp. 783–4.

[78] Caesarius of Heisterbach, *Dialogus miraculorum*, ii.25, 2 vols, ed. Joseph Strange (Cologne, Bonn, and Brussels: Sumptibus J. M. Heberle [H. Lempertz & comp.], 1851), vol. 1, p. 96; Rudolf Cruel, *Geschichte der deutschen Predigt im Mittelalter* (Detmold: Meyer'sche Hofbuchhandlung, 1879), p. 621.

[79] Bernhard Blumenkranz, *Le juif médiéval au miroir de l'art Chrétien* (Paris: Etudes augustiniennes, 1966), p. 32. See Ruth Mellinkoff, *Outcasts: Signs of Otherness in Northern European Art of the Later Middle Ages*, 2 vols (Berkeley, Los Angeles and Oxford: University of California Press, 1993), vol. 1, pp. 127–8.

Our second ploy is to return to the friars' audiences, and to mull over and ponder the later medieval compendia that were compiled by and for the friars who talked to them. One starting point is provided by a literary commonplace about human curiosity, provided by the anonymous author of one compendium of scientific knowledge about bodies and the world, *Omnes homines*. He chose to invoke natural human curiosity about such things, beginning his work with the opening words of Aristotle's *Metaphysics*, 'all men naturally desire to know'. What follows in the text, a sequence of questions and answers, constituted in itself a formal literary counterpart of this commonplace about human beings asking questions and wanting answers, as did also the title of Conrad von Halberstadt's compendium of questions and answers, *Responsory to the Curious*. Conrad's preface spells out the rationale of his collection of scientific data. His fellow Dominicans mingle among 'laymen of all estates'. In order to be better received among them, these friars will find it useful to have a compendium of scientific knowledge about bodies and the natural world, which is what laymen are interested in.[80]

If Conrad's preface suggests a topic that is partly confined to literary analysis (of a tradition of rhetorical commonplaces in such introductions), it also points to a *reality*, that of the audiences for Dominican sermons. It hints at the divide between the aims of the friars and the interests of those who were listening. The religious men who were the friars (*religious* was the medieval name for monks and friars, not for anyone who was pious) were concerned to hammer home doctrinal truths and moral lessons, while what really interested ordinary people was the ordinary world seen in natural or scientific terms rather than through the lens of religion. The conjecture follows: that where ordinary people's minds turned to the characteristics of peoples, religion may not have played as large a part as it did in the texts and minds of the literate clerical elite.

Let us turn to one striking characteristic of Albertus's *Questions* and Pietro d'Abano's commentary on the *Problems*: the scattering of references to the characteristics of particular named peoples, sometimes with attribution of these thoughts in phrases such as 'as many say'. Caution is needed. The references are few. Any particular example may have an earlier textual root that has not been identified. The 'many' may be

---

[80] Conrad von Halberstadt, *Responsorium*, fol. 15r: '<Q>uia multi homines libenter de raris et curiosis querunt et delectabiliter audiunt et loquuntur, ideo ut fratres nostri predicatores quos frequenter apud homines diversorum statuum et condicionum esse oportet inter eos gratius conversentur quo ad talia valeant aptius respondere et de talibus sciunt etiam convenientius conferre, presens opusculum quod de raris et curiosis questionibus ex diversis breviter compilavi.'

another group of scholastics rather than common people. The names of peoples are in a continuum with names taken from older texts (above all Scythians and Ethiopians). The proposition is usually a commonplace. It may also be mainly an exercise in wit.

Nevertheless, let us take as an example two adjacent *Questions* of Albertus, where he raises comparisons of peoples in hot, cold, damp and dry regions. Naming begins with Avicenna's Ethiopians, old at thirty. It continues in a proposition about eating, viz. that digestive capacity is larger in cold regions. A Pole or a German eats in one day what a Lombard or Frenchman eats in four days. Naming occurs again in connection with the bodily size and courage of different peoples. Men are of larger size and boldness in Germany, Flanders and Poland. Although this is attributed to Avicenna, Albertus then invokes what is said *vulgariter*. 'It is said *vulgariter*, that men of hot regions are naturally timid, and inept for war.' If men of hot regions are bold, 'they are inordinately and rashly bold, and they quickly give up, like the French, who do wonderful things at the beginning and nothing at the end, and in French people like this are called *hardi*, bold'.[81] Albertus's sarcasm about the word *hardi* and his *Bild Zeitung* views of the French seem clear, as does also Albertus's use of *vulgariter*, combining 'commonly' and 'in the vernacular'.

Albertus intends a juxtaposition of two sorts of opinion, one from a learned authority and another from common opinion, by implication not ancient, authoritative, textual and Latin. The quotation attributed to Avicenna cannot be found – and if Albertus invented it, this underlines the polarity at which he was aiming. The opinion that is juxtaposed to Avicenna's is held 'commonly', it is backed up by quotation of a French word in an exercise of heavy humour, and it is made a contemporary matter. Above all, this common contemporary view holds that the characteristics of these peoples are theirs according to nature, *naturaliter*. Both ancient learned opinion and contemporary common opinion ground the characteristics of peoples in nature.

We conclude here, repeating the point that the usual situation of the modern historian of medieval thought is to know a great deal about the ideas of the tiny elite of Latin-literate men, and virtually nothing about the thoughts that were in the minds of ordinary people. The final

[81] Albertus Magnus, *Quaestiones*, vii.28, pp. 183–4: 'Oppositum patet per Avicennam. Dicit enim, quod in Alemannia et Flandria et Polonia, quae sunt loca frigida, homines sunt magnae quantitatis et audaciae. Dicitur enim vulgariter, quod homines calidae regionis sunt naturaliter timidi et ad bella inepti ... Sed in hominibus regionis calidae calor dispergitur et, si intendatur, hoc est per accidens per calorem accidentalem et inordinantum. Unde si sint audaces, hoc est inordinate et cum impetus et cito desistunt, ut Gallici, qui volunt facere mirabilia in principio et in fine nulla, et tales vocantur "hardi" in Gallico.'

point in this prospectus is that one important task in a longer account would be to put under the microscope every point of possible of contact between academic and non-academic thought, in order to investigate the degree to which common people's proto-racial thought also had a strong 'natural' element.

8   Physiognomy, science, and proto-racism 1200–1500

Joseph Ziegler

One of the important sources for medieval and renaissance Latin physiognomy which reemerged in the twelfth century after almost seven centuries of neglect and oblivion is *De physiognomonia liber* by Marcus Antonius Polemon of Laodicea, probably written in Greek in the fourth decade of the second century and preserved in a ninth-century Arabic translation. It is available today, in a modern Latin translation based on a 1356 Arabic manuscript made in Damascus and kept now in Leiden, in two manuscripts of a different recension of the text now in the library of the Topkapı Sarayı museum in Istanbul, in a fourth-century Greek paraphrastic epitome by Adamantius the Sophist, and incorporated into an anonymous fourth-century Latin treatise known as *Anonymus latinus*. Georg Hoffmann, who edited Polemon's physiognomy book for Richard Förster's edition of the Greek and Latin physiognomic texts, translated the title of chapter 35: 'On the Greeks and their pure race' (*De Graecis et eorum genere puro*),[1] which perhaps echoes the nineteenth-century marriage of physiognomy and racism. But it essentially conforms to the content of the chapter, which introduces the Greek Ionic man (*al-yūnānī* in the Arabic translation)[2] as the physiognomic ideal type (medium stature, firm and erect, broad-shouldered, square face, slim lips, straight and evenly proportioned nose, and, perhaps most importantly, of pure

---

[1] *Scriptores physiognomonici graeci et latini*, ed. Richard Förster (Stuttgart and Leipzig: Teubner, 1893), I, pp. 242–4. See also Robert Hoyland's new translation and edition in Simon Swain (ed.), *Seeing the Face, Seeing the Soul: Polemon's Physiognomy from Classical Antiquity to Medieval Islam* (Oxford: Oxford University Press, 2007), p. 427 ("Regarding the Greeks and the Pure Race among Them"). For the problematic use of "race" when translating the Latin word *gens* or the Greek γένος see Susan Reynolds, *Kingdoms and Communities in Western Europe 900–1300* (Oxford: Clarendon Press, 1984), p. 255 and "Our Forefathers? Tribes, Peoples, and Nations in the Historiography of the Age of Migration", in Alexander Callander Murray (ed.), *After Rome's Fall: Narrators and Sources of Early Medieval History. Essays Presented to Walter Goffart* (Toronto: University of Toronto Press, 1998), pp. 17–36 (25–6, 31).

[2] Simon Swain, "Polemon's Physiognomy", in Swain, *Seeing the Face*, pp. 197–9 (which discusses Greek concepts of national and racial purity with respect to Romans) and pp. 200–1 (which discusses the Islamic perception of Greek racial purity).

breeding). Its beauty, owing to a perfect form and proportions, and its consequent superiority also derive from its biological purity (the word *purus*/καθαρώς appears three times in this short chapter). The matter is repeated in chapter B32 in *The Physiognomy* of Adamantius the Sophist who produced in the fourth century an abridgement of Polemon's treatise.[3]

Benjamin Isaac analysed classical physiognomy in general and this story in particular as evidence of distinct clear tendencies of "the denial of individuality and variation both between individuals and generations, so typical of racist thinking".[4] It is indeed tempting to present eighteenth- and nineteenth-century racist physiognomy, which embraced some of the ancient physiognomic approaches and theories, as a product or a mere continuation or perhaps fruition, of ancient influences. But when it comes to the history of physiognomy, looking at the much-neglected medieval and early renaissance period sheds intriguing light on the direct relationship between ancient and modern physiognomy. Below I first survey my findings on ethnic or racist physiognomy in learned physiognomy from 1200 to 1500, and then try to explain why the available concepts describing the biological transmission of character could not constitute a solid foundation for a racist theory. In other words, the development of ancient physiognomy into racist physiognomy was not one-way. For over 300 years classical physiognomy flourished in Western scientific thought in a way that reinforced rather than denied individuality and variation. While some regard physiognomy as an irrational belief, hence a pseudo-science, I treat medieval and early renaissance physiognomy as a rational science, because this is how contemporary thinkers treated it.[5] Critique and suspicion of physiognomy left their mark, but some of the brightest minds in politics, natural philosophy, medicine, and theology (Albertus Magnus, Giles of Rome, John Buridan, Pietro d'Abano, Rolandus Scriptor) cultivated the study and practice of this body of knowledge. Their work supplied classical physiognomy with the missing part, namely a theoretical, explanatory framework for the physiognomic signs, whose absence had ignited the most devastating criticism by people like Pliny and Galen.

First back to Polemon, one of the main sources of late-medieval and renaissance physiognomers such as Pietro d'Abano and Bartolomeo della

[3] Ian Repath, "*The Physiognomy* of Adamantius the Sophist", in Swain, *Seeing the Face*, p. 532.
[4] Benjamin Isaac, *The Invention of Racism in Classical Antiquity* (Princeton and Oxford: Princeton University Press, 2004), pp. 161–2.
[5] Joseph Ziegler, "Philosophers and Physicians on the Scientific Validity of Latin Physiognomy, 1200–1500", *Early Science and Medicine* 12.3 (2007), 285–312.

Rocca Cocles. A chapter like chapter 35 is not found in any of the Latin physiognomic texts until at least 1500. All the medieval discussions of the well-tempered person who is well bred and has an ideal physiognomic portrait, hence an ideal character, ignore the existence of an ethnic ideal type. Greek physiognomers sought signs deviating from the ideal Greek type, a quest that derived from an ethnocentric approach holding that Greece and Ionia were the geographical centre of the earth.[6] The non-Greek types included the Barbaric, and people from other climatic zones such as Ethiopians, Egyptians, and Scythians. Consequently, ancient physiognomy has most recently been described as an important factor of Greek and Roman stereotypical thinking.[7] None of this can be detected in medieval physiognomy. Since it is unclear what part of Polemon's physiognomy was actually available to thinkers in the medieval West, it is impossible to determine with certainty whether this was a deliberate omission or when exactly it happened (it may already have been a fourth-century development). But the conspicuous absence of a physiognomic discourse reinforcing the superiority of one ethnic group deserves an explanation. Was there an alternative physiognomic ideal type for the medieval person? Indeed there was, and a rather surprising one.

According to the physician Michele Savonarola (towards 1450), two of the foremost characteristics of the well-tempered person (*homo temperatus*) were a well proportioned mixture of white and red colour, combined with fine, brilliant skin.[8] Savonarola linked the description of the well-tempered person who was well proportioned and characterized by *mediocritas* – the key physiognomic category for the ideal personality – to the widely disseminated thirteenth-century Latin text describing the face of Christ along what seem to be clearly physiognomic lines.[9] This description, which Savonarola transcribed in full immediately after he identified the bodily signs of the well-tempered person as well as those of the

---

[6] Maud W. Gleason, *Making Men: Sophists and Self-Presentation in Ancient Rome* (Princeton: Princeton University Press, 1995), pp. 29–54 (33).

[7] Isaac, *Invention*, pp. 149–63.

[8] Michele Savonarola, *Speculum physonomie*, Paris, BnF, MS lat. 7357, fol. 54rb.

[9] On the history of this text, which is a thirteenth-century invention reflecting the growing distance between Eastern (Byzantine) and Western representations of the face of Christ, see Ernst von Dobschütz, *Christusbilder. Untersuchungen zur christlichen Legende* (Leipzig: J. C. Hinrichs, 1899), vol. II, pp. 308–30 [*Texte und Untersuchungen zur Geschichte der Altchristlichen Literatur*, ed. Oskar von Gebhardt and Adolf Harnack, vol. III NF, Bd. III]. For more evidence on the physiognomic context of this literary portrait see Joseph Ziegler, "Text and Context: On the Rise of Physiognomic Thought in the Later Middle Ages", in Yitzhak Hen (ed.), *De Sion Exibit Lex et Verbum Domini de Hierusalem. Essays on Medieval Law, Liturgy and Literature in honour of Amnon Linder* (Turnhout: Brepols, 2001), pp. 159–82 (170–2), and "Skin and Character in Medieval and Early Renaissance Physiognomy", *Micrologus* 13 (2005), 511–35 (529–30).

philosopher (*homo sapiens*), included the assertion that Christ's face was without a wrinkle or any spot, and that a moderate touch of red beautified it. The imaginary skin of Christ, his medium-sized and erect stature, his moderately straight hair, and his blue, variegated or changeable and bright eyes thus became the model for the ideal body which contains the morally perfect personality. Like Adam he enjoyed a perfectly balanced complexion,[10] which rendered him the handsomest in all mankind (*speciosus inter filios hominum*).

So for the medieval physiognomer the ideal physiognomic type (characterized by a perfectly balanced complexion as attested by a perfectly proportioned body, hence perfect character and behaviour) was not an individual belonging to a specific ethnic group. It was Christ – a super-national second Adam, representative of mankind in general. Consequently, medieval physiognomy was generally non-ethnic. Its basic unit of reference was the human being (*homo*) so that physiognomic texts between 1200 and 1500 can easily be described as universally humanistic.[11] This reading of the nexus physiognomy/racism in the Latin medieval world is at variance with Steven Epstein's view that the legacy of ancient physiognomy to the Middle Ages was a form of racism that still valued or devalued people on the basis of skin colour and even the colour of the iris.[12] Epstein further maintains that colour prejudice did take the form of a sustaining ideology and was deeply ingrained in Western culture at least from the eleventh century onwards and coexisted with the belief in the universalizing effects of baptism.[13] His study attempts to show how the fates of mixed relationships demonstrate the underlying durability of the prescribed divisions among people. Darkness imposed images of evil on anyone who could be perceived as black and the diverse Mediterranean world trained people to see human difference in terms of colour. Epstein detects the long history of colour prejudice and suggests that dark skin colour during the Middle Ages became a way to justify oppression. The language of physiognomy became the best way to

---

[10] Here and throughout this essay complexion or temperament is the balance of the elementary qualities of hot, wet, cold, and dry in the body. It is unique for each person.

[11] One could expect the exclusion of women from such texts. But even in this respect medieval physiognomy is more open and attentive than its classical model.

[12] Steven A. Epstein, *Purity Lost: Transgressing Boundaries in the Eastern Mediterranean, 1000–1400* (Baltimore: The Johns Hopkins University Press, 2007), p. 183. See also Maaike van der Lugt, "La peau noire dans la science médiévale", *Micrologus* 13 (2005), 439–75 (at 447) who maintains that the medico-physiognomic model of skin colour concerns the individual rather than groups. It refers only to the white man and hence has nothing to do with the modern classification of human races.

[13] See above Denise K. Buell's contribution which challenges the idea that Christianity's universalizing claims protected society from racism.

discuss human difference in terms that referred to meaningful signs like the eyes or the colour of the skin. This literal valuing of people crossed beyond simple colour symbolism or even prejudice into a way of thinking that closely resembled modern forms of racism, in a vocabulary suited to the times. Faces and colour proved to be the best clues indicating the deeper unalterable truths. Nothing from physiognomy, he concludes, taught strong lessons about human equality.[14]

I do not maintain that people ignored ethnic specificities in the shape of the body and in their mentalities. But in the texts of learned physiognomy they always remained marginal digressions. Let me quickly summarize the sort of material one can find in these texts.

First there were recurrent references to the Aristotelian, Pseudo-Aristotelian and Hippocratic north/south divide in bodily shape and in character. Northerners (often called *Teutonici* or *Sclavi*) were regarded as naturally brave and daring (*fortes audaces*) as well as intellectually capable, while Southerners (Ethiopians) were deemed timid. It was stressed that this was due to the Northeners' essentially hotter complexion than the Southerners'. The key to this paradoxical phenomenon was the belief that cutaneous pores in the north were constricted by the cold exterior, preventing the natural heat from leaving the internal organs, for it was not attracted by its like (external heat). The opposite applied in the case of the open pores in hot regions, through which internal heat was sucked out by the external heat.

Then there were local physiognomic traits which applied to particular groups in specific political environments. Thus, Italian physiognomers were fond of allotting behavioural traits to inhabitants of specific Italian cities. According to the Bolognese physiognomer Bartolomeo della Rocca Cocles (d. 1504), every town and province in Italy has a specific characteristic which is occasionally caused or reflected by bodily structure. The Lombard people of Modena are foolish or have a fiery brain (hence inclined to violence). Ruled by asinine character, the people of Siena and Ferrara are uncultivated or rude. Lombardy normally confers upon its inhabitants liberality and fidelity. Tuscany imposes on its inhabitants infidelity and avarice. But at the end Cocles reiterates that the most significant variable determining one's character is the parental contribution, which determines, for example, that stupidity runs in the family.[15] The Tuscan head, according to Pietro d'Abano and his commentator Rolandus Scriptor, is long and mallet-shaped, which makes Tuscans

---

[14] Epstein, *Purity Lost*, pp. 201–3.

[15] Bartolomeo della Rocca Cocles, *Chiromantie ac physionomie anastasis cum approbatione magistri Alexandri de Achillinis* (Bologna, 1504), I.7 (henceforth Cocles, *Anastasis*).

cautious and prudent. This shape allows the spirit carrying the images of imagination, judgement, and memory to pause, and devote due time to every intellectual stage.[16]

Along the same line of argumentation, a spherical head is a distinguishing mark of the French, according to Pietro d'Abano and Rolandus Scriptor. It is related to poor judgement and memory since the head's roundish shape creates an excessively mobile spirit.[17] Particular national groups have characteristics that often defy the standard meaning of the physiognomic sign. The English are courageous (*viri animosi*) even though their hair is soft (normally a sign of timidity, being associated with a combination of extreme cold and moisture). Despite the cold and moist climatic conditions, the English body is robust and the English are audacious. The Germans (*alemani*), who live in cold and dry climatic conditions, have thick, rough, and darker hair because of internal heat, which coexists with the external cold air. The hair of Indians is soft and pleasant, so they are consequently timid and their bodies are weak because of the distemperate climate and the weak innate heat.[18] From the second third of the thirteenth century lists of proto-national stereotypes appear in a variety of literary texts, mainly in polemical contexts. These stereotypes refer to English drinking habits and deviant sexual mores, to French pride, to German fury, to Scottish treachery, to Burgundian brutishness and stupidity, to Lombard avarice, to Roman violence or to Sicilian cruelty.[19]

---

[16] Rolandus Scriptor, *Reductorium physonomie*, in Lisbon, Biblioteca Ajuda, MS 52.XIII.18, fol. 56v.

[17] Rolandus, *Reductorium*, fols 51v–52r.

[18] Savonarola, *Speculum*, fol. 18vb; Rolandus, *Reductorium*, fol. 49r–v.

[19] According to Jacques de Vitry, *Historia occidentalis*, c. vii: De statu parisiensis ciuitatis, in John Frederick Hinnebusch (ed.), *The Historia Occidentalis of Jacques de Vitry: A Critical Edition*, Spicilegium Friburgense 17 (Fribourg: The University Press, 1972), p. 92, the polemic environment in Paris was characterized by ethnic abuse which accompanied the academic disputations:

> multas contra se contumelias et obprobria impudenter proferebant, anglicos potatores et caudatos affirmantes, francigenas superbos, molles et muliebriter compositos asserentes, teutonicos furibundos et in conuiuiis suis obscenos dicebant, normanos autem inanes et gloriosos, pictauos proditores et fortune amicos. Hos autem qui de Burgundia erant brutos et stultos reputabant. Britones autem leues et uagos iudicantes, Arturi mortem frequenter eis obiciebant. Lombardos auaros, malitiosos et imbelles; romanos seditiosos, uiolentos et manus rodentes, siculos tyrannos et crudeles; brabantios uiros sanguinum, incendiarios, rutarios et raptores; flandrenses superfluos, prodigos, comessationibus deditos, et more butyri molles et remissos, appellabant.

See also Benoît Grevin, "De la rhétorique des nations à la théorie des races: L'influence des théories scientifiques sur la pensée des stéréotypes nationaux à partir du XIII⁰ siècle", at http://gas.ehess.fr/document.php?id=106.

The infiltration of such stereotypes into medieval physiognomic discourse is hardly detectable.[20]

The observation of menstruating Jewish men, which appears in two different versions in the physiognomy of Michael Scotus and of Michele Savonarola, is to my knowledge the only reference to Jews in the learned medieval physiognomic treatises.[21] I found no reference to the Saracens. The Mongols (or Tartars) appear only once. None of the literary descriptions of the Tartars (stressing their small stature, short legs, broad face and space between the eyes, high cheekbones, eyes covered with lids, almost hairless face, their flat nose (*simus nasus*) and their peculiar eyes – all signs which were loaded with physiognomic significance) includes a physiognomic judgement of the race. The Western observers were content to suggest uncritically that these were signs of a beastly, foul (*turpissimi*), and inhuman group, but in doing so they could not rely on a learned analysis by physiognomers.[22] The sole reference I found in medieval physiognomic texts to the Tartars is when the physician and physiognomer Rolandus Scriptor discusses flat nose (*simus nasus*), normally a sign of impetuosity and lust, for it was related to extreme bodily heat and moisture at the stage of organ formation. Curly hair was often found to coexist with flat nose. This was the case among the Moors and Tartars, whose sperm was consumed by the extreme heat in the territory they inhabited, and their blood was blackened. The disturbed spirits and vapours responsible for the curliness of the hair also introduced a characteristic common to both peoples: the smoothness (*lenitas*) of facial and cranial skin. This,

---

[20] For the infiltration of these national stereotypes into early-modern physiognomy see Peter Burke, "Frontiers of the Monstrous: Perceiving National Characters in Early Modern Europe", in Laura Lunger Knoppers and Joan B. Landes (eds.), *Monstrous Bodies / Political Monstrosities in Early Modern Europe* (Ithaca: Cornell University Press, 2004), pp. 25–39 (at 32).

[21] Peter Biller, "A 'Scientific' View of Jews from Paris around 1300", *Micrologus* 9 (2001), 137–68 (141 n. 3). See also Maria Garbaczowa, "Mikołaja z Brzegu Komentarz do *De physionomia* Pseudo-Arystotelesa w Zbiorach Rękopiśmiennych Biblioteki Jagiellońskiej", *Studia Mediewistyczne* 19/2 (1978), 127–64 at 160 (ch. 14) for the reappearance of the allegation in the scholastic commentary on Pseudo-Aristotle's physiognomy by the Krakow theologian Nicolai de Brega (*c.* 1440). For a broader discussion of Jewish physiognomy in the Middle Ages see Irven Resnick's forthcoming *Marks of Distinction: Christian Perceptions of Jews in the High Middle Ages*.

[22] Simon de St-Quentin, *Histoire des Tartares*, ed. J. Richard (Paris, 1965), XXXII. 71, p. 31; Felix Faber, *Evagatorium in terrae sanctae, arabiae et Egypti peregrinationem*, ed. Conrad Dieterich Hassler, 2 vols (Stuttgart: sumtibus Societatis literariæ stuttgardiensis, 1843–49), II. 40; Johannes de Plano Carpini, *Storia dei Mongoli*, ed. Paolo Daffinà, Claudio Leonardi, Maria Cristiana Lungarotti, Enrico Menestò, and Luciano Petech (Spoleto: Centro italiano di studi sull'alto Medioevo, 1989), p. 32. For the representation of Tartars in medieval art see Debra Higgs Strickland, *Saracens, Demons, and Jews: Making Monsters in Medieval Art* (Princeton and Oxford: Princeton University Press, 2003), pp. 192–200. I am indebted to Felicitas Schmieder for many of the references in this note.

however, was not associated with positive behavioural traits normally connected to smooth facial skin, but with lust and impetuosity.[23] Similarly missing from physiognomic texts are references to the Gypsies, whose dark skin, shrivelled face, curly hair, and general ugliness appeared typically in eyewitnesses' accounts which also occasionally stressed their preoccupation with chiromantic practices.[24]

Some physiognomic distinguishing marks were class-specific. Unculti-vated peasants (*rudes rustici*) were intellectually incapacitated (*insensibiles, male intelligentes*), hence marked with copious hard flesh (*caro dura et habituosa*).[25] But this does not amount to a systematic attempt by the learned physiognomers to categorize groups (social or ethnic) according to distinctive physiognomic signs. It is therefore wrong to draw the learned physiognomy of the later Middle Ages into the debates about the virulent delegitimization of non-Christian minorities. The distinctive features of Jewish faces in thirteenth- and fourteenth-century iconography cannot be physiognomical in the sense that they draw on specific physiognomic texts and theory. The prominent hooked nose which often identifies the Jew in medieval illuminations simply did not appear as such in texts of learned physiognomy. At most one can venture the vague hypothesis that the rise of physiognomic thought highlighted the bodily shape/human character nexus, and that consequently artists were inclined to adopt specific icono-graphic codes when depicting members of enemy minority groups.

Racist or proto-racist thought must entail some sort of scientific doc-trine acceptable to contemporary thinkers and explaining how a man's behaviour and character are inherently constant and unchangeable through human will. Could not the newly emerging theory explaining causally the relationship between bodily sign and behavioural pattern (the great contribution of late-medieval thinkers to the science of physiog-nomy) provide the hinge on which a racist type of physiognomy would turn? It was after all a material process based in physical spirits and blood which essentially determined how a human being was formed and later developed.[26]

---

[23] Rolandus, *Reductorium*, fol. 105v: "Istud apparet in tartaris et mauris. In quibus ex natura regionis calide nimis comburentis sperma et denigrantis etiam et sanguinem formationis, constituto cerebro secundum naturam frigido respectu aliorum membrorum implentis caput potissime propter erectionem figure, talibus vaporibus et spiritus turbantis. capilli crispantur cum quadam lenitate cutis capitis et faciei potissime."

[24] For the 1427 arrival of the Gypsies to Paris see Alexandre Tuetey (ed.), *Journal d'un bourgeois de Paris (1405–1449)* (Geneva: Slatkin Reprints, 1975), 468, p. 220. I am grateful to Jean-Patrice Boudet for this reference.

[25] William of Mirica, Oxford, Bodleian Library, MS Can. Misc. 350, fol. 85v.

[26] The following discussion is a concise summary of the theoretical debate in Rolandus, *Reductorium*, fols. 26r–28r and Savonarola, *Speculum*, fols. 60va–61ra.

According to this theory, innate formative spirit (*innatus seu complanta-tus*) mixed with frothy moisture (*spumosa humiditas*) forms the heart and consequently the other organs from blood, which is its passive agent. This spirit is responsible for the shape of all these organs. The diversity of the spirit and blood involved in this primary activity at the stage of foetal formation affects character traits, and not only the external shape of the body. In addition to the formative spirit each organ has an innate spirit, which is attributed to it at the moment of generation and through which the organ can start performing its activities. The bodily spirits, all materially defined as temperate vapour of blood (*uapor sanguinis temperatus*), are the primary instruments of the soul. They can be affected by food: for example, one wishing to increase the chances of generating males may take a proper heat-stimulating diet, which will induce the heating up of the sperm and the spirit.

The body's essential form (*forma corporeitatis*) is elemental, and the complexion and quality of the formative spirit determine in *hora formationis*, the period of formation of the embryo and the shape of the organs, which consequently are firmly linked to the behavioural patterns.[27] The formative spirit is constantly affected by natural and counter-natural things, and it transmits these influences to the animal's shape and character. Celestial movements affect the body's shape and the character traits. In addition, a purely material process, which takes place throughout the stage of foetal formation and is centred in the left ventricle of the heart – the first bodily organ to be formed – is the sole determinant of personality and bodily shape, which are closely interconnected. The innate formative spirit can be too hot, cold, dry, or moist, in which case it creates a similar configuration in the menstrual blood (the material-constructing component of the organs) and affects distinctive physical marks that signify specific personality flaws or virtues. Confusion and disturbance (*permixtio, commotio*) emerge from excessive heat; condensation or compression (*constrictio*) rise from excess cold.

Such a theory rendered inevitable tensions between the material concepts of complexion and formative spirit and the spiritual/religious concept of the soul as the cause for behavioural patterns. But there was always a way out. A person may be naturally disposed to anger by astral constellation or by the power of God, the creator of the soul, William of

---

[27] Rolandus, *Reductorium*, fol. 26r–v: "Quare igitur secundum diuersitatem ipsius spiritus sicut et esse forme variatur, ita et morum habituum et actuum magna fit alteritas. Et quia prima formarum diuersitas eductarum de materia formata forma corporeitatis est elementalis et elementorum. Ideo secundum diuersam complexionem qualitatemque spiritus diuersimode membra formantur et figurantur ut antea satis est declaratum. Quare et actus et mores variantur conformiter secundum hanc diuersitatem."

Mirica (the fourteenth-century commentator of Pseudo-Aristotle's *Physiognomy*) tells us, and Galen's words concerning the complexion of the heart as the fundamental explanation for the variety in behavioural patterns do not mean that complexion is the cause of natural character but rather its sign. Even though the search for causes of some bodily signs may lead one to complexion and the four qualities, the principal causes of character and behaviour will always remain in the souls, hence are preternatural.[28] When Dante asks in *Paradiso* VIII. 93 how "from sweet seed can come bitter fruit" and how a mean nature can descend from a generous one, he replies through the mouth of Charles Martel (d. 1295; the oldest son of Charles II of Naples, titular King of Hungary, and heir to Naples and Provence) that congenital character is not hereditary but comes by divine appointment through the stars. Through the celestial Intelligences controlling the spheres God, "the Primal intelligence", gives to all things and all souls the qualities suited to their use in His providence (*provedenza*). The stars give souls their individual temperament without regard to their family. So Esau differed in the womb from Jacob, and Romulus (Quirinus), a peasant's son, became the founder of Rome and was believed to be the son of Mars.

Interspersed in every medieval physiognomic text are various declarations, marks, and signs suggesting that physiognomy is about inclinations, not deterministic predispositions; that it is about teaching us what we are in order to enable us to resist what should be resisted.[29] One could wave aside these assertions saying that their writers were just paying lip service to ecclesiastical discomfort with the potential threat to free will lurking in physiognomy. But beyond the Christian barrier that prevented the racialization of physiognomy in the medieval period, another, perhaps as powerful, blocked this course: medieval thinkers (natural philosophers and physicians) lacked the notion of a solid, inherent, unalterable category to which they could anchor a belief in the biological inalterability of character. In what follows I shall examine the theoretical concepts shared

---

[28] William of Mirica, fol. 153r–v: "Unde quod aliquis naturaliter irascibilis vel mansuetus ex astris contingit saltem disposite et ex virtute dei creantis ipsas animas cum talibus virtutibus et possibilis que ultra requirit tales ver tales dispositiones corporis. Unde minor istius rationis falsa est que dicit. Quod dicit quod talis diuersitas non eueniat ex parte anime ad dictum Galeni dicendum quod ipse intendit declarare per complexionem cordis mores naturales non intelligens quod complexio sit causa morum naturalium, sed pocius signum. Sicut effectus significant suam causam et hoc dicendum intendit Hally. Vel potest dici quod licet aliqua signa reducantur in complexionem naturalem et per consequens in 4^{or} qualitates complexionales et similiter alique passiones signate reducantur in ipsas tamquam in causas inmediatas et contrarias. Anime tamen sunt cause earum principales et primarie..."

[29] Ziegler, "Text and Context", pp. 161–4.

by learned physiognomers, physicians, and natural philosophers when they discussed issues relating to the connection between body and soul, and more specifically between physical and mental characteristics.

Three key theoretical concepts which came to be used in Western medical and biological thought during the thirteenth century could potentially serve as a foundation for a scientific discussion of the biological transmission of individual and group characteristics.

The theory of pangenesis, that the seed comes from all parts of the body, gave scientists (at least since Hippocrates' *Airs, Waters, Places* 14) a physical basis for positing the inheritance of diseases as well as of acquired character.[30] It could provide thinkers with a reasonable physical mechanism for the inter-generational transmission of abnormalities within groups. But in opposition to its growing popularity from the sixteenth century onwards as an explanatory tool of bodily characteristics among national groups (possibly related to the revival of interest in Hippocratic writings among the humanists), the sporadic and inconsistent use of pangenesis theory in the Middle Ages, particularly from the thirteenth century (due mainly to the assimilation into the natural philosophical and medical discourses in the Latin West of Aristotle's reservations in *On the Generation of Animals* I.18, 725a), hampered linking it to a systematic explanation of the transmission of group characteristics. Aristotle's view in *On the Generation of Animals* I.17–20 that seed originates in the blood as a residual product derived from nourishment in its final form, and that it transmits not material but a source of movement and of development (the *virtus informativa* or *spiritus informativus*), elicited a set of questions among embryologists regarding the nature of the seed.[31] Common questions were: what is really in the seed? Does the male sperm enter the substance of the foetus? What part of the father's soul is in it, and how does it affect the child's soul? What exactly is the *virtus informativa* that emerges from the genitor's heart? I have found no debate about the transmission of mental or bodily characteristics among groups in the major embryological treatises of the thirteenth–fifteenth centuries.

---

[30] Conway Zirkle, "The Early History of the Idea of the Inheritance of Acquired Characters and of Pangenesis", *Transactions of the American Philosophical Society*, n.s 35.2 (1946), 91–147; Danielle Jacquart and Claude Thomasset, *Sexuality and Medicine in the Middle Ages*, trans. Matthew Adamson (Cambridge: Polity Press, 1988), pp. 53–5; Paivi Pahta, *Medieval Embryology in the Vernacular: The Case of* De Spermate (Helsinki: Société neo-philologique, 1998).

[31] For a general survey of the philosophical and medical discourses on embryology around 1300 see Joseph Ziegler, "The Scientific Context of Dante's Embryology", in John C. Barnes and J. Petrie (eds.), *Dante and the Human Body* (Dublin: Four Courts Press 2007), pp. 61–88.

The other two useful concepts, which became fundamental in medical theory from the second quarter of the thirteenth century, could perhaps also be used as an anchor to a stable and rigid theory for explaining the transmission of bodily and mental characteristics – a prerequisite for the development of a scientific racist approach to the differences between nations. First is the concept of radical moisture (*humidum radicale*), which was developed in classical antiquity and the Middle Ages to help explain the nature of life and the occurrence of aging and of fevers. The radical moisture or moistures was the term used by Avicenna to character- ize the fourth moisture, constitutive of the members since birth, and the subject of its natural heat (*humidum radicale*) is actually derived purely from the sperm of generation, hence is indistinguishable from the *humidum spermaticum* (Avicenna), or is only one of its constituent parts. One thing is clear: it is acquired in generation and our life fully depends upon its survival. Once it disappears (at the end of a long process of desiccation) we cease to be. But the radical moisture helped to explain the processes of aging and death; it was not used, to my knowledge, to explain the hereditary transmission of character and physical traits. This is clearly visible in *Libellus de humido radicali* of Arnau de Vilanova (active at Montpellier between 1292 and 1309 with a few intervals), which discusses two questions: first, is the *humidum radicale* actually derived purely from the sperm in generation? Second, can the *humidum radicale* be replen- ished, recreated by the process of nutrition? Nowhere in this unique treatise is the *humidum radicale* linked to the hereditary transmission of physical or intellectual traits.[32] Furthermore, throughout our lives we remain the same beings even though the radical moisture dwindles.

The second key concept in medical theory was that of complexion. It too could not provide a solid foundation for a biological/scientific elabo- ration of a racist theory. True, we are what we are as human beings and as individuals by virtue of our complexions, and complexion was defined by Avicenna as "the sum quality (*summa qualitas*) which emerges from the mutual action and passion of opposing elemental qualities within the

---

[32] Arnau de Vilanova, "Libellus de humido radicali", in *Opera* (Lyon, 1520), fols 38vb– 42va. Forthcoming as vol. V.2 in the series *Arnaldi de Villanova Opera Medica Omnia* (Granada/Barcelona: Seminarium Historiae Scientiae Barchinone (C.S.I.C.), 1975–) is a critical edition of the text accompanied by a detailed introduction and a commentary by Chiara Crisciani, Giovanna Ferrari, and Michael R. McVaugh. Still pertinent is Michael R. McVaugh, "The *Humidum Radicale* in Thirteenth-Century Medicine", *Traditio* 30 (1974), 259–83. See also chapter 87 of Arnau's *Speculum medicine* in *Opera*, fol. 26ra–b and discussed in Peter Biller's essay as an example for the infiltration of a proto-racist thought into medical discourse.

body",[33] and was hence a purely material category which determined our identity from birth and was affected by parental and environmental inputs.

One normally distinguished accidental or natural complexion (*complexio naturalis*), that is subjected to environmental and generational variables and, hence fluid and changeable, from the innate complexion (*complexio innata* or *radicalis*), that qualifies the generational process and its agents (i.e., the sperm and the menstrual blood) and is much more constant and less prone to change during one's lifetime.[34] In his commentary on Ps.-Aristotle's *Problem* XXX.1 (which discusses the famous connection between genius and melancholy complexion), Pietro d'Abano elaborates on the similarity between the behavioural and moral effects of wine and melancholy – an observation already made by the author of the Ps-Aristotelian *Problems*. While the effect of wine is temporary, nature effects through complexion long-lasting behavioural and moral traits. But here Pietro inserted a crucial warning and clarification:

Note that because of this [difference between wine and melancholy complexion] one should not conclude that natural complexion (*complexio naturalis*) could not be completely changed (*permutari*), and if character (*mores*) [could be changed] minimally, even though it follows the unalterable form [i.e., the rational soul], surely natural complexion remains subjected to transmutation and change.[35]

Well, so far so good. But what about the radical complexion? According to Pietro d'Abano, even the innate, radical complexion is subject to change.[36] Sanguine people can gradually become choleric; choleric can change into melancholic; and melancholic into phlegmatic. Fundamental complexional change may occur, gradually, within the given latitude, and from one complexion to the neighbouring one (so it is extremely difficult to convert from melancholy to sanguine complexion). A lapsing, innate imbalance of health (*discrasia lapsa*) can change into a temperate state through medical intervention, which would be useless without the

---

[33] Avicenna, *Liber canonis* (Venice, 1507), I.1.3.1, fol. 2ra: "qualitas que ex actione ad inuicem et passione contrariarum qualitatum in elementis inuentarum".

[34] Pietro d'Abano, *Conciliator* (Venice, 1565), diff. 17, fol. 26va: "Complexionem quoque innatam, seu radicalem audio, quae primo qualificat principia generationis, spermatis scilicet, et sanguinis menstrui, in qua complexio misti et viventis continetur et conterminatur".

[35] *Problemata Aristotelis cum duplici translatione antiqua et noua, scilicet Theodori Gaze cum expositione Petri Aponensis...* (Venice, 1519), fol. 246vb: "Notandum quod non propter hoc concludendum est quod complexio naturalis non possit permutari, et si mores possint minime cum ipsi sequantur formam inalterabilem, complexio vero naturalis manet transmutationi et variationi subiecta."

[36] Pietro d'Abano, *Conciliator*, diff. 22, fols 34vb–35vb ("utrum complexio innata, seu radicalis permutari possit, necne").

possibility of a complexional change. Human character changes according to geography and climate, and certain poisonous mushrooms become edible when they are moved from Persian to Egyptian soil. Women's practice of making pointed and elongating the skull of the new-born child to render him bolder and more courageous in fighting suggests that nature follows custom and may be affected by artificial intervention. Abano's conclusion is unequivocal: innate complexion necessarily changes.[37] All this proves that however powerful and lasting the impact of radical complexion may be, it too is subject to change and therefore cannot constitute a solid foundation for a doctrine of biological continuity and determinism.

A highly popular genre of short scientific treatises dealing with complexions and celebrating the overwhelming presence of this concept in biological, physical, chemical, and medical thought from the thirteenth century onwards transmits the same ideas. These treatises, mostly entitled *De complexionibus*,[38] describe the normal phenomenon by which parental complexion is transmitted to the offspring. For example, according to one such treatise compiled in 1352 by a certain Magister Iohannes Par., a phlegmatic person will generate a phlegmatic offspring and a choleric will generate a choleric. This is particularly true if both parents share the same fundamental complexion. While this was the rule, emotional, nutritional, and environmental variation could lead to a change in the offspring's complexion. This could be radical, producing a third complexion from the combination of two different complexions (e.g., choleric and phlegmatic producing a sanguine, which combines the active qualities of the two corrupted complexions: the heat of the choleric and the moisture of phlegmatic). Furthermore, all complexions can mutually permutate so that a choleric can turn sanguine, a melancholic can turn choleric, and vice versa.[39] Despite their differences, all complexions shared a fundamental qualitative conjunction or common ground (*conuenientia*), which facilitated this natural fluidity from one to the other. Thus diet was a major agent of change which enabled complexional transformation if there was affinity (*symbolum*) between the two interacting objects (the choleric and sanguine had such affinity, which was lacking between the phlegmatic and

---

[37] Pietro d'Abano, *Conciliator*, fol. 35va: "Haec igitur omnia complexionem innatam, a qua deciduntur praedicta, demonstrant permutari necessario. Neque est fluens tantum, vel quaecunque acquisita, quae permutetur solum, sed tandem quae innata vere, cum omnium talium causet, aut recipiat immutationem et sibi reddatur."

[38] Lynn Thorndike, "*De complexionibus*", *Isis* 49 (1958), 398–408.

[39] Erfurt, Un. Bib., MS CA 4^0 15, fols 59v–61v (61r): "In prima dicendum est quod omnes complexiones ad inuicem transmutantur ut ex colerico fit sanguineus et ex melancholico colericus et econtra."

choleric). The nature of the diet in pregnancy and the infant's food in his early days was crucial for the smooth transmission of parental complexion, or its change.

A balanced (hence healthy) complexion (*complexio equalis*) (that complexion which the physicians sought in their clinical investigation) did not have a single, absolute, ideal value. In *Liber canonis* I.1.3.1 Avicenna mentions eight modes by which the scope (*latitudo*) of complexion can and should be measured. The third mode is the congruence between climate and complexion. The complexion of the Indians and the Slavs, both belonging to the human species and sharing the human complexion, is adapted to their environmental and regional setting. The Indians' balanced complexion differs from that of the Slavs (Indians being the generic name for Southerners living in extremely hot regions and Slavs for Northerners). What was regarded as a healthy complexion in India would be regarded as an imbalanced and diseased complexion in the northern regions and vice versa, and would lead a person to disease and even death. So, the Slavs and the Indians have different, indeed opposing physical constitutions. And one would expect such an assertion to lead to a racist discourse about the inherent and immutable physical and mental differences between these people. But the medieval commentators of Avicenna did not choose this path. On the contrary, they made an effort to convince others not to follow it.

After explaining who an Indian or a Slav is, and what it means to have a balanced complexion in India or among the Slavs, Jacques Despars (Jacobus de Partibus (d. 1458), who was regent master in Paris in the second decade of the fifteenth century and composed his great commentary on Avicenna's *Liber canonis* between 1432 and 1453) asks his readers to observe that the inhabitants of different regions do not differ in their (human) form (*in specie*) according to their substance but only according to place.[40] Despars then adds a second warning. The complexion of the Indian can slowly but surely change into a Slavic complexion when an Indian spends time from childhood on Slavic soil and slowly acquires Slavic physical characteristics. An Indian thus will be stronger and live longer in a Slavic environment, just like the Ethiopians (blacks) in France

---

[40] Jacques Deaspars, *Commentum*, in *Hic merito inscribi potens vite liber corporalis Abohali Abynsceni canonis libros quinque duflici fere per totum commento munos nuperque translatos…/ doctores circa textum positi ut locis suis apparebit hi sunt: Gentilis de Fulgineo … [et al.], 4 partes* (Venice: Benalius, 1503), fol. 22r: "Attende hic circa hoc quod dicit princeps et unaqueque earum per comparationem ad suam speciem quod habitatores diuersorum locorum non differunt specie secundum substantiam, sed secundum ubi vel locum." I am indebted to Karine van't Lund who directed me to this source and provided me with a hard copy.

who live longer than in Ethiopia.[41] For because of excess heat Ethiopians are wasted and aged by the time they are thirty while the Slavs flourish in their youth. This does not eliminate the inherent mental differences between Southerners and Northerners living in their own lands (Southerners being weak and feeble, easily penetrated by heat and cold, fearful and lean though highly agile; Northerners fleshy with thick and dense flesh, strong and powerful, audacious and having a stronger resistance (presumably to external infiltrations into the body)). Generally Northerners (the inhabitants of Scotland and Ireland according to Jacques Despars) who move to southern regions sustain the heat better than Southerners who move to northern regions sustain the cold. This is due to their natural strength to resist better external threats to the body. Thus the nature of their flesh provides them with better defences against extreme heat. Moreover extreme cold constitutes a graver danger to health since superfluous cold is the main cause of the extinction of innate heat, which is one of the definitions of death.[42] By introducing the possibility of a change in one's natural complexion, of even acquiring in one's lifetime some of the physical traits of those living in the opposite geographical and climatic regions, Jacques Despars largely dismantled the racist potential in such a medical discourse.[43]

Such views regarding the possibility of a long-term complexional change were common not only in fourteenth- and fifteenth-century medical discourse. Readers of philosophical texts from the mid-thirteenth century on environmental thought would already have been exposed to the idea that a complexioned entity (*res complexionata*) transferred to a different climatic zone would slowly become similar in complexion to the one typical of the new place. For example, in *Liber de natura loci*

---

[41] The view that immigrants are generally affected by the particular conditions of a place and over time become like its inhabitants was current among ninth-century Islamic belletristic writers. See Robert Hoyland, "The Islamic Background of Polemon's Treatise", in Swain, *Seeing the Face*, p. 255.

[42] Jacques Despars, *Commentum*, fol. 22r: "Attende tertio quod sclauus translatus ad terram indie minus moleste sufferret calorem patrie quam indus translatus in scotiam vel hiberniam frigua hibernum, Quia sclauus est natura fortior et densior carne et adipe et magis abundans in principiis vite. Indus vero rarus, tenuis et nudus carne cito penetratus a frigore forti usque ad intima. Maius autem periculum est in infrigidando quam in calefaciendo quoniam superflua frigiditas est mors innati caloris."

[43] *Ibid.*: "Attende secundo quod si complexio indi gradatim posset a pueritia reduci ad complexionem sclaui transeundo et acquirendo habitum per media loca paulatim. Indus ipse fortior fieret et diutius viueret sicut ethiopes in francia diutius viuunt quam in ethiopia. Ethiopes etenim pre calore nimio resoluti senescunt anno trigesimo dum sclaui florent in iuuentute. Et sunt ethiopes in regione propria debiles viribus, cito penetrati a calore, et frigore pauidi macri, sed agiles valde. Sclaui vero sunt carnosi carnis spisse, fortes, audaces et magne resistentie."

Albertus Magnus discusses in detail the fundamental physical diversity (*diversitas*) between Southerners (specifically Ethiopeans and Indians) and Northerners (Dacians, Goths, Slavs, and Germans).[44] This diversity is the result of the environmental impact (mainly the combination of temperature and levels of humidity) on the seed (*semen generationis*) and the womb, producing, in the case of the extreme heat in the southern regions and the first climatic zone, humans with blackened humour and cooked blood. The combination of a porous and an extremely dry body and a hot environment, maintains Albertus, results in the rapid evaporation of both the natural power (*virtus naturalis*) and the animal spirit (*spiritus animalis*). This is why blacks age quickly and die approaching the age of thirty. Black skin is directly related to physical agility and mental failure; the Ethiopians are *leves corpore ... et fatui mente*. But first, there can be black-skinned people whose mental and intellectual capacities flourish due to the subtlety and sharpness of their animal spirits. This is the case in India, where people, aided by powerful stellar influence typical of the region, excel in philosophy and in particular in mathematics and magic.[45] Second, and more significantly in the context of this paper, it is possible that black people who are sometime born in different climatic zones, such as in the fourth or fifth one, even though they receive their blackness from their original begetters who were complexioned in the first or second climates, slowly change to whiteness when they are transferred to other climatic zones.[46]

Similar views can be detected among Islamic thinkers of the fourteenth century who maintained that distinctions between nations are determined by custom and geographical location, and not only by descent, and that change is a typical trait of national character or physique. Thus, for example, Ibn Khaldūn (1332–1406) expressed the view that

Negroes from the south who settle in the temperate fourth zone or in the seventh zone that tends toward whiteness, are found to produce descendants whose colour gradually turns white in the course of time. Vice versa, inhabitants from the north

---

[44] Albertus Magnus, *Liber de natura loci* 2.3, in *Opera omnia*, vol. 5.2, ed. P. Hossfeld (Münster: Aschendorff, 1980), pp. 26–7.

[45] *Ibid.*, p. 26 ll. 85–92: "In operationibus autem animalibus, qui sub aequinoctiali sunt, vigent propter subtilitatem spirituum et plus in inveniendo propter calidum movens et acumen spirituum eorum. Cuius signum est, quia praecipui in philosophia in India fuerunt et praecipue in mathematicis et magicis propter fortitudinem stellarum super climata illa super quae perpendiculares radios proiciunt planetae."

[46] *Ibid.*, p. 27 ll. 6–11: "Licet autem huiusmodi nigri aliquando nascantur etiam in aliis climatibus, sicut in quarto vel in quinto, tamen nigredinem accipiunt a primis generantibus, quae complexionata sunt in climatibus primo et secundo, et paulatim alterantur ad albedinem, quando ad alia climata transferuntur."

or from the fourth zone who settle in the south produce descendants whose colour turns black. This shows that colour is conditioned by the composition of the air.[47]

So despite the powerful impact of the environment in creating physical and mental group characteristics, these can slowly change once the environment has changed. Complexion, not only skin colour, was deemed mutable despite its overwhelming power. This should not deter us from identifying other domains in medieval society and culture where proto-racist ideas and feelings could thrive. For racism can emerge in a purely religious context without any scientific or biological input. One such domain is the encounter between Christians and converts. The clear signs in theological and legal sources of a growing suspicion from the twelfth century onwards of Jewish converts suggest that for many clerics Jewish identity was an immutable, physical characteristic which could not be effaced by baptism or eradicated by conversion.[48] The anti-Anacletus II rhetoric (Anacletus being Petrus Pierleoni, the great-grandson of the converted Jew Baruch-Benedict, the "Jewish Pope" whose election in 1130 caused a papal schism) loudly echoes this sense of inherent difference separating Christians and Jews even when generations have elapsed since a conversion. For example, Arnulf, archdeacon of Sées, and later bishop of Lisieux, referred to Anacletus's face as displaying the Jewish image and perfidy. He thus expressed the wide belief that Anacletus's family had still not been purified from the yeast of Jewish corruption.[49] Similarly, late-medieval romance (frequently cited by scholars are certain versions of *Parzival* and the Middle English *King of Tars*) is replete with instances in which conversion to Christianity is insufficient to cancel out differences of colour or race and with references to embodied representations of Islamic and Jewish racial otherness. Religious difference thus came to mean also a theory of biological essence which was indivisible from religion itself.[50]

[47] Ibn Khaldūn, *The Muqaddimah: An Introduction to History*, trans. Franz Rosenthal, 3 vols, Bollingen Series XLIII (Princeton: Princeton University Press, 1958), I.153, p. 171.

[48] Steven F. Kruger, *The Spectral Jew: Conversion and Embodiment in Medieval Europe* (Minneapolis/London: University of Minnesota Press, 2006), pp. 67–109; Jonathan M. Elukin, "From Jew to Christian? Conversion and Immutability in Medieval Europe", in James Muldoon (ed.), *Varieties of Religious Conversion in the Middle Ages* (Gainesville: University Press of Florida, 1997), pp. 171–89; and David Nirenberg's contribution to the present collection.

[49] Mary Stroll, *The Jewish Pope: Ideology and Politics in the Papal Schism of 1130* (Leiden: Brill, 1988), pp. 160–1, 167 (for an insinuation of Bernard of Clairvaux that Jewish character could remain unaffected by conversion).

[50] Lisa Lampert, "Race, Periodicity and Neo-(Middle Ages)", *Modern Language Quarterly* 65 (2004), 392–421; Geraldine Heng, *Empire of Magic: Medieval Romance and the Politics of Cultural Fantasy* (New York: Columbia University Press, 2003), pp. 226–37; Jeffrey J. Cohen, *Medieval Identity Machines* (Minneapolis/London: University of Minnesota Press, 2003), pp. 190–206.

Between 1200 and 1500, Latin thinkers from the various domains of natural philosophy, medicine, and theology were increasingly engaged in biological thinking. Why do wise people (*sapientes*) often generate stupid children? How can one explain the sweat of blood of the suffering Christ? Did Christ resemble Mary? How exactly did Adam's body function before sin? What was the effect of the tree of life on one's body? This is just a sample of intriguing questions which received complicated answers saturated with up-to-date scientific bio-medical information and steering these debates onto a highly material track. The new physiognomic discourse, which ensconced the classical physiognomic treatises in a thick explanatory frame deeply rooted in humoral theory, is part of this biological shift. But despite this trend, medieval and early renaissance physiognomers largely circumvented ethnic or proto-racist usages of their knowledge. Lacking a stable or unalterable analytical category, they kept physiognomy a universal practice geared to decipher the personality of individuals, not of groups. In fact, medieval and early renaissance physiognomy was so individualistic that questions of parental transmission of traits and of heredity were relegated to a marginal position in the physiognomic discourse and practice. Physiognomy would thus disappoint any of its students who were looking for a sustained and coherent explanation of human mixing.[51]

Valentin Groebner has recently traced the path by which the notion of complexion, originally designating the balanced proportion of humours specific to each individual, came to be used as a term for a person's bodily appearance and skin colour.[52] When *complexio* turned into complexion the investigation became visual, surfaced to the skin (mainly its colour), and increasingly became prominent in the description of classification marks of groups. *Complexio* established itself as a collective category. Having shifted from the invisible internal blend of fluids in one's body to something identifiable on the skin, it became a congenital and immutable category. He located this shift in the second half of the sixteenth century, when the concept of complexion became crucial for describing the differing bodily and mental natures of inhabitants of Africa and the Americas. This was already an entirely different world from the one described above.

---

[51] Epstein, *Purity Lost*, p. 178; Joseph Ziegler, "Hérédité et physiognomonie", in *L'hérédité entre Moyen Âge et Époque moderne: Perspectives historiques*, ed. Charles de Miramon and Maaike van der Lugt (Florence: Sismel, 2008) pp. 245–72.

[52] Valentin Groebner, "*Complexio*/Complexion: Categorizing Individual Natures, 1250–1600", in Lorraine Daston and Fernando Vidal (eds.), *The Moral Authority of Nature* (Chicago: Chicago University Press, 2003), pp. 357–83, and *Who are You? Identification, Deception, and Surveillance in Early Modern Europe* (New York: Zone, 2007), pp. 139–41.

9 Noble dogs, noble blood: the invention of the concept of race in the late Middle Ages

Charles de Miramon

The *Thrésor de la langue françoise* (Treasure of the French Language) is one of the first comprehensive French dictionaries. It was composed by Jean Nicot and printed in 1606. A twenty-first-century reader opening the *Thrésor* at the entry *race* might be surprised to learn a lot about dogs.[1] The entry starts,

> Race ... means descent. Therefore, it is said that a man, a horse, a dog or another animal is from good or bad race ... And that the race of Spanish horses and French hounds came from etc. ... Du Fouilloux in his *Venery* explains that the Trojans used to hunt in these forests with such a race of dogs, which when they found a stag, they would not let go of it before it was dead, i.e., such a kind, sort, nature of dogs ... A gentleman of ancient race: *Longo sanguine censetur* (Juvenal, *Satires* 8)....[2]

The word *race* does not exist in Greek, nor in classical and medieval Latin. It is a neologism that has no root in Latin. In his 1552 French–Latin dictionary, Robert Estienne explains that race should be translated *stirps*, *gens* or *sanguine* (stock/stem, people/tribe, from the blood of). When, where, and why was *race* invented? Nicot gives us a rare clue by citing Du Fouilloux's *Venery* (1561), the foremost French hunting encyclopaedia of the sixteenth century. Du Fouilloux writes extensively about the

---

[1] Several digitised old French dictionaries (including the *Thrésor*) can be found at http://artfl. atilf.fr/dictionnaires/.

[2] Jean Nicot, *Thrésor de la langue françoise* (Paris: D. Dovcevr, 1606): 'Race, f. penac. Est fait du genitif du Latin Radix par syncope de la syllabe du milieu, et signifie extraction. Ainsi dit on homme, cheval, chien, et autre animal de bonne ou mauvaise race, Laudatae aut Illaudatae propaginis, Et la race des chevaux d'Espagne, ou la race des chiens courans en France estre venue de etc. Race se prent aussi pour maniere, sorte, espece. Du Fouillous en sa venerie, fut adverti que les Troyens chassoyent ordinairement en ses forests avec telle race de chiens que depuis qu'ils avoyent trouvé le cerf ils ne l'abbandonnoyent jamais qu'il ne fut mort, c'est à dire avec telle maniere, sorte et naturel de chiens etc. Cum eo genere canum, Canibus hac vi praeditis. Gentilhomme d'ancienne race, Longo sanguine censetur, Iuuen. sat. 8.'

different races of hunting dogs,[3] but hunters used the word earlier. The oldest occurrence of *race* can in fact be found in a little-known poem of Jacques de Brézé, *The Hunt.* Jacques de Brézé, scion of a wealthy Norman family and a great seneschal of Normandy, married Charlotte de France, the natural daughter of Charles VII and Agnès Sorel. A keen hunter, this Capetian courtier describes in his poem a deer hunt that took place around 1481 at which Anne of Beaujeu, daughter of Louis XI and future regent, was present. Brézé names several leading hounds of the pack and indicates their pedigree. During the pursuit, Anne praises two bitches, Fricaulde and Ligière: 'Against them (the deer), you have a fair quarrel [They are fair game for you]. Your race is their enemy.'[4] Naming two female dogs constitutes subtle support for Anne, who was intent on seizing power when normal rules – albeit never applied – excluded women during regencies. Drawing a parallel with humans, Jacques de Brézé explains that hunting is the 'nicest possible trade. It should come to nobles by race when they are not soldiering.'[5] A later poem, *The Deeds of the Good Dog Souillard,* where the term *race* occurs is a eulogy for Souillard, the best hound of his time. Brézé describes its kin – the oldest example of a canine pedigree in Western Europe – and relates that the cub Souillard was offered to Louis XI 'as a dog of good race'.[6]

The glorious clamour of hounds, horns, and worn-out horses; a ray of light through the damp trees; the glassy stare of a dead stag and the odour of entrails – these form the physical and social environment where race was born. This was far indeed from what is commonly associated with racism during the late Middle Ages. The word was not coined to denigrate a despised minority or an alien people with a strange skin colour. It was first uttered in France, not Spain or Portugal. It was not invented to justify colonisation or enslavement. In his classic *Race and History,* Claude Lévi-Strauss firmly grounds race in anthropology. He explains that before scientific racism race was how a tribe, a nation, or an ethnic group defined itself, by rejecting all others.[7] Subsequent historiography based itself on this humanistic foundation and bypassed the origins of the word race.[8]

---

[3] Jacques du Fouilloux, *La Vénerie et l'Adolescence*, ed. Gunnar Tilander (Karlshamn: ABEG Johanssons Boktryckeri, 1967) also on the internet: http://www.chass.utoronto.ca/~wulfric/rentexte/fouillou/fouilloux_table.htm.

[4] 'Contre eulx [les cerfs] avez bonne querelle, / Vostre race est leur ennemye!'. Jacques de Brézé, *La chasse; les dits du bon chien Souillard et Les louanges de Madame Anne de France*, ed. Gunnar Tilander (Lund: C. Bloms boktr., 1959), p. 44.

[5] '[La chasse est] le plus beau mestier que l'on face. / Aux nobles doit venir de race, / Au temps qu'ilz ne suivent pas les armes'. *Ibid.*, p. 41.

[6] *Ibid.*, p. 57.   [7] Claude Lévi-Strauss, *Race and History* (Paris: UNESCO, 1952).

[8] For example, George M. Fredrickson, *Racism: A Short History* (Princeton N.J.: Princeton University Press, 2002).

This paper attempts to fill this void by describing the forge where race was minted, namely the discourse on nobility in the late Middle Ages. This will allow us to determine whether the concept of race was racist from its birth.

Before returning to Jacques de Brézé, let us look at the muddled lexicography of *race* in the fifteenth century.[9] Some authoritative dictionaries still uphold the theory of an Italian origin for *race*.[10] They point out that in a medieval translation of the *Faits des Romains*, a compendium of Roman history, we are told about Caesar's horse that 'l'uomo diceva che re Nicodeme di Bettinia li 'l dono, e altri affermavano ch'elli fu nato in suo raza'. However, the French original reads: 'Li un disoient que Nicodeme li donna, li autre afferment qu'il fu nez en son haras' ('Some said that Nicodemus gave it to him, others that it was born in his brood-herd').[11] *Razza* translates *haras*, which means a stud farm in modern French. In the Middle Ages it meant a reproductive herd of broodmares and foals, as reflected in the English phrase *haras of horses*. Haras is an old Norman word, used with its zoo-technical meaning in regions under Norman influence such as southern Italy.[12] Initially *Arazza* and its variant *razza* did not go beyond the equestrian jargon. Only in the Early Modern period did the word acquire a metaphorical sense owing to its phonetic proximity to *race*.

Another word close to *race* is *generation*. In biblical Latin, *generatio* can mean *tribe, people*.[13] In fifteenth-century French, *génération* can render *generatio* in translations or adaptations of the Old Testament but it can also have a more general meaning of *lineage*. In the late fifteenth century *race* could replace *generation*, as in the *Mystère du vieil Testament* (around 1480), but also in the tortuous language of the astrologer Simon de Phares. In his catalogue of great magicians (1494), Simon states that Phines was *de la race entre les Juifs* (from a Jewish tribe) that enjoyed a hereditary gift of performing magical fumigations. Later in his book Simon speaks of the English race.

Perusing dictionaries and lexicographical databases, I have found nine occurrences of *race* before 1500. Four (three in Jacques de Brézé and one

---

[9] To shorten references, unless otherwise stated, citations are drawn from the following databases: *Base de Lexiques du Moyen Français (DMF1)* available on the website of the *Analyse et Traitement Informatique de la Langue Française* Institute (http://www.atilf.fr/dmf) and the *Corpus de la littérature médiévale* (CD-ROM, Paris, 2001).

[10] *Französisches Etymologisches Wörterbuch* (Bonn/Leipzig/Basel 1922–).

[11] Gianfranco Contini, 'I più antichi esempi di *razza*', *Studia di Filologia Italiana* 17 (1959), 319–27.

[12] Francesco Sabatini, 'Conferme per l'etimologia di razza dal francese antico haraz', *Studia de Filologia Italiana* 20 (1962), 365–82.

[13] For example, Numbers 1: 20.

in Commynes) are related to hounds, hunting, nobles, and war. One occurrence, in Commynes, is a translation of the Italian *razza* (= *haras*). In four occurrences (two in the *Mystère du vieil Testament* and two in Simon de Phares) it is a synonym of generation (tribe, people). In this paper, I concentrate on the zoological and aristocratic race, the usage apparently the most common in the fifteenth century. It also forms the nucleus of dictionary entries in the sixteenth and seventeenth centuries. In a few years' time progress in the digitisation of medieval texts will certainly yield a richer harvest with a more detailed picture of this lexicographical phenomenon.

Noble races of animals

Recent research has stressed the importance of selection and improvement of cattle races during the seventeenth and eighteenth centuries for modelling the 'epistemic space' that later gave rise to the Darwinist theories of heredity and to scientific racism.[14] Gentlemen farmers around Europe elaborated new zoo-technical knowledge that paved the way to a new approach to animals. Import of new species and experiments logged in stud books mark this change. Selection of natural races is crucial for the application of the natural sciences to separate hereditary and external influences better.[15] What was the situation in the Middle Ages? What practical interest did medieval breeders have in selecting animals and monitoring their reproduction? And to what extent can a theoretical concept of race or sub-species be found in learned zoology, hunting books, and husbandry treatises?

In the late Middle Ages pastoral economy underwent substantial transformations. Modest breeding of a few cattle by every farmer was partially superseded by extensive regional pastoral economies.[16] Still, zoo-technical innovations were not the cause of pastoral transformations.[17]

---

[14] Staffan Müller-Wille and Hans-Jorg Rheinberger, 'De la génération à l'hérédité. Continuités médiévales et conjonctures historiques modernes', in Maaike van der Lugt and Charles de Miramon (eds.), *L'hérédité entre Moyen Âge et Époque moderne. Perspectives historiques* (Florence: Sismel, 2008) pp. 355–89; Staffan Müller-Wille and Hans-Jorg Rheinberger (eds), *Heredity Produced. At the Crossroads of Biology, Politics, and Culture 1500–1870* (Cambridge, Mass./London: MIT Press, 2007).

[15] Staffan Müller-Wille and Hans-Jorg Rheinberger, 'Heredity: The Formation of an Epistemic Space', in Müller-Wille and Rheinberger (eds.), *Heredity Produced*, pp. 3–34.

[16] Robert-Henri Bautier, 'Les mutations agricoles des XIVe et XVe siècles et les progrès de l'élevage', *Bulletin philologique et historique* (1967), 1–27.

[17] See the bibliography in Maaike van der Lugt and Charles de Miramon, 'Penser l'hérédité au Moyen Âge: une introduction', in van der Lugt and de Miramon (eds.), *L'hérédité entre Moyen Âge et Époque moderne*, pp. 3–40.

Data of archaeological cattle bones and husbandry treatises alike attest to the continuous mediocrity of cattle races throughout the Middle Ages. Farmers were not concerned to control the reproduction of their cattle and had very little interest in selecting animals. Learned agronomic treatises like Petrus de Crescentiis's *Ruralia Commodia* and zoological literature like Albertus Magnus's *De animalibus* here and there described regional species. Drawing on Aristotle's observations on the uneven geographical distribution of animals – called biotopes nowadays – treatises link climate to variations in animals' colour or size.[18] But even in Albertus Magnus's masterworks this extension of climatic theories to animal populations adduces no theoretical concept of race or sub-species. In everyday medieval life taxonomy of domestic animals was mostly functional, not racial. Horses were divided into chargers, rounceys, palfreys, and so on. Dogs were divided into bloodhounds, pointers, scent hounds, watchdogs, and so on.

Husbandry, zoology and common taxonomy seem to leave no room for animal races, yet a closer look reveals a more contrasting landscape. Some regions were famed for their horses.[19] For example, English sources speak of *powys*, horses bred in the Welsh county of Powys. Gerald of Wales explained that powys horses descend from Spanish horses imported by Robert of Bellême in the late eleventh century.[20] Gerald's story, like Du Fouilloux's Trojans dogs, clings to the model of the classic legend of colonisation, which Foucault has aptly named 'the war of the races'.[21] A noble alien warrior tribe conquers a country and subjugates the degenerate locals. New customs and new animals are symbols of their conquest. Nevertheless, regional animal races have extremely feeble foundations. Most European regions were at one time or another famous for their horses, and archaeozoologists still debate the existence of a specific race of great warhorses in the Middle Ages.[22]

Only for two animals, birds of prey and dogs, can a proto-concept of race detached from geographical determinism be found. In zoological and hunting literature specific species of hawks and dogs are said to be noble.

---

[18] *Ibid.*

[19] Philippe Contamine, 'Les robes des chevaux d'armes en France au XIVe siècle', in Robert Durand (ed.), *L'homme, l'animal domestique et l'environnement du Moyen Âge au XVIIIe siècle* (Nantes: Ouest editions, 1993), pp. 257–68.

[20] R. H. C. Davies, 'The Warhorses of the Normans', *Anglo-Norman Studies* 10 (1987), 67–89.

[21] Michel Foucault, *Il faut défendre la société. Cours au Collège de France (1975–1976)* (Paris: Seuil/Gallimard, 1992), pp. 51–74.

[22] Contamine,'Les robes des chevaux d'armes', pp. 257–68; Frédérique Audoin-Rouzeau, *La taille du cheval en Europe de l'Antiquité aux temps modernes* (Juan-les-Pins: APDCA, 1994).

For birds of prey, the association of *courtois* civilisation with hawks started very early, well before the diffusion of technical falconry literature.[23] But the ennoblement of birds became evident when, from the twelfth century onwards, a hierarchy of birds of prey was drawn from the less to the most noble. Every bird was paired with a level of nobility and a social class. For example, the count was paired with the peregrine falcon, the priest with the sparrowhawk, and so on.[24] This social hierarchy is based on a triple partition of hawks, goshawks and sparrow-hawks. Most medieval falconry tracts contain a list of birds. Some of the lists are essentially ornithological, based on Arabic sources or on the author's direct observations.[25] Others focus on the social ladder of birds. The end result is a complex and shifting system which mixes in varying degrees bird watching, hunting practices, learned tradition, and social ideology. [26]

Albertus Magnus composed the most sociologically induced list. In his encyclopaedia of birds (book 23 of *De animalibus*) he includes a comprehensive falconry manual, which lists ten races of noble falcons, ten races of commoners, three bastard races, and one mixed breed race.[27] Bastards are the result of interbreeding between nobles and commoners. The mixed breed is the offspring of two different noble races and is good for hunting. Albertus particularises falcons' anthropomorphism. He gives a physiognomonic description for every sub-species and spells out its complexion and natural virtues. Moreover, he posits a far sounder hereditary theory than the one he had introduced into his discussion about human reproduction.[28] He explains that the black falcon and the white falcon are geographical variants of peregrine falcons: the white comes from cold

---

[23] Baudouin Van den Abeele, *La fauconnerie dans les lettres françaises du XIIᵉ au XIVᵉ siècles* (Leuven: Leuven University Press, 1990).

[24] D. Evans, 'The Nobility of Knight and Falcon', in Christopher Harper-Bill and Ruth Harvey (eds), *The Ideals and Practice of Medieval Knighthood III* (Woodbridge: Boydell, 1990), pp. 79–99, at pp. 90–91.

[25] The *Ur* text is al Ġiṭrīf ibn Qudāma al Ġassānī, *Traité des oiseaux de vol (Kitāb Ḍawārī aṭṭayr)*, trans. François Viré and Detlef Möller (Nogent-le-Roi: J. Laget, 2002), pp. 68–70.

[26] Baudouin Van den Abeele, *La fauconnerie au Moyen Âge* (Paris: Klincksieck, 1994), pp. 45–91 presents these lists from an ornithological point of view.

[27] Albertus Magnus, *De animalibus*, XXIII, 1, ed. Hermann Stadler, 2 vols (Münster: Aschendorff, 1916–22), II, pp. 1453–93. Albertus's list is indeed not devoid of ornithological problems, see Van den Abeele, *La fauconnerie au Moyen Âge*, pp. 45–91. Frederick II had no interest in the nobility of falcons (Frederick II, *De arte venandi cum avibus*, ed. Carl Arnold Willemsem (Leipzig: In aedibus Insulae, 1942)). See also Robin S. Oggins, 'Albertus Magnus on Falcons and Hawks', in James A. Weisheipl (ed.), *Albertus Magnus and the Sciences* (Toronto: Pontifical Institute of Mediaeval Studies, 1980), pp. 441–62.

[28] For the place of heredity in human generation see Joseph Ziegler, 'Hérédité et physiognomonie', in van der Lugt and de Miramon, *L'hérédité*, and Maaike van der Lugt 'Les maladies héréditaires dans la pensée scolastique (XIIᵉ – XVIᵉ siècles)', in *ibid.*, pp. 273–320.

regions and the black from hot regions.[29] The form (*figura*) is what counts: the colour is accidental and depends on the region of origin. This extension of the peregrine race is enlightening. The peregrine falcon holds fourth place in the middle of Albertus's hierarchy. It is the most common hawk in Europe, hence the generic symbol of nobility. In his chapter on bastard races Albertus states that a half-blood where the father is a peregrine falcon and the mother a blue foot falcon (from a bad stock) is nobler than the other way around.[30] He supplies an Aristotelian reason for this phenomenon. The father's virtue is transmitted by the male seed. In the context of falconry this explanation is counter-intuitive because female birds of prey are bigger than males, capable of catching bigger fowl and therefore more prized. Clearly, Albertus's hawk hierarchy can be read as an imaginary projection of hereditary nobility. This ideological bias led Albertus to positions close to the selection of animal races in the seventeenth and eighteenth centuries. Very soon, hawks become animals for which race purity and the value of crossbreeding are taken into account.

As noted, dogs too are animals with noble races. In dogs, racial differences are very easy to spot. Iconography and archaeology show the presence of a wide variety of dogs in the Middle Ages, from midget lapdogs to huge, fierce watchdogs.[31] However, dogs were ennobled much later than birds of prey. This may be because dogs have ambiguous moral value. The dog is man's best friend but also 'returns to its vomit' (Proverbs 26: 11).[32]

The first mention of noble dogs can be found in Thomas de Cantimpré's *De naturis rerum* (*c.* 1225/6–41). Thomas distinguishes three races of dogs.[33] The noblest is the greyhound. Scent hounds with long drooping ears are noble. At the bottom of the ladder are the commoners, the watchdogs. Albertus Magnus broadly followed Thomas de Cantimpré's triple division.[34] The hierarchy of dogs' races follows a similar pattern to the hawks'. Nobility lies between a top princely crust and a bottom commoner layer. This middle noble layer is the linchpin of the hierarchy and is occupied by hounds. Note that pointers are absent from this hierarchy. Thirteenth-century literature and iconography often depict

---

[29] Albertus Magnus, *De animalibus*, XXIII, 1, 10 (n. 27), II, 1465.
[30] Albertus Magnus, *De animalibus*, XXIII, 1, 16 (n. 27), II, 1470.
[31] Jacques Bugnion, *Les chasses médiévales: le brachet, le lévrier, l'épagneul, leur nomenclature, leur métier, leur typologie* (Gollion: Infolio, 2005).
[32] An Smets, 'L'image ambiguë du chien à travers la littérature didactique latine et française (XIIe –XIVe siècles)', *Reinardus* 14 (2001), 243–53.
[33] Thomas de Cantimpré, *Liber de natura rerum*, IV, 13, ed. H. Boese (Berlin / New York: Walter de Gruyter, 1973), p. 115.
[34] Albertus Magnus, *De animalibus*, XXII, 2, 1 (n. 27), II, 1365. I leave open the question of the relationship between the *De animalibus* and the *Liber de natura rerum*.

the *brachet*, that sits on the back of his master's horse, points the game and retrieves it when downed in a bow hunt or after hawking.[35]

The paths of noble dogs and of noble hawks crossed in the middle of the fourteenth century, during the golden age of medieval hunting literature.[36] Several debates written at the Capetian court contrast venery and hawking.[37] Henri of Ferrières penned the model for this peculiar rhetorical battle in his *Livres du roy Modus et de la royne Ratio* (1360–79).[38] Two ladies dispute the respective values of hunting with dogs or hunting with birds. The Count of Tancarville is chosen as an arbiter and hands down his verdict after each lady has pleaded the cause of her champion animal. At stake here is the social hierarchy of two types of hunting.[39] It is also about choosing the nobler between the hound and the hawk. Dogs start with a handicap: they are said to be filthy and raucous beasts whereas hawks are naturally beautiful and noble. In his Salomonic verdict the Count of Tancarville declares that venery is the more enjoyable hunt, but that the hawk is without doubt the nobler creature.[40] Dogs slowly closed the gap on hawks and overtook them at the beginning of the sixteenth century.[41] Whereas birds were deemed noble as individuals, dogs were noble as a group. In his *Livre de chasse* (1389) Gaston Phébus writes an emotional eulogy for dogs:

[Dogs] are the most noble animals, the most reasonable, the most learned ever created by God ... And when I see the dogs that hunt today and when I recall the dogs I saw in bygone times and when I remember the goodness and loyalty that were common between the lords of the world and between other people and when I see what is happening today, I insist that there is no possible comparison. And every reasonable man cannot but agree.[42]

---

[35] In the fourteenth century the brachet would be replaced by the spaniel; Bugnion, *Les chasses médiévales*.

[36] Armand Strubel and Chantal de Saulnier, *La poétique de la chasse au Moyen Âge. Les livres de chasse du XIVᵉ siècle* (Paris: Presses universitaires de France, 1994).

[37] Baudouin Van den Abeele, *La littérature cynégétique* (Turnhout: Brepols, 1996), pp. 47–8.

[38] Henri de Ferrières, *Les livres du roy Modus et de la royne Ratio*, ed. Gunnar Tilander (Paris: Société des anciens textes français, 1932), I, pp. 230–66.

[39] Strubel and Saulnier, *La poétique de la chasse*, pp. 138–43.

[40] Henri de Ferrières, *Les livres du roy Modus*, I, p. 264.

[41] In Gace de la Buigne, *Le roman des deduis*, ed. Åke Blomqvist (Karlshamn: E. G. Johansson, 1951) (before 1377) birds are still winning the contest. In the later anonymous *Débat du faucon et du lévrier*, ed. Gustaf Holmér (Stockholm: Almqvist & Wiksell International, 1978), the part about the dog is twice as long as the part about the falcon. In Guillaume Crétin, *Débat de deux dames sur le passetemps de la chasse des chiens et oyseaulx* (Paris, 1526), the dog is declared more noble than the falcon.

[42] Gaston Phébus, *Livre de chasse*, ed. Gunnar Tilander (Karlshamn: E. G. Johanssons Boktryckeri, 1971), pp. 106–7.

A pack of brave hounds represented an ideal noble society of the four-teenth century. The hawk was associated with *courtoisie* values. Hawking highlights the eyas, the hawk fledgling, which could be trained but never tamed. Flight was associated with freedom. The downing of fowl was associated with the raptorial domination of the many by the few. Birds were assembled like a medieval court, with the eagle crowning the pyr-amid. By contrast, the dog embodied the new aristocratic values of the late Middle Ages: loyalty to the master, virility, cohesion of the company, a passion to fight. The domination of the dog replaced the sovereignty of the hawk.[43] I will come back to this new set of values, which is associated with a change from heredity to acquired characters. The shift of interest to the hound led to increased attention to descriptions of sub-species and breed-ing advice.[44] In his *Livre de chasse* Gaston Phébus described in detail several sub-species of dogs: the *alant* (a mastiff), the greyhound, the *chien courant* (bloodhound), the spaniel, and the *mâtin* (a large mastiff).[45] Gaston does not care for spaniels. He says that they are brawlers and howlers because they are from Spain: their bad nature derives from their bad *generation*.[46] Two centuries later, in his *Vénerie* (1561), Jacques du Fouilloux is much more precise about races of dogs, pedigrees, and selection methods.[47]

Jacques de Brézé's use of the word race must therefore be understood in the context of a transformation of the conception of aristocratic heredity during the fourteenth century. This transformation is subtle: nothing like a central concept of heredity exists in the Middle Ages.[48] Changes are more visible on the fringes of medieval cultural history, like hunting literature, than in discourses normally associated with nobility and repro-duction. The transformation of heredity is not limited to the invention of the noble race of hounds. The revival of hereditary blood early in the fourteenth century is another fine example of the cultural and political evolutions that explain the birth of race.

Noble blood and princes of the blood

Jean Nicot and before him Robert Estienne gave *sanguis* (blood) as a possible Latin translation of race. Early Modernity indeed displays a large conceptual overlap between race and hereditary blood. I will call

---

[43] For the shift from sovereignty to domination see Foucault, *Il faut défendre la société*, p. 42.
[44] Pierre Tucoo-Chala, 'Les chiens de chasse dans les traités de vénerie du XIVe au XVIe siècle', in Durand, *L'homme, l'animal domestique et l'environnement*, pp. 269–78.
[45] Gaston Phébus, *Livre de chasse*, pp. 125–38.   [46] *Ibid.*, pp. 136–7.
[47] Jacques du Fouilloux, *La Vénerie et l'Adolescence*.
[48] Van der Lugt and Miramon, *Penser l'hérédité au Moyen Âge*.

hereditary blood the specific symbolic use of blood in genealogical and kinship contexts, in contrast with other uses of blood: bodily fluid, blood of Christ, blood shed, and so on.[49]

In his dictionary entry for *race*, Jean Nicot gives a reference to Juvenal. In his eighth Satire Juvenal mocks the decadent aristocrat Ponticus who boasted his blood and pedigree (*stemmata*).[50] In Roman culture, blood had a strong symbolic value and was associated with nobility and family descent.[51] This ancient tradition could easily lead to the conclusion that down the centuries blood was the symbolic backbone of European kinship. This very idea permeates the abundant anthropological literature on Western kinship.[52] Generations of medievalists have explained that noble lineages were bonded by blood ties.[53] The sources tell a different history. From late Antiquity onwards, hereditary blood waned. Expressions inherited from Antiquity survived as imprints, but new ones, such as *nobility of the flesh* (*nobilitas carnis*), were more common.[54] Moreover, from the seventh to the twelfth centuries, thinkers exalted the nobility of virtue and belittled the nobility of the flesh.[55] I will not delve here into this well known paradox: medieval society represents itself as a meritocracy of the virtuous even though social reproduction is based on heredity.

Through the cracks of the veneer of virtuous nobility a new hereditary blood discourse nevertheless appeared. The chronology and the sources of this new discourse closely coincided with the emergence of animal noble races. The first traces of the idea of a hereditary blood are found

---

[49] In the following, I summmarise Charles de Miramon, 'Aux origines de la noblesse et des princes du sang. France et Angleterre au XIVe siècle', in van der Lugt and de Miramon, *L'hérédité*, pp. 157–210.

[50] Juv. 8, 1.

[51] Gianni Guastella, 'La rete del sangue; simbologia delle relazioni e modelli dell'identità nella cultura romana', *Materiali e discussioni per l'analisi dei testi classici* 15 (1985), 49–123; Francesca Menacci, 'Sanguis/Cruor. Designazioni linguistiche e classificazione antropologica del sangue nella cultura romana', *Materiali e discussioni per l'analisi dei testi classici* 17 (1986), 25–91; and for Greece, Jérôme Wilgaux, 'David M. Schneider en Attique: le sang, le sperme dans les représentations de la parenté en Grèce ancienne', *Incidence* 1 (2006), 75–89.

[52] For example, David. M. Schneider, *American Kinship: A Cultural Account*, second edition (Chicago: University of Chicago Press, 1980).

[53] For example, Marc Bloch, *La société féodale*, seventh edition (Paris: Éditions Albin Michel, 1949, 1989), p. 395.

[54] Nobility of flesh is twice as frequent as nobility of blood in the *Patrologia Latina*, Cetedoc and *e-MGH* databases.

[55] The bibliography on medieval ideology of nobility is very large. See Andrea Robiglio, 'The Thinker as a Noble Man (*bene natus*). Preliminary Remarks on the Medieval Concepts of Nobility', *Vivarium* 44 (2006), 205–47 and Guido Castelnuovo, 'Revisiter un classique: noblesse, hérédité et vertu d'Aristote à Dante et à Bartole (Italie communale, début XIIIe – milieu XIVe siècle)', in van der Lugt and de Miramon, *L'hérédité*, pp. 105–56. Both with extensive bibliographies.

in thirteenth-century scholastic literature. In the *Nicomachean Ethics* Aristotle wrote about friendship among brothers, explaining that brothers share the same identity and could be said to come 'from the same blood'.[56] In one of his two commentaries on the *Ethics*, Albertus Magnus expands on this brotherly blood using his physiological knowledge and likens it to consanguinity.[57] Brothers love each other because they share the same degree of consanguinity. But later commentators are silent on this topic.[58] A more fruitful scholastic context is the legal discussion on the heredity of penalties. There is a strong tradition rooted in Canon Law of the personality of punishments.[59] Children do not inherit their parents' curse. But there are exceptions: children can suffer the punishments of their parents if the latter have committed crimes of lesemajesty or heresy. To explain this anomaly the jurist Cynus of Pistoia argued, at the start of the fourteenth century, that in this case children are said to come from faulty blood (*a sanguine improbato*).[60]

The link between hereditary blood and lese-majesty echoes the link between good race and loyal hounds. Treason is a major topic of political life in late medieval France and England.[61] The countless magnate rebellions that reverberate through the political stories of these two kingdoms

---

[56] '*Fratres* autem ad invicem in ex eisdem nasci. Ad illam enim ydemptitas ad invicem idem facit propter quod aiunt idem sanguinem et radicem et talia'; Aristotle, *Ethica nicomachea* VIII, 13–14, ed. René-Antoine Gauthier, Aristoteles Latinus XXVI (Leiden/Bruxelles: Brill/Desclée de Brouwer, 1974), p. 537. On friendship in medieval commentaries on the Ethics see Bénédicte Sère, *Penser l'amitié au Moyen Âge. Étude historique des commentaires sur les livres VIII et IX de l'Éthique à Nicomaque (XIIIᵉ – XVᵉ siècle)* (Turnhout: Brepols, 2007) and on the diffusion of the vocabulary at a princely court Klaus Oschema, *Freundschaft und Nähe im spätmittelalterlichen Burgund. Studien zum Spannungsfeld von Emotion und Institution* (Cologne/Weimar/Vienna: Böhlau Verlag, 2006).

[57] Albertus Magnus, *Super Ethica*, VIII, 12, in *Opera Omnia* XIV:2, ed. Wilhelm Kübel (Münster: Aschendorff, 1987), p. 641, and Albertus Magnus, *Ethicorum libri decem*, VIII, 3, 6, in *Opera Omnia*, ed. Auguste Borgnet (Paris: apud Ludovicum Vivès, 1891), VII, p. 549.

[58] Thomas Aquinas, *Sententia Libri Ethicorum* (Rome: Ad Sanctae Sabinae, 1969), p. 487, summed up in Giles of Rome, *De regimine principum*, 2.2.4 (Rome, 1566), p. 175. See also Jean Buridan, *Super decem libros ethicorum*, 8, 17 (Paris, 1513 = repr. Frankfurt, 1968), fol. 184r.

[59] Vito Piergiovanni, *La punibilità degli innocenti nel diritto canonico dell'età classica* (Milano: Giuffré, 1974).

[60] Cynus of Pistoia, *Super Codicem*, ad C. 9, 8, 5, *Quisquis* (Frankfurt, 1578), fol. 543. For heresy see VI° 5, 2, 15. John of Andrea, *Novella in Sextum*, VI° 5, 2, 15 (Venezia 1499 = repr. Graz 1963), p. 255 reuses Cynus. See also Bracton in Samuel E. Thorne and George E. Woodbine, *Bracton on the Laws and Customs of England* (Cambridge, Mass.: Published in association with the Selden Society, the Belknap Press of Harvard University Press, 1968), II, p. 366.

[61] John G. Bellamy, *The Law of Treason in England in the later Middle Ages* (Cambridge University Press, 1970); Simon Hirsch Cuttler, *The Law of Treason and Treason Trials in Later Medieval France* (Cambridge University Press, 1981).

are analysed by historians in the cold language of geopolitics. Yet contemporaries perceived them in an emotional framework. They dreamed of an aristocratic society regulated by natural love and natural lordship, devoid of plotting, civil wars, and disunion. The proverb *bon sang ne saurait mentir* ('a fair blood cannot lie') conveys the idea that a good nature will always reveal itself, and that lies and deceit will disappear from the ideal society of fair blooded and virtuous nobles. The proverb appears for the first time in the anonymous chanson de geste *Beaudoin de Sebourc* in the Valenciennois in the 1310s.[62] *Beaudoin de Sebourc* is a lengthy chanson with a complex and long-winded plot whose complete summary is beyond the scope of this essay. Suffice it to say that fair blood is characteristic of the hero Beaudoin, his brothers, and his bastard sons. Blood is a heroic male virtue that reveals itself on the battlefield or in the natural bonding of family kin. The author contrasts hereditary blood with the normal world where fidelity is bought by money, gifts, or marriage.

Beaudoin de Sebourc was written in Artois, one of the hot spots of the 1314 rebellion of the nobility. In this kingdom-wide rising at the start of Philip V's reign, regional leagues of nobles petitioned the king for bills of rights.[63] They presented themselves as 'the nobles of Burgundy, etc.'.[64] It was a semantic turning point. Previously, 'noble' was mostly used as an epithet. In the high Middle Ages the aristocracy defined itself with feudal words – knight, lord, baron – or with expressions of power such as magnate.[65] The vocabulary is intrinsically hierarchical. By contrast, when the rebellious leagues of 1314 used the substantive 'noble' they presented themselves as a single estate defined by a common norm in the same way

---

[62] Giuseppe di Stefano, *Dictionnaire des locutions en Moyen Français* (Montréal: CERES, 1991) s.v. sang. On the fourteenth-century chanson de geste see the collected studies of François Suard, *Chanson de geste et tradition épique en France au Moyen Âge* (Caen: Paradigme, 1994), and particularly his 'L'épopée française tardive (XIVe–XVe siècles)', in Jean-Marie d'Heur and Nicoletta Cherubini (eds.), *Études de Philologie Romane et d'Histoire Littéraire offertes à Jules Horrent* (Liège, 1980), pp. 449–60 and 'Hugues Capet dans la chanson de geste au XIVe siècle' in Dominique Iogna-Prat and Jean-Charles Picard (eds.), *Religion et culture autour de l'an Mil* (Paris: Picard, 1989), pp. 215–25. Text: *Li romans de Baudouin de Sebourc IIIe roy de Jhérusalem*, ed. [L. N. Boca] (s.l. 1841); Study: Edmond-René Labande, *Étude sur Baudouin de Sebourc. Chanson de geste* (Paris: E. Droz, 1940).

[63] André Artonne, *Le mouvement de 1314 et les chartes provinciales de 1315* (Paris: F. Alcan, 1912).

[64] In the 1317 bill of rights for Burgundy, Louis X addressed the 'nobles', 'religious', and 'non-nobles of these lands'. Eusèbe Jacob de Laurière, *Ordonnances des roys de France de la troisième race* (Paris: Imprimerie Royale, 1742–), I, p. 558.

[65] Bloch, *La société féodale*, pp. 395–402 and Joseph Morsel, *L'aristocratie médiévale* (Paris: Armand Colin, 2004), pp. 121–2 on ternary nomenclature.

as clerical law rules the mighty bishop and the lowly chaplain.[66] Although *Beaudoin de Sebourc* is not a political pamphlet it shares some values with the rebels and shows the transformation of the self-representation of the nobility: noble used as a substantive, the new hereditary blood, the switch from the noble individual bird to the collective pack of hounds. All these elements exemplify fresh conceptions of heredity that emerged in the fourteenth century. Heredity is not the ordered genealogical tree of a pedigree but the more diffuse soul of a group. The notion of race developed out of this legacy. Moreover, far from being confined to the realm of symbolism, these new conceptions were strong enough to give shape to an institution: 'the princes of the blood'.

The institution of the princes of the blood assumes the existence of a royal blood. The expression appears in 1330, the year Edward III got rid of Roger Mortimer. One of Roger's allies, Simon of Basford, was tried for treason and felony in Parliament. Simon was accused of forfeiting 'royal power', murdering his 'liege lord' and destroying 'royal blood'.[67] I have found two examples from 1317, one French and one English, of the use of hereditary blood in a royal context.[68] The 1330 Parliament Roll is the first text with the expression 'royal blood'. It also shows that hereditary blood has entered the wide world of politics. In the same Parliament where Simon of Basford was tried, Richard of Arundel was pardoned. Richard's father had been executed for treason in 1327. The estates and honours of his father were restored to Richard, who was said to be 'like from the blood

---

[66] Howard Kaminsky, 'Estate, Nobility and the Exhibition of Estate in the Later Middle Ages', *Speculum* 68:3 (1993), 684–709.

[67] 'Mes pur ce que notoire chose est et conue a touz que l'avantdit Simon estoit aidant et conseillant au dit Roger en totes les tresons, felonies et malveistes susditz, lesquelles choses sont en purpris de roial poer, murdre de seign' lige et destruction de sank real', John Strachey, John Pridden, and Edward Upham (eds.), *Rotuli parliamentorum* (London 1767–1832), II, p. 53. I was unable to access the new digital edition: Chris Given-Wilson (ed.), *The Parliament Rolls of Medieval England*, 2005 (http://www.sd-editions.com/ PROME/). In the same context see also the London Chronicle description of the coup against Roger Mortimer: 'Et en le mesme temps, comme Dieux y voleit, le roy ove son counseil fist prevément prendre sire Roger le Mortimer en son lit en le chastel de Notingham, et autres ovesques luy, si les fist maunder à le tour de Londres, les queux avoyent purpensée d'avoir forfait le roy et tot le saunk de luy', in George James Aungier (ed.), *Chroniques de London, depuis l'an 44 Hen. III* (London: J.B. Nichols and son, 1844), p. 63.

[68] A letter from Jean de Fiennes to Edward II (Pierre Chaplais, 'Un message de Jean de Fiennes à Édouard II et le projet de démembrement du royaume de France (janvier 1317)', *Revue du Nord* 43 (1961), 145–8 at 148 (new edition in Pierre Chaplais, *Essays in Medieval Diplomacy and Administration* (London: Hambledon, 1981)) and a letter from Eudes duke of Normandy, defending the rights of Jeanne, daughter of Louis X, in Gustave Servois, 'Documents inédits sur l'avénement de Philippe le Long', *Annuaire-bulletin de la Société de l'histoire de France* 2 (1864), 44–79, at 71.

of the Count of Arundel'.[69] Arundel's pardon is the first example of the 'corruption of blood' procedure, whereby sons of executed magnates got back their father's properties from the merciful king.[70]

A vast bibliography exists on late medieval royal ideology, but royal blood is rarely mentioned. Perhaps this is because royal blood was treated *en passant* in Ernst Kantorowicz's classic *The King's Two Bodies* as nothing more than an exemplification of the mysticism of royal continuity.[71] The 1330 text, by contrast, shows that blood was set apart from both the royal public body and feudal power. Royal blood is not invented to strengthen the devolution of the crown from father to son. Therefore, it does not fit Kantorowicz's model as can be seen for the French princes of the blood.

In medieval France, royal blood had a slightly more specific meaning than in England. Royal blood did not refer to an abstract concept but to a group of the king's kin: those of the royal blood. The first mention of those of the royal blood can be dated to 1340 but the concept crystallises a little later.[72] The treaty of Mantes, crafted in 1354, is the first Capetian text to mention what would later be called the princes of the blood. In 1354 the young Charles, king of Navarre, also known as Charles the Bad, had the Constable Charles of Spain, king Jean le Bon's favourite, murdered. Meanwhile the English threat loomed large. Jean swallowed his pride and negotiated a humiliating reconciliation treaty with his nephew/son-in-law.[73] The treaty of Mantes was formulated like a forgiveness letter (*lettre de rémission*). The king swore forgiveness to Charles and so did 'Mylord the Dauphin, Mylord of Anjou, Mylord of Orléans, Mylord of Bourbon and all other Lords of the Blood of France (*Seigneurs du sanc de France*)'.[74] The initial list of the 'Lords of the Blood of France' matches more or less the 'company' of the *Dauphin*. The company was a group of youths created in 1350 at Philip VI's court around the *Dauphin* and his younger brothers, and headed by Philip d'Orléans, Jean le Bon's younger

---

[69] *Rotuli parliamentorum* (n. 67), II, p. 56. On Richard's efforts see Bellamy, *Law of Treason*, p. 84.

[70] J. Enoch Powell and Keith Wallis, *The House of Lords in the Middle Ages: A History of the English House of Lords to 1540* (London: Weidenfeld & Nicolson, 1968), pp. 445–6 gives examples from the beginning of the fifteenth century.

[71] Ernst H. Kantorowicz, *The King's Two Bodies: A Study in Mediaeval Political Theology* (Princeton, N.J.: Princeton University Press, 1957), pp. 332–4.

[72] *Chronique latine de Guillaume de Nangis*, ed. H. Géraud (Paris 1843), Société de l'histoire de France, p. 180.

[73] Raymond Cazelles, *Société politique, noblesse et couronne sous Jean le Bon et Charles V* (Genève: Droz 1982), pp. 157–9. Denis-François Secousse, *Mémoires pour servir à l'histoire de Charles II...* (Paris: Durand, 1758) is still useful.

[74] Denis-François Secousse, *Recueil de pièces servant de preuves aux mémoires sur les troubles excités en France par Charles II dit le Mauvais, roi de Navarre et comte d'Évreux* (Paris: Durand, 1755), p. 36.

brother.[75] The company had its own budget and its own livery worn for festivities.[76] In European court life companies were an element of the *courtois* renaissance, similar to (though less institutionalised than) royal chivalrous orders. As a token of friendship and fealty, identical luxurious clothes or heraldic badges were given to a select group of people.[77] Some similarities in fact exist between hereditary blood and heraldry. In some documents of the first half of the fourteenth century, princes of blood are called princes of the lis or lily (*seigneurs du lys*), a reference to the royal coat of arms.[78]

Like heraldry, hereditary blood mixes genealogical determinism and a certain amount of free will. The list of Mantes mentions Louis de Bourbon. Bourbons have some Capetian ancestry through males but their proximity to the Valois stems from alliance. Isabelle de Valois, the wife of Pierre I, duke of Bourbon, is Philip VI's half-sister. Bourbons are included among the 'Blood of France' because the king wants it, not owing to an essential quality.[79] Integration of outsiders in the select group of 'princes of the blood' was nevertheless very rare. Even if no rules ever define the limits of royal blood, it is generally limited to the king's brothers, sons, and bastards. Traitors like Charles II are excluded. From the reign of Jean le Bon until the Revolution, princes of the blood are familiar figures at the French court. They have more power and clout or less, depending on the historical circumstances.[80]

[75] Françoise Lehoux, *Jean de France, duc de Berri. Sa vie, son action politique*, 4 vols (Paris: A. et J. Picard, 1966–68), I, pp. 19–25.

[76] Françoise Piponnier, *Costume et vie sociale. La cour d'Anjou XIVᵉ – XVᵉ siècle* (Paris/The Hague: Mouton, 1970), p. 25.

[77] Laurent Hablot, 'La devise, mise en signe du prince, mise en scène du pouvoir. Les devises et l'emblématique des princes en Europe à la fin du Moyen Age' (Ph.D. thesis, Université de Poitiers, 2002).

[78] Hervé Pinoteau, *La symbolique royale française Vᵉ – XVIIIᵉ siècles* (La Roche-Rigault: PSR Éditions, 2003), p. 581, n. 592; Brigitte Bedos-Rezak, 'Idéologie royale, ambitions princières et rivalités politiques d'après le témoignage des sceaux (France 1380–1461)', in *La "France anglaise" au moyen âge: colloque des historiens médiévistes français et britanniques*, Congrès national des sociétés savantes. Section d'histoire médiévale et de philologie, Poitiers, 1986. 111th, vol. 1 (Paris: C.T.H.S., 1988), pp. 483–511.

[79] The special position of the Bourbons is clear in the creation of the peer-dukedom in 1327 by Charles IV. Hereditary blood is not used, but is implied in the statement that duke Louis is 'sicut de stirpe regum Francie claram et propinquam originem traxisse non ambiguitur'; M. Huillard-Bréholles, *Titres de la maison ducale de Bourbon* (Paris: H. Plon, 1867), I, n° 1850.

[80] No comprehensive study of princes of the blood exists. A multi-century pecking-order conflict between peers and princes of blood has left a large documentation already published in Jean Du Tillet, *Recueil des rois de France, leurs couronnes et maison* (Paris 1602), and used by Richard A. Jackson, 'Peers of France and Princes of the Blood', *French Historical Studies* 7 (1971), 27–46.

Royal blood entered, albeit rather slowly, Capetian theories about crown devolution. It was used in the dynastic conflict of the Hundred Years' War against English claims to the crown. Capetian lawyers explained that Edward III could not become king of France because he was not 'from the blood of France'.[81] This argument was very weak because it had no legal grounds. French and English lawyers were battling in the realm of Roman-canonical law. *Ius sanguinis* is used in the *Corpus iuris civilis* but it does not have the signification of hereditary blood. Consanguinity also had a different and very technical meaning.[82] Adapting hereditary blood to the learned law system thus needed mastery. It was the great Baldus who at the end of the fourteenth century created a legal theory of hereditary blood, first applied to devolution of the crown and then to other matters.[83] The place of the prince of the blood in Valois's defence against English claims does not mean that royal blood was rejected by English kings. Royal blood never had the same importance in England as in France but it is by no means absent.[84]

Conclusion

The first mention of the word 'race', in Jacques de Brézé's poems at the end of the fifteenth century, can be linked to transformations of ideas of heredity during the fourteenth century. These transformations can be spotted in the ennobling of dogs, the rebirth of noble blood, and the invention of the 'princes of the blood'. All these transformations are related to the self-consciousness of European nobles but are peripheral and even against the ideological core of nobility, which insists on individual virtue. At the beginning of this chapter, I mentioned the classic definition of racism as the rejection of others. Alternatively, racism could be defined as a discourse justifying the social domination of a

---

[81] 'Item obicitur [Philipe VI] predicto regi Anglie quod ipse non est de sanguine domus Francie nisi per medium mulieris, videlicet domine Isabelle, matris sue'. Pierre Chaplais, *English Medieval Diplomatic Practice*, 2 vols in 3 (London: H.M.S.O., 1982), II, p. 449. On these negotiations see Eugène Déprez, *Les préliminaires de la guerre de Cent ans. La papauté, la France et l'Angleterre (1328–1342)*, second edition (Genève: Slatkine-Megariotis Reprints, 1975 (1902)), pp. 223–36, and 'La conférence d'Avignon (1314). L'arbitrage pontifical entre la France et l'Angleterre', in Andrew George Little and Frederick Maurice Powicke (eds.), *Essays in Medieval History Presented to Thomas Frederick Tout* (Manchester/ Edinburgh: R. & R. Clark, 1925), pp. 301–20; Clifford J. Rogers, 'The Anglo-French Peace Negotiations of 1354–1360 Reconsidered', in James Bothwell (ed.) *The Age of Edward III* (Woodbridge: York Medieval Press/Boydell, 2001), pp. 193–213.

[82] Frank Roumy, 'La naissance de la notion canonique de *consanguinitas* et sa réception dans le droit civil', in van der Lugt and de Miramon, *L'hérédité*, pp. 41–66.

[83] Miramon, 'Aux origines de la noblesse'.   [84] *Ibid.*

group by virtue of an essentialist component.[85] Even with this alternative definition, race and hereditary blood are not the main components of the self-justification discourse of the nobility. Race and hereditary blood were not initially racist, even if the scientific racism of the twentieth century incorporated patches of the old discourse of the 'war of the races'.[86] In the Middle Ages religious and medical anthropology were mostly individualistic and unitarian.[87] The dominant medieval discourse leaves little room for a concept of race or human sub-species. The word 'race' is the product of a minority trend that must be understood in the framewok of a complex cultural change that took place at the end of the Middle Ages. The medieval prehistory of 'race' models the cultural matrix that was to witness the growth of the uses of race and hereditary blood in the second half of the sixteenth century.[88]

[85] Pierre Bourdieu, 'Le racisme de l'intelligence', in *Questions de sociologie* (Paris: Éditions de Minuit 1984).

[86] For example, the Nazi Richard Walther Darré, *Neuadel aus Blut und Boden* (Munich: J. F. Lehmann, 1938).

[87] Alain Boureau, 'Hérédité, erreurs et vérité de la nature humaine *(XIIe–XIIIe siècles)*', in van der Lugt and de Miramon; *L'hérédité*, pp. 67–82; Ziegler, 'Hérédité et physiognomonie'.

[88] Arlette Jouanna, *L'idée de race en France au XVIe siècle et au début du XVIIe siècle (1498–1614)* (Lille/Paris: Atelier reproduction des thèses, Université de Lille III / H. Champion, 1976); André Devyver, *Le sang épuré: les préjugés de race chez les gentilshommes français de l'Ancien Régime, 1560–1720* (Bruxelles: Éditions de l'Université de Bruxelles, 1973).

10   The carnal knowing of a coloured
      body: sleeping with Arabs and Blacks
      in the European imagination, 1300–1550

Valentin Groebner

In 1928, the brother of the Italian anthropologist Ridolfo Livi posthumously published the book for which Livi had collected material for nearly thirty years: *La schiavitù domestica nei tempi di mezzo e nei moderni* – Household Slavery in Medieval and Modern Times. The author, in his introduction, set a disquieting tone. In the very moment when Italy had finally begun to build up an overseas colonial empire in North and Northeast Africa to rule over large numbers of people of different colour, he stated solemnly, it was time to reassess the purity of the noble Italian race itself. Medieval and Renaissance history, according to Livi, had disturbing lessons to tell on the 'slow and hidden transformations of race'. Presenting hundreds of pages of edited source material from the twelfth to the sixteenth century on slaves of non-European descent in Italian cities, Livi wanted his Italian readers to wake up to the fact that they counted among their medieval ancestors not only Romans, Greeks and Normans, but also Arabs, Turks and Canary Islanders, not to mention considerable numbers of Tartar and Black men and women. The slit eyes of peasants in the Veneto, the dark complexion of Sicilian peasants: from the perspective of racial anthropology, he stated, these features pointed to a difficult, if not downright dangerous burden on the health of the Italian nation, a burden inherited from the Renaissance.[1]

The following deals with what most studies on ethnicity or race in pre-modern times elegantly encapsulate with terms like 'mixing', 'merging', 'miscegenate', or, in a particularly coy way, 'integration', even 'accultura-tion'. It is what arriving immigrants do with residents and vice versa, con-querors with the subjugated, slaves with their masters: the coitus between the persons of different sex and visibly different ancestry – different, as I

---

[1] Ridolfo Livi, *La schiavitù domestica nei tempi di mezzo e nei moderni* (Padua: C.E.D.A.M., 1928), pp. 7–8. For a broader analysis of the Italian racial anthropology see Claudio Pogliano, *L'ossessione della razza: antropologia e genetica nel XX secolo* (Pisa: Scuola Normale Superiore, 2005).

would want to specify, in skin pigmentation. 'Sex is at the very heart of racism', Ronald Hyam stated somewhat bluntly several years ago in his study on the sexual politics of the British Empire.[2] The same, I want to show, can be said for a broad range of European texts between the thirteenth and the sixteenth centuries. The medieval historian William Chester Jordan, in his afterword 'Why Race?' to the 2001 volume of the *Journal of Medieval and Early Modern Studies* dedicated to the concept of race, has emphasized 'the apparent conflation of misogyny and racism in medieval texts' which raises, he holds, 'a number of vexing questions'. Speaking about race inescapably means defining sexual roles, with masculinity as the ability to impregnate at its core. 'Race' is a notion with a complicated history, attributed to humans relatively late, in the fifteenth century, as Spanish *raza*, Italian *razza*, French *race*. The term was used for drawing boundaries in the realm of the sexual, but its meanings and the context of its uses as a label in late-medieval and Renaissance Europe are difficult to describe. I would therefore like to start with a simple (and probably naïve) question. What were the categories in which Christian writers between the thirteenth and sixteenth centuries described carnal relations between Europeans and non-Europeans? I do not have a ready answer for this question. Rather, I would like to sketch a number of problems that arise in describing the complex relations between race, sex and religion, and to end up with even more open questions.

1.

In a recent article, Peter Biller has drawn attention to the fact that the black woman appears as a definitely sexualized figure in the learned culture of a Christian Europe where Africans still were a very rare sight – that is, in the twelfth and thirteenth centuries. It was Albertus Magnus's writings from the middle of the thirteenth century, especially *De natura loci*, written in Cologne between 1250 und 1254, which, as Peter Biller puts it, 'kickstarted the theme of sex', offering detailed descriptions of the allegedly greater bodily heat of black women, the special qualities of their milk, and, very prominently, their greater sexual lust. Albertus's treatment of black women is, according to Biller, 'the most powerful and comprehensive natural-philosophical account of black people in any Western text of the period'.[3]

---

[2] Ronald Hyam, *Empire and Sexuality: The British Experience* (Manchester: Manchester University Press, 1990), p. 203. See also Naomi Zack (ed.), *Race/Sex: Their Sameness, Difference, and their Interplay* (London: Routledge, 1997).

[3] Peter Biller, 'Black Women in Medieval Scientific Thought', in *La Pelle umana / The Human Skin* (*Micrologus* 13) (Firenze: Sismel, 2005), pp. 477–92, at 488 and Biller's contribution to the present collection at pp. 170, 172, 174.

But the passages from *De natura loci* had their counterparts in the European literary imagination – the courtly epics abound in descriptions of eroticized encounters between men and women of different colour. Let me start with a couple of examples from the German-speaking realm I am most familiar with. In Wolfram von Eschenbach's *Parzifal*, the hero's father marries a beautiful black Moorish princess who then gives birth to a son, Feirefiz, whose skin-colour is spotted, partly black, partly white – a most noble and virtuous knight.[4] These positive figures, however, had their negative counterparts. A German author named *Der Stricker* (literally: the knitter) deplored in his poem 'The Queen of the Moors' written in the 1230s, the decline of chivalric virtue. In his account, a heathen queen sends out hundreds of beautiful black women as erotic secret agents into the realm of a Christian queen to seduce Christian knights, and to lure them away from the Christian faith into pagan superstition and idolatry, sweetened by sexual bliss. In the courtly epic *Apollonius von Tyrlant*, written around 1300 by one Heinrich von Neustadt, the Christian hero conquers large territories in a fictitious and exotic Middle East. Although already married to a white Indian princess, he falls in love with Palmina, a beautiful black queen who, in the poet's words, proudly declares the special abilities of her kind to provide sexual delight: 'ain mörinne gibt vil dick süsser minne'. She bears Apollonius two children, a son, Garamant, of black and white skin colour, the future ruler of Mesopotamia and the Land of the Moors, and a daughter, Marmacora, 'black as a crow'. Palmina's counterpart in the epic is the violent and sexually hyperactive black tyrant Glorant, who boasts he has raped more than 400 white Christian women. After capturing another white princess – she must first serve his lust in the royal bed, then work in a huge subterranean carpet factory – the tyrant finally meets his fate, being overthrown and beheaded by the Christian hero Apollonius.[5]

The biblical motive of the powerful and seducing black queen from a mythical Orient could be expanded in more ambiguous variants. Taking up a passage from Flavius Josephus on Moses' first wife, of African origin, and extensively borrowing from Petrus Comestor's *Historia scholastica*, the German poet Rudolf von Ems amplified the theme in his thirteenth-century *Weltchronik* (Chronicle of the World) into a complex tale.

---

[4] More examples in Alfred Ebenbauer, '"Es gibt ain mörynne vil dick süsse mynne". Belakanes Landsleute in der deutschen Literatur des Mittelalters', *Zeitschrift für deutsches Altertum und deutsche Literatur* 113 (1984), 16–42.

[5] *Ibid.*, 30–2. Heinrich von Neustadt, *Apollonius von Tyrlant*, Codices Illuminati medii aevii 49 (Munich: Lengenfelder, 1988); Wolfgang Wilfried Moelleken, Gayle Agler and Robert Lewis (eds.), *Die Kleindichtung des Strickers* (Göppingen: Kümmerle, 1974), vol. 2, pp. 236–42.

Moses, on behalf of the Egyptian Pharaoh waging war against the Africans, falls in love with a black African princess, Tarbis. She promises him, as princesses usually do in courtly literature, that he can rule her country if he agrees to marry her; which he does, fathering two children. But Moses in his African kingdom is soon overcome by something his black wife cannot satisfy, homesickness. Being trained in magical arts, Moses owns a ring with an inbuilt antique image possessing special supernatural powers. With its help, he can make a person forget what he or she loves most. Erasing himself from the memory of his black princess, Moses is able to escape from Africa, back to Egypt, and then, remarried, to wander further to the Promised Land.[6]

Medieval literary and scholarly imagination from the thirteenth century concentrated on dark skin colour as a label for sexualizing figures – female ones. The figure of the virtuous, black-skinned saint and martyr Mauritius had no female counterparts: medieval hagiography knew no saintly black women of virtuous behaviour. But literature abounded, in the fourteenth and fifteenth centuries, not only with lustful, dark-skinned oriental tyrants, but with moorish princesses as well. Such a powerful female protagonist stood at the centre of Hermann von Sachsenheim's *Mörin*, an epic written in Swabia in the 1450s. Hermann presented her to his German readers as priestess of the pagan deity Venus, her lips, teeth, golden earrings, breasts and her skin 'soft like black velvet' meticulously described, driving the hero mad with sexual promise and delight in a piece of literature that was written as a *roman à clef* with allusions to contemporary politics at a small Wurttemberg court.[7] Such a tradition obviously worked in the complete absence of real men and women of dark complexion, and the name of Hermann's smashing black princess is telling enough: Brunhilde she is called – not exactly a name with a true African ring.

2.

With fictive black partners in imagined sexual unions abounding, what was the quality of whiteness evoked, on the other side of the bed, as it were? Europeans between the thirteenth and the sixteenth century did not

[6] I owe the reference to Petrus Comestor to Robert Bartlett. For the history of the motif in the medieval German literature see Andreas Mielke, *'Nigra sum et formosa': Afrikanerinnen in der deutschen Literatur des Mittelalters* (Stuttgart: Helfant, 1992), and the valuable critical comments of Maaike van der Lugt, 'La peau noir dans la science médiévale', in *La Pelle umana*, pp. 439–76.
[7] Hermann von Sachsenheim, *Die Mörin*, ed. Hans Dieter Schlosser (Wiesbaden: Brockhaus, 1974); on the epic see Ebenbauer, '"Es gibt ain mörynne"', 36, and the important remarks in Mielke, *Nigra sum*.

describe themselves as being white. Different skin colours served as signs of an individual's physical *complexio* – an ever-changing, fluid combination of one's bodily liquids.[8] Some medieval medical writers like Arnau de Vilanova even held that the human skin had no colour in itself; rather, like a fingernail, it made visible the colour of the flesh and liquids underneath. In treatises on medicine, physiognomy and natural philosophy as well as in novellas and courtly epics, an astonishing range of skin colours ascribed to European individuals can thus be found, from *albus* to *nigra*, from *ulivigna* (olive-coloured), to 'deep red', *vermeille* (crimson) and even *verdâtre* or *verdastro* (greenish). Following the medical authorities from antiquity, the ideal was of course a well-balanced middle position between the extremes of heat and dryness, associated with black, and coldness and moisture, visible through very white and pale skin.[9]

This middle position between white and black was the ideal *complexio* the Greek authorities of Antiquity had already claimed for themselves. Arab writers in the tenth and eleventh centuries would follow their model, contrasting their own ideal well-tempered *complexio* to those of dark-skinned Africans in the South and barbarous white-skinned Franks and Turks in the North and Northeast. Learned Europeans did the same. Petrarca, in his famous 'Letter to posterity' written in the 1360s, described himself as having 'sparkling eyes, my skin colour between white and dark' (*inter candidum et subnigrum*).[10] In the first description of the Canary Islands, translated in the same years by Boccaccio from Italian to Latin, the skin colour of the inhabitants of these 'Happy Islands' was the same, perfectly balanced between black and white.[11]

The detailed description of a person's outward appearance could be used to deliver explicit messages – political physiognomics, as it were – on their well or badly balanced bodily fluids and temperament. The humanist Enea Silvio Piccolomini wrote in the 1420s of the Austrian Duke Albrecht that he had 'a black, fear-inspiring face'. A Nuremberg merchant, member of a diplomatic mission, described the French king Louis in 1466 as

[8] On medieval concepts of skin colours, see my '*Complexio*/complexion. Categorizing Individual Natures 1250–1600', in Lorraine Daston and Fernando Vidal (eds.), *The Moral Authority of Nature* (Chicago: University of Chicago Press, 2003), pp. 133–56, and 'Nature's Way: The Colours of Things', in *Who Are You? Identification, Deception, and Surveillance in Early Modern Europe* (New York: Zone, 2007), pp. 117–50.
[9] *Ibid.*, pp. 130–31; important additions in van der Lugt, 'La peau noir', 446 (on Arnau de Vilanova) and 451–7 (on theories of generation).
[10] Francesco Petrarca, *Posteritati: Lettere ai posteri*, ed. Gianni Villani (Rome: Salerno editrice, 1990), pp. 35–6.
[11] Robert Bartlett, 'Medieval and Modern Concepts of Race and Ethnicity', *Journal of Medieval and Early Modern Studies* 21 (2001), 39–56 at 45–7; Groebner, *Who Are You?*, pp. 130–3.

'a small man with a long nose, deep-seated dark eyes' and 'of brown appearance'. Such skin colours did not necessarily point to exotic origins, but rather to individual complexions and living conditions that resulted in physical differences. Climate played an important role, but so did individual temperament, age (old people, losing natural heat, would get paler), diet and sex – women, with moist and cold fluids dominating, were held to appear lighter than the dryer and hotter men. Marco Polo and, a generation later, at the beginning of the fourteenth century, Odorico da Pordenone, described the Tartar and Chinese as light-skinned and white; their women being 'the most beautiful in the world'.[12]

With the boom of the European slave trade in the second half of the fourteenth century, and with the arrival of large numbers of slaves of non-European origin in Italian cities, these categories underwent a rapid change. In 1367, Petrarca complained in a letter to a friend about the beauty of Venice being 'tainted' by the growing number of 'Scythian faces' on its streets, that is, slaves with Asian facial features.[13] The above-mentioned anthropologist Ridolfo Livi, worried about Italy's early racial miscegenation, edited in his 1928 volume the complete Florentine *Registro degli schiavi*. Its registers offer long lists of slaves bought and sold in Florence between 1366 and 1397, the overwhelming majority of them female, 329 out of a total 357, with detailed descriptions of their outward appearances. They speak for example of an 18-year-old woman of Tartar origin, *de natione Tartarorum*, sold in July 1366 as 'being above medium height, with olive-coloured skin (*ulivigna*), a big nose and a black mole above the nose and two scars on her left hand'. Or of another of 'quasi black skin, with some marks on the left side of her nose'; or of a woman from the Black Sea port of Caffa, 'of white skin, with pierced ears and a black mole on the left side of her forehead'. These extensive descriptions, however, focus less on skin colour than on partic-ular bodily signs such as birthmarks on hands and faces, scars and tattoos by which a fugitive slave could be identified. Moreover, the categories used for skin pigmentation – *flava* or yellow, *bruna*, *nigra*, *ulivigna*, *rossa*, or even *verdastro*, greenish – were the same as those applied to contem-porary Italians.[14]

---

[12] Johann August Schmeller (ed.), *Des böhmischen Herrn Leo von Rozmital Ritter-, Hof- und Pilgerreise* (Stuttgart: Bibliothek des literarischen Vereins, 1844), p. 164; Folker Reichert, *Begegnungen mit China. Die Entdeckung Ostasiens im Mittelalter* (Sigmaringen: Thorbecke, 1992), pp. 104–5.

[13] Steven Epstein, *Speaking of Slavery: Color, Ethnicity, and Human Bondage in Italy* (Ithaca and London: Cornell University Press, 2001) p. 105.

[14] Livi, *Schiavitù*, pp. 141–217; for the broader context, see Epstein, *Speaking*, pp. 84–5.

Nearly all the women in Livi's Florentine register came from the Northern and Northeastern shores of the Black Sea. When the Ottoman conquest of Byzantium in 1453 blocked European access to the formerly main slave exporting region, the northern shores of the Black Sea, the slave traders turned to the Atlantic. Slaves from Muslim Spain had appeared already in the twelfth and thirteenth centuries at the slave markets in Sardinia and Genoa. From the mid-fifteenth century on, Portuguese and Spanish slave traders intensified their raids into North and West Africa, and reached out into the Atlantic, bringing tens of thousands of Africans to the Iberian Peninsula. It was the booming Renaissance slave trade that finally decided the fate of the inhabitants of the Canary Islands – and the way their skin colour was perceived by Europeans. Sources from Florence, Pisa and Genoa indicate the presence of female household slaves from the islands in these cities: two women called Caterina delle Canarie appear as slaves in Sienese court records in the 1480s. The German traveller Hieronymus Münzer saw Canary Islanders in chains working in the port of Valencia. 'Their women are beautiful', he wrote, 'with long and strong limbs'. But their customs were brutish, *bestiales*, he added, they were all idolaters, and their skin colour was nearly black, a dark brown.[15] Within 150 years, the appearance of the inhabitants of the 'Happy Islands' who, in Boccaccio's account, had looked like Petrarca, described by ideal categories borrowed from Antiquity, had undergone drastic change.

3.

Münzer's labelling of the Canary Islanders as 'idolaters', infidels, is crucial in his account. From the Black Sea to the Atlantic, Europe from the fourteenth to the sixteenth centuries was characterized by the presence of relatively large numbers of men and women of un-free status, of slave raids and slave trades. In a series of papal bulls (*Illius qui*, 1442; *Dum diversas* and *Divino amore communitati*, 1452) the Holy See had authorized Portugal 'to conquer, subdue and enslave all enemies of Christ and pagans' and take possession of their property and territory. Slave trade was justified in *Inter cetera* (1464) on the ground that slaves would be converted. In a Christian Europe, where powerful fraternities like the Italian Trinitarians or the Spanish Order of Merced deplored the fate of Christian slaves in the hands of the infidels and successfully raised large

[15] Groebner, *Who Are You?*, p. 134; Ludwig Pfandl (ed.), 'Itinerarium Hispanium Hieronymi Monetarii, 1494–1495', *Revue Hispanique* 48 (1920), 1–179, at 23–4.

amounts of money for their liberation, slavery was legal, as Steven Epstein reminds the readers of his great study on Renaissance household slaves. It was permitted under the condition that the master was Christian. No Jew in Italy, no Jew or Muslim in Spain could legally own slaves, regardless of their religion.

The European slave trade in the fourteenth and fifteenth centuries was to a considerable extent a trade in female slaves, particularly in the Italian cities, and we have ample evidence of the functions of these slaves as concubines of their masters. Skin colour was a strong factor in the price of a person, as Epstein has shown. In fifteenth-century Sicily, prices for female slaves of African origin were considerable lower – roughly two-thirds – than those from Georgia, Turkey and the Caucasus. In extant contracts of purchase from Genoa, women from Russia and the Balkans were sold for prices more than 50 percent higher than those labelled as *mora* – dark-skinned, of West or North African origin.[16]

As detailed as the physical descriptions of the young women in the Florentine *registro* may seem – and with their information on birthmarks and scars, they have no equivalents in contemporary sources – they lack one detail, highly important for buyer and seller: whether the slave was pregnant or not. What happened to such children? A general answer seems difficult; the practice seems to have varied according to regional circumstances. In a recent article on status and slavery in Italy and in the Venetian colonies in the Eastern Mediterranean, Sally McKee has shown that slave women were remarkably successful in securing freedom for the children born out of sexual relations with their masters. Contrary to the statutes of Roman Law and to the *ius commune*, in Italian judicial practice children between slaves and masters inherited their fathers' status instead of their mothers'; in short, they were no more slaves, but free – and were baptized Christian. This happened not only on Crete, McKee argues, but also in the cities of the Italian mainland. In Venice, the Great Council even passed, in 1422, a law that explicitly prohibited the practice of Venetian patricians to put up their illegitimate sons by slave women for seats in that Council. Unlike earlier references that spoke more vaguely and coyly of 'women of low and vile condition', the 1422 edict explicitly labels the women the Venetian patricians had slept with: *ancillae* – their female slaves.[17]

McKee deliberately avoids the term 'ethnicity' and suggests 'ancestry' instead: 'the awareness', she defines, 'of who a person's parents and

---

[16] Epstein, *Speaking*, pp. 185–90.
[17] Sally McKee, 'Inherited Status and Slavery in Late Medieval Italy and Venetian Crete', *Past and Present* 182 (2004), 31–53.

grand-parents were and sometimes where they came from'. But what differences in ancestry counted?

Anxiety over inter-faith sex was a discourse extremely prominent in medieval Christian Spain, as David Nirenberg has recently shown. As every Christian woman, wed or unwed, was the bride of Christ through baptism, the thirteenth-century Spanish code, *Siete partidas*, ruled, sleeping with a Muslim or Jew was adultery. In the *Cantigas de Santa Maria*, the Virgin herself miraculously intervenes to save a young Christian wife falsely accused by her mother-in-law of intercourse with her Muslim slave. As Christian women were not only God's wives, but also his daughters, the Dominican preacher Vicent Ferrer stated in his sermons, engaging in inter-faith sex meant that they disobeyed their fathers and turned themselves into prostitutes. He also thundered against the alleged lusts of Christian men for Muslim and Jewish women. In a sermon in 1415, Vincent Ferrer warned his audience in Saragossa, many Christian men believed their children to be their own, when they had actually been fathered by Muslims or Jews. Nirenberg shows how prostitutes became the focal point for anxiety about sexual frontiers between Christians, Muslim and Jews in fourteenth-century Spain, many of the stories emphasizing that the Christian woman could detect her infidel customer by his circumcised penis. Accusations of sexual intercourse of a Jew or a Muslim with a Christian woman were spread deliberately to spark pogroms and massacres. Even after the forced mass conversions of Jews and Muslims in the late fourteenth and the first half of the fifteenth centuries, the motif was still widely used. The town council of Valencia complained that the Christian brothel was so crowded with newly converted Moriscos exercising their new sexual privilege that the regular Christian customers could not get in the door.[18]

Vincent Ferrer and his contemporaries chose sexual terms to express what they perceived as a crisis of religious identification: the language of sexual danger was a symptom of the crisis and a promise of its potent cure, simultaneously fortifying boundaries and marking them as already breached. The new anxieties were not the result of any increase in the amount of sexual contact between people of different faiths, Nirenberg argues. Rather, they were sparked by the mass conversions of Spanish Jews and Muslims, the disappearance of the Jew and the Muslim as stable

---

[18] David Nirenberg, 'Conversion, Sex, and Segregation. Jews and Christians in Medieval Spain', *American Historical Review* 107 (2002), 1065–93. See also his: 'Das Konzept von Rasse in der Forschung über mittelalterlichen iberischen Antijudaismus', in Christoph Cluse, Alfred Haverkamp and Israel J. Yuval (eds.), *Jüdische Gemeinden und ihr christlicher Kontext in kulturräumlich vergleichender Betrachtung von der Spätantike bis zum 18. Jahrhundert* (Hanover: Hahnsche Buchhandlung, 2003), pp. 49–74.

figures that had so long served to define, as Anti-Christian, what being Christian meant. In the 1430s, a generation after the forced mass conversions, the first Christian Spanish writers began to articulate the view that the converts and their descendants were essentially different, that is, inferior to 'natural' Christians. The infamous laws of the *limpieza de sangre* sought to ban all children and grandchildren of converted Jews and Muslims from climbing into royal offices and high up church hierarchies. Fifteenth- and early sixteenth-century Spanish authors were convinced that these 'New Christians' – as opposed to 'natural Christians' – and their children could, among other things, be detected by their outward appearance, dark complexion and curly hair.[19]

Yet in the Italian cities at the same period, sexual relations between Christian masters and their infidel female slaves seem not to have been a reason for deep concern and sexual panic, unlike the alleged sexual acts between Christians, Jews and Muslims in medieval Spain. As both McKee and Nirenberg emphasize, Christian law codes clearly stipulated that children born of a mixed union were fully Christian and were to be raised as such. I have not come across any judicial or administrative measures against the descendants of female slaves of non-European origin in fifteenth- and sixteenth-century Italy so long as the children were baptized – with the exception of the Venetian law of 1422 mentioned above that prohibited Venetian patricians from putting up their illegitimate sons by slave women for seats in the Great Council: a decree, it seems, made for a singular case.

4.

Fourteenth- and fifteenth-century slaves, sold, taxed or pursued by the law, are among the best described people in the late medieval past, as Steven Epstein has remarked in *Speaking of Slavery*. Scribes registered meticulously their names, origin and price. They noted their height and stature, described their scars, moles and tattoos and whether their ears were pierced or not. But once freed and baptized, all these men and women disappear from the records, however exotic their outward

---

[19] Nirenberg, 'Conversion', 1088–91, with extensive bibliography and his contribution to this collection at pp. 242–60. See also Henry Kamen, 'Race, limpieza et noblesse dans l'Espagne du XVIe siècle', in Joël Fouilleron, Guy Le Thiec and Henri Michel (eds.), *Sociétés et idéologies des temps modernes: Hommage à Arlette Jouanna* (Montpellier: Université de Montpellier III, Centre d'histoire moderne et contemporaine de l'Europe méditerranéenne et de ses périphéries, 1996), pp. 721–30, and Max Sebastian Hering Torres, 'Limpieza de sangre – Rassismus in der Vormoderne?', *Wiener Zeitschrift zur Geschichte der Neuzeit* 3 (2003), 20–37.

appearance may have been – thus disquieting, four centuries later, our worried anthropologist Ridolfo Livi. The procedures of juridical exclusion created the written sources the modern historian's analysis depends on. According to their logic, not ethnicity or skin pigmentation, but religion and juridical status – the condition of slavery – made the difference.

The lack of juridical sources brings us back to the literary traditions I started with; narratives and categories themselves marked by the conditions of slavery. Within a century, the light-skinned Asian beauties of Marco Polo and Odorico da Pordenone underwent a profound change, transforming, in the vernacular Florentine literature of the fourteenth and early fifteenth centuries, into much coarser literary stereotypes. The female slave appeared as comical and grotesque, greedy and lustful, uttering obscene wordplay in transmogrified Tuscan dialect – a sexualized figure to make a male audience laugh.[20] But the comical always signifies ambivalence: we joke about what we fear. With the arrival of ever larger numbers of slaves from Northern and Western Africa in the second half of the fifteenth century, the sexualized black woman, the seducing Moorish princesses and the sexually hyperactive princes from African or Oriental lands so prominent in the courtly literature of the twelfth and thirteenth centuries gave way to a new literary paradigm that, with quite different means, expressed a deep-seated anxiety.

In his *Novellino*, a collection of novellas written in the 1460s, the Italian poet Masuccio Guardati developed a new variant of the topic. The slaves he portrays in his novellas – all situated in Southern Italy and, partly, at the Mediterranean shores of France – were quite unlike the grotesquely sexualized Tartar women of the Florentine literary tradition. They are described as *moros* – an ambivalent term that could mean Arabs as well as Africans, emphasizing difference in faith as well as in skin colour in comparison with Italians. Masuccio's Moors resemble their earlier dark-skinned counterparts from the courtly epics of earlier centuries I have described above. Yet they no longer act as princesses and princes in exotic lands, but as slaves in Italian households. And they use their bodies – partly described as seductive and beautiful, partly as hideous and ugly – as weapons against their masters.

---

[20] Piero Guarducci and Valeria Ottanelli, *I servitori domestici della casa borghese toscana nel basso medio evo* (Florence: Salimbeni, 1982); Agostino Zanelli, *Le schiave orientali a Firenze nei secoli XIV e XV* (Bologna: Forni, 1976). See also the classic accounts of Iris Origo, 'The Domestic Enemy: The Eastern Slaves in Renaissance Tuscany in the 14th and 15th century', *Speculum* 30 (1955), 321–66; Charles Verlinden, *L'esclavage dans l'Europe médiévale*, vol. 2 (Ghent: de Tempel, 1977); Jacques Heers, *Esclaves et domestiques au Moyen Age dans le monde méditerranéen* (Paris: Fayard, 1981).

In one of Guardati's stories, a noble woman in Sicily falls for her beautiful male Moorish slave and flees with him to the North African coast, taking the money and jewels of her cuckolded Christian husband with her. Only by seducing his wife's female Moorish slave is the husband able to find her and her dark-skinned lover in the land of the infidels, and to take (as Italian readers probably expected) sanguinary revenge. In another, even more drastic novella, Guardati tells the tale of a Christian woman. Although married to a loving and attentive husband, she engages 'in perverse lust', as the author puts it, with her black slave who, although being a hideous dwarf, has a huge penis. Here, it is not the husband but another Moorish slave servant who, surprising the two unequal lovers in bed, is so shocked and ashamed that she pierces them in the act with a huge lance, thus offering the returning nobleman the shocking evidence of both adultery and its punishment.[21] Guardati's stories, dedicated to the King of Naples and intended to amuse an elegant courtly audience, no longer concentrate on the eroticized body of the exotic dark-skinned Other. Rather, they emphasize the sexual contact between Christians and dark-skinned Moors as grotesque, appalling and menacing – the black-and-white coitus becoming the centre of the plot, the physical difference turned into pornography.

A generation later, in the mid-sixteenth century, the Tuscan-born Matteo Bandello told in his 'Novelle' the terrifying tale of the Moorish slave who takes the absence of his master as the opportunity for a cruel revenge. He locks himself up in a tower with the master's wife and three children, rapes and tortures the wife and torments the returned owner with the threat of destroying his family. In order to get his wife and children back, the Moor in the tower cries down to his helpless master, he must cut off his own nose; and after the desperate man does that, the slave replies, this life-long disfigurement was only the well-deserved punishment for the master's excessive cruelty toward his slaves. He finally kills his master's wife and children, jumps from the tower and kills himself. The lesson was clear enough, the author Bandello explains to his readers. Never trust a slave; they were sex-crazed and cruel, the Moors being the worst.[22]

---

[21] Masuccio Salernitano, *Il Novellino*, ed. Salvatore Nigro (Milan: Rizzoli, 1990). I have used the German edition: Il Masuccio, *Novellino* (Berlin: Wagenbach, 1988), vol. 1, pp. 28–35 and 54–5.

[22] Matteo Bandello, *Tutte Le Opere*, ed. Francesco Flora (Verona: P.S.E.M. 1943), vol. 2, pp. 374–8; see also Epstein, *Speaking*, pp. 44–5. The German translation of Bandello's collection has a slightly misleading title that does not really prepare its readers for the stronger stuff of sixteenth-century storytelling: Dirk Blask (ed.), *Matteo Bandello. Mit List und Leidenschaft. Italienische Liebesgeschichten aus der Renaissance* (Munich: Winkler, 1985).

It is not very likely that these narratives, impressive as they may be, describe real encounters of real fifteenth- and sixteenth-century people of different creed and complexion. Bandello's story is a mere variation of a much older account, written nearly four centuries earlier by Gerald of Wales in his *Topographia Hibernica* of 1188. Gerald set his story in a savage Ireland peopled by wondrous creatures, fairies, barbarians and, among other things, women copulating with he-goats; a wild place waiting, in the logic of the *Topographia*, for the civilizing, ordering forces of the English king's rule. In the Tuscan adaptation of the 1550s, this wilderness has definitely entered European households. Yet Bandello's account is clearly influenced by the medieval narrative tradition of sex between people of different colour I have tried to sketch. The words of the cruel Moor's justification of his sexual suicide attack imply that Bandello's readers were well aware of the fact that some slaves were treated cruelly by their Christian masters; as they were aware of the entanglements of violence and sexual desires between light-skinned and dark-skinned human bodies. This is a story about sexual horrors. In Gerald's twelfth-century version, the outraged prisoner in the tower forces the one on the ground not to cut off his own nose, but to emasculate himself. Sixteenth-century Italian readers were familiar with the equation of nose and penis, with the *denasatio* (cutting off somebody's nose) as a frequently used and depicted metaphor for castration.[23] The thrill Bandello gave his readers was based, among other things, on the imagination of a deadly rivalry between a white Christian, and a black Moorish *cazzo*.

5.

The history of the European perception of skin colours is deeply marked by the rapid expansion of the Western slave trade in the second half of the fifteenth century. Among the manifold varieties between humans, those categories were highlighted as marking the racially Other that matched the outward appearances of the women and men brought in from Northern and West Africa. Describing a person's skin colour, between the thirteenth and sixteenth centuries, was not only closely linked to juridical and religious categories of exclusion. At the beginning of the sixteenth century, a new term was coined to describe qualities transferred from one generation to the next by way of ancestry and consanguinity – Spanish *raza*, Italian *razza*, French *race*.

---

[23] On the imagery of late medieval and Renaissance cut-off noses, see my *Defaced: The Visual Culture of Violence in the Late Middle Ages*, trans. Pamela Selwyn (New York: Zone, 2004), pp. 67–86.

It was not a new word; in the centuries before, it had been used for the lineage and traits that dogs and horses inherited by pedigree.[24] From around 1500, it was applied to humans. Spanish theologians and jurists claimed that the children of both baptized Jews and Muslims differed in their *raza* from pure *cristianos de natura*. A new category was established, inscribed irrevocably in a person's flesh (and skin) 'by nature'. By its very definition, it should preclude anyone's capacity to name and change themselves. Thus it not only contains the violent exclusion and expulsion of Jews and Muslims from the Iberian peninsula and the history of Renaissance slavery; but also the reshaping of eroticized, exotic bodies in the complex, pornographic *mis-en-scènes* of Guardati's and Bandello's Renaissance novellas.

How can we thus describe the Mongol, Moorish and Black ancestors of the inhabitants of twentieth-century Europe that preoccupied so intensely the racial anthropologist Ridolfo and his colleagues in the 1920s? Tracing their history in fifteenth- and sixteenth-century documents and narratives leads us, at the end, into a paradox. Imagined, fictitious sexual encounters between people of different ancestry, it seems, had stronger effects and consequences than real ones.

And here we are back to sex as part of a particular libido, a libido not necessarily typical of the relationship between Renaissance masters and their slaves, but characterizing contemporary historians. There is a historian's desire for the desires of others, long ago, to fulfil some of his or her own wishes, it seems. We may, from a twenty-first-century point of view, too easily see the coitus as 'das Eigentliche', as the very moment when hidden desires and stark power relations finally become manifest and visible, the moment of the unveiling of naked truths.

Yet the medieval discourse on sex between masters and slaves and between men and women of different faith followed rules quite different from the ones that govern our own discourse. The medieval language of sexual danger was a symptom of crisis – much more a crisis of identification of a person's juridical status and religion than one of adherence to a group defined by skin colour – and simultaneously the promise of a potent cure for it, marking and fortifying social and religious boundaries by presenting them as endangered.

There is a second aspect. I'm aware that I run here the risk of committing one of the worst of sins of my profession, anachronism. But I cannot help but point to what seems to me a remarkably durable category in talking about sex, one that might link our own experiences in bed with

---

[24] See Charles de Miramon's chapter in the present volume.

those of the people five or six centuries ago. Sex is not always and not necessarily the moment of the unveiling of the truth. On the contrary, sex is the very field of deception, of the masking of one's identity. Sexual partners lie to the ones they lie with, and this is exactly what so many of the medieval and Renaissance narratives made the very centre of their plot. It is pitch dark when the beautiful black queen Palmina in Heinrich von Neustadt's epic slips into the white hero's bed and makes him believe he is making love to his own wife. Moses, in Rudolf von Ems' chronicle, manipulates the mind of his black wife with magical devices, erasing himself from her memory. Guardati's novellas and finally Bandello's terrifying tale of the cruel Moor speak of sex as a weapon in plots of revenge, dissimulation and deceit.

The physical fulfilment of sexual desire with its complicated relations to volition and submission is not only about the real thing, but also, inescapably, it seems, about changing one's mind. The sexual act has the uncanny power to change the mutual perception of the two partners involved. This power can bring about transformations in the desired other that may be sobering, frightening or repulsive. Sex is able, to put it simply, to turn the beloved one into a stranger, a savage, a person from the wilderness whom we have not known before.[25] And maybe that is why talking about sex served so well the purpose of telling tales of deceit, dissimulation and changing roles; because this, too, was what late medieval discourse on race and sex was about.

---

[25] More in Wendy Doniger, *The Bedtrick: Tales of Sex and Masquerade* (Chicago: Chicago University Press, 2000).

11   Was there race before modernity?
The example of 'Jewish' blood
in late medieval Spain

David Nirenberg

> What is known as the history of concepts is really a history either of our
> knowledge of concepts or of the meaning of words.
>
> Gottlob Frege, *Die Grundlagen der Arithmetik*, vii.

Less than a lifetime ago many scholars agreed that racial concepts offered
reasonable explanations for the differences they perceived between certain
human populations. That consensus extended, not only to such "colour"
distinctions as those between "white" European and "black" sub-Saharan
African, but also to less chromatic classifications such as "Indo-European"
and "Semite." It extended backward in time, as well. In the nineteenth
century, for example, the most eminent historians did not hesitate to
describe medieval and early-modern conflicts between Christians and
Jews (or Muslims) as racial. Today the situation has so reversed itself that
no scholar of any stripe or period can strip the word "race" of its scare-
quotes without inviting polemic.

It is not difficult to find the turning point in the fate of race as theory. It
came at mid-twentieth century, with the German National Socialists'
implementation of an explicitly racial ideology that culminated in the
extermination of millions of members of those races deemed most dangerous or degenerate. Opponents of fascism often pointed critically to the
brutality of Nazi racial policies, even if they made relatively little effort to
help the victims of those policies, and this critique in turn strengthened
the arguments of those who sought to challenge the authority of racial
ideologies in the countries and colonies of the eventual Allies.
Throughout the 1930s and 1940s in the United States, for example,
African-American journalists drew frequent comparisons between the
treatment of Jews in Germany and blacks at home. In those same decades,
social scientists like Ruth Benedict and Ashley Montague took up Franz
Boas's invitation to demonstrate the arbitrariness of any definition of
"race." In *Man's Most Dangerous Myth: The Fallacy of Race* (1942),

Montague made the point through the then timely example of the Jews. For centuries, he claimed, the persecution of Jews

> was always done on social, cultural, or religious grounds ... [W]hatever was held against them was never attributed to clearly defined biological reasons. The 'racial' interpretation is a modern 'discovery.' That is the important point to grasp. The objection to any people on 'racial' or biological grounds is virtually a purely modern innovation.

The goal of arguments like Montague's was to demolish the scientific grounds upon which racial regimes justified their discriminations between human populations, thereby unmasking those discriminations as the contingent product of the workings of power in modernity. So great was the success of such arguments that by 1950 race was discredited as a mode of discourse in the biological and social sciences, if not in more regional or popular dialects. For evidence of the impact of this discursive shift, we need look no further than the United Nations' post-war declarations on human rights, or the deliberations of the United States' Supreme Court about the constitutionality of segregation.[1]

The dismantling of racism's claims to provide a natural explanation for the existence of cultural, economic, and social difference, or for the persistence of such difference through time, was one of the most important achievements of the mid-twentieth-century social sciences. Since that time, those sciences have been struggling with mixed success to find new terms and theories with which to describe and explain the persistence of group identity and group difference across time and space.[2] Historians too are struggling with the consequences of the dismantling of race, but theirs is a slightly different problem, for their task is not only that of criticizing the ontological status of key words and concepts such as race, but also that of understanding the concepts and categories that their

---

[1] Ashley Montague, *Man's Most Dangerous Myth: The Fallacy of Race*, revised edition (New York: Oxford University Press, 1974[1942]), pp. 21–22. At p. 56 he quotes Boas: "[W]e talk all the time glibly of races and nobody can give us a definite answer to the question what constitutes a race" (quoted from Franz Boas, "History and Science in Anthropology: A Reply," *American Anthropologist* 38 [1936], 140.) Thurgood Marshall's successful arguments before the Supreme Court in the case of Sweatt vs. Texas (1950) provide a good example of some of the legal consequences of the de-legitimization of racial theory in academic circles. Marshall called on Robert Redfield, chair of the anthropology department at the University of Chicago, to explain to the justices that "there is no understandable factual basis for classification by race." See Richard Kluger, *Simple Justice* (New York: Vintage Books, 1977), p. 264. My thanks to Jane Dailey for these references.

[2] See, *inter alia*, Michael Banton, *Racial Theories*, second edition (Cambridge: Cambridge University Press, 1998), p. ix. On the struggle for a vocabulary to apply to the case of Jews and Judaism specifically, see Gavin Langmuir, "Prolegomena to Any Present Analysis of Hostility against Jews," *Social Science Information = Information sur les sciences sociales* 15 (1976), 689–727, here 691.

historical subjects used to make sensible (at least to them) claims about the formation and reproduction of group identities in their own societies.

These two goals are not always compatible. When, for example, scholars make use of the word race in their analyses of nineteenth- and twentieth-century United States history, as they so often do, they are deploying what they know to be a "myth" incapable of definition. But if they were to follow the injunctions of the more radical among them to erase such fictions from their vocabulary, they would lose purchase on the language of their subjects. (Besides, such a logic would require us to expunge many other words from our analyses, among them "God.")[3] It is for this reason, among others, that modernists, insofar as they are describing the thought-world of their subjects rather than their own, continue to write about "race" and "racism" with relatively little controversy. But the further we move toward the pre-modern, the more controversial such usage becomes. Why should we apply words denoting concepts that we ourselves believe have no value as explanations of difference, to societies whose protagonists were not only ignorant (except, as we shall see, in Romance-speaking lands) of the word "race" itself, but also untutored by the scientists (Lamarck, Mendel, Darwin, Huxley...) who would give that word teeth? On both sides of the chronological divide between the modern and the pre-modern (wherever it may lie), there is today a remarkable consensus that the earlier vocabularies of difference are innocent of race.

Like every consensus, this one has costs as well as benefits. But before exploring those, it is worth pointing out the more or less mutual disinterest upon which the consensus is based. Among advocates of pre-modern innocence, the dismissal of race too often relies on the most cursory engagement with the complex history of the modern racial concepts whose relevance is at issue.[4] Some take refuge in lexicography, arguing (for example) that because the word *Rasse* did not enter German until the eighteenth century and the word *Anti-Semitismus* until the nineteenth, we need not look for these concepts in the earlier history of German-speaking lands. Others embrace narrow definitional strategies which succeed, not in solving the problem but in rendering it uninteresting. It is not

[3] The more radical among them: for Barbara Fields's argument against the explanatory value of race in American history, see Barbara Fields, "Ideology and Race in American History," in Joseph M. Kousser and James McPherson (eds.), *Region, Race, and Reconstruction: Essays in Honor of C. Vann Woodward* (New York: Oxford University Press, 1982), pp. 143–177.

[4] Rainer Walz, "Der vormoderne Antisemitismus: Religiöser Fanatismus oder Rassenwahn?," *Historische Zeitschrift* 260 (1995), 719–748, offers an excellent review of some of the definitions of race proposed in the debate, as well as some new suggestions.

surprising, for example, that those who define race as the application of eighteenth- and nineteenth-century vocabularies of biological classification to human populations differentiated by skin color are certain that it cannot be found in earlier periods.[5] Such definitions cannot tell us much about the pre-modern, since they fail to make sense even of modern racial ideologies against which they define themselves, ideologies which are themselves not only tremendously diverse, but also change a great deal over time.

Perhaps the most widespread and intuitively persuasive argument against the relevance of race for the pre-modern period is the common view that medieval (for example) classifications of peoples were not sufficiently biological to qualify as racism, no matter how much they might smack of natural history. Robert Bartlett put this consensus particularly well: "while the language of race [in medieval sources] – gens, natio, 'blood,' 'stock,' etc. – is *biological*, its medieval reality was almost entirely *cultural*."[6] Although it is not absolutely clear what "reality" of language means here – perhaps the reality of the differences described by the language? – what is clear is that the procedure of establishing a difference between the terms of a distinction (biological) and the reality of that distinction (cultural) is meant to relieve the Middle Ages of the charge of racism.

We need not pronounce judgment on the charge in order to wonder if this defense is adequate. All racisms are attempts to ground discriminations, whether social, economic, or religious, in biology and reproduction. All claim a congruence of "cultural" categories with "natural" ones. None of these claims, not even the most "scientific" ones of the twentieth century, reflects biological reality. Modern population genetics has of course discovered some real differences between, say, sub-Saharan African populations and Swedish ones, or between Jewish and non-Jewish

[5] A criticism I would make also of Walz. This tendency is manifest even in the otherwise excellent article "Rasse," in Otto Brunner *et al.* (eds.), *Geschichtliche Grundbegriffe: Historisches Lexicon zur politisch-sozialen Sprache in Deutschland*, 8 vols. (Stuttgart: E. Klett, 1984), vol. V, pp. 135–178. On the other hand, neither is it very helpful to describe as racial every ideology that assigns to lineage a role in the production of identity, as many proponents of pre-modern "racism" do. Thus for Arlette Jouanna, race is an idea "according to which the qualities that classify an individual within society are hereditarily transmittable through blood." Arlette Jouanna, *L'idée de race en France au XVIème siècle et au début du XVIIème siècle (1498–1614)*, 3 vols. (Lille/Paris: Université Lille III, 1976), vol. I, p. 1.
[6] Robert Bartlett, *The Making of Europe: Conquest, Colonization, and Cultural Change, 950–1350* (Princeton: Princeton University Press, 1993), p. 197 (emphasis added). Bartlett's insights on the topic are very helpfully expanded in his "Medieval and Modern Concepts of Race and Identity," *The Journal of Medieval and Early Modern Studies* 31 (2001), 39–56, which, however, largely avoids both Jews and the Romance languages.

populations (as any student of breast cancer or Tay-Sachs disease knows).[7] But these real biological differences have no obvious or natural relationship to the cultural work they are asked to do in systems of racial discrimination, systems which are products of culture, not of nature. If this lack of congruence does not suffice to make modern racist ideologies less "racial," then it cannot suffice to excuse pre-modern discriminations from the charge.[8]

We can generalize this objection: rather than engage in a systematic comparison of the discursive power of natural histories deployed in specific pre-modern and modern arguments about the reproduction of group difference, we pre-modernists too often rely on the questionable axiom that modern racial theories depend upon evolutionary biology and genetics, in order to leap to the demonstrably false conclusion that there exists a truly biological modern racism against which earlier forms of discrimination can be measured and judged innocent.[9] But the certainties of modernists about the origins of race are equally partial, and equally questionable. In one of a series of lectures at the Collège de France in 1976, Michel Foucault (to pick a prominent example) insisted that racism

---

[7] The possibility of identifying genetic markers whose relative frequency varies markedly between specific populations has long been known. See, for one example of such variation, Surinder S. Papiha, "Genetic variation and Disease Susceptibility in NCWP [New Commonwealth with Pakistani] Groups in Britain," *New Community* 13 (1987), 373–383, on the genetic causes of the varying susceptibility to specific diseases in Britain of Anglo-Saxon populations and populations of immigrants from the Asian subcontinent.

[8] For similar reasons, arguments like that of David Romano, who insists that "els antropòlegs seriosos ... estableixen clarament que no hi ha races," and that therefore there was complete racial equality of Christians and Jews in medieval Catalonia, seem to me beside the point. On that argument, there can have been no racial inequality in 1930s Germany, either. See David Romano, "Característiques dels jueus en relació amb els cristians en els estats hispànics," in *Jornades d'història dels jueus a Catalunya* (Girona: Ajuntament de Girona, 1987), pp. 9–27, here pp. 15–16.

[9] I call the axiom questionable on two grounds. First, the late-eighteenth-century efflorescence of racial theory (e.g., in Immanuel Kant's 1775 "Von den verschiedenen Rassen der Menschen" in *Gesammelte Schriften, Akademie-Ausgabe* [Berlin: Georg Reimer, 1902], vol. II, pp. 429–443, and Johann Friedrich Blumenbach, *De generis humani varietate nativa* [On the Natural Varieties of Mankind] [Göttingen: Vandenhoeck und Ruprecht, 1795]) depended much more on Montesquieu's updated version of climate theory than on genetic arguments. (For an early example of the impact of such theories on writing about Jews see Johann David Michaelis's critique of Christian Wilhelm Dohm, *Ueber die bürgerliche Verbesserung der Juden*, 2 vols. [Berlin and Stettin: Friedrich Nicolai, 1781–83], vol. II, pp. 51, 63.) Second, even after the widespread dissemination of Darwinian evolution, many of the examples of hybridity and its dangers most favored by nineteenth- and twentieth-century racist writers (like Alfred Schultz, *Race or Mongrel: A Brief History of the Rise and Fall of the Ancient Races of Earth* [Boston: L. C. Page & company, 1908]) were drawn from an agricultural domain of animal breeding that was already well known in the ancient and medieval worlds. I know of no comparative study on this topic, and will myself no more than gesture toward one below.

was a uniquely modern phenomenon, the product of a European struggle for sovereignty that did not occur before the seventeenth century. According to Foucault, medieval sovereignty had been organic and corporatist. It was of course hierarchical and therefore often conflictual, but that conflict was always contained by a ritual regime and a historical discourse that were celebratory and inclusive. Even warring nations never forgot their common ancestry, going back, if not to Rome, then to Troy. And from this memory sprang as well a common historiography. "What is there in [medieval] history," Foucault asked, quoting Petrarch, "that is not in praise of Rome?"[10]

Race arose out of the collapse of this system. By the early seventeenth century, society was no longer thought of as an organic system, but as a binary. The governing metaphor was no longer that of society as a harmonious body, but of society as a war between two irreconcilable groups or bodies. And although those groups could be characterized and classified in a number of ways (as classes, for example), the symbolic logic underlying these classifications was always racial, in that it imagined one group as polluting and the other pure, one to be isolated or exterminated, the other to be protected and reproduced. The emerging nation state was at first the venue for this struggle between groups, then eventually its arbiter, the chief guarantor of racial purity. This final nineteenth-century stage Foucault referred to as "state racism." And just as history in the Middle Ages had been a reflection of the symbolic order that articulated power in terms of organic unity, in modernity history became a battlefield, an accounting of losses and victories in the eternal war of the races.

Even if we were to grant (as many would not[11]) that the struggle for sovereignty within Europe was the key conflict in the emergence of race, we could easily object that Foucault's arguments for the modern origins of race depend upon a falsely organic view of the Middle Ages. Have not R.I. Moore, Dominique Iogna-Prat, Tomaž Mastnak, and many other medievalists shown us the dependence of medieval arguments about sovereignty on the identification of Jewish, Muslim, or heretical threats to Christian society, and on claims to defend Christian society against those threats? It is relatively easy to demonstrate the importance of such religious "enmities" to the formation of Western European notions of a Christendom threatened from without and within by impurity and

---

[10] Michel Foucault, *Il faut défendre la société: Cours au Collège de France, 1976* (Paris: Seuil/Gallimard, 1997), p. 65.
[11] Although my conclusion here is not quantitative, my sense is that scholars of the emergence of race and racism are generally more interested in the external challenges of European exploration, expansion, and colonialism than in internal European conflicts over sovereignty.

pollution.[12] Why should these enmities not be considered a sufficient stimulus to the symbolic logic Foucault associated with the origins of race? Clearly Foucault's audience shared some of these doubts, for he began his next lecture (of February 4) by addressing them. "During the last week or two, people have sent me a number of objections, both oral and written," asking in particular "what does it mean to have racism originate in the sixteenth or seventeenth century, to attach it only to problems of state sovereignty, when we well know, after all, that religious racism (anti-Semitic racism in particular) has existed since the Middle Ages?" Foucault did not respond to these objections. He merely restated his conviction, and concluded with the greatest evasion available to a professor: "come see me during office hours."

The proceedings of Foucault's office hours, unlike those of his lectures, have not been transcribed and published, so we cannot say whether or how he engaged these questions. It is unlikely that he was sympathetic, given that history was for him a scythe, to be swung against the giant stalks of genealogical fantasy with which Europeans attempted (according to Nietzsche) to climb down into their distant past. "History," Foucault insisted in an essay on Nietzsche's genealogies, "is for cutting." When it comes to the question of race, nearly an entire generation of historians – most of whom share neither Foucault's general program for the writing of history, nor his specific sense of the struggle for sovereignty as the driving force of race – seems to agree, forgetting that a history that cuts too often or too deep is just as fantastic as one whose filiations are too thick.[13]

---

[12] John Marshall's recent *John Locke, Toleration and Early Enlightenment Culture* (Cambridge Studies in Early Modern British History, Cambridge University Press, 2006) is, among many other things, a masterful demonstration of the ongoing power of these religious models of enmity and pollution in the very age where Foucault sees the emergence of his binaries.

[13] Following Nietzsche, Foucault (somewhat confusingly) used the term "genealogy" to describe his antithetical alternative to the histories produced by this fantasy, a history that does not "go back in time to restore an unbroken continuity that operates beyond the dispersion of forgotten things ... [that] does not resemble the evolution of a species or map the destiny of a people." See Michel Foucault, "Nietzsche, Genealogy, History", in Donald Bouchard (ed.), *Language, Counter-Memory, Practice*, trans. Donald Bouchard and Sherry Simon (Ithaca, NY: Cornell University Press, 1977), pp. 154, 162; and Foucault, *Il faut défendre la société*, p. 10. Numerous scholars have castigated Foucault for some of his periodizations, most notably his argument for a transition from pre-modern "blood" regimes to modern "sexual" ones. Kathleen Biddick, for example, finds in medieval texts a simultaneous insistence on the importance of blood and of pedagogy, and concludes that Foucault's insistence on the modernity of blood regimes and disciplinarity is therefore incorrect. "Disciplinarity (pedagogy) was always already folded within this colonial symbolics of blood." See Kathleen Biddick, "The Cut of Genealogy: Pedagogy in the Blood," *Journal of Medieval and Early Modern Studies* 30 (Fall, 2000), 453. Biddick's "always already" may, however, obscure as much as it reveals.

Hence Nietzsche had insisted on an element of formal continuity to the ideas whose history interested him: a "terrifying mask" that these ideas wore across time, impressing them upon generations of human memory and concealing their transformations behind features of unchanging horror. For Nietzsche (unlike Foucault), the history of ideas consisted less in stripping the "mask" from the "actor," than in developing a dramaturgy appropriate to their interplay.

Be that as it may, the snipping of several generations of historians has by now separated race from whatever masks it may once have worn. Precisely for this reason it seems to me useful to stroll through some more ancient museums of natural history, and imagine race placed amongst their exhibits. What if, for example, we treat race as but one chapter in the long history of the conviction that culture is produced and reproduced in the same way as the species procreates itself? I cannot, in the pages that follow, pretend to provide anything so cosmopolitan as a critical history of this conviction. Nor do I aspire to anything so provincial as a proof that late medieval discriminations were racial. My goal is only to demonstrate that too easy a certainty about where each chapter in a "natural history" of culture begins and ends represses the very processes of contextualization, comparison, and analogy out of which a critical understanding of such histories should emerge. To shift metaphors: it is painfully clear why for the last half century it has been so important to cut a modern straitjacket for histories of race. Perhaps our analyses have reached the point where we may loosen the sleeves, and begin comparing the mad certainties of different times and places. I have chosen one example of what such a comparison might look like, the same example with which Ashley Montague confronted his readers, and with which Foucault's audience confronted him – I mean, of course, the venerable debate over the nature of Christian attitudes toward the Jews – and will focus within that example on the Crowns of Aragon and of Castile in the Middle Ages: the polities that we today call Spain.

★★★

Like the more general questions of race with which we began, the debate over the racial nature of anti-Semitism was taken up with new urgency after the rise of National Socialism. Some historians, such as Cecil Roth, saw real affinities between pre-modern ideologies of discrimination (particularly those of late medieval Spain toward Christians descended from Jews) and modern (particularly German) ones, affinities which he explored in an essay published in 1940, entitled "Marranos and Racial anti-Semitism: A Study in Parallels." Others, like Guido Kisch,

categorically denied any racial element in pre-modern anti-Judaism, and
criticized those who thought otherwise for "reading modern racist conceptions into medieval sources."[14]

The extermination of nearly all the Jews of Europe during the Second
World War raised the ethical stakes of these debates to heights far greater
than those that historical argument generally affords. For some, the gravita-
tional pull of Auschwitz is so strong that all earlier ideologies about Jews
become coordinates in a trajectory clearly spiraling toward destruction.
Historians of this school (Benzion Netanyahu is an example) make relatively free use of the words "race" and "racism" to describe discriminations
against Jews, whether they occurred in Hellenistic Egypt, fifteenth-century
Spain, Nazi Germany, or the present.[15] For others, indeed the vast majority, such stakes are unbearably high. They prefer to understand modern
racial anti-Semitism as the specific and contingent product of the intersec-
tion of capitalism, imperialism, and post-Enlightenment natural science, a
phenomenon radically discontinuous with other and earlier histories. The
deep cuts of this historicism are (at least in part) designed to relieve more
distant pasts from responsibility for an ideology that has come to stand for
all that is evil in Europe. Thus Heiko Oberman can reassure us that the
Reformation is untainted by racism, because the many negative comments
that Reuchlin, Erasmus, and Luther made about Jews, about converts from
Judaism, and about their descendents, were based on a purely theological
understanding, not a biological one, that we might term anti-Judaism but
not anti-Semitism.[16]

[14] Salo Baron took an intermediate position, agreeing that medieval people did not have a
conscious concept of race in its modern form, but seeing real similarities between the
ideologies. See Salo Baron, *Modern Nationalism and Religion* (New York: Harper, 1947),
p. 276, n. 26, and p. 15, reformulated in Baron, *A Social and Religious History of the Jews*,
18 vols (New York: Columbia University Press, 1969), vol. 13, pp. 84ff. Kisch rejected this
approach as well, in Guido Kisch, *The Jews of Medieval Germany* (Chicago: The University
of Chicago Press, 1949), pp. 314–316 and 531, n. 60. The debate is summarized in Yosef
Haim Yerushalmi's classic pamphlet on the topic, *Assimilation and Racial Anti-Semitism: the
Iberian and the German Models* (New York: Leo Baeck Institute, 1982), p. 29.
[15] On this tendency in Benzion Netanyahu's *The Origins of the Inquisition in Fifteenth Century
Spain* (New York: Random House, 1995), see David Nirenberg, "El sentido de la historia
judía", *Revista de Libros* 28 (April 1999), 3–5.
[16] Heiko Oberman, *Wurzeln des Antisemitismus. Christenangst und Judenplage im Zeitalter von
Humanismus und Reformation*, second edition (Berlin: Severin & Siedler, 1983), p. 63.
Oberman's work is also characteristic of this scholarship in that it makes no attempt to
demonstrate assumed differences in the biological knowledge that underlay modern racist
anti-Semitism, and that encoded in comments like Martin Luther's observation
(*Weimarer Ausgabe*, vol. 53, p. 481) that the Jews' poisonous hatred "dass es ihnen
durch blut und fleisch, durch Marck und bein gegangen, ganz und gar natur und leben
geworden ist. Und so wenig sie fleisch und blut, Marck und bein koennen endern, so
wenig koennen sie solchen stoltz und neid endern. Sie muessen so bleiben und verderben,
Wo Gott nicht sonderlich hohe wunder thut."

This distinction between a "biological" anti-Semitism associated with modernity and a "cultural" anti-Judaism associated with pre-modernity did not, of course, originate with Oberman. It is what we might call the "Jewish corollary" to the broader axiom about the modernity of race.[17] Every bit as widespread as that axiom, the corollary has itself assumed in most historical circles the status of article of faith, even if a few heretics remain.[18] But there is room for doubt, and the scholarly expression of that doubt tends to cluster around Spain in the late Middle Ages.[19]

Iberian history has long served as a focal point for arguments about pre-modern race because, as is well known, large populations of Muslims and

---

[17] The bibliography on the question of anti-Judaism (non-racial) vs. anti-Semitism (racial) is vast. In addition to the works already cited (e.g. Walz), see, *inter alia*, Peter Herde, "Von der mittelalterlichen Judenfeindschaft zum modernen Antisemitismus," in Karlheinz Müller and Klaus Wittstadt (eds.), *Geschichte und Kultur des Judentums* (Würzburg: Kommissionsverlag F. Schoningh, 1988); Christhard Hoffmann, "Christlicher Antijudaismus und moderner Antisemitismus. Zusammenhänge und Differenzen als Problem der historischen Antisemitismusforschung," in Leonore Siegele-Wenschkewitz (ed.), *Christlicher Antijudaismus und Antisemitismus. Theologische und kirchliche Programme Deutscher Christen* (Frankfurt am Main: Haag & Herchen, 1994), pp. 293–317; Winfried Frey, "Vom Antijudaismus zum Antisemitismus. Ein antijüdisches Pasquill von 1606 und seine Quellen," *Daphnis* 18 (1989), 251–279; Johannes Heil, "»Antijudaismus« und »Antisemitismus« – Begriffe als Bedeutungsträger," *Jahrbuch für Antisemitismusforschung* 6 (1997), 91–114. Gavin Langmuir divided the vocabulary differently in *History, Religion, and Antisemitism* (Berkeley: University of California Press, 1990), positing a (medieval) shift from rational anti-Judaism to irrational anti-Semitism.

[18] Jonathan Elukin, for example, argued for an "incipient racial ideology" evident in the Christian treatment of converts from Judaism in the Middle Ages. See Jonathan Elukin, "From Jew to Christian? Conversion and Immutability in Medieval Europe," in James Muldoon (ed.), *Varieties of Religious Conversion in the Middle Ages* (Gainesville: University Press of Florida, 1997), pp. 171–189, here p. 171. One of the best known cases was addressed by Aryeh Grabois, "From 'Theological' to 'Racial' Anti-Semitism: The Controversy over the 'Jewish' Pope in the Twelfth Century," [Hebrew] *Zion* 47 (1982), 1–16. Such arguments tend to see evidence of racial thought in medieval assertions about the ongoing Jewishness (or "immutability") of converts or their descendents, but do not engage in the comparative exploration of medieval theories of immutability with modern racial ones that would seem to me to be a prerequisite for such a claim. For an important survey of medieval Christian attitudes toward converts from Judaism in the eleventh- and twelfth-century Rhineland, see Alfred Haverkamp, "Baptized Jews in German Lands During the Twelfth Century," in Michael Signer and John van Engen (eds.), *Jews and Christians in Twelfth Century Europe* (Notre Dame, IN: University of Notre Dame Press, 2001), pp. 255–310 (who does not, however, engage the question of "racial anti-Semitism").

[19] This case was of course implicit in the question posed to Foucault, and explicit in the debates between Roth, Kisch, *et al.* Yosef Haim Yerushalmi took up the debate in 1982 (*Assimilation and Racial Anti-Semitism*), comparing late medieval Spanish ideologies that understood Jewishness as carried in the blood with nineteenth-century German anti-Semitic ideologies, and understanding both as recognizably racial. The line of argument was pursued further by Jerome Friedman, "Jewish Conversion, the Spanish Pure Blood Laws, and Reformation: A Revisionist View of Racial and Religious Antisemitism," *Sixteenth Century Journal* 18 (1987), 3–31.

Jews made the peninsular kingdoms the most religiously diverse in medieval Western Europe. The late fourteenth and fifteenth centuries witnessed massive attempts to eliminate that diversity through massacre, segregation, conversion, Inquisition, and expulsion. In one sense these efforts toward homogeneity were successful. Over the course of the hundred years from 1391 to 1492, for example, all the Jews of Spain either converted or were expelled.[20]

But the conversion of a large number of people whom Christians had perceived as profoundly different transformed the old boundaries and systems of discrimination rather than abolished them, as categories that had previously seemed primarily legal and religious were replaced by the genealogical notion that Christians descended from Jewish converts (*Cristianos nuevos, confessos, conversos, marranos*) were essentially different from "Christians by nature" (*Cristianos de natura, cristianos viejos, lindos, limpios*). Moreover, the ideological underpinning of these new discriminations claimed explicitly to be rooted in natural realities, as is most evident in what came to be called the doctrine of "limpieza de sangre." According to this doctrine, Jewish and Muslim blood was inferior to Christian; the possession of any amount of such blood made one liable to heresy and moral corruption; and therefore any descendent of Jews and Muslims, no matter how distant, should be barred from church and secular office, from any number of guilds and professions, and especially from marrying Old Christians.

The debate over the utility of concepts such as race and racism in explaining these conflicts, discriminations, and ideologies has been quite heated. It has remained, however, bedeviled by the fiction of true race. In the early years of history as *Wissenschaft*, of course, this fiction enabled racial analysis, because historians themselves believed in the racial logic they were attributing to their historical subjects. In writing of conflict between Christians, Muslims, and Jews, historians constantly employed the vocabulary of race, although they meant very different

---

[20] The population of Jews in the Crown of Aragon dropped from a high of 27,000–50,000 just before the massacres of 1391, to approximately 9,000 at the time of the expulsion of 1492 (and thereafter, of course, to zero). These figures, which are far below those offered by many historians, are meant primarily to illustrate the scale of the decline. They are taken from Jaume Riera, "Judíos y Conversos en los reinos de la Corona de Aragón durante el siglo XV," in *La expulsión de los judíos de españa* (Castilla–La Mancha: Asociación de Amigos del Museo Sefardí, 1993), pp. 71–90, here p. 78, who, however, provides no evidence for them. Henry Kamen, in his self-consciously revisionist "The Mediterranean and the Expulsion of Spanish Jews in 1492," *Past and Present* 119 (1988), 30–55, provides very similar numbers, but also adduces no evidence.

things by it.[21] An early example is that of Leopold von Ranke, who believed that the Old Christian refusal to intermarry with New Christians was an extension of the ancient abhorrence that the "Germanic" and "Romanic" races felt toward amalgamation with "Semitic" Jews and Muslims.[22] Half a century later (c. 1882) the great historian Marcelino Menéndez y Pelayo, in whose honor Spain's Real Academia de la Historia is named, could echo Darwin unselfconsciously: "It is madness to believe that battles for existence, bloody and century long struggles between races, could end in any way other than with expulsions and exterminations. The inferior race always succumbs." Elsewhere he opined that "the matter of race [by which he meant the existence of "Semitic" Jews and Muslims] explains many phenomena and resolves many enigmas in our history," and "is the principal cause of decadence for the [Iberian] Peninsula." At much the same time, though an ocean and an ideology away, Henry Charles Lea also accepted racial categories in order to make the argument that the Spanish Inquisition was an instrument of racism.[23]

But as we have already seen from the debate between Cecil Roth and Guido Kisch, such certainties began to fade in the mid-twentieth century. Within the ambit of Spanish historiography, Américo Castro became perhaps the most influential critic of racial vocabulary. Castro was interested in debunking not just notions of Jewish or Muslim racial identity, but the idea of a "raza hispanica" as well. As he put it in one of his later works, "faith in the temporally uncertain biological continuity of the Spaniard has inspired the works both of respected men of wisdom and

---

[21] Though in this chapter I will be focussing on the Jewish case, the same phenomenon applies to the historiography of Muslims in the Iberian Peninsula. Examples of racial language in the description of Christian–Muslim relations abound in José María Perceval, *Todos son uno. Arquetipos, xenofobia y racismo. La imagen del morisco en la Monarquía Española durante los siglos XVI y XVII* (Almería: Instituto de Estudios Almerienses, 1997), *passim*, but see for example p. 63.

[22] See Leopold von Ranke, *Fürsten und Völker von Süd-Europa im sechszehnten und siebzehnten Jahrhundert*, 2 vols. (Berlin: Duncker und Humblot, 1837), vol. I, p. 246.

[23] "Locura es pensar que *batallas por la existencia*, luchas encarnizadas y seculares de razas, terminen de otro modo que con expulsiones o exterminios. La raza inferior sucumbe siempre y acaba por triunfar el principio de nacionalidad más fuerte y vigoroso." Marcelino Menéndez y Pelayo, *Historia de los heterodoxos Españoles*, 8 vols. (Madrid, 1882/Mexico City: Editorial Porrua, 1982), vol. II, p. 379. Compare vol. I, p. 410; vol. II, p. 381. Despite the Darwinian overtones of this passage, and though he everywhere utilizes the vocabulary of race, Menéndez y Pelayo nevertheless also claims to reject some of the racial theories of his day (compare vol. I, p. 249: "Sin asentir en manera alguna a la teoría fatalista de las razas ... los árabes ... han sido y son muy poco dados a la filosofía"). Compare Henry Charles Lea, *A History of the Inquisition of Spain*, 4 vols. (New York: AMS Press, 1906/1966), vol. I, p. 126.

of superficial scholars."[24] His task, as he saw it, was to demonstrate the falsity of any model of Spanish identity based on such a faith. To this end, Castro began nearly all of his books with an attack upon the relevance of the concept of race to Spanish history.[25] In the opening of *The Spaniards*, for example, he explains that he speaks of Muslim, Jewish, and Christian "castes," not races, "for in that Spain of three religions everyone was light-skinned, with horizontal eyes, except for a few black slaves brought in from Africa" (p. v). Similarly in the Introduction to the 1965 edition of *La realidad*, he writes:

A much wider detour will be necessary in order to include in future historiography the positive and decisive presence of the Moorish and Jewish castes (not races!). Because the resistance is notable to the acceptance that the Spanish problem was of castes, and not of races, [a term] today only applicable to those distinguished, as the Dictionary of the Academy has it, "by the color of their skin and other characteristics."[26]

[24] Américo Castro, *The Spaniards, An Introduction to their History* (Berkeley: University of California Press, 1971), p. 20. If such a faith lasted longer in Spain than it did in the rest of Western Europe, this is partly because Franco's triumph allowed Falangist historians to continue celebrating the achievements of the "raza hispanica" for many years. But it should be added that the "faith ... in biological continuity" of Spanish fascists had its own distinctive flavor. Primo de Rivera, for example, could proclaim: "España no se justifica por tener una lengua, ni por ser una raza, ni por ser un acervo de costumbres, sino que España se justifica por una vocación imperial para unir lenguas, para unir razas, para unir pueblos y para unir costumbres en un destino universal." Cited in Eduardo Gonzalez Calleja and Fredes Limon Nevado, *La hispanidad como instrumento de combate: raza e imperio en la prensa franquista durante la guerra civil española* (Madrid: Consejo Superior de Investigaciones Científicas, 1988), pp. 27–28. Can we imagine a similar statement from a German fascist?

[25] An approach common to Américo Castro's *España en su Historia: cristianos, moros y judios* (Buenos Aires: Editorial Losada, 1948); *La realidad historica de España*, Biblioteca Pourra 4 (Mexico City: Editorial Porrua, 1954); *De la edad conflictiva*, Collección Persiles 18 (Madrid: Taurus, 1963); *"Español", palabra extranjera: razones y motivos* (Madrid: Taurus, 1970), and *The Spaniards*.

[26] Castro, *La realidad historica*, third edition (1965), p. 5 of the 1965 introduction: "Un viraje mucho más amplio será necesario para incluir en la historiografia futura la presencia positiva y decisiva de las castas (¡no razas!) mora y judía. Porque es notable la resistencia a aceptar que el problema español era de *castas* y no de *razas*, hoy sólo aplicable a quienes se distinguen, como dice el Diccionario de la Academia, 'por el color de su piel y otros caracteres'." In this context it is worth pointing out that the *Diccionario* itself actually uses the word "raza" in its definition of the word "antisemita": "enemigo de la raza hebrea, de su cultura, o de su influencia" (my thanks to Daniel Waissbein for bringing this to my attention). Writing at much the same time as Castro, Nicolas López Martinez, "Teologia española de la convivencia a mediados del siglo XV," *Repertorio de las Ciencias Eclesiásticas de España* 1 (Siglos III–XVI), (Salamanca, 1967), 465–476 embraced the vocabulary Castro rejected. He saw the fifteenth-century drive toward assimilation as "un fenómeno casi biológico" (p. 466), and did not hesitate to speak of race: "Si añadimos la notoria eficacia de la raza hebrea para hacerse con las claves económicas del país, comprenderemos ... que, a veces, por motivos inmediatos aparentemente fútiles, se haga

This repudiation of race depends upon familiar strategies: the focus on the *Diccionario's* definition of race as referring only to skin color (he ignored the ominous "Y otros caracteres"); and the conjuration of an easily dismissed "true" biological racism based solely on external physical characteristics.[27]

Castro's approach to race is the one point of his *oeuvre* with which nearly all Spanish and French scholars of peninsular history concur. In the words of a devoted "Castrista," F. Márquez Villanueva: "The problem of the New Christians was by no means a racial one; it was social and in the second line religious. The *converso* did not carry in any moment an indelible biological stigma." Historians with less enthusiasm for many of Castro's broader arguments agree. As Adeline Rucquoi recently put it, "Loin d'être lié à des concepts plus ou moins biologiques de 'race', loin aussi d'être un simple mécanisme d'exclusion d'un groupe social par un autre, le problème de la pureté du sang nous paraît être un problème ontologique, lié dans l'Espagne du début des Temps Modernes au problème du salut." The fact that the few dissenting voices are mostly North American has perhaps contributed to the polarization, as Spanish scholars have sought to distance themselves from what they perceive to be an excessive willingness of "Anglo-Saxon" scholars to project the racial histories of their own lands onto that of Spain.[28]

---

guerra sin cuartel" (p. 467). "Como se ve, pretendía una discriminación semejante a la que, todavía en nuestros tiempos, se basa exclusivamente en motivos de raza o del color de la piel" (p. 468).

[27] One might further complain that late medieval and early modern Spaniards were perfectly capable of believing that Jews and *conversos* actually *were* distinguished by physical characteristics, such as large noses. Lope de Vega pokes fun at precisely this belief in Vega, *Amar sin saber a quién, Edición de Carmen Bravo-Villasante* (Salamanca: Anaya, 1967), p. 10, "Largas hay con hidalguía/ y muchas cortas sin ella." See Maria Rosa Lida de Malkiel, "Lope de Vega y los judíos", *Bulletin Hispanique* 75 (1973), 73–112, here 88.

[28] Francisco Márquez Villanueva, "El problema de los conversos: Cuatro Puntos Cardinales", in Joseph Sola-Solé *et al.* (eds.), *Hispania Judaica I: History*, (Barcelona: Puvill-Editor, 1985), p. 61: "Por lo pronto, el problema de los cristianos nuevos no era, en absoluto, de índole *racial*, sino social, y secundariamente, religioso. No se pierda de vista que el converso no llevaba consigo en todo momento un estigma biológico indeleble"; Adeline Rucquoi, "Noblesse des conversos?" in *"Qu'un Sang Impur..." Les Conversos et le pouvoir en Espagne à la fin du moyen âge*, Etudes Hispaniques 23 (Aix-en-Provence: Publication de l'Université de Provence, 1997), pp. 89–108. For a representative critique of "Anglo-Saxon" historiography on these grounds, albeit on a slightly different issue, see Mercedes García-Arenal and Béatrice Leroy, *Moros y judíos en Navarra en la baja Edad Media* (Madrid: Hiperion, 1984), pp. 13–14:

El interés por la cuestión ha sido promovido principalmente por estudiosos anglosajones preocupados por problemas actuales de minorías dentro de sus propios países, y en ocasiones planteamientos u ópticas válidas para sociedades posteriores a los imperialismos occidentales han sido aplicadas a la Edad Media española con resultados deformantes y anacrónicos. Sobre todo ha hecho que se barajen conceptos muy semejantes a

Each of these repudiations of race has been of undoubted strategic importance. There were, for example, many Spanish scholars who did maintain that Jews and Muslims were members of races inferior to the "raza hispanica," and Américo Castro's attack against that vocabulary helped bring these groups back into the mainstream of Spanish history and culture. But such strategic skirmishes cannot alone conquer the vast complex of ideas about the reproduction of culture that they claim to target. Indeed unless they open a path for heavier engagements, they risk being stranded behind enemy lines. Castro's easy isolation of race in the epidermis, for example, blinded him to the ways in which his methodology simply displaced many of the naturalizing and essentializing functions of "race" into the less charged term of "caste" (much as many speakers today use "ethnicity"). There is in fact a close kinship between Castro's "Semitic caste" and "Semitic culture" and Ernest Renan's "Semitic race."[29] Both posited stable, essential, and inescapable forms of group identity continuously reproduced across time. Castro, like Renan, combed "Jewish" texts beginning with the Old Testament for Semitic characteristics whose entrance into Spain he then attributed to Jews and *conversos*. He found a number of them. "Inquisitorial fanaticism and recourse to slandering informants – what one might call in Spanish 'malsinismo' – frantic greed and plundering, the concern over purity of blood ... the concern with public reputation ..., the desire of everyone to be a nobleman ... somber asceticism ..., the negative view of the world ..., disillusionment, and the flight from human values," all of these were the "poisons ... that seeped into Spanish life, Spanish Christendom, in the increment of forced converts."[30]

---

los de la vieja bibliografía polémica de finales del siglo pasado, conceptos que en este estudio se intentarán evitar.

In Mercedes García-Arenal, *Inquisición y moriscos, los procesos del Tribunal de Cuenca*, second edition (Madrid: Siglo Veintiuno, 1983), p. 116, she suggests that although today anti-Muslim attitudes are racial, four centuries ago they were religious. On the question of an Anglo-American vision of Spanish history, see Ángel Galán Sánchez, *Una visión de la 'decadencia española': la historiografía anglosajona sobre mudéjares y moriscos, siglos XVIII–XX*, Colección "Monografías" 4 (Málaga: Servicio de Publicaciones, Diputación Provincial de Málaga, 1991). Nevertheless the word "raza" is still sometimes applied to the Jews by Spanish historians writing today, e.g. Ramon Gonzálvez Ruiz, "El Bachiller Palma y su obra de polémica proconversa," in *"Qu'un sang impur..."*, p. 48: "Palma ... guarda una natural vinculación con los hombres de su raza convertidos al cristianismo."

[29] On the racial nature of Renan's categories see Shmuel Almog, "The Racial Motif to Renan's Attitude to Jews and Judaism," in Shmuel Almog (ed.), *Antisemitism through the Ages* (Oxford: Pergamon Press, 1988), pp. 255–278.

[30] The quotes are from Américo Castro, *The Structure of Spanish History*, translated by Edmund L. King (Princeton, NJ: Princeton University Press, 1954), pp. 542–543, 569. In a review of the Spanish version of the work (Castro, *España en su historia*) Yakov Malkiel rather mildly observed that Castro's approach resembled theories of cultural transmission discredited by association with National Socialism. Marquez Villanueva, on the other

These "cultural" traits of Jews and converts are startlingly similar, not only to those "racial" ones listed by Renan or his disciples (which on this score included the champion of the "raza hispana" and Castro's arch-rival, Claudio Sánchez Albornoz[31]), but also to those of fifteenth- and sixteenth-century anti-*converso* tracts advocating *limpieza*. Nor are the means of their reproduction so very different, for though Castro and his students reject biological explanations for cultural transmission, they rely heavily on genealogical ones, frequently mapping a particular intellectual position or literary style onto a family tree in order to prove the "Semiticness" of either the idea or of its exponent, a type of logic that has turned many Iberianists into methodological disciples of Inquisitors.[32] Like many other historians and philologists, Castro fled from the horrifying embrace of race straight into the arms of another genetic fantasy. Small wonder that, far from having banished race and racism, he found himself accused of replicating it under another name.[33]

★★★

Thus far my argument has been entirely "negative," first criticizing the terms in which questions about race in the pre-modern period have been asked by others; then suggesting that, at the rather gross level of historiography, those terms are much the same whether we are talking of race generally, of the Jewish case more specifically, or of the singular example of Spain. But of course each case differs a great deal in its particulars, and it is through a focus on those particulars in the Spanish case that I will attempt to provide a more "positive" example of the cognitive benefits that may flow from emphasizing, rather than eliding, the medieval vocabularies through which "naturalizations" of difference were expressed. The history of the Romance word "raza," from whence the English "race,"

---

hand, praised precisely these pages as "the most acute and fruitful of [Castro's] oeuvre." See his "El problema de los conversos", pp. 51–75, here p. 69. The piece originally appeared in a Castro Festschrift in 1965.

[31] A convergence pointed out by Benzion Netanyahu in his *Toward the Inquisition: Essays on Jewish and Converso History in Late Medieval Spain* (Ithaca, NY: Cornell University Press, 1997), chapters 1 and 5. For a good example of Sánchez-Albornoz's agreement with Castro on this score, see Claudio Sánchez-Albornoz, *España: un enigma histórico*, 2 vols. (Buenos Aires: Editorial Sudamericana, 1962), vol. 2, pp. 16, 255.

[32] Thus Márquez Villanueva, seeking to prove that (*pace* Horace) the literary figure of the procuress or go-between is a "semitic" trope, writes of one author (Feliciano de Silva) that, although his ancestry is not certain, he "looks highly suspicious, given his marriage to a lady of known Jewish lineage and his life-long affinity with the *converso* literary milieu." See Francisco Márquez Villanueva, "*La Celestina* as Hispano-Semitic Anthropology," *Revue de Littérature Comparée* 61 (1987), 425–53, here 452, n. 2. The association of particular intellectual positions or literary interests with "judaizing," so prominent a feature of the Inquisition, has also become a prominent strategy of essentialization among a particular school of Spanish philologists in the United States.

[33] Castro expressed surprise at this in his introduction to *The Spaniards*.

provides an obvious starting point. The Castilian word does cover a broad semantic field,[34] yet certain corners of that field deserve closer cultivation than they have received. Castro's invocation of the Real Academia's modern definition of "raza" in order to dismiss the possibility of pre-modern "Spanish" racism is in fact a startling procedure, given that Castro was a philologist who had elsewhere, for example, deployed the history of the word "Español" to suggest that the concept of "Spanishness" was a late import to Spanish culture. Had he been willing to apply the same technique to the word *raza*, he would have found that it too is a word with a suggestive history in the various Romances of the peninsula.

Already in the early fifteenth century "raza," "casta," and "linaje" (race, caste, lineage) were part of a complex of closely associated terms that linked both behavior and appearance to nature and reproduction. Some of these words, like the word "lineage" itself, had long been used to tie character to genealogy, and the history of that usage was largely independent of "Jewish" questions, although it could easily be extended to them. Writing around 1435, for example, the chronicler/historian Gutierre Díez de Games explained all treason in terms of Jewish "linaje": "From the days of Alexander up till now, there has never been a treasonous act that did not involve a Jew or his descendants."[35]

The Castilian word "raza," however, was much newer, and it seems to have come into broad usage as a term in the animal and the human sciences more or less simultaneously. Although the earliest use I know of in Castilian deploys the term to refer to a hoof disease in horses, among breeders the word "raza" quickly came to mean, in the first quarter of the fifteenth century, something like "pedigree."[36] Thus Manuel Dies's

---

[34] Ricardo del Arco Garay, for example, could speak of a "raza Aragonesa," and José Plá of a "raza hispanica" which encompassed all of Spain and Latin America. See Ricardo del Arco Garay, *Figuras Aragonesas: El genio de la raza* (Zaragoza: Tip. Heraldo de Aragón, 1923-96), and José Plá, (ed.), *La misión internacional de la raza hispánica* (Madrid: Javier Morata, 1928), just two among countless examples.

[35] Juan de Mata Carriazo (ed.), *El Victorial: Crónica de don Pero Niña, conde de Buelna, por su alférez Gutierre Díez de Games* (Madrid: Espasa-Calpe, 1940), p. 17: "desde la muerte de Alexandre acá nunca traición hizo que no fuese judío o su linaxe." For the dating of these lines, see p. xiii.

[36] See Teodorico Borgognoni, "Libro de los Caballos", Ms. Escorial b-IV-3, in John O'Neill (ed.), *Electronic Texts and Concordances, Madison Corpus of Early Spanish Manuscripts and Printings* (CDROM), (Madison and New York: Hispanic Seminary of Medieval Studies, 1999): "La.x. titulo dela enfermedat. que dizen raza. // Faze se alos cauallos una malautia quel dizen Raça. Et faze se de sequedat dela unna." Gianfranco Contini gave a related etymology for "raza" in his "Tombeau de Leo Spitzer", in *Varianti e altra linguistica. Una raccolta di saggi (1938–1968)* (Turin: Einaudi, 1970), pp. 651–660. There he argued that Spitzer's derivation of Romance "raza" from Latin "ratio" was incorrect, and drew the etymology instead from "haraz/haras," the breeding of horses, the stallion's deposit.

popular manual on equine care (written *c.* 1430) admonished breeders to be careful in their selection of stock:

For there is no animal that so resembles or takes after the father in virtues and beauties, nor in size, or coat, and similarly for their contraries. So that it is advised that he who wishes to have good race and caste of horses that above all he seek out the horse or stallion that he be good and beautiful and of good coat, and the mare that she be large and well formed and of good coat.[37]

At more or less the same time in Castilian poetry, "raza" emerged as a way of describing a variety of defects linked to poetic speech, to sexuality, and especially to Judaism.[38] Francisco Imperial, whose Italianate verse had an important impact on the Castilian lyric tradition, addressed an exhortatory poem to the king in 1407 which provides an ambiguous but early example of this last: "A los tus suçessores claro espejo / sera mira el golpe de la maça./sera miral el cuchillo bermejo/que cortara doquier que falle Raza/... /biua el Rey do justiçia ensalça." Scholars have not seen in this early use an association of "raza" to "lineage of Jews." But the poet's condemnation of the "bestia Juderra" a few lines before (line 321) suggests

---

[37] Manuel Dies, "Libre de la menescalia," *c.* 1424–1436, Biblioteca General i Històrica de la Universitat de València, Ms. 631, llib. I (Libre de cavalls), cap. 1 (Com deu ésser engendrat cavall): "car no ha animal nengú <que> tant semble ne retraga al pare en les bondats hi en les bellees, ni en la talla, ni en lo pèl, e axí per lo contrari. Axí que cové qui vol haver bona raça o casta de cavalls que sobretot cerch lo guarà o stalló que sia bo e bell e de bon pèl, e la egua gran e ben formada e de bon pèl." There is a forthcoming edition by Lluís Cifuentes in the series *Els Nostres Clàssics*. For the Castilian translation by Martín Martínez de Ampiés, see Manuel Dies, *Libro de albeytería* (Zaragoza: Pablo Hurus 1495, reprinted 1499). There is a transcription of the 1499 edition by Antonio Cortijo and Angel Gómez Moreno in the Archivo digital de manuscritos y textos españoles [= ADMYTE], (Madrid: 1992), disc I, number 32:

lib. I (Libro de los cavallos), cap. 1 (En qué manera deve el cavallo ser engendrado): El cavallo deve ser engendrado de garañón que haya buen pelo, y sea bien sano y muy enxuto de manos, canillas, rodillas y piedes. Y deve mirar en ésto mucho, que en él no haya mal vicio alguno, porque entre todos los animales no se falla otro que al padre tanto sea semejante en las bondades, belleza ni talle, ni en el pelo, y por el contrario en todo lo malo. Por ende, es muy necessario a qualquier persona que haver codicia raça o casta buena y fermosa cercar garañón muy escogido en pelo, tamaño y en la bondad, y la yegua creçida y bien formada y de buen pelo.

[38] For an example of "raça" as referring to a defect in poetic performance, see Brian Dutton and Joaquin Gonzalez Cuenca (eds.), *Cancionero de Juan Alfonso de Baena* (Madrid: Visor Libros, 1993), Baena to Lando, #363, pp. 641–642: "Fernand manuel, por que versefique / donaires mi lengua sin raça e polilla, / sabed que vos mando de mula pardilla / dozena de festes en el quadruplique" (ll. 9–12. festes: horse turdlets). In early usages the word seems also to have designated sexual defects, and was in this sense used to refer to procuresses and prostitutes. Compare in the same Cancionero #496 (p. 339, line 17) and (perhaps the earliest usage) #100, by Alfonso Álvarez de Villasandino (p. 127, line 10).

otherwise, as does his echo of the exhortation, commonly addressed to Trastamaran kings of Castile, that they defeat that Jewish beast.[39]

In any event, the "Jewishness" of the defects encoded in "raza" soon became more obvious, and as they did so they were enriched with meanings drawn from the more agricultural corners of the word's semantic field. Alfonso Martínez de Toledo, writing around 1438 in the midst of an evolving conflict over *converso* office-holding in Toledo (on which see more below), provides a clear example of the developing logic. You can always tell a person's roots, he explains, for those who descend from good stock are incapable of deviating from it, whereas those of base stock cannot transcend their origins, regardless of whatever money, wealth, or power they may obtain. The reasons for this, he asserts, are natural. The son of an ass must bray. This can be proven, he suggests, by an experiment. If one were to take two babies, the one a son of a laborer, the other of a knight, and rear them together on a mountain in isolation from their parents, one would find that the son of the laborer delights in agricultural pursuits, while the son of the knight takes pleasure only in feats of arms and equestrianship: "Esto procura naturaleza."

> Thus you will see every day in the places where you live, that the good man of good raça always returns to his origins, whereas the miserable man, of bad raça or lineage, no matter how powerful or how rich, will always return to the villainy from which he descends ... That is why when such men or women have power they do not use it as they should.[40]

I will return in a moment to the strenuous debate that developed over this incipient claim that political rights should be dependent on proper "race." But first it is worth insisting that the language of this claim was already saturated with resonance to what contemporaries held to be

---

[39] "Dezir de miçer Francisco a las syete virtudes," lines 393–400, in Dutton and Gonzalez Cuenca, *Cancionero*, p. 316. Writing *c.* 1432, Juan Alfonso de Baena also linked good kingship to the elimination of "Raza": "quitastes/del reyno todas las raças". See his "Desir que fiso Juan Alfonso de Baena," lines 1183–1184, in p. 766. Against my view of this early association between "raza" and Judaism see María Rosa Lida, "Un decir más de Francisco Imperial: Respuesta a Fernán Pérez de Guzmán," *Nueva Revista de Filología Hispánica* 1 (1947), 170–177, and Leo Spitzer's article, "Ratio>Race," in *Essays in Historical Semantics* (New York: Russell and Russell, 1948), pp. 47–69, cited therein. See also Joan Corominas, *Diccionario crítico etimológico de la lengua castellana*, 4 vols. (Bern: Editorial Francke, 1954), vol. III, pp. 1019–1021, s.v. "raza."

[40] Alfonso Martínez de Toledo and Michael Gerli (eds.), *Arcipreste de Talavera o Corbacho*, fourth edition (Madrid: Catedra, 1992), ch. 18, pp. 108–9. : "así lo verás de cada día en los logares do bivieres, que el bueno e de buena raça todavía retrae do viene, e el desaventurado de vil raça e linaje, por grande que sea e mucho que tenga, nunca retraerá sinón a la vileza donde desçiende .... Por ende, quando los tales o las tales tienen poderío no usan dél como deven, como dize el enxiemplo: 'Vídose el perro en bragas de cerro, e non conosçió a su compañero.'"

"common sense" knowledge about the reproductive systems of the natural world.[41] It is the marriage of these two domains, of political disability and of reproductive fitness, which is so well reflected in the famous definition of the word "raza" that Sebastián de Covarrubias provided in his Spanish dictionary of 1611: "the caste of purebred horses, which are marked by a brand so that they can be recognized ... Race in [human] lineages is meant negatively, as in having some race of Moor or Jew."[42]

The natural science upon which such wisdom was based was not that of the nineteenth century, but it was nonetheless capable of generating conclusions startlingly similar to those of a later age.[43] Nor, I hasten to add, was this logic in any way peculiar to Spain. Writing in 1538, in praise of the King of France, the Italian Jacobus Sadoletus would urge the readers of his child-rearing manual "that what is done with horses and dogs should also be done with men ... so that out of good parents there might be born a progeny useful to both the king and the fatherland." Joachim du Bellay (c. 1559) admonished the French parliament in a similar vein:

> For if we are so careful to preserve the race
> Of good horses and good hounds for chase
> How much more carefully should a king provide
> For the race, which is his principal power?[44]

---

[41] Of course much of this knowledge predated the Middle Ages, as a glance at Aristotle's *History of Animals* (7.6 on the resemblance of children to their parents, and compare his *On the Generation of Animals* I.17–18), or Xenophon's *On Hunting* (III, VII on breeding of dogs), makes clear.

[42] Sebastián de Covarrubias, *Tesoro de la lengua castellana o Española* (Madrid: Por L. Sanchez, impressor del rey n.s, 1611) s.v. "raza": "La casta de cavallos castizos, a los quales señalan con hierro para que sean conocidos ... Raza, en los linajes se toma en mala parte, como tener aguna raza de moro o judío." Examples of such usage are legion. A particularly famous one is that of Juan de Pineda, *Diálogos Familiares de la Agricultura Cristiana*, 5 vols. (Salamanca: P. de Adurça y Diego Lopez, 1589), vol. II, xxi, sec. 14: "Ningún cuerdo quiere muger con raza de judía ni de marrana."

[43] The topic of medieval knowledge about animal breeding is only now beginning to be studied. See, for example, Charles Gladitz, *Horse Breeding in the Medieval World* (Dublin: Four Courts Press, 1997). The well known contribution of knowledge about animal breeding to the development of biological discourses about evolution in the eighteenth and nineteenth century suggests that for our purposes the topic would repay further research.

[44] Jacobus Sadoletus, *De pueris recte ac liberaliter instituendis* (Basel, 1538), p. 2: "Maxime autem in hoc laudanda Francisci Regis nostri sapientia est, et consilium summo principe dignum, qui quod caeteri fere in equis et canibus, ipse praecipue in uiris facit, ut prouidentiam omnem adhibeat, quo ex spectatis utrinque generibus electi in hoc sanctum foedus matrimonii conueniant, ut ex bonis parentibus nascatur progenies, que postea et Regi , et patriae possit esse utilis." Cited in Walz, "Der vormoderne Antisemitismus," p. 727. Joachim du Bellay, "Ample Discours au Roy sur le Faict des quatre Estats du Royaume de France," in Henri Chamard (ed.), *Oeuvres Poétiques* (Paris: Droz, 1931), vol. XI, p. 205, and Jouanna, *L'idee de Race en France*, vol. III, p. 1323: "Car si des bons chevaux et des bons chiens de chasse/Nous sommes si soigneux de conserver la

The point, in short, is that words like *raza, casta,* and *linaje* (and their cognates in the various Iberian romance languages) were already embedded in identifiably biological ideas about animal breeding and reproduction in the first half of the fifteenth century. Moreover, the sudden and explicit application of this vocabulary to Jews coincides chronologically (the 1430s) with the appearance of an anti-*converso* ideology (already encountered in the example of Alfonso Martínez de Toledo) which sought to establish new religious categories and discriminations, and legitimate these by naturalizing their reproduction. One of the earliest legislative examples comes from 1433. It was on the 10th of January of that year that Queen María decreed on behalf of the converts of Barcelona that no legal distinction could be made between "natural" Christians on the one hand and neophytes and their descendents on the other, a decree which implies that some people were attempting to make precisely those distinctions.[45] The following year the Council of Basel decreed that

> since [the converts] became by the grace of baptism fellow citizens of the saints and members of the house of God, and since regeneration of the spirit is much more important than birth in the flesh ... they enjoy the privileges, liberties, and immunities of those cities and towns where they were regenerated through sacred baptism to the same extent as the natives and other Christians do.[46]

A few months later King Alfonso of Aragon rejected attempts in Calatayud to impose disabilities on neophytes; in 1436, the councilors of Barcelona moved to bar converts and those whose parents were not both "cristianos de natura" from holding the office of notary; in 1437 the town council of Lleida attempted to strip *conversos* of broker's licenses.[47] The converts of Catalonia and Valencia felt compelled to appeal to the pope, and in 1437

---

race, / Combien plus doit un Roy soigneusement pourvoir / A la race, qui est son principal pouvoir?" I cite non-peninsular texts in order to stress that, *pace* the Black Legend, there is nothing specifically Iberian about these strategies of naturalization. They are pan-European, as much Protestant as Catholic. See, e.g., the citation from Martin Luther above.

[45] Archive of the Crown of Aragon (ACA):C 3124:157r–v: "separatio aut differentia nulla fiat inter christianos a progenie seu natura et neophytos ... et ex eis descendentes." The use of the word "by nature" to distinguish Old Christians was already common by this date.

[46] "Et quoniam per gratiam baptismi cives sanctorum & domestici Dei efficiuntur, longeque dignius sit regenerari spiritu, quam nasci carne, hac edictali lege statuimus, ut civitatum & locorum, in quibus sacro baptismate regenerantur, privilegiis, libertatibus & immunitatibus gaudeant, quae ratione duntaxat nativitatis & originis alii consequuntur." Joannes Dominicus Mansi, *Sacrorum conciliorum nova et amplissima collectio,* 54 vols. (Florence, 1759 f./reprint Graz: Akademische Druck-u. Verlagsanstalt, 1961), vol. 29, p. 100.

[47] ACA:C 2592:21r–22v; Raimundo Noguera Guzmán and José Maria Madurell Marimón (eds.), *Privilegios y ordenanzas históricos de los notarios de Barcelona* (Barcelona: [s.n], 1965), doc. 57; Pedro Sanahuja, *Lérida en sus luchas por la fe (judíos, moros, conversos, Inquisición, moriscos)* (Lleida: [s.n], 1946), pp. 103–110. See Riera, "Judíos y conversos," pp. 86–87.

Eugene IV condemned those "sons of iniquity ... Christians only in name," who suggested that recent converts be barred from public office and who "refuse to enter into matrimony with them."[48] Similar attempts took place in Castile. In Seville, an anti-monarchical rebellion may have planned to murder the *converso* population in 1433–4, and ten years later, still in the midst of civil war, King Juan II was obliged to instruct the cities of his kingdom that the *conversos* were to be treated "as if they were born Christians," and admitted to "any honorable office of the Republic."[49]

The vocabulary of race evolved under the pressure of this conflict, as words like "raza," "casta," "linaje," and even "natura" herself were applied to converts and their descendents. By 1470 the word "race" was so common in poetry that Pero Guillén included it (along with other useful words like "marrano") in his *Gaya ciencia*, a handbook of rhymes for poets.[50] The "cristiano de natura" mentioned by Queen María became a common (though by no means exclusive) term of reference for "Old Christians." The exclusionary genealogical logic of the term was perfectly clear to *conversos*, some of whom coined a rebuttal: "cristianos de natura, cristianos de mala ventura" ("Christians by nature are Christians of bad fortune"). By this they meant (or at least so they told the Inquisition decades later) that *conversos* shared the lineage of the Virgin Mary, whereas old Christians were descended from idol-worshiping gentiles.[51] Such remarks encode histories that are too complicated to address here, but they suggest that the converts responded to the *Naturgeschichte* of "clean Christians" with genealogies of their own.[52] In any event the wide extension of such vocabulary in the 1430s and following decades makes clear that the role of lineage in determining character, which had become an increasingly important aspect of chivalric and aristocratic ideology in Iberia in the decades following the Trastamaran civil war, was now becoming more explicitly biological, and being applied

[48] Vicente Beltrán de Heredia, "Las bulas de Nicolás Vacerca de los conversos de Castilla," *Sefarad* 21 (1961), 37–38. Recall that the council of Basel had included an exhortation to the conversos that they marry Old Christians: "curent & studeant neophytos ipsos cum originariis Christianis matrimonio copulare."
[49] Juan de Mata Carriazo (ed.), *Crónica del Halconero de Juan II*, Colección de Crónicas Españolas 8 (Madrid: Espasa-Calpe, 1946), p. 152; Netanyahu, *Origins of the Inquisition*, pp. 284–292.
[50] See José María Casas Homs (ed.), *La gaya ciencia de P. Guillén de Segovia*, 2 vols. (Madrid: CSIC, 1962), s.v. "raça."
[51] Encarnación Marin Padilla, *Relación judeoconversa durante la segunda mitad del siglo XV en Aragón: La Ley* (Madrid: [s.n.], 1988), pp. 60–67.
[52] For a fuller exploration of the dialogic evolution of genealogical thinking among Jews, Christians, and converts in fifteenth-century Spain, see David Nirenberg, "Mass Conversion and Genealogical Mentalities: Jews and Christians in Fifteenth-Century Spain," *Past and Present* 174 (Feb. 2002), 3–41.

extensively to converts from Judaism.[53] This logic of lineage was not a priori prejudicial to converts: some writers on nobility and genealogy even argued, as did Diego de Valera *c.* 1441, that descent from the "chosen people" ennobled rather than debased the "New Christians."[54] But in fact throughout the middle decades of the fifteenth century, these naturalizations came increasingly to be deployed against them.

The Toledan revolt of 1449 against the monarchy and the *conversos* as its perceived agents provides a good example of such deployment. The Toledans and their sympathizers were clearly anxious that the converts posed a threat to the reproduction of social and political status. Thus they claimed that "baptised Jews and those proceeding from their damaged line" were waging an implacable and cruel war against Christianity. Their conversions were motivated only by ambition for office and "carnal lust for nuns and [Christian] virgins." *Marrano* physicians even poisoned their Christian patients in order to get hold of their inheritance and offices, "marry the wives of the old Christians they kill" and stain their "clean blood" (sangre limpia).[55] Arguing that all those "descended from the

[53] On these changing notions of nobility see Rucquoi, "Noblesse des conversos?," pp. 89–108, and Adeline Rucquoi, "Etre noble en Espagne aux XIVᵉ–XVIᵉ siècles," in Otto G. Oexle and Werner Paravicini (eds.), *Nobilitas: Funktion und Repräsentation des Adels in Alteuropa* (Göttingen: Vandenhoeck & Ruprecht, 1997), pp. 273–298. On evolving chivalric ideology, see Jesus D. Rodríguez Velasco, *El debate sobre la caballería en el siglo XV: la tratadística caballeresca castellana en su marco europeo*, Collection de estudios de historia (Valladolid [Salmanca]: Junta de Castilla y León, Consejería de Educación y Cultura, 1996).

[54] Diego de Valera, "Espejo de la verdadera nobleza," in Mario Penna (ed.), *Prosistas castellanos del siglo XV*, Biblioteca de Autores Españoles 116 (Madrid: Ediciones Atlas, 1959), pp. 102–103: "si los convertidos ... retienen la nobleza de su linaje después de christianos ... en quál nasció tantos nobles fallarse pueden ... Dios ... el qual este linaje escogió para sí por el más noble?" The converts' possession of the blood of Jesus and Mary remained a standard argument in defense of *converso* rights well into the sixteenth century (more on this below). Apologizing for any embarrassment he might cause to the descendents of *conversos*, Joan Antonio Llorente, the author of the first critical history of the Inquisition, used the same argument to insist that such descent was cause not for shame but for pride. See Joan Antonio Llorente, *Histoire Critique de l'Inquisition dupuis l'époque de son établissement par Fedinand V, jusqu'au règne de Ferdinand VII, tirée des pieces originales des archives du Conseil de la Supreme, et de celles des tribunaux subalternes du Saint-office* (Paris: Treuttel et Würz, 1817), p. 24.

[55] These accusations are made by the Bachelor Marco García de Mora in his brief defending the anti-*converso* activities of the rebel government of Toledo. See Eloy Benito Ruano, "El Memorial del bachiller Marcos García de Mora contra los conversos," *Sefarad* 17 (1957), 314–351 [reprinted in his *Los orígenes del problema converso* (Barcelona: El Albir, 1976), pp. 95–132, here pp. 103, 111, 118]. Similar charges, with the addition of those against Marrano physicians, are made in a fifteenth-century manuscript by an anonymous author whose relationship to the Toledan rebels is unclear. See the "Privilegio de Don Juan II en favor de un Hidalgo," BNM, MS 13043, fols. 172–177. The text is edited in *Sales españolas; o, Agudezas del ingenio nacional. Recogidas por Antonio Paz y Melia*, Biblioteca de Autores Españoles 176 (Madrid: Ediciones Atlas, 1964), pp. 25–28, here p. 26.

perverse lineage of the Jews" were, like their ancestors in ancient times, "enemies" who sought above all "to destroy all the Old Christians," the Toledans set about confronting the danger, first with violence, and then with a "Sentencia-Estatuto" banning descendents of converts from holding public office for at least four generations: the first of what would soon be many Spanish statutes of "purity of blood."[56]

The texts produced by the rebels and their allies in defense of their position, and by opponents like Alonso de Cartagena, Juan de Torquemada, Lope de Barrientos, and Fernán Diáz de Toledo against it, became central texts in the Spanish debate over the "Jewishness" of converts and their descendents. The eventual victory of the anti-*converso* genealogical arguments in the debate was not obvious or easy, for medieval people had a great many ways of thinking about the transmission of cultural characteristics across generations, such as pedagogy and nurture, which did not necessarily invoke nature, inheritance, or sexual reproduction.[57]

Nevertheless the genealogical turn was taken, and it proved to be one of extraordinary power. The reasons for its success are many and complex, but one which should not be underestimated is the power of its appeal to medieval "common knowledge" about nature. Consider, for example, the language of a treatise like the *Alborayque*, an anonymous work composed *c.* 1455–65. The treatise maps the moral attributes and cultural practices of the *conversos* onto diverse body parts of the Alborayque, the Qur'anic composite beast (part horse, part lion, part snake, etc.) who carried Muhammad to heaven. The use of this hybrid to stand for the converts, though often treated by modern critics as a mere conceit, is in fact a

---

[56] The "Sentencia-Estatuto" is published by Fritz Baer, *Die Juden im christlichen Spanien*, 2 vols. (Berlin: Akademie-Verlag, 1936), vol. II, #302, pp. 315–317. On these texts see especially Eloy Benito Ruano, "La 'Sentencia-Estatuto' de Pero Sarmiento contra los conversos Toledanos," *Revista de la Universidad de Madrid* 6 (1957), 277–306; Benito Ruano, "D. Pero Sarmiento, repostero mayor de Juan II de Castilla," *Hispania* 17 (1957), 483–454; Benito Ruano, "El Memorial del bachiller Marcos García de Mora," 314–351.

[57] The lines of difference between these various ways are, however, not always easy to establish. Pope Pius II, for example, authorized an annulment for Pedro de la Caballeria in 1459, on the grounds that his wife was a heretic who had been taught to judaize by her mother. "Pedro, a true Catholic, is prepared to endure … every danger of death rather than consummate a marriage of this sort, lest [any] begotten offspring follow the insanity of the mother, and a Jew be created out of a Christian" (ASV, Reg. Vat. 470, fol. 201r-v [=Simonsohn #856]). Since Pedro de la Caballeria was himself also a *converso*, the problem here is one of pedagogy and nurture, not inheritance. Steven Kruger seems not to realize that Pedro is a *converso*, and argues for this text as evidence of a racial notion of Judaism in his "Conversion and Medieval Sexual, Religious, and Racial Categories," in Karma Lochrie *et al.* (eds.), *Constructing Medieval Sexuality* (Minneapolis: University of Minnesota Press, 1997), pp. 158–179, here pp. 169–70.

systematic strategy of argument from nature. The converts are not only Alborayques. They are bats, unclassifiable as animal (wings) or bird (teeth); they are a weak alloy rather than pure metal; and above all, they are a mixed lineage, a mixture of Edom, Moab, Amon, Egypt, and more. These unnatural mixtures support the conclusion (and here is the leap to culture) that the *conversos* can never be classified as Christian, for "si los metales son muchos ... segun la carne, quanto mas de metales de tantas heregias."[58] Similarly the negative imagery of mixed species in the treatise leads ineluctably to its conclusion: a prayer that the "clean" lineages of the old Christians not be corrupted through marriage with the new.[59]

Like a number of polemicists before him, the author of the *Alborayque* chose to focus on the corruption of the Jewish lineage in historical time, but other approaches were possible.[60] Writing at about the same time, for example, Alonso de Espina verged on a polygenetic approach when he related the lineage of Jews to the offspring of, first, Adam with animals and second, Adam with the demon Lilith. As a result of these unions, he wrote, Jews are of the lineage of demons and of monsters, the mule and

[58] "Tratado del Alborayque," BNM, MS 17567. The quote is from fol. 11r. Dwayne Carpenter is preparing a critical edition of the manuscript and printed versions of this important text. In the meantime Moshe Lazar provides an edition of the text based on BNP ms. Esp. 356: Moshe Lazar, "Anti-Jewish and anti-*Converso* Propaganda: Confutatio Libri Talmud and Alboraique," in Moshe Lazar and Stephen Haliczer (eds.), *The Jews of Spain and the Expulsion of 1492* (Lancaster, CA: Labyrinthos, 1997), pp. 153–236.

[59] Once again these argumentative strategies seem to be quickly mirrored in Jewish sources. Shem Tov b. Joseph ibn Shem Tov, writing in the 1480s, made a similarly "metallurgical" argument: "If a person is of pure blood and has a noble lineage, he will give birth to a son like himself, and he who is ugly and stained (of blood?) will give birth to a son who is similar to him, for gold will give birth to gold and silver will give birth to silver and copper to copper, and if you find some rare instances that from lesser people sprang out greater ones, nevertheless in most cases what I have said is correct, and as you know, a science is not built on exceptions." Shem Tov ben Joseph ibn Shem Tov, *Derashot* (Salonika 1525/ Jerusalem 1973), 14a col. b, cited in Eleazar Gutwirth, "Lineage in XVth Century Hispano-Jewish Thought," *Miscelanea de estudios arabes y hebraicos* 34 (1985), 85–91, here 88.

[60] A number of fourteenth-century polemics stressed the hybrid nature of the Jewish people. One influential tradition maintained that since Titus had put no Jewish women aboard the ships that carried the survivors of the siege of Jerusalem into the Diaspora, the males had taken Muslim or pagan women to wife, so that their descendents were not real Jews but only bastards, with no claim to the covenant. See Josep Hernando i Delgado, "Un tractat anònim *Adversus iudaeos* en català," in Frederic Raurell (ed.), *Paraula i història. Miscel. lània P. Basili de Rubí* (Barcelona: Edicions Franciscanes, 1986), p. 730; Jose María Millás Vallicrosa, "Un tratado anónimo de polémica contra los judíos," *Sefarad* 13 (1953), 28; and the Castilian polemic written *c.* 1370 but preserved in a fifteenth-century manuscript: "Coloquio entre un Cristiano y un Judío," Biblioteca del Palacio, MS 1344, fol. 106r–v. (Also in the recent edition by Aitor García Moreno, *Coloquio entre un cristiano y un judío*, [London: Queen Mary, University of London, 2003], pp. 154–5.)

the sow their adoptive mother.[61] Such genealogies doubtless seemed as fantastic to many medieval readers as they do to us. They provided an important theoretical underpinning, however, for the doctrine of "limpieza de sangre," or purity of blood: the idea that the reproduction of culture is embedded in the reproduction of the flesh.

It is upon this logic that new boundaries would be built between Christian and "Jew" in Spain. These new boundaries were enormously controversial.[62] I know of no more extensive pre-modern discussion about the relationship between biology and culture than that in the literature produced in the debate over *converso* exclusion between 1449 and 1550.[63] But the logic of the *Alborayque*, with its mapping of "Judaizing" corruption onto reproductive hybridity, was eventually victorious. The victory of this logic was due, in part, to the fact that it resonated so well with other registers of cultural reproduction in late medieval Iberian society. Defenders of the *conversos* could insist, as they all did, that the reproduction of the flesh could not limit the miraculously transforming power of God working through the sacrament of baptism: it was, after all, dogma that in Christ there is neither Jew nor Greek. But when it came to other areas of culture in which behavior and lineage were traditionally tightly linked, even the most eloquent among them could not attempt to dissociate the two.

Perhaps the most important of such questions was whether or not descendents of Jews could form part of the nobility. A negative answer like that of the Toledan rebels (not even the king's grace could make descendents of such a debased lineage noble) would effectively bar the New Christians from any number of rights and privileges. But a positive one seemed to require the discovery among them of either an aristocratic

---

[61] Alonso de Espina, *Fortalitium Fidei, consideratio* ii, editio princeps, (Nuremberg: Anton Koberger, 1494), fol. 79, col. d. See Alisa Meyuhas Ginio, *De bello iudaeorum: Fray Alonso de Espina y su* Fortalitium Fidei, Fontes Iudaeorum Regni Castellae 8 (Salamanca: Universidad Pontificia de Salamanca, 1998), pp. 16–17. See also Netanyahu, *Origins of the Inquisition*, p. 83; Ana Echevarria, *The Fortress of Faith: the Attitude toward Muslims in Fifteenth-Century Spain* (Leiden: Brill, 1999), p. 167.

[62] The arrival of the *Tratado del Alborayque* in Guadalupe, for example, provoked a bitter schism that was later remembered by the friars as the defining moment in relations between Old and New Christians in the monastery. See Gretchen D. Starr-Lebeau, *In the Shadow of the Virgin: Inquisitors, Friars, and Conversos in Guadalupe, Spain* (Princeton, NJ: Princeton University Press, 2003).

[63] The scholarship on purity of blood statutes is too large to summarize here. Early and foundational contributions include Albert Sicroff, *Les controverses des statuts de "pureté de sang" en Espagne du XVe au XVIIe siècle* (Paris: Didier, 1960); Antonio Domínguez Ortiz, *La clase social de los conversos en Castilla en la Edad Moderna* (Madrid: Consejo Superior de Investigaciones Científicas, 1955); I. S. Revah, "La controverse sur les statuts de pureté de sang", *Bulletin Hispanique* 63 (1971), 263–316.

lineage or an aptitude for heroism – since military valor was generally
understood as the causal foundation of nobility in fifteenth-century peninsular society. Thus advocates for the New Christians found themselves
simultaneously preaching "woe to those who build a city on blood"
(Habakkuk 2:12); and insisting through genealogies of extremely "longue
durée" that the converts recuperated the nobility of the Israelites – which
had lain dormant within the Jews for the millennium and a half that they
had denied Jesus – and shared the same blood as God and His virgin
mother.[64]

Similarly with the question of courage: the Bachelor Marcos deployed a
common prejudice when he wrote that the "ruinous lineage" of the Jews
conveyed cowardice to their Christian descendents, for the timidity of the
Jews was proverbial in the Middle Ages.[65] Again, Alonso de Cartagena's
counter-argument did not entirely reject his opponent's theses about the
biological reproduction of culture, but argued rather for a different starting point. The Old Testament had famously chronicled the courage of the
ancient Israelites, and

> as Aristotle would have it, among dispositions toward virtue none is more derived
> among descendents through propagation of the blood than the disposition that
> tends toward fortitude .... Therefore since, considering their small number,
> proportionally more from among these [descendents of Jews] rise to investiture
> in the orders of knighthood, than from among those who descend from some
> rustic family of ignoble commoners ... it follows that we should presume that the
> nobility that some of them had in ancient times, lies latent enclosed within their
> breasts.

[64] Diego de Valera, "Espejo de la verdadera nobleza," pp. 102–103 is an early example of
such an argument. Alonso de Cartagena, *Defensorium unitatis christianae* ed. P. Manuel
Alonso (Madrid: C. Bermejo, 1943), is another prominent example. The citation of
Habakkuk is from Cardinal Juan de Torquemada, who then goes on to suggest that the
converts deserve special honor because of the genealogy they share with Jesus. See Juan de
Torquemada, Nicolas López Martinez, and Vicente Proaño Gil Burgos (eds.), *Tractatus
contra Madianitas et Ismaelitas* (Burgos: Seminario Metropolitano de Burgos, 1957),
p. 123.
[65] Proverbially timorous: Alonso de Cartagena, *Defensorium unitatis christianae*, II.iv.20,
p. 215: "when we want to express excessive timidity, we call it Jewishness, and we usually
call a man who is excessively fearful a Jew." This passage (as well as the next I will quote
from Cartagena) is helpfully discussed (toward a different conclusion) in Bruce
Rosenstock, *New Men: Conversos, Christian Theology, and Society in Fifteenth-Century
Castile* (London: Queen Mary and Westfield College, 2002), pp. 47–49. Marcos on
"ruin linaxe": "El Memorial del bachiller Marcos García de Mora," p. 112. A few decades
earlier, St. Vincent Ferrer bemoaned that Christians would insult as "Jews" other
Christians who refused to participate in violence or vengeance. See St. Vincent Ferrer,
Sermons, vol. I, pp. 42, 93, 155; III, 16; V, 190.

Once the Jewish vessel is baptized, the fortitude encoded in its ancient blood is free to shine once more, like a bright light whose concealing bushel is removed.[66]

Alonso de Cartagena's claims about the "deep heritability" of courage and nobility, like those of other pro-*converso* writers, are based on a reading of Aristotelian natural science that is very similar to that of Manuel Dies' horse-breeding manual, or indeed to that of those anti-*converso* writers who emphasized the "ruinous lineages" of the Jews.[67] This congruence is not evidence of the pro-*converso* party's hypocrisy (as many of their opponents claimed at the time, and some scholars still do today), but of the differential densities of reproductive logics across the many registers of a complex culture. The victory of the anti-*converso* movement consisted in extending the power of ideas about heritability from certain areas where they were already thickly rooted (such as in discourses of animal breeding and of aristocratic genealogy) to previously inhospitable soil (such as sacramental theology). To the degree that this victory extended the cultivation of "raza" into new corners of culture and society, we can literally say that it made fifteenth-century Spain more "racial."

The consequences of this victory were momentous. The argument that *converso* morals were habitually corrupt, for example, led to the establishment of the first "proto-Inquisition" under Alonso de Oropesa in the 1460s. Oropesa, a prominent opponent of discrimination against descendents of *conversos*, believed that rooting out the heresies of the few would prove the innocence of the majority. Indeed he found little evidence for the charges against the converts, but their increasingly effective reiteration was used to justify the establishment of the Inquisition itself in 1481. And this Inquisition operated according to a logic strikingly similar to that of the *Alborayque*. Judaizers were to be identified by their behavior, but that behavior only gained meaning in light of their flesh's genealogy.

---

[66] Alonso de Cartagena, *Defensorium unitatis christianae*, II.iv.20, p. 217.

[67] There were other readings available, since Aristotle had said diverse things on the subject. In *Politics* 7.7, for example, he (like Hippocrates) put forward a more climatological model of courage according to which the cold regions of Europe produce fortitude (and therefore comparatively free peoples), whereas those who live in the warmth of Asia are more fearful, and therefore "ruled and enslaved." Alonso de Cartagena, however, could not embrace such a climatological reading (*avant* Montesquieu) without calling into question crucial axioms of fifteenth-century Castilian aristocratic culture. On knowledge of Aristotle's politics in the fifteenth century, see Christoph Flüeler, *Rezeption und Interpretation der aristotelischen Politica im späten Mittelalter*, 2 vols. (Amsterdam–Philadelphia: B. R. Grüner–J. Benjamins, 1992); and Anthony R. D. Pagden, "The Diffusion of Aristotle's Moral Philosophy in Spain, ca. 1400–ca.1600," *Traditio* 31 (1975), 287–313.

Already in 1449 Fernán Díaz, the Relator of Juan II, had pointed out the dangers of such a system. There was scarcely a noble house in Spain that had no *converso* in its family tree. If Jewishness were attached to blood, the Relator warned, the nobility of Iberia would be destroyed.[68] Moreover, since the effects of genealogy were primarily expressed culturally, the religio-racial classification of cultural practice became an important part of the accusational economy. Virtually any negative cultural trait could be presented as "Judaizing." We have seen the *Alborayque*'s list, and there were many others, each sounding more and more like Borges' Chinese encyclopedia. The characteristics encoded in Jewish blood, according to the bishop of Cordoba in 1530, included heresy, apostasy, love of novelty and dissension, ambition, presumption, and hatred of peace. (Note the similarity with the list produced by Américo Castro.) The effectiveness of such claims in attracting the attention of Inquisitional courts made them strategically useful, and thereby judaized ever more extensive cultural practices. By 1533, even the son of the then Inquisitor General, Rodrigo Manrique, could write to the self-exiled humanist Luis Vives: "You are right. Our country is a land of … barbarism. For now it is clear that no one can possess any culture without being suspect of heresy, error, and Judaism."[69]

★★★

It would be a mistake to see, in this attachment of "Jewishness" to culture, evidence that these late medieval discriminations were not "racial." On the contrary, this "judaization" of Spanish culture was the direct result of the increasingly widespread use of ideas about the biological reproduction of somatic and behavioral traits in order to create and legitimate hierarchies and discriminations, within a society where extensive intermarriage (as well as strategic practices like the falsification of genealogies and proofs of purity of blood) made the reproductive segregation of "Judaism" impossible.

---

[68] For the Relator's text see Alonso de Cartagena, *Defensorium unitatis christianae*, Appendix II, pp. 343–56, here pp. 351–355. Note that though the Relator condemns the anti-*converso* aspects of this genealogical approach, he (like Alonso de Cartagena, Juan de Torquemada, and other pro-*converso* writers) nevertheless utilizes genealogical arguments, referring constantly (for example) to the converts as of the lineage of Christ. On the Relator see *inter alia*, Nicholas Round, "Politics, Style and Group Attitudes in the *Instrucción del Relator*," *Bulletin of Hispanic Studies* 46 (1969), 289–319.

[69] Henry de Vocht, "Rodrigo Manrique's Letter to Vives," *in Monumenta Humanistica Lovaniensia: Texts and Studies about Louvain Humanists in the First Half of the XVIth Century* (Louvain: Charles Uystpruyst, 1934), pp. 427–458, here p. 435: 'Plane uerum est quod dicis inuidam atque superbam illam nostram patriam; adde, & barbaram. Nam iam pro certo habetur apud illos neminem bonarum literarum mediocritur excultum, quin heresibus, erroribus, Judaismis sit refertus." See also Enrique González González, "Vives, un humanista judeoconverso en el exilio de Flandres," in Luc Dequeker and Werner Verbeke (eds.), *The Expulsion of the Jews and their Emigration to the Southern Low Countries (15th–16th C.)* (Leuven: Leuven University Press, 1998), pp. 35–81, here p. 77.

It would, however, be just as great an error to conclude that we have shown these discriminations, and the theories of cultural reproduction that underlay them, to be "racial." All we have done is demonstrate the inadequacy of some influential arguments for dismissing the relevance of race to the pre-modern by finding in medieval Spain some of the attributes of race that various scholars have located in modernity (such as theories of selection in animal breeding, Foucault's binary enmities, and of course the word "race" itself). From this we can conclude only that the vocabularies of difference and the natural histories available to the residents of the Iberian Peninsula in the fifteenth and sixteenth centuries can be fruitfully compared to those of other times and places. We have barely begun the process of comparison itself. We have not explored, for example, the robustness of the binary opposition between "Christian" and "Jew" posited by the enemies of the *conversos*, or asked how the cultural work of such a binary within the state structures of the late Middle Ages differed from or was similar to the work Foucault had in mind in the Modern. We noted some broad similarities in the theoretical underpinnings of Toledo's purity of blood statutes and the "racial anti-Semitism" of later periods, but we did not note how different the uses, applications, functions, and effects of these medieval theories were from those more modern ones. We have, in other words, only arrived at the most provisional and banal of conclusions: more work needs to be done.

This, it seems to me, is the most that can be expected of any history of race, and I would like to end by defending the humility of this conclusion. It is an ancient tendency of the historical imagination to think of ideas and concepts as having a discrete origin in a particular people, whence they are transmitted from donor to recipient cultures across space and time.[70] There may be some concepts whose histories are well described by such etymological and genealogical approaches.[71] Here, however, we are concerned with the history of an idea – the conviction that culture is produced and reproduced in the same way as the species procreates itself – so venerable and widespread that Giambattista Vico elevated it to a universal in his *Principles of the New Science*. It is, moreover, an idea that has produced so heterogeneous a set of discourses and outcomes – even when limited to its most modern forms, such as "race" and "racism" – that these can scarcely be subsumed into a "concept" or a "theory." The

---

[70] A tendency as well represented in fifteenth-century Castile as in other times and places: see, e.g., the "Invencionario of Alfonso de Toledo," BNP, MS Esp. 204, fols. 1–105v.

[71] Given Nietzsche's and Foucault's success in redefining the meaning of the term "genealogy," it is important to note that here and throughout I am using the term "genealogical" in its traditional, non-Foucauldian sense.

history of this idea is not the history of a train of thought, whose wagons can be ordered by class and whose itinerary may be mapped across time and space, but that of a principle of locomotion so general that any account of its origins, applications, and transmission will always be constrained by our ignorance (or to put it more charitably, by what we recognize as significant). We cannot solve this difficulty by cutting ("race did not exist before modernity"), by stitching ("race has always already existed") or by refusing to talk about what cannot be clearly defined ("races do not exist, and race does not have a history").

None of this means that we should paralyse history with the cautions of a logician – "what is known as the history of concepts is really a history either of our knowledge of concepts or of the meaning of words" – only that we should keep such cautions in mind. There will always be strategic reasons for choosing to represent the relationship of ideas about the natural reproduction of culture that are scattered across time and space in terms of filiations or, conversely, in terms of disjuncture (or even to refuse the possibility of such an idea at all). Yet the choice can only be situational and polemical, in the sense that its recognition of significance springs from the needs and struggles (theological, political, philosophical, professional, etc.) of a specific moment. The polemics produced by such choices are invaluable when they stimulate us to comparison and self-consciousness. If, however, we treat them as anything but strategic, we simply exchange one lack of consciousness for another.

Race demands a history, both because it is a subject urgent and vast, and because its own logic is so closely akin to that of the disciplines (etymology, genealogy, history) with which we study the persistence of humanity in time. For these same reasons, any history of race will be at best provocative and limited; at worst a reproduction of racial logic itself, in the form of a genealogy of ideas.[72] In either case, histories of race are

---

[72] Thus, for example, many of the Spanish scholars mentioned in these pages came to the conclusion that, whatever "raza" might be, it originated with the Jews. Already in the nineteenth century Marcelino Menéndez y Pelayo, "founding-father" of Spanish historiography, wrote that "the fanaticism of blood and race ... we probably owe to the Jews." The quote is from his letter to Valera, 17 October 1887, in Juan Valera, *Epistolario de Valera y Menéndez Pelayo* (Madrid: Espasa-Calpe, 1946), p. 408. See also Menéndez y Pelayo, *Historia de los heterodoxos Españoles*, vol. I, p. 410; vol. II, p. 381. Within the context of Spanish history, the opinion has been embraced by writers as diverse as Américo Castro and Claudio Sánchez Albornoz (see note 20, above). Conversely, an equally diverse group of Jewish scholars (which includes Yitzhak Baer, Cecil Roth, Haim Hillel Ben-Sasson, Yosef Yerushalmi, Benzion Netanyahu, and Yosef Kaplan) has strenuously argued the opposite thesis, that these ideas were invented by gentiles (in this case Iberian Christians) as a way of denying converts from Judaism full membership in the Christian spiritual and social communities they sought to enter. Yosef Kaplan, "The Self-Definition of the Sephardic Jews of Western Europe and their Relation to the Alien and

best read by pre-modernist and modernist alike, not as prescriptive, but as polemical stimuli to comparison. We can each draw energy from the collision of such polemics with our own particles of history, and find new elements of both past and present in the wreckage. Put another way, we might read such histories as metaphors. I mean metaphor not in the sense of model or map, as some anthropologists and scholars of comparative religion have recently championed, but in the medieval sense articulated in the eleventh century by Albert of Monte Casino: "it is the function of metaphor to twist, so to speak, its mode of speech from its property; by twisting, to make some innovation; by innovating, to clothe, as it were, in nuptial garb; and by clothing, to sell, apparently at a decent price."[73] As in Albert's understanding of good metaphor, good histories and theorizations of race are a source of productive deceit. The associations they provoke are seductive, communicative, startlingly revealing, but also in some sense fraudulent. We cannot reject their power without impoverishment, but neither can we accept their suggestions without suspicion.

The same is true, of course, in reverse. Just as modernity provokes the medievalist, so should medieval encounters disturb the troubled certitudes of the modernist. The latter will, however, not travel without guides: yet another reason why it is important that pre-modernists (or at least those interested in specific problems, such as the transformations of religious categories in fifteenth century Spain) confront their subjects' natural histories, rather than hiding behind over-easy rejections of race. But it is equally important that we not confuse the strategic comparisons and heuristic polemics produced by such confrontations, with a history of "race" or "racism." The suggestion that we can benefit from the systematic juxtaposition of various strategies of naturalization need not imply that these strategies can be arranged into an evolutionary history of race, just as the argument that we can learn from the similarities we discover between, say, fifteenth-century ideologies and twentieth-century ones

---

the Stranger," in Benjamin R. Gampel (ed.), *Crisis and Creativity in the Sephardic World, 1391–1648* (New York: Columbia University Press, 1997), p. 128; Henry Méchoulan, "The Importance of Hispanicity in Jewish Orthodoxy and Heterodoxy in Seventeenth-Century Amsterdam," in Bernard Cooperman (ed.), *In Iberia and Beyond: Hispanic Jews Between Cultures* (Newark, DE: University of Delaware Press, 1998), pp. 353–372.

[73] "Suum autem est metaphorae modum locutionis a proprietate sui quasi detorquere, detorquando quadammodo innovare, innovando quasi nuptiali amictu tegere, tegendo quasi praecio dignitatis vendere." Mauro Inguanez and Henry M. Willard (eds.), *Alberici Casinensis Flores rhetorici* (Montecassino: Miscellanea Cassinese, 1938), p. 45. For a modern statement of a similar epistemology see FitzJohn Porter Poole, "Metaphors and Maps: Towards Comparison in the Anthropology of Religion," *Journal of the American Academy of Religion* 54 (1986), 411–457.

need not suggest that one followed from the other.[74] Admittedly the danger of such a fallacy is great, for the subject of race tends to bewitch its historians with the same philo-genetic fantasies and teleological visions that underwrite racial ideologies themselves. But if we wish to study how medieval people sought to naturalize their own histories, while at the same time attempt to denaturalize our own, it is a risk worth taking.

---

[74] As George Fredrickson implicitly suggests by beginning his *Racism: A Short History* (Princeton, NJ: Princeton University Press, 2002) with a treatment of "limpieza de sangre."

12 Religion and race: Protestant and Catholic discourses on Jewish conversions in the sixteenth and seventeenth centuries

Ronnie Po-chia Hsia

Prologue

Ethnocentric pride is nothing new. The ancient Greeks felt their civilization was superior to their neighbours, as did the ancient Chinese. Yet, in the writings of Herodotus or Zima Qien, the descriptions of foreign peoples were not necessarily disparaging. Rather, the narratives focus on customs and beliefs: the manner of clothing, marriage customs, behavior in war; and, for Herodotus, whether foreign peoples resembled Greeks in that they erected temples, columns, and statues to their gods, such as the Egyptians; or not, such as the Persians and Scythians. There were particular things that interested our Greek and Chinese historians: for Herodotus, the thinness of skulls on the part of the Persians, and the contrary for Egyptians; whereas for Zima Qien and Chinese ethnography in general, writing and food-ways always signified the level of civilization. Ethnography, in other words, is not necessarily linked to feelings of racial superiority, for the ancient Greek and Chinese sources devote little attention to the physical description of alien peoples. It was customs, not looks, cultural practices and not physique, which gave ancient civilizations their sense of superior identity. And to the extent that a people can adopt the cultural practices of another, there was no immutable barrier to the change of identity. In Chinese history, for example, the adoption of the Chinese script, Confucian ethics, Chinese imperial institutions, and Han city life by a succession of nomadic invaders qualified them for "sinicization" and upward advance in the ladder of civilized hierarchy in the view of Chinese historiography. In the West, a similar process characterized the adoption of Roman ways by the conquered peoples of the Empire. In short, identity was not static; and physical appearance measured lightly in the scale of civilization that weighed speech, dress, rituals, and beliefs in heavier measures.

Yet, in the history of the medieval West, the emergence of a particular link between culture and ethnicity, or, to be more specific, between religion and race, would shape the discourse of the modern world. At the center of this development was the relationship between Jews and Christians. By definition a matter of diverse cultic practices, the perception of differences between the two religious groups developed in the course of the centuries into one that was marked by blood. In other words, the permeability of the religious-cultural boundaries was re-defined as an immutable divide between peoples of different blood lineages. It was no longer a matter of Egyptians or Scythians or Chinese disliking foreign customs; it became a question of essential identity on the part of the Jews, seen from the Christian perspective, which no cultural adaptation or religious conversion could erase.

Christian–Jewish relations in the pre-modern West, therefore, formed a prism through which were refracted the ethnic or racial attitudes that shaped the modern world. In this paper, I propose to analyze two case studies: the German Protestant discourse on Jews and Judaism after the Reformation, and the Catholic discourse on conversions, Jewish and otherwise, in the context of post-Tridentine missions outside Europe. I shall argue for the emergence of an attitude of racial superiority during the sixteenth and seventeenth centuries, one common to both Protestant and Catholic countries, that began to represent religious differences between Christianity and all other religions in reference to non-cultural criteria: blood and physique.

Anti-Judaism, anti-Semitism: What's in a name?

First, let me introduce two definitions of anti-Semitism. The late Heiko Oberman, a leading expert on the Reformation, wrote in *The Roots of Antisemitism*:

Anti-Judaism is the concerted assault by humanism and the Reformation against all externalizations of inner values; it is the triumph over the dead letter in the name of the living spirit. Anti-Judaism in this form is destined to become an integrated component of the reform program of the sixteenth century. In the struggle for the renewal of church and society, Jews and Judaism will be adduced as comprehensible and unambiguous proofs of the spiritual chaos of the time. Although the boundaries to the later anti-Semitism are clearly marked out, the crossovers and points of transgression have equally clearly been mapped in.[1]

In drawing a distinction between anti-Judaism and anti-Semitism, Oberman bore in mind the great Protestant Reformer, Martin Luther. Sympathetic to

---

[1] Heiko A. Oberman, *Wurzeln des Antisemitismus. Christenangst und Judenplage im Zeitalter von Humanismus und Reformation*, second edition (Berlin: Severin & Siedler, 1983), p. 28. In the English translation: Oberman, *The Roots of Anti-Semitism in the Age of Renaissance and Reformation*, trans. James I. Porter (Philadelphia: Fortress Press, 1984), p. 22.

Luther's theology of Justification, Oberman could not circumvent the strident anti-Jewish treatises of the old Luther. By placing a boundary between religious controversy and racism, Oberman avoids the anachronism that marks some works on anti-Semitism, but at the risk of downplaying the tensions that Luther's legacy would leave for his Church.

The second position, one closer to my own view of things, is enunciated by the medievalist Gavin Langmuir in his book on anti-Semitism:[2]

Christian anti-Judaism thus seemed an important precondition for European anti-Semitism, a halfway station between a very common kind of ethnocentric hostility and the peculiarly irrational hostility of Hitler.

Later in his book, Langmuir attributes an importance to Christian doubts about Jews for the emergence of anti-Semitism, arguing for the transition from a medieval anti-Semitism (that had not obtained in Antiquity) to a modern, racist anti-Semitism.[3]

In the long process of the transformation of anti-Judaism into anti-Semitism, myths of Jewish atrocities against Christians developed in northern Europe: host desecration and the blood libel devastated the Ashkenaz communities of England, France, the Holy Roman Empire, and Poland from the twelfth to the seventeenth centuries. In countries where the Sephardim predominated – Portugal, Spain, and Italy after 1494 – these myths assumed a less powerful force, but the notion of blood was articulated in the well-known *limpieza de sangre* decrees of the Iberian kingdoms. In the following sections, I shall first address the case of the Holy Roman Empire and examine the legacy of Luther in the transformation of a religiously motivated anti-Judaism into a form of anti-Semitism that made no distinction between religious practices and physical essence. Then, I shall turn my attention to the discourse and practices of the Catholic Counter-Reformation in overseas missions. Under the patronage of the Portuguese and Spanish monarchies, the anti-Jewish prejudices of some of the missionaries would be carried over to the non-European world.

Luther's legacy: Jewish ethnographies in the Holy Roman Empire

With the Protestant Reformation came an intense and more widespread interest in all things Jewish in the Holy Roman Empire. The Hebrew

---

[2] Gavin I. Langmuir, *Toward a Definition of Antisemitism* (Berkeley: University of California Press, 1990), p. 7.
[3] Ibid., pp. 301–52.

language, the Hebrew Scriptures, the history of the Jewish people, the customs of the Ashkenazim, and the religious practices of contemporary Judaism found a broader audience beyond the narrow clerical circles of the late Middle Ages. The dialogue between *Ecclesia* and *Synagoga* was no longer one conducted only in Latin and Hebrew, but was represented in the many German language works penned by Jewish converts, Christian Hebraists, and popular writers. I have elsewhere described this phenomenon as the emergence of a Christian ethnography of Jews.[4] Suffice here to say that one of the major motivations came from the Reformation's fixation on the Bible, and the consequent identification of Protestantism with "A New Israel." That this identification was much more than metaphoric is clear: Luther's followers felt they were Israelites persecuted by the idolatrous Roman Church, and that they represented the true Israelites, the spiritual descendants of the Old Testament Israelites, as opposed to the Jews of their times, the blood descendants of Israel.[5] In territories with a strong Calvinist presence, this self-identification with Israel could lead to philo-Semitism, due to the experience of exile and suffering by the Reformed Church; in the Dutch Republic, it led to the admission of Portuguese Jews and the rise of Christian biblical and rabbinical scholarship in the seventeenth century.[6] In Lutheran Germany, in spite of the emergence of Hebraic studies and a Jewish ethnography, many negative images of Jews from the Middle Ages survived into the early modern period.[7] Jewish converts in Germany were torn between allegiance to their new faith and sympathy for their racial identity, which seemed difficult to evade in the eyes of many German Christians.[8] The New Protestant Israel in Germany, instead of fostering philo-Semitism, marginalized further the Jewish communities. In this context, Luther's

---

[4] Ronnie Po-chia Hsia, "Christian Ethnographies of Jews in Early Modern Germany," in Raymond B. Waddington and Arthur H. Williamson (eds.), *The Expulsion of the Jews, 1492 and After* (New York: Garland Publishers, 1994), pp. 223–236.

[5] See for example Stephen G. Burnett, *From Christian Hebraism to Jewish Studies: Johannes Buxtorf (1564–1629) and Hebrew Learning in the Seventeenth Century* (Leiden: E. J. Brill, 1996).

[6] Miriam Bodian, *Hebrews of the Portuguese Nation: Conversos and Community in Early Modern Amsterdam* (Bloomington, IN: Indiana University Press, 1997) and Peter T. van Rooden, *Theology, Biblical Scholarship and Rabbinical Studies in the Seventeenth Century* (Leiden: E. J. Brill, 1989).

[7] Petra Schöner, *Judenbilder im deutschen Einblattdruck der Renaissance, Ein Beitrag zur Imagologie* (Baden-Baden: Valentin Koerner, 2002); see also the contributions by Petra Schöner and Edith Wenzel in *Jews, Judaism, and the Reformation in Sixteenth-Century Germany*, ed. Dean Phillip Bell and Stephen G. Burnett (Leiden/Boston: Brill, 2006).

[8] See Elisheva Carlebach, *Divided Souls: Converts from Judaism in Germany, 1500–1750* (New Haven, CT: Yale University Press, 2001).

anti-Jewish writings served as the foundational texts for the elaboration of a more racialized anti-Jewish discourse.

Georg Schwartz, better known by his pen name Nigrinus (1530–1602), was a Lutheran cleric who came of age during the troubled times of the Schmalkaldic Wars. Luther's death in 1546, the military defeat of the Protestant princes in 1547, and the Interim declared by Emperor Charles V all heralded in a new urgency for the new Evangelical Church, which saw itself in the throes of the Last Age. A strong eschatological fervor seized the theological heirs of Luther: Flacius Illyricus, Martin Chemnitz, Spangenberg, and other leading Lutheran clerics of the second generation would attach a stern face to Lutheran orthodoxy in the second half of the sixteenth century. Nigrinus belonged very much to this movement.

A prolific writer of more than twenty works, Nigrinus started out as a writer denouncing drunkenness and exhorting Bible-reading to his flock. In the 1570s and 1580s he won a name for himself as an indefatigable polemicist against Catholicism, publishing ten works against the Franciscans and Jesuits in Germany, refuting the decrees of the Council of Trent, and castigating the Catholic Church as the Antichrist. One of the works that appeared in these decades is a voluminous rabid anti-Jewish book: *Jüden Feind*.[9] The long subtitle of the book already spells out the full litany of anti-Jewish charges.[10] The sins of the Jews consisted in this: they blaspheme against Christ; they are allies of the Turks; they practice usury and mint false coins. In the long polemic, Schwartz would pile on further accusations, commonplaces in the history of anti-Semitism: blood libel, host desecration, well poisoning, bribery of officials, idolatry, followers of the Devil, etc. *Jüden Feind* was dedicated to the dukes and counts Wilhelm Ludwig, Philipp, and Georg of Hesse, in order to persuade them to expel the Jews from their territories. To bolster his arguments, Schwartz also invokes a long genealogy of anti-Jewish writers from the Church Fathers

---

[9] Georgius Nigrinus [Georg Schwartz], *Jüden Feind. Von den Edelen Früchten der Thalmudischen Iüden*, reprinted edition (Oberursel: Drucker Nik. Henricus, 1570/ Frankfurt am Main: Johann Saurn, 1605).

[10] Schwartz describes his book as dealing with "von den edelen Fruchten der Thalmudischen Jüden / so jetziger Zeit in Teutschlande wonen / ein ernste / wolgegründe Schrifft / darin kurtzlich angezeiget wird / Das sie die grösste Lesterer vnd Verechter unsers Herrn Jesu Christi / Darzu abgesagte und unversündliche Feinde der Christen sind. Dargegen freunde und Verwande der Türcken / Über das / Landschinder und Betrieger / durch iren Wucher und falsche Müntz. Die auch über das viel unleidlicher böser stücke treiben. Derhalben sie billich von einer jedem Christlichen Oberkeit nicht geduldet warden solten / oder dermassen gehalten / wie in Gott selbs / die Weltliche und Geistliche Recht auffgeleget / in zur Straffe / und allen Völckern / sonderlich den Christen Menschen zum Exempel."

to his day; and among his contemporaries none other wrote more power-fully than Luther:

In German, nobody has written against them [the Jews] more vehemently, ear-nestly, and thoroughly than the late Martin Luther. And with such proof and reason, that Satan, the father of all lies, especially of Jewish ones, could not refute him.[11]

In Schwartz's familiar echo of hateful rhetoric against the Jews, one finds a new motif that is noteworthy: the Lutheran polemicist claimed that the Jews of his day were not worthy of that name because they were not Jews but Talmudists. The Jews of the Diaspora were totally different from the Jews of the Old Testament from whom Jesus descended; rather, they belonged to "Satan's synagogue."[12] To separate the Jews of his days from Jesus, Schwartz resorts to a theory of race and blood: it was almost 1,500 years after the Diaspora; many Jews had been killed. He writes:

Therefore whoever wants to believe it go ahead, but I do not, that there are many amongst them, who are descended from the unmixed Jewish seed of Abraham. They are well bastards and half-breeds.[13]

Even the Old Testament bore evidence that in ancient times, Egyptians, Gentiles, and Israelites could not be clearly distinguished. The Jews have fallen away from Mosaic Law for 1,500 years; the Jewish religion and Kingdom had long been destroyed. The Jews of the Holy Roman Empire must be called "Talmudists, cabalists, and half-Muslims."[14]

Behind this discursive marginalization of Jews was an unspoken replace-ment: the Old Israel (the destroyed Jews of the Old Testament) has been replaced by a new chosen people, the New Israel of Protestants. While this theological argument works metaphorically in most Protestant texts, Schwartz drives his anti-Jewish rhetoric to an extreme by advancing a racial reasoning: the pure seed of Abraham has been polluted over the centuries by conquest, intermarriages, and the mixing of Israelites and Gentiles, resulting in a race of "mixed blooded half-breeds." Yet, this process of miscegenation, this creation of a mestizo people, in Schwartz's view, was paradoxically responsible for the essentially immutable character of the Jews:

[11] "Aber im teutschen ist keiner der so hefftig/ernstlich und gründlich wider sie geschrie-ben/als Martin Lutherus seliger. Und das mit solchem grund und beweise/das im der Satan/aller Lugen Vater/sonderlich der Jüdischen/selbs nicht widerlegen kan." Ibid., B6ᵛ.

[12] Ibid., B7ᵛ–B8ᵛ.

[13] "Darumb gleube es wer da wil/ich gleube nicht/das unter in viel ubrig seien/die aus unvermischtem Jüdischen Samen von Abraham herkomen. Es mögen wol Bastern und Mengling sein." Ibid., C1.

[14] Ibid., C1ᵛ–C5.

I see Jews as Jews, whether baptized or circumcised,
If not all from one delivery, they still belong to one Livery,
All serving the one God, which Christ calls Mammon,
Who shall with his servants all, into the Devil's dominion fall.[15]

Hence, the water of baptism could not wash away the sign of Jewishness. In short, Schwartz held a view that any cultural and religious adaptation remained ineffectual in altering the essential and unchanging racial characteristics attributed to a people. He concluded that Christians who argued for toleration were either bribed by the Jews or completely misguided. Allowing Jews to live amongst Christians "means warming snakes in one's bosom, and raising wolves at home."[16]

The definition of Jews in the Empire as a "half-breed, mixed race" found an echo in the sixteenth century in the wider global context of the expansion of the Spanish and Portuguese empires. In encountering the peoples of the Americas, Africa, and Asia, Iberian writers elaborated on ethnography of national differences, in which the notion of mesticization plays a significant role, a notion that owed its elaboration to the tensions of Christian–Jewish relationships in the Christian West.[17]

Catholic missions and the peoples of the world

The rise of an ethnography of Jews in the Holy Roman Empire coincided with the emergence of a Christian ethnography of non-European peoples in the Iberian overseas missions. While the earliest Spanish debates on the nature of Amerindians focused on questions of enslavement and conversion,[18] a more nuanced discourse of non-European peoples was articulated during the last decades of the sixteenth and the early seventeenth centuries, as a result of European experience with Asian civilizations. Positioning Christian Europeans at the top of a hierarchy of peoples, this Catholic discourse acknowledged the equal status of Chinese and Japanese, similar if not superior in political and material cultures to Europeans, deficient only in their ignorance of the Christian truth. While South Asians and Amerindians were placed in the middle rungs,

---

[15] "Ich halte Jüden für Jüden / Sie seyen getaufft oder beschnitten / Sind sie nicht all einer Ankunft / gehören sie doch all in ein Zunft / Sie dienen all gleich einem Gott / Den Christus Mammon genant hat. Welchen mit sein Dienern entlich gleich / wird faren in des Teuffels Reich." Ibid., H5ᵛ–H6.
[16] Ibid., L2ᵛ ("heisset Schlangen im Büsem wermen / und Wölffe im Hause auffziehen").
[17] See Serge Gruzinski, *Les Quatre Parties du Monde: Histoire d'une Mondialisation* (Paris: La Martinière, 2004). Gruzinski stresses the cultural mesticization of the Iberian expansion and not specifically the creation of mixed-blood populations.
[18] Anthony Pagden, *The Fall of Natural Man: The American Indian and the Origins of Comparative Ethnology* (Cambridge: Cambridge University Press, 1982).

Black Africans found themselves at the bottom of a ladder of ethnic hierarchy that used language, books, cities, economy, and political organization as criteria for differentiation.[19] The one commonplace that joined these inner and outer discourses of race and religion in Europe was the Jew, and we shall turn our attention to finding its traces in the voluminous missionary records of the Iberian empires.

On 15 August 1668, Gabriel de Magalhães (1610–77), a Portuguese Jesuit in Beijing and a kinsman of the circumnavigator of the globe, wrote to the vice-provincial and the visitor of the mission, putting his case for ordaining indigenous clergy to advance the cause of Catholicism in China.[20] In the recent persecutions against Christianity, Magalhães stated, the European fathers were all arrested and confined, whereas the few native clerics managed to escape detection and continue their work. The case in China differed from India, where plenty of European clergy ensured the survival of Catholicism, and it differed from the Americas, where the native peoples were too feeble to drive away the Catholic clergy, protected by the arms of the Catholic monarchs. Turning back to China, Magalhães argues that Buddhism, a foreign religion, survived and thrived in China in spite of sporadic and fierce persecutions in its history because of the growth of a native clergy, who ensured the domestication of Buddhism.[21] This development is reminiscent of the situation in Portugal, Magalhães lamented: "Why is it not possible to extinguish, until now, in Portugal and in her possessions, profaning Judaism, even when it is rigorously prohibited and castigated, as we see every day how we sigh and cry? It is impossible because the faithless and ingrate people has mixed with Portuguese blood."[22] Strange argument perhaps for advocating the training of an indigenous clergy, but the logic seemed sound. In faraway Beijing, Magalhães was thinking of his native Portugal.

In the same year that Magalhães wrote this letter, the Jesuit missionaries in China debated fiercely a problem of conversion: whether to require Chinese Buddhists and sectarians who practiced vegetarianism to break their fast before admitting them to baptism. The issue was indeed complicated, as it involved the Jesuit polemic against the doctrine of

---

[19] An example of this discourse can be found in the first systematic introduction of the world to a Chinese readership, by the Italian Jesuit Giulio Aleni (1582–1649). Giulio Aleni, *Zhifang waiji* (1623), (Areas outside the Concern of the Chinese Imperial Geographer).

[20] Bibliotheca Ajuda (BA), Jesuitas na Ásia (JA) , 49–IV–62, fols. 149ʳ–154ᵛ.

[21] Ibid., 49–IV–62, fol. 151ᵛ.

[22] "Porque se não pode ate agora extinguir, em Portugal, e seus etados, a Judaica profanado, sendo tão rigorozamente prohibida, e castigada como cada dia vemos e sem reme gememos e choramos? Se não porque a infiel, e ingrata gente se misturou com o sangue portuguez." Ibid., 49–IV–62, fol. 152ʳ.

metempsychosis or reincarnation, a key doctrine in Buddhism; it also involved the question whether to admit members of prohibited sects, generically labeled "White Lotus" or "Sect of Vegetarians" by imperial authorities, who, rightly or wrongly, suspected the sectarians to be potential rebels. The question: "The vexing question on how to proceed with those who refuse to break their fast (Utrum quaestio inter nos hactenus agitatam circa jejunantes procedat de iis qui obstinate renuunt frangere jejunium? Nec ne?)" was submitted to the Jesuits in China.[23] A majority of 23 responded negatively: those who refuse to break their fast cannot be baptized. A minority of 13 fathers stated that in extraordinary cases baptism should be permitted, that arguing in some cases it would be impossible for the fasters to break their fast.

Among those who forcefully argued the two opposites, the French father André Grelon (1618–96) fiercely upheld the negative opinion, while the Italian Prospero Intorcetta (1625–96) pleaded for leniency and flexibility. Intorcetta argued for the good intentions of the Chinese fasters and the fact that they only refused certain foods, arguments which Grelon vehemently rejected.[24] For Grelon the argument that the Chinese fasters were only refusing certain foods would also invalidate the arguments and work of the Inquisition in Europe, which had cracked down on the dietary restrictions of the *conversos* as a sign of their adherence to the old faith. Besides, the situation was worse in China because whereas the Jews were tolerated in Europe, the sect of fasting was prohibited in China. Would the Holy Office give permission to the Jews who wanted to convert that for the love of God they would want to abstain from pork, blood, and other unclean foods, etc. not only for one day, but for years, and for the whole lifetime? Grelon did not think anyone would have had the temerity to ask that of the Inquisition in Portugal, Spain, or in Rome. For Grelon good intentions, or intentions at all, did not count. If a Jew kneels before a statue of Christ, this is an act of respect, but if a Christian genuflects before an idol while mocking the idol in his heart, this is still an act of sin. Moreover, the breaking of a fast does not occur in private or in a forest, but in the full light of day among friends, relatives, family, and the entire community.[25]

It is the public act and not the private intention that counts. So Grelon claims. This, of course, goes to the heart of the dilemma, namely the ambivalence of religious identity in an age of a Christendom torn asunder and the deep fears it unleashed. In the Iberian Catholic missions this anxiety over identity expressed itself thus: whether being Christian

---

[23] Ibid., 49–IV–62, fols. 95^r–115^v, 262^v–294^r.   [24] Ibid., 49–IV–62, fols. 289^r–291^v.
[25] Ibid., 49–IV–62, fols. 291^v–292^r.

implied, necessarily, adopting Christian names, speaking Spanish and Portuguese, wearing European clothes, and generally accepting the cultural superiority of Europe. The presence of Iberian colonial power bore a direct bearing on this question of religious identity: the greater colonial control, the closer the identification of Catholic beliefs and Iberian ways; the more numerous the colonists, the sharper the racial superiority on the part of Spaniards and Portuguese. Nowhere was this issue more pronounced than in the ordination of indigenous clergies. The policy of the Society of Jesus, for example, closely followed the racial hierarchy elaborated in western discourses of non-European peoples: namely, the greater readiness to accept Japanese and Chinese into the Catholic clergy, persistent resistance to ordaining indigenous clergy in South Asia and Latin America, and the absence of any effort to train a native African clergy.[26]

India was a case in point.[27] The Portuguese divided the indigenous clergy into four categories: first, sons of Portuguese parents born in India called *Indianos*; second, mestizos; third, native Indians; and finally, the Syriac-Thomas Christians. In 1558 André Vaz was the first Goan to be ordained priest. In the 1594 catalogue of the Goan Province of the Jesuits, there were 312 Jesuits, and only 37 were "Indians," of whom 28 were fathers. But most of these "Indians" were Portuguese born in India, and only Luis of Quilon from a Brahmin class was a full-blooded Indian. There was great reluctance to accept native-born Portuguese, not to mention Indian converts; this mentality persisted until the dissolution of the society. Although the generals in Rome (Ignatius, Lainez, Borja) repeatedly directed the provincials in Goa to accept Indians into the Society, there was adamant opposition. Under the generals Mercurian (1573–80) and Acquaviva (1581–1615), there were clear guidelines against acceptance. All the provincials, including Francis Xavier, argued against accepting Indians and effectively blocked the directive from Rome. These provincials included men who accepted the Japanese, such as Francisco Cabral (1592–1609), provincial in Goa, and Alessandro Valignano (1583–87), Visitor in India and later Japan. Valignano wrote in 1575:

Now that I come to speak of the natives (I speak here of the dark-coloured, and not of the whites, such as for examples the Japanese, on whom I spoke earlier): no one should be accepted because the dark-coloured in general are little qualified to be

[26] Johannes Beckmann SMB (ed.), *Der Einheimische Klerus in Geschichte und Gegenwart. Festschrift P. Dr. Laurenz Kilger OSB zum 60. Geburtstag dargeboten* (Schöneck-Beckenried: *Neue Zeitschrift für Missionswissenschaft* = Supplementa II, 1950).
[27] Josef Wicki, S. J., "Der einheimische Klerus in Indien (16. Jahrhundert)," in Johannes Beckmann, *Der Einheimische Klerus*, pp. 17–72.

accepted, and tended toward evil and filled with low instincts, and further because they enjoy very little esteem with the Portuguese, and even from their own kind in relationship to the Portuguese.[28]

Valignano, however, held the Chinese and Japanese in great esteem and strongly advocated the training of a Japanese clergy during his Visitorship in Japan. But even for the Japanese and Chinese, considered "white peoples" like Europeans, there was a notable difference of opinion between Portuguese and other European missionaries. In the Jesuit Mission of seventeenth-century China for example, many Portuguese resisted elevating the Chinese members to the priesthood, whereas Italian and Belgian fathers strongly supported their inclusion.[29]

Could one perhaps associate Portuguese resistance to the ordination of indigenous clergies with lingering anxieties about *converso* apostasy back in the home country? Does Gabriel de Magalhães' association of Buddhist and Jewish conversions, analyzed above, signal a deeper and far more widespread mentality of the age? Is it a coincidence that the Jesuit who pioneered the Tamil Mission in sixteenth-century India – a missionary flexible in his conversion approaches and open to Tamil language and culture – was the Portuguese *converso* Henrique Henriques?[30]

In a Christian Europe split into rival confessional camps, an early modern European society that produced martyrdom, dissimulation, conversions, and the multiple crossings of religious frontiers, an expanded world inhabited by Lutherans, Calvinists, Anabaptists, Anti-Trinitarians, Jews, Hindus, Muslims, Buddhists, and Confucians, the European Middle Ages must have been seen by some as simple and comforting. Gone was the contrast between *ecclesia* and *synagoga* in the lands of Ashkenaz, or the tripartite interplay between Christianity, Islam, and Judaism in the lands of the Sephardim. In the early modern world, the traditional certainty of opposition between Christian and Jew in Europe would provide a guide to mapping a path through the complicated religious and cultural landscapes of a global world.

---

[28] Wicki, "Der einheimische Klerus in Indien," p. 36.
[29] See Ronnie Po-chia Hsia, "La questione del clero indigeno nella missione cattolica in Cina nel sedicesimo e diciassettesimo secolo," in *Studia Borromaica: Saggi e documenti di storia religiosa e civile della prima età moderna*, vol. 20 (Milan: Biblioteca Ambrosiana, 2006), pp. 185–194.
[30] Henriques worked in southern India from 1549 to 1600. See Ines G. Zupanov, "Compromise: India," in Ronnie Po-chia Hsia (ed.), *A Companion to the Reformation World* (Oxford: Blackwell, 2004), p. 362.

13   Vagrants or vermin? Attitudes towards Gypsies in early modern Europe

Miriam Eliav-Feldon

The forgotten group

In the heroic age of the "Discovery of Man and the World", to use Jacob Burckhardt's capitalized slogan, Europeans were almost incessantly debating the question of attitudes towards hitherto unfamiliar peoples encountered in other continents. The chapters in the last section of this volume present some of the reactions and consequences of facing, conquering or enslaving the inhabitants of Asia, Africa and America. These encounters were such huge dramas, involving so many millions of human beings and producing such large amounts of records, that they could not but absorb the full attention of scholars searching for the foundations of modern categorizations and classifications of human "races". In addition, transformations and upheavals in Europe itself were causing the reformulation of attitudes and policies towards those ethnic or religious minorities that had resided in Europe for many centuries.

It is therefore not surprising that these revolutionary developments overshadowed the appearance of a small, unfamiliar people in Western Europe itself, the only new ethnic group to enter these countries after long centuries of stability in the composition of their populations. The Gypsies,[1] moving gradually westward, arriving in Italy, Germany, France, the Netherlands and the Iberian states sometime during the early fifteenth century and in England only in the sixteenth century, were at first no more than small bands of strangers (their relative unimportance symbolized by the fact that the name of their group was often written without an initial capital, "gypsies", as it is sometimes still

---

[1] Although "Gypsies" is considered today a pejorative name for the Roma and Sinti, I shall continue to use the different variations on "Gypsies" (Egyptians, Gitanos) which were the common names for them in the early-modern period. They themselves claimed at the time to have come out of Egypt, and most Europeans believed that they had originated in Egypt itself or in some place called "Little Egypt" or "Egypt Minor" (which was probably added to the imaginary geography of the Renaissance as a result of a traveler exclaiming when he saw a settlement of Gypsies outside the town of Modon that it was a veritable Little Egypt).

written today). During the early-modern period, however, they were probably encountered by more Europeans than were Africans, Amerindians or Chinese. And yet, the Gypsies are seldom discussed in studies of early-modern attitudes to minorities or aliens; they are hardly ever mentioned in studies of racism which refer to pre-Nazi periods; in the special issues of two prestigious journals, which were dedicated to pre-modern race and racism,[2] not one author discussed attitudes to the Roma; there is not a word about them in the vast literature on the early-modern encounters of civilizations; and even in the pages of the numerous studies of policies in Spain towards Jews, Muslims and New Christians, there are but rare and brief references to the newly arrived Gitanos as another persecuted ethnic minority on Iberian soil. Life on the margins, in the full sense of the word, led also to the marginalization, if not to the exclusion, of the Gypsies in modern historical scholarship concerned with attitudes to "the Other".

More than the Jews

The Gypsies "are a people more scattered than Jews, and more hated", wrote the English playwright, Thomas Dekker, in his most successful work, *Lantern and Candle-Light* (1608). He named them "Moon-men" because they appeared, he said, to be mad and changeable.[3]

From a twenty-first-century viewpoint it is easy to see, despite some important differences, the similarities and parallels between the history of the Jews and that of the Gypsies. Until the first groups of Gypsies appeared in the fifteenth and sixteenth centuries, there were no "alien" populations except the Jews in most parts of Europe. Thus in some places the Gypsies were called at first "pseudo-Jews", as there was no other group they could be compared to and no other compartment in which they could be placed within the contemporary mental cabinet of curiosities. Andrew Boorde, author of one of the earliest travel guides, *The First Book of the Introduction of Knowledge* (1547), devotes chapter 38 to "Egypt", describing in fact the appearance and customs of the Gypsies in Europe, and offers a few phrases in their language with their translation into English (probably the first ever published text of Romani speech). In the very next chapter Boorde writes of Jews and the land of Judah with a sample of

---

[2] The *William and Mary Quarterly* 54 (1) (January 1997), and the *Journal of Medieval and Early Modern Studies*, 31 (1) (Winter 2001).

[3] Thomas Dekker, "Lantern and Candle-Light", in A. V. Judges (ed.), *The Elizabethan Underworld* (London: George Routledge & Sons Ltd., 1930), pp. 312–365, ch. 8: Of Moon-Men, pp. 344–347.

Hebrew sentences.[4] His descriptions indicate that he did not actually visit the Middle East but rather met both Jews and Gypsies on his travels in Europe, and regarded them equally as representatives of ancient nations which had somehow wandered into contemporary Europe.

A wandering people with a widespread diaspora were indeed attributes of both groups, although obviously on a different scale and with a different history. At the time discussed here, the two groups were moving in fact in opposite directions: as the Gypsies were slowly making their way westward, the Jews, as a result of policies of expulsion and forced conversion, were practically disappearing from most parts of Western and Central Europe and migrating mostly eastward – towards Eastern Europe and the Ottoman Empire. But in both cases, being a "scattered" nation helped to feed similar stereotypes and prejudices against its members. Rootlessness, faithlessness, suspicious liaisons and contacts abroad, sympathies for the Turks, willingness to serve as enemy spies or even as saboteurs – all these were accusations hurled equally at both Gypsy and Jew.

Both communities were perceived as voluntarily keeping themselves apart, avoiding exogamic marriages, dressing differently, maintaining strange customs and using a foreign language. This refusal to assimilate emphasized and prolonged their otherness in the eyes of authorities and the local population. It also increased the resentment of neighbors who believed that these "aliens" regarded themselves as superior to the gentile or the gadje.

Fear, suspicion, hatred, resentment and stigmatization, mixed with some envy and admiration, would accompany the history of Jews and Gypsies in Europe (or in the West – for men and women of both peoples migrated to the New World as well) down to the present, and would cause the holocaust of both nations by the monstrous racist machinery erected by the Nazis. Nevertheless, and without suggesting a hierarchy of suffering, I would like to propose that shortly after their first appearance in Europe, the persecution of the Gypsies and the discourse regarding them contained elements which were more virulent than any other (budding) racist attitude towards minorities in Europe or towards peoples on other continents.

Neither heretics nor witches

Yet, before we proceed to the question of how the Gypsies were perceived, it is important to stress in what categories of hounded persons they were *not* included.

[4] Andrew Boorde and Frederick J. Furnivall (eds.), *The First Book of the Introduction to Knowledge* (London: N. T. Trübner & Co., 1870), pp. 217–221.

Contrary to what one would expect when looking at Reformation Europe, neither the Catholic inquisitions nor the Protestant consistories were concerned with the Gypsies. In an era obsessed with minute differences in faith, with attempts to impose religious uniformity and to extirpate anything which could be regarded as heresy by the dominant church, the indifference of the authorities to the religious affiliation and behavior of the – nominally Christian – Gypsies is quite surprising.

Admittedly in certain areas of Europe they were named "heathens" (*heiden*) – despite the facts that they presented themselves as Christians and that, when there was an advantage in being known as indigenous, they were careful to baptize their children in local churches with non-Gypsies serving as godparents. Here and there we hear of church dignitaries forbidding church services to the Gypsies, but little else. And it seems that neither authorities at the time nor scholars nowadays were too concerned with what these nomads believed or how they practiced their version of Christianity.

As a result of large numbers of forced conversions and feigned conversions – first of Jews and Muslims in Spain and then of all manner of Christians across Reformation Europe, particularly after it had accepted the *cuius regio, eius religio* principle – both church and secular authorities became obsessed with dissimulation, investing enormous efforts in ferreting out religious impostors. But there is no indication that this collective paranoia influenced policies towards the Gypsies. Although their adherence to the official faith was worn very lightly, they were neither listed in public warnings against secret heretics (such as the Edicts of Faith in Spain), nor branded as Nicodemites or hidden enemies of the true church. Marginality could be one possible explanation for the indifference shown towards the Gypsies' beliefs: the various inquisitions had their hands full with intellectuals, merchants and other leading citizens effectively spreading pernicious ideas; they had no time to worry about the creed and practices of the riffraff. But perhaps more important was precisely the overriding concern with pretence and deception: since these travelers were so clearly and visibly different, no one could suspect they were *disguised* heretics.

Both the powers-that-be and the population soon stopped believing the Gypsies' "cover story" (or the "Great Trick" as Angus Fraser calls it[5]) – that they were Christian pilgrims (from Egypt or from somewhere in the East) who for some obscure sin had to embark on a seven-year journey of penance. The exposure or the fading out of the lie, however, although it

---

[5] Angus Fraser, *The Gypsies* (Oxford: Blackwell, 1992), ch. 4: The Great Trick, pp. 60–83.

reduced the amount of alms and protection they received, did not seem to increase the concern about their true identity – no one seemed to be asking who or what these so-called Egyptians "really" were from the religious point of view.

If at all, Gypsies entered the discourse on imposture and dissimulation by another door altogether. Oddly, we find numerous expressions of concern that some vagabonds were pretending to be Gypsies: legislation in England, for example, often referred to "Egyptians" and "*counterfeit Egyptians*".[6] Was this suspicion part of the obsession with fraud and deception on the part of the authorities? Or were there indeed people who pretended to be Gypsies? Were Irish tinkers and perhaps other "undesirables" joining the Gypsy bands at this early date? These are questions which are difficult to answer on the basis of existing documentation, but they do emphasize the vagueness of the notions regarding the identity of these newcomers to the scene.

Even more surprising perhaps than the fact that they were not persecuted as heretics is the absence of accusations of witchcraft against the Gypsies. After all, the appearance of the Gypsies in the West coincided with the "witch-craze", i.e. with the waves of persecutions in most European countries which claimed the lives of tens of thousands of people who were tried and executed for signing pacts with the Devil and for *maleficium*. One would have thought that these exotic men and women – known for trickery, palm reading, fortune-telling and other magic – would loom large among those indicted for witchcraft.

Some modern-day scholars turn assumption into fact by simply stating that the Gypsies were often prosecuted in witch trials.[7] But in the vast amount of research on the subject published in recent decades, which has brought to light most of the extant records on witch persecutions, there is no real evidence that this was the case. In fact, modern-day research has revealed that persons accused of witchcraft were practically always members of the local community, not passing strangers. Moreover, *maleficium* was seldom attributed to known magicians, healers or wise women. Satanic witchcraft was considered so dangerous precisely because it was practiced in secret by people who outwardly had nothing to do with magic.

Some histories of the Gypsies in the British Isles refer to a book by Samuel Rid, *The Art of Juggling* (1612), as evidence of the association of Gypsies with witchcraft. Rid plagiarized the well-known book by Reginald

---

[6] Compare Thomas W. Thompson, "Consorting with and Counterfeiting Egyptians", *Journal of the Gypsy Lore Society* 3 (2) (1923), 81–93.

[7] See, for example, Henry Kamen, *Early Modern European Society* (New York: Routledge, 2000), p. 171.

Scot, *Discoverie of Witchcraft* (1584), but turned it into a pseudo-history of the Gypsies and attributed all of Scot's descriptions of the witches' activities to feats of the "Egyptians". Scot's book, however, was a skeptic's attack on witch beliefs and persecutions. He set out to prove that every supernatural wonder attributed to them was mere trickery and fraud, not satanic magic. Thus Rid, by borrowing from Scot, was in fact disassociating the Gypsies from witchcraft and not vice versa.[8]

Vagrants

The main context in which Gypsies were discussed in Europe in the fifteenth, sixteenth and seventeenth centuries was that of vagrancy – without doubt the most acute social problem of those days. No one disputes, I believe, that there was a gradual process of criminalization of poverty in both Protestant and Catholic countries: i.e., towns and states throughout Europe adopted policies that were intended to restrict charity and poor relief only to the "deserving" poor, and, more specifically, to the *local* deserving poor, while applying the severest measures of exclusion and punishment to all other beggars. Gypsies, obviously, were the ultimate alien vagrants, and thus were deemed undesirable everywhere *(cajoux,* as they were defined in Paris in the early fifteenth century, when they were confined to La Chapelle[9]).

Laws and statutes referring to the vagrant Gypsies were draconian: calling for flogging, branding, expulsion and execution of the "Egyptians", sometimes labeled "Land-Pirates"[10] – but measures just as harsh were proclaimed against all rogues and vagabonds. Thus, some say, these nomadic groups of people simply chose a bad time to appear in Western Europe. Not only were Protestantism and budding capitalism limiting charity everywhere, even towards those who succeeded in convincing the locals that they were pilgrims doing penance; not only did they roam among

[8] Samuel Rid, "The Art of Juggling", in Arthur F. Kinney (ed.), *Rogues, Vagabonds and Sturdy Beggars: A New Gallery of Tudor and Early Stuart Rogue Literature Exposing the Lives, Times, and Cozening Tricks of the Elizabethan Underworld,* reprinted edition (Amherst: University of Massachusetts Press, 1990), pp. 265–291.

[9] Colette Beaune (ed.), *Journal d'un Bourgeois de Paris (1405–1449)* (Paris: Livre de Poche, 1990).

[10] Comparing the Gypsies to pirates, in addition to including them with all other vagrants, helped to emphasize their association with what were considered the worst economic and social problems of the time. The term "Land-Pirates" was first used as a description of Gypsies by Aeneas Silvius Piccolomini (Pope Pius II) *c.* 1461 (see Leonardo Piasere, "De Origine Cinganorum", *Études et Documents Balkaniques et Méditerranéens* 14 [1989],105–126, here 107), and this epithet would later appear in several documents in different European countries, including Dekker's chapter on the Moon-Men. Dekker, "Lantern and Candle-Light", p. 346.

a settled population that viewed foreigners, particularly mendicants, with suspicion, but they happened to enter Western Europe precisely when the fight against masterless men – sometimes named "sons of Cain" (later to be confused with Canaan)[11] – was at its peak. If Gypsies were to be found in all prisons and in disproportionate numbers on the galleys[12] – as most historians of the period claim – it was because they indeed stole and cheated, were regarded as rabble, and because all European countries were conducting at the time a systematic campaign to rid their territories of the parasitic poor. A. L. Beier summarizes: "The Gypsies ... were covered by a distinct body of legislation [in England], but were essentially viewed as vagabonds".[13]

This is the position taken by practically all historians of the poor and the marginal in early-modern Europe, beginning with R. H. Tawney and continuing more recently with Bronislaw Geremek, Henry Kamen, Robert Jütte, Paul Slack, Piero Camporesi, Jan Lucassen and many others.[14] And if that was the case, if they were universally viewed only as a category of vagabonds, simply part of the rabble, then anti-Gypsy attitudes had nothing to do with racism.

More evidence could be cited to argue the "not racism" case further. For example, the notorious "Act against certain persons calling themselves Egyptians" (England, 1554) declared that, because of their "abominable living" or "devilish and naughty practices and devices", they would not be allowed to enter the kingdom; those already in England were to be

---

[11] The biblical verse, in which Cain says: "I shall be a fugitive and a vagabond in the earth; and it shall come to pass that every one that findeth me shall slay me" (Genesis 4:14) was often quoted in connection with the vagrants in general and with the Gypsies in particular. In some cases the two figures to be eternally punished, Cain and Canaan (Genesis 9:25) were confused and vagabonds or Gypsies became the accursed "sons of Canaan" – which would be presented as biblical justification for enslavement or banishment. On the identification of Africans with the sons of Canaan see David M. Goldenberg, *The Curse of Ham: Race and Slavery in Early Judaism, Christianity and Islam* (Princeton, NJ: Princeton University Press, 2003).

[12] For Gypsies sent to prisons and the galleys see, for example, I. A. A. Thompson, "A Map of Crime in Sixteenth-Century Spain", *The Economic History Review* 21 (1968), 244–267.

[13] A. L. Beier, *Masterless Men: The Vagrancy Problem in England 1560–1640* (London: Methuen, 1985).

[14] Piero Camporesi (ed.), *Il libro dei vagabondi* (Turin: G. Einaudi, 1973); Bronislaw Geremek, *Poverty: A History* (Oxford: Blackwell, 1997), and *The Margins of Society in Late Medieval Paris* (Cambridge: Cambridge University Press, 1997); Robert Jütte, *Poverty and Deviance in Early Modern Europe* (Cambridge: Cambridge University Press, 1994); Kamen, *Early Modern European Society*; Jan and Leo Lucassen (eds.), *Migration, Migration History, History: Old Paradigms and New Perspectives* (Bern: P. Lang, 1997); Leo Lucassen, Wim Willems and Annemarie Cottaar, *Gypsies and Other Itinerant Groups: A Socio-Historical Approach* (London: Macmillan Press, 1998); Paul Slack, *Poverty and Policy in Tudor and Stuart England* (London: Longman, 1988); Richard. H. Tawney, *The Agrarian Problem in the Sixteenth Century* (New York: Longman, 1912).

expelled; and if they remained, they would be executed. The law, how-ever, did not extend to those "Egyptians" who "shall leave that naughty, idle and ungodly Life and Company, and be placed in the Service of some honest inhabitant", implying that it was their *way of life*, not their nature, which was abhorrent.[15]

Furthermore, the law did not extend to Gypsy children under thirteen, who apparently could be saved by re-training which would correct their "naughty, idle and ungodly" tendencies (a vision similar to the policy adopted in Australia towards the Aborigines as late as the 1960s). And in addition, a parliamentary act in 1562 emphasized that the harsh laws of the previous reign applied to the same extent to "real" Egyptians as to those who disguised themselves as Egyptians and led the same kind of life: "commonly called or calling themselves Egyptians, or counterfeiting, transforming or disguising themselves by their apparel, speech or other behaviour, like unto such Vagabonds, commonly called or calling them-selves Egyptians"[16] – an emphasis which also made it very clear that the fight was against vagabonds and their behavior, not against an ethnic group whose members were inherently bad.

In a similar manner the law in Spain of 1619, which ordered all the Gypsies to leave the peninsula on pain of death, also stated that they would be allowed to remain if they settled and abandoned the dress, name and language of the Gitanos.[17] This was an option resembling the one offered over a century earlier to Jews and to Muslims – convert and abandon all your customs, or leave – but a choice which was not offered to the Moriscos who were expelled *en masse* from all of Spain between 1609 and 1614, regardless of how assimilated they were willing to become. In certain cases, it seems, belief in the possibility of assim-ilation overcame racist views that attributed irredeemable qualities to a stigmatized group.

In sum, Gypsies in early-modern Europe were often viewed, as they are still viewed today by most historians, not as a religious minority, not as witches, not as an ethnic group (they were not defined as a "race" until the 1938 Nazi decree "Combating the Gypsy Plague"), but rather as a social or a socio-economic problem.

---

[15] For the English laws concerning Gypsies see Thompson, "Consorting with and Counterfeiting Egyptians", 81–93.

[16] Ibid., and also in Gamini Salgado, *The Elizabethan Underworld* (London: J. M. Dent, 1977), pp. 151–158.

[17] Spanish law of 1619 quoted in Fraser, *The Gypsies*, p. 161. The Spanish government oscillated for generations between policies of banishment and forced assimilation towards its minorities.

Danger signals

Nevertheless, when reading early modern texts pertaining to Gypsies it is impossible to ignore certain expressions which indicate that a number of authors and legislators regarded them as different from simple vagrants and as a unique category among the masses of masterless men. I consider such expressions to be black flags – signals that should alert us to the existence of (at least) roots of racism in the discourse about the Gypsies.

Let me begin with an example which is sometimes cited in support of the other side of the argument and as evidence of sympathy and admiration for this exotic nation. One of Cervantes' exemplary tales, "The Little Gipsy Girl" ("La Gitanilla", 1613), is often presented as the earliest version of the *topos* of the beautiful and enticing Gypsy girl (a figure best known to us from Georges Bizet's opera *Carmen* [1875], which was based on Prosper Mérimée's novella by that name [1845]). In a recent book on the *Novelas ejemplares*, Joseph Ricapito, a leading scholar on Golden Age Spanish literature, sets out to re-affirm that Cervantes was a "Cristiano Nuevo", and therefore felt empathy for other marginalized groups such as the Moriscos and the Gypsies.[18] Yet, regardless of the author's origins, a little black flag can be detected on the very first page of "La Gitanilla". The story begins:

> Gipsies seem to have been born into the world for the sole purpose of being thieves: they are born of thieving parents, they are brought up with thieves, they study in order to be thieves, and they end up as past masters in the art of thieving. Thieving and the taste for thieving are *inseparable from their existence* [emphasis added].[19]

A devil's advocate could still argue that these negative words should be interpreted as a variation on the anti-poor propaganda and within the context of anti-vagrant literature. Moreover, one could say, the Gitanos were described by Cervantes in this passage as undesirables not for what they *were* but because of what they *did*: they stole. In other places and at other times they were accused of starting fires (for example in Prague in 1541), of spying for the Ottomans, and – as accusations became all the more vicious – of practicing cannibalism, incest, and kidnapping children (the latter charge still believed today in many parts of the world). The useful distinction (made by David Wiesen and quoted in David Goldenberg's article),[20] between doing and being, is probably one of the

---

[18] Joseph V. Ricapito, *Cervantes's Novelas Ejemplares: Between History and Creativity* (West Lafayette, IN: Purdue University Press, 1996).

[19] Miguel de Cervantes, "The Little Gipsy Girl", in *Exemplary Stories*, trans. C. A. Jones (London: Penguin Classics, 1972), p. 19.

[20] David Wiesen, "Juvenal and the Blacks", *Classica et Mediaevalia* 31 (1970), 132–150, quoted in David Goldenberg's article, above p. 88.

better yardsticks by which to differentiate racism from other forms of hatred or xenophobia. And stealing was indeed something the Gypsies could be accused of *doing*. If, however, it was a quality "inseparable from their existence", did not thieving become something they *were*, inherent to their nature and not simply a habit or a way of life which they could learn to overcome?

Cervantes then went on to describe the beautiful Preciosa, in what was to become the traditional manner of romanticizing the heart-breaking Gypsy dancer. Yet he immediately insisted that this paragon was:

> the most beautiful and discreet girl to be found, not only among the gipsies, but among all the most famous the world has ever known for their beauty and discretion. The heat of the sun, the winds and every kind of inclement weather, to which gipsies are more exposed than other folk, had failed to spoil the beauty of her face or to harden her hands. Not only that, but despite the rough upbringing she had received, she gave every sign of *having been born of better stock than gipsies* [emphasis added].[21]

The white, beautiful, honest, shy, talented and precious young girl – Cervantes first implies and then reveals – was not really a Gypsy at all; she *could not be* of Gypsy stock.[22]

More than skin deep

Gypsies, according to a consensus among European authors, were black and ugly. One of the earliest descriptions of Gypsies in Western Europe, the Chronicle of Bologna in 1422, stated that "they were the ugliest brood ever seen in these parts".[23] Shortly afterwards, in 1435, Hermann Cornerus concurred: "A certain strange, wandering horde of people, not seen hitherto, came out of eastern lands … they were excessively given to thievery … very ugly in appearance and black as Tartars".[24] Thomas Dekker offered an original explanation for the skin colour of these "tawny devils": they are "not born so, neither has the sun burnt them so, but they are painted so".[25]

One could continue with innumerable quotations about their dark skin, filthy complexion and ugly features. But in themselves, as has been argued in some of the articles in this volume and elsewhere, these were not

---

[21] Cervantes, "The Little Gipsy Girl", p. 19.
[22] David Mayall, *Gypsy Identities: From Egypcyans and Moon-Men to the Ethnic Romany* (London: Routledge, 2004), p. 18: "such examples [of claiming that those Gypsies who did not fit pre-conceived ideas were stolen] are so frequent that they now appear unremarkable".
[23] Fraser, *The Gypsies*, p. 72.   [24] Ibid., p. 67.
[25] Dekker, "Lantern and Candle-Light", p. 344.

necessarily racist pronouncements. Peasants, as Paul Freedman shows,[26] could also be described as black, ugly and dumb. Nevertheless to say, as Cervantes did, that white and beautiful must inevitably mean "not Gypsy" is definitely a warning signal. Cervantes adopted the same attitude in his play "The Baths of Algiers" ("Los baños de Argel"), in which the beautiful Moorish girl who helped the protagonist escape from the hands of cruel Muslim pirates, also turned out to be a nice Christian girl who had been kidnapped as a child. According to Cervantes, beauty and virtue, ingrained characteristics, could only indicate that the person did not belong to the tainted groups of Gypsies or Moors.

Such assumptions, implicit and perhaps even subconscious, suggest that by the end of the sixteenth century the premise that the people known as Gypsies were, in fact, an inferior "stock", with certain biological qualities that neither water nor education could erase, was not unknown even among the relatively tolerant literate classes.

Hardened racists

A further "black flag" which should alert us to the existence of racist attitudes in the sixteenth century is the position taken by persons who went on record to express their fierce hatred towards more than one minority.

A letter written in 1658 by a certain Spanish judge (*alcalde*), Juan de Quiñones, is probably one of the earliest full-fledged anti-Semitic (rather than anti-Jewish) texts. In it Quiñones, worried like so many of his contemporaries about the plague of dissimulation and deception, expressed his gratitude to God for providing indelible bodily signs that could not be faked or removed.[27] The Marranos, i.e., New Christians of Jewish extraction and their descendants for all generations, had – according to Quiñones and to the various authorities that he quoted or interpreted to suit his purpose – very distinct physiological characteristics: big noses, a unique smell, a tail, and in addition, the males of the species bled once a month from their posterior. The notion that Jewish men "menstruate" was apparently first suggested in the early thirteenth century (by Jacques

---

[26] Paul Freedman, *Images of the Medieval Peasant* (Stanford, CA: Stanford University Press, 1999), and also his article, "The Representation of Medieval Peasants as Bestial and as Human", in Angela N. H. Creager and William Chester Jordan (eds.), *The Animal/ Human Boundary: Historical Perspectives*, (Rochester, NY: University of Rochester Press, 2002), pp. 29–49.

[27] "Juan de Quiñones al Antonio de Sotomayor", MS 868 (Colecção Moreira), fols. 73–89, Biblioteca Nacional Lisbon.

de Vitry).[28] Quiñones' innovation, however, was the claim that baptism would cure them only if their conversion had been sincere, but if they "Judaized" the affliction would return. And, he said, it was precisely this monstrous (or, if you like, feminine) trait which caused the special Jewish smell – and not just the food cooked in olive oil, as some contemporaries suggested. Not much given to hesitation, Quiñones was nevertheless uncertain whether this monthly loss of blood was also the reason why Jews and crypto-Jews needed to imbibe the blood of Christian children, as was asserted by some of his predecessors. In any case, he urged the inquisitors to conduct a thorough physical examination of suspects: first for circumcision in both Marranos and Moriscos, and then for other tell-tale marks, inborn rather than self-inflicted, which would reveal the true identity of persons attempting to pass themselves off as pure Old Christians. Attributing specific physical characteristics, which could nei-ther be erased nor overcome by any means, to all members of a certain group, was (by all definitions proposed in this volume) a clear and distinct racist conception.

Furthermore, the very same Juan de Quiñones, exposed by scholars studying the history of the *conversos* as one of the earliest exponents of biological anti-Semitism,[29] was also known as a "hanging judge" for Gypsies. Early in his career, in 1631, he wrote a fierce diatribe calling on the king not to show them any leniency and to enforce to the letter the law calling for their expulsion, applying it to their children as well since they could never be redeemed. He was one of the first authors in Europe to accuse the Gypsies of practicing incest and cannibalism among other horrific vices.[30]

Quiñones was not alone in targeting more than one group for branding as undesirable. "In order for Spain to stay clean, it remains to do the same with the Gypsies", wrote Salazar de Mendoza after the expulsions of the Moriscos in 1609–1614.[31] The obsession with purity, the idea that irre-spective of their faith or culture, men and women born to certain groups defile and contaminate society, was part of the mentality that bred the "limpieza de sangre" laws pertaining to Marranos, led to the expulsion of

---

[28] For the history of the notion of male menstruation as a Jewish characteristic see, for example, Irven M. Resnick, "Medieval Roots of the Myth of Jewish Male Menses", *The Harvard Theological Review* 93 (3) (July 2000), 241–263.

[29] See Yosef Hayim Yerushalmi, *From Spanish Court to Italian Ghetto. Isaac Cardoso: A Study in Seventeenth-Century Marranism and Jewish Apologetics* (New York: Columbia University Press, 1971), pp. 124–133.

[30] Quiñones on the Gypsies is quoted in Fraser, *The Gypsies*, p. 161.

[31] Quoted in Anwar G. Chejne, *Islam and the West: The Moriscos, A Cultural and Social History* (Albany, NY: S.U.N.Y Press, 1983), pp. 13–14.

approximately 300,000 Moriscos (despite their formal adherence to Christianity) by the government of Philip III, and was part and parcel of the policies concerning Gitanos. The sixteenth century in Spain witnessed a turn (though far from absolute or universal) from policies of enforced conversion and assimilation to acts of ethnic cleansing.

However, one might say, a handful of racists do not Racism make (in the same manner as Lucien Febvre argued about atheists and Atheism in the sixteenth century). This is probably true: there were only occasional manifestations of what we would all agree to define as a racist frame of mind, not a systematic ideology or government policy based wholly on racist premises. Nevertheless, these manifestations should not be ignored, especially when combined with other pronouncements of the supposition that certain characteristics – of Jews, Moriscos or the Gypsies – were "inseparable from their existence".

Verminization

Dehumanization, claiming that certain groups of people are not quite human but closer to animals (because they have a different skin color, because they wear no clothes, because they speak a "barbaric" language, because they have no property, because they eat with their hands, because they live in caves, etc.) has always been a tell-tale sign of a fully developed or, at the very least, a nascent racist doctrine. True, bestiality was sometimes applied to peasants, but more often than not putting people on a level below Man served as justification for conquest, enslavement and persecution of foreign peoples. Africans and Amerindians were frequently compared to apes, wild beasts or beasts of burden, or – in a manner typical of the Renaissance – to monstrous creatures culled from classical literature: troglodytes, for example, were a favorite simile for natives of other continents, for they were creatures who dwelled in caves rather than houses.

Gypsies were dehumanized in early-modern literature no less than Jews, Moors, Africans or Amerindians. As with the other groups, they were most often described as "swine", but they were sometimes also compared to wolves: in a plea to the Spanish king in 1619, for example, calling on him not to show leniency towards the Gypsy children, they were said to be "wolf-whelps, to the assured future detriment of the flock".[32] And, again like the other groups, they were sometimes defined as creatures between ape and man. In Italian literary works of the late fifteenth

---

[32] "Sancho de Moncada to King Philip III", quoted in Fraser, *The Gypsies*, pp. 160–161.

century Gypsies were depicted as monstrous hybrid creatures,[33] while in the most frequently quoted sixteenth-century description of Gypsies, included by the erudite Sebastian Münster in book 6 of his *Cosmographia Universalis* (1544), Gypsies were said to be frightening and hideous.[34]

But far more worrying than such comparisons to animals or even to mythological "monstrous races" were, I believe, the vermin similes. "Vermin", writes historian Mary E. Fissel, "is not a timeless category. It has a history".[35] Not only did the kinds of animals defined as vermin change over time and habitat, but they were not always necessarily associated with dirt and disease. However, she adds, "vermin are animals who it is largely acceptable to kill ... these small animals are the enemy, poaching human food rather than decently eating animal food."

Like Jews ever since the Black Death, Gypsies were sometimes accused of being carriers of the plague (as for instance in a Milan decree in 1506[36]). In seventeenth-century Europe quarantine imposed on travelers by authorities in certain towns referred particularly to Gypsies as potential carriers of syphilis and the sweating sickness.[37] Such an association with the cause of pestilence, whether as deliberate poisoners or as inadvertent transmitters, was bad enough, but it was not identical to the image of an army of harmful creatures, for prior to the nineteenth century epidemics were not linked to vermin.

Thomas Dekker, quoted above comparing his "Moon Men" to Jews, wrote of "Egiptian grasshoppers that eat up the fruits of the earth, and destroy the poor corn fields", and elsewhere he complained of the "swarming Egiptian lice".[38] Plague might not have been caused by vermin in early modern medical theories, but both epidemics and invasions of harmful creatures spread at the same frightening rate, and the expression "a plague of godless vagabonds infesting the land" seemed to appear only when Gypsies were involved. Although Gypsy companies in the sixteenth and seventeenth centuries seldom numbered more than a few dozen

---

[33] Antonio Campigotto and Leonardo Piasere, "From Margutte to Cingar: The Archeology of an Image", in Matt T. Salo (ed.), *100 Years of Gypsy Studies: Papers from the 10th Annual Meeting of the Gypsy Lore Society* (Cheverly, MD: The Society, 1990), p. 19. For similar descriptions of the Jews – as snakes, wolves and a mixed breed – see above in Ronnie Po-chia Hsia's quotations from Nigrinus' text.

[34] Sebastian Münster, *Cosmographia Universalis* (Basel: [s.n], 1544), lib. III: De Gentilibus Christiani. The Latin text of this chapter in D. M. M. Bartlett, "Münster's 'Cosmographia universalis'", *Journal of the Gypsy Lore Society* 31 (3) (1952), 83–90.

[35] Mary E. Fissel, "Imagining Vermin in Early Modern England", in Angela N. H. Creager and William Chester Jordan (eds.), *The Animal/Human Boundary: Historical Perspectives* (Rochester, NY: University of Rochester Press, 2002), pp. 77–114.

[36] Fraser, *The Gypsies*, p. 106.   [37] Mayall, *Gypsy Identities*, p. 60.

[38] Dekker, "Lantern and Candle-Light", p. 346.

people, they were "swarming", and "infesting" and "plaguing" and "flooding" in all published warnings, whether in legislation, in literary texts, or in local chronicles. And like these pests, Gypsies, it was believed, were thieves *by nature*. They poached on human territory and stole man's food (at the time when famine was always at the doorstep), and could no more be civilized than locusts or lice.

Verminization, if I may coin a term, could serve no purpose if the author wished to justify discrimination, segregation, exploitation, enslavement or control and repression; it could justify however not only expulsion but extermination as well. Twentieth-century experience taught us this lesson only too well: it would suffice to evoke here the Nazi film "The Eternal Jew", in which Jews were represented as hordes of rats, or the Hutu in Rwanda referring to the Tutsi as "cockroaches" just before the genocide of 1994, to indicate how dangerous verminization could be.

"[T]o sweep those swarms out of this kingdom there are no other means but the sharpness of the most infamous and basest kinds of punishment", wrote Thomas Dekker.[39] Such verminization helps to explain why Gypsies were the sole target of organized manhunts in Germany, Switzerland and the Netherlands from the late sixteenth century well into the eighteenth century.[40] Local authorities in these countries either organized official hunts or incited the population to do so by offering rewards on Gypsy men and women, dead or alive. This was happening simultaneously with the campaign for vermin hunts: across Europe parishes and town councils were encouraged to provide payments for the killing of vermin injurious to crops, and bounties were offered for animal heads.[41]

Beasts of burden, farm animals, performing bears and monkeys, exotic creatures to be placed in cages for people's delight, cute pets – all these non-human creatures have always had their uses for Man, the Lord of Creation, instructed by God to "have dominion over the fish of the sea, and over the fowl of the air, and over every living thing that moveth upon the earth" (Genesis 1:28). But vermin cannot be domesticated and they are by definition dangerous, harmful beings, which Man had been exterminating as best as he could since the world began. Thus defining human beings as vermin is potentially the most lethal form of dehumanization and cannot be regarded as anything but racism.

---

[39] Ibid., pp. 346–347.
[40] On such *heidenjachten* in Germany, for example, see Robert A. Scott Macfie, "Gypsy Persecutions", *Journal of the Gypsy Lore Society* 22 (3) (1943), 71–73; and Fraser, *The Gypsies*, p. 147.
[41] Fissel, "Imagining Vermin", p. 79.

The small companies of "Egyptians" that entered Central and Western Europe in the fifteenth and sixteenth centuries aroused a whole spectrum of feelings and attitudes among the local population and the authorities, notions and emotions which were mostly also applied to other groups both within and outside the European world. Nevertheless, for a number of reasons, the Gypsies were singled out, and they evoked on occasion reactions which clearly constituted one of the early origins of racism in the West.

14 The peopling of the New World: ethnos, race and empire in the early-modern world

Anthony Pagden

I

The concept of race, and thus of racism, is of relatively recent origin which is not, of course, to say that something amounting to ethnic differentiation is not to be found in all cultures and at all times. In the form in which it is most often employed today, however, races are taken to be genetically specific groups of people – biological, or rather pseudo-biological – not cultural, entities.[1] Because of this, and the properties they supposedly possess, they cannot vary very much over time or space. Racism, thus understood, is clearly the product of nineteenth-century positivism, and it has therefore often been argued that any attempt to apply the term to an earlier period is merely anachronistic.

It is certainly the case that without any reference to some degree of physiological, biological or even psychological determinism the very notion of race in the ancient or early-modern world becomes highly problematical. With a few obvious exceptions – most obviously those applied to sub-Saharan Africans – most of the classificatory schemes dreamt up before 1700 were not in any obvious modern sense "racial". True, the peoples of the globe were organized into large groups, races, nations, tribes, etc. and each was ascribed a number of defining features. But all of the features which these groups were supposed to possess were essentially what we today would call "cultural". The word "race" – *race, razza, raza* etc. and their equivalents – is itself of relatively recent coinage. It has some affinities with the term *ratio* in the sense of "the order of things", but in its modern sense it is of uncertain origin and, not insignificantly, probably reached Europe via Spain. It is also significant that it first achieved widespread recognition during the sixteenth century when the cultures of Southern Europe, Spain, Portugal and Italy were

[1] The general consensus among modern biologists, however, is that no such thing as "race" actually exists. An excellent account of the current scientific debate is to be found in Colin Kidd, *The Forging of Races: Race and Scripture in the Protestant Atlantic World, 1600–2000* (Cambridge: Cambridge University Press, 2006), pp. 1–18.

increasingly coming into contact with a large number of "new", or at least unfamiliar, "races".

Its earliest uses are zoological, having first been applied to falcons and horses. The transference from animals to humans was, at least initially, seemingly both unproblematical and non-prejudicial. It was used, for instance, by Edmund Spenser in the *Faerie Queene* in 1589:

> And thou, fair imp, spring out from English race
> How ever now accompanied Elfin's son
> Well worthy doest they service for her grace
> To aid a virgin desolate foredone   (X.6)

It seems clear that for Spenser, at least, a number of other terms would have done just as well – in particular "nation" – had the rhyme scheme, and the meter, called for it. Race continued to be used in this way as a synonym for "people", "nation", "breed" or even "kind", until at least the early nineteenth century. Byron, in 1823, could even speak of stone statues as "a race of mere impostors".[2]

It was probably the French doctor, disciple of Gassendi and tireless traveler (he spent twelve years as physician to the Mughal emperor Aurangzeb) François Bernier, who, in 1648, first used the term in something like its modern meaning, by equating the word race with the unambiguously biological "species" in a brief essay entitled: "A new division of the earth by the different species or races which inhabit it." Geographers, he said, have hitherto divided the world into countries or regions, but his "long and frequent travels" had suggested to him another way of classifying humankind. Men, he had seen, may vary greatly from one to another as far as their appearance is concerned, even within the same nation. "I have nevertheless observed that there are four or five Species or Races of men, the difference between whom is so marked, that it may serve as the basis for a new division of the Earth." The first of these groups included the Europeans, most of the peoples of North Africa, India and much of the Far East; the second all the Africans, except the coastal peoples; the third those living in areas of the Far East, central Russia and Mongolia; and in the fourth – by themselves – the Laps. No fifth group is mentioned, but the Amerindians, although they are olive skinned and "have faces which are cast differently from ours", are said to be "not sufficiently unlike us to constitute a separate species". But even

---

[2] A race of mere impostors, when all's done –
    I've seen much finer women, ripe and real
    Than all the nonsense of their stone ideal
    Don Juan, canto II, lines 942–944.

Bernier nowhere suggests that his division could be employed to impute different mental characteristics to his four races. Much of the essay is taken up with a discussion of female beauty, and although it is obvious that his aesthetics are wholly European, such beauty, he says, can be found in every race, "even among the blacks of Africa".[3]

The closest approximations to anything like modern racial classifications in the early-modern world are, perhaps, to be found in the "national characters" supposedly possessed, largely if not consistently, by the various peoples of Europe. The English were perfidious, the Germans brutal but courageous, the Italians cunning and so on. The multinational mercenary armies of early-modern Europe were often organized along these lines, although non-racial qualities were frequently muddled in with the apparently racial ones. The Germans were put out in front not only because they were ferocious, but because they were good pike-men; the English were placed a little way behind not only to prevent them from sneaking off in the heat of battle, but because they were skilled archers, etc. But supposed natural attributes could, in this way, easily become confused with acquired skills. Were the Germans, for instance, good pike-men *because* they were ferocious, the English good archers because they were cowardly and unsuited to hand-to-hand combat? Whatever the answer, the source of "national character" was not anything that could plausibly be described as race; but rather as custom and education; cultural, that is, not natural. "As to *physical* causes", wrote David Hume, "I am inclined to doubt altogether of their operation in this particular; nor do I think that men owe anything of their temper or genius to the air, food or climate."[4]

There was also the question of the blood line. Although the transference of identity via the blood has no place in ancient medicine, by the late Middle Ages, if not earlier, the idea that certain features of a person's identity could be passed down in this way appears to have become a commonplace. Yet this was less a means of distinguishing between peoples from different races than it was a way of marking distinctions within the

---

[3] [François Bernier], "Nouvelle division de la Terre, par les différentes Espèces ou Races d'hommes qui l'habitent", *Journal des Sçavans* 12 (April 1684), 148–155.

[4] David Hume, "Of National Characters", in Knud Haakonssen (ed.), *David Hume. Political Essays* (Cambridge: Cambridge University Press, 1995), pp. 80–81. This, however, is the essay which contains the infamous footnote which begins "I am apt to suspect that negroes, and in general all other species of men … [are] naturally inferior to the whites", which has earned Hume a reputation as a racist. But the note, inserted in the essay in the edition of 1753 – five years after it was written – is not merely a denial of the basic premise of all of Hume's anthropology, which assumed a universal and unchanging human nature, it also, in Colin Kidd's words, "runs … against the argumentative thrust of the essay which it supplements". Kidd, *The Forging of Races*, pp. 93–94.

same race. As the European aristocracy lost its traditional military role in the late Middle Ages, so it increasingly came to defend itself against the newer aristocracies of commerce and service by appealing to origins *ex nobili genere, ex nobili prosapia*. Even the notorious *limpieza de sangre* statutes in Spain aimed at denying *conversos* – Christians of Jewish ancestry – access to positions in the Church or the administration, although it would be absurd to deny that they were in some sense racist, belong to this category.[5] They were, in effect, the extension to a particular people of an essentially social classification.

An early, and unusually conventional, classification of these categories is provided by the canon lawyer Regino of Prüm, writing in about 900. He offers four ways of distinguishing between what he calls the "various Nations" of the world: they are "descent, custom, language and law".[6] If we add religion to this list, with relatively few modifications these criteria will remain largely unchanged until the eighteenth century.[7] Of these only the first – "descent" – really qualifies as a true racial category. Ever since Hesiod – perhaps ever since mankind has been organized into societies – descent, lineage, genealogy, mostly spurious and contrived, have been employed to establish differences, generally of course differences of status.[8] Yet even here the usage is problematical. Certainly to be, say, German "by descent" distinguished one from those who were Norman "by descent". Yet precisely because there was no theoretical argument underpinning the notion of "descent", the only way to differentiate one descent group from another was by reference to the other categories in Regino's list. If, that is, we were to ask what made the lineage of Germans distinct from the Normans all we could reply would be: "custom, language and law".

---

[5] See Albert A. Sicroff, *Les Controverses des statuts de "pureté de sang" en Espagne du XIVe au XVIIe siècles* (Paris: Didier, 1960), pp. 290–297, and Gil Anidjar, "Lines of Blood: Limpieza de Sangre as Political Theology", in Mariacarla Gadebusch Bondio (ed.), *Blood in History and Blood Histories* (Florence: SISMEL/Edizioni del Galluzzo, 2005), pp. 119–136.

[6] Quoted in Robert Bartlett, *The Making of Europe: Conquest, Colonization, and Cultural Change, 950–1350* (Princeton, NJ: Princeton University Press, 1994), p. 197.

[7] Colin Kidd is surely right, however, in saying that the "absence of racialist doctrine did not mean that racist prejudice was similarly invisible. Racist attitudes existed, but, significantly, did not rest upon clearly articulated theories of racial difference. Race – like ethnicity and even national consciousness (as distinct, say, from allegiance to one's monarch) – was a matter of second order importance behind primary commitments to church and state." Kidd, *The Forging of Races*, p. 54.

[8] See the comments by Judith Shklar in "Subversive Genealogies", in *Political Thought and Political Thinkers*, ed. Stanley Hoffman (Chicago: University of Chicago Press, 1998), pp. 132–160.

The whole thing becomes in the end inescapably circular. In 1539 the Portuguese chronicler João de Barros – who evidently had not given much thought to these matters – describes, or makes Vasco da Gama describe, the Hindus as being "all from one race" (*geracâo*) precisely because they were "very alike in their customs", and, he added, because they shared a belief in the Trinity, they were also "friends of the Christians *by nature*"; a piece of nonsense to be sure, but enough for Barros to lump together all the peoples of southern India as belonging to a single descent group.[9]

If race is ultimately a matter of languages, customs, laws and even religion, it is evidently highly unstable. Customs can be acquired, religion and laws can be accepted and observed. Languages may be learned. But language acquisition presented a rather more complex problem, since for most language theorists, from Aristotle to Condillac, speech was believed to provide something akin to a cognitive map of the mind of the speaker. Initially "barbarian" (*barbaros*) had been a linguistic category, since the *barbaroi* were believed to be those who had no access to rational speech, knowing only how to say *bar bar bar*. The widely held assumption was that if you lacked a word for something, then you probably also lacked the understanding of that thing. Similarly, if the Inuit famously have dozens of words for "snow" this is not because they are highly imaginative, but because they cannot formulate general categories.

This deficiency may, perhaps, broadly be understood as a "racial' characteristic. It may, on the other hand, be merely a consequence of history. Although some supposedly primitive peoples, such as the Tahitian "Aotourou", whom the French navigator Antoine de Bougainville took with him to France in 1769, might have found it impossible to master a more "advanced" language (in this case French), this was never attributed to anything resembling race. In Aotourou's case it was ascribed by Bougainville to the simplicity and transparency of the world in which he lived. He would, he said of his Tahitian guest, have had to "create, so to speak, in a mind as indolent as his body, first a world of ideas, before being able to adapt them to the words in our language which corresponded to them".[10] And it was certainly neither his "race" nor his "descent" which prevented him from doing this, but rather the incommensurability of his culture with the French, and the brevity of his exposure to European mores.

[9] João de Barros, *Asia de João de Barros: Dos feitos que os Portugueses fizeram no descobrimento e conquista dos mares et terras do Oriente*, 8 vols. (Lisbon, 1781), vol. I, pp. 154–155 (I.iv.9).
[10] Louis-Antoine de Bougainville, *Voyage autour du Monde par la frigate la Boudeuse et la flute l'Étoile; en 1766, 1767, 1768 et 1769*, reprinted edition (Paris: Saillant & Nyon, 1771/ F. Maspero, 1980), pp. 161–162.

The most extreme expression of cultural transformation – which was clearly and crucially open to all – was religious conversion. Conversion to Christianity, if St. Paul was to be believed, guaranteed admission to a community in which the distinctions between "Greek or Jew, circumcision and non-circumcision, barbarian, Scythian, bondman, freeman" would all be dissolved.[11] Lineage may not change. The Christian Scythian remains a Scythian, but his character, his *ethnos*, has become something else. As the Jesuit historian José de Acosta, one of the first to attempt a systematic analytical history of the peoples of the Americas, said in 1590 about those he called the "Ethiopians" – that is black Africans – if they were brought up "in a palace", they would be in all respects, save the colour of their skin, "just like other men".[12] What significance, then, could skin color possibly have?

The answer would seem to be, none. But what is it then that leads certain peoples to adopt certain kinds of customs, laws, languages and even religions, and not others? If (in Greek eyes) the laws and customs of the Persians inclined them to slavishness and those of the Greeks to liberty, is this something inherently Persian and Greek or, in other circumstances, could Greeks become slavish – as it was later believed that they had done under Turkish rule – and the Persians freedom-loving? One answer, offered by Aristotle, embellished by Polybius, picked up by Aquinas and his Spanish commentators, by Jean Bodin in the sixteenth century, and elaborated into a full-scale theory of cultural (not racial) differentiation by Montesquieu in the eighteenth century, was climate – or to be rather more precise, since a significant number of factors other than climate itself were involved, "environment".

Crudely stated, this argued that the Asians who lived in hot climes reacted to their environment by becoming lethargic and indolent; that those who lived in the cold northern climes became hyperactive, aggressive and uncouth; only the Greek, and in later versions Europeans generally, because they were poised midway between these two extremes, could achieve the necessary balance to remain free, in control of their passions, reflective and morally active.

But even climate could determine only disposition. Aristotle's lethargic Asians, and un-civil northerners, might well become perfectly balanced Greeks were they to take up residence in the Mediterranean – not perhaps within a single generation, but certainly within two. Similarly those Europeans born in places remote from Europe might, it was feared, lose

---

[11] Colossians 3:11.
[12] José de Acosta, *De promulgatione evangelii apud barbaros*, sive *De procuranda indorum salute libri sex* (Cologne: Birkmann, 1596), pp. 150–151.

something of their identity under unfamiliar skies and in extreme climates. The debilitating force of the environment, so obvious in the lethargic and indolent lives of the native Americans, was clearly visible to the (Spanish-born) Franciscan Bernardino de Sahagún, the first European to attempt a systematic description of a Mesoamerican people. Those Europeans born in the Americas, he wrote, "are born very much like the Indians, for in appearance they are Spaniards, but in disposition they are not ... and I believe that this is due to the climate and constellations of this land". For this same reason, the provincial council of the Jesuits in Lima ruled in 1582 that Creole neophytes should not be admitted to the order until they were twenty (the age for those born in Europe was eighteen) and subjected them to a more rigorous training.[13]

One more deterministic and, I think, genuinely racist – or as Benjamin Isaac characterizes it, "proto-racist" – theory to come out of antiquity was to have a longer after-life even than the theory of climates: Aristotle's discussion of natural slavery in the *Politics*. This has been much debated and given the fragmentary nature of Aristotle's argument it is unlikely that any consensus will ever be reached as to just what he intended by the category.[14] But on the most minimal account it claimed that slaves should by their nature be inferior beings in comparison with their masters. A "natural" slave is one who, rather than being defined by his legal status, is defined by his psychological identity, since he is one who, contrary to the norm, possesses no independent autonomous self. [15]

The definition of this anomalous creature was grounded in a distinction between what was called in Greek psychology the "rational" and the "irrational" souls. For "all things rule and are ruled according to their nature", since "such duality exists in living creatures, but not in them alone; it originates in the constitution of the universe".[16] What this means is that in fully developed human males (although not in either children or women) the rational will invariably triumph over the irrational, unless it is diseased. This is what it means to possess the capacity for deliberation or moral choice. The natural slave, however, lacks this capacity. In this respect he is akin – but also inferior – to women and children, "for the

---

[13] Bernadino de Sahagún, *Historia de las cosas de Nueva España*, 5 vols. (Mexico City: P. Robredo, 1938), vol. III, p. 82.

[14] See Benjamin Isaac, *The Invention of Racism in Classical Antiquity* (Princeton, NJ: Princeton University Press, 2004), pp. 175–181, and Peter Garnsey, *Ideas of Slavery from Aristotle to Augustine* (Cambridge: Cambridge University Press, 1996), pp. 124–127.

[15] For the most compelling modern discussion of the implications of Aristotle's views see Bernard Williams, *Shame and Necessity* (Berkeley: University of California Press, 1993), pp. 110–116.

[16] Aristotle, *Politics*, 1254ᵃ 28f.

slave has no deliberative faculty at all; the woman has but it is without authority and the child has but it is immature".[17] While being a fully developed adult male, he nonetheless has, as Aristotle characterizes it, only a share in the faculty of reason, without being in full possession of it. He is said to be capable of understanding but incapable of practical wisdom (*phronesis*) for "practical wisdom issues commands ... but understanding only judges".[18] While free he is violating what nature had intended him to be, for his master does his thinking for him, and he is himself almost literally a "living but separate part of his master's frame".[19]

Slaves are a feature of the natural world, and a necessary requirement for the proper functioning of the only true political form, the *polis*. There could never exist a *polis* composed only of slaves, just as there could not be one made up solely of women and children.[20] On the other hand "a *polis* cannot be administered without them".[21] Slaves also – and this is crucial – benefit by being enslaved, although they may not be immediately aware of it, since this is the proper fulfillment of their nature.

What this could be taken to mean is that the slave is a kind of useful automaton, able, as Aristotle says, to carry out commands, but not to initiate them. "Almost an animated instrument of service", Saint Thomas Aquinas said later.[22] As such there is nothing inherently racist about such a claim. It is merely condescending. Most European aristocrats until recently would have said something similar about their servants. What makes it racist – or proto-racist – is Aristotle's identification of the slave with a particular group of people: namely what he calls "the barbarians". "Among barbarians", he said,

no distinction is made between women and slaves, because there is no natural ruler among them: they are a community of slaves male and female. That is why the poets say "it is meet that the Hellenes should rule over the barbarians".[23]

The "barbarians", then, are merely communities of un-mastered slaves; a race of slaves in other words. And war on them is not only justified: it may be likened to hunting.[24]

---

[17] Ibid., 1324[b] 21–2.   [18] Aristotle, *Nichomachean Ethics*, 1143[a] 11.
[19] Aristotle, *Politics*, 1254[a] 8. For a more extensive, and more nuanced account of Aristotle's views on this see Isaac, *The Invention of Racism*, pp. 175–176.
[20] In *Politics* 1252[b] 5, however, the *barbaroi* are said to be made up entirely of slaves. But then such peoples do not live in *poleis*, and are merely biding their time until they will be enslaved and thus put to their proper purpose.
[21] Aristotle, *Politics*, 1283[a] 14–23.
[22] Thomas Aquinas, *In decem libros ad Nicomachum exposition*, third edition, ed. Raymundi M. Spiazzi (Rome–Turin: Marietti, 1964), p. 1447 (*lectio*, 7.I.9).
[23] Aristotle, *Politics*, 1252[b] 5.   [24] Ibid., 1255[b] 34; cf. 1333[b] 38.

But who exactly are these "barbarians"? Aristotle leaves this question unanswered – or unasked – but given the general use of the term it would seem to include the peoples of Asia described conventionally as "more servile than those in Europe". Although being more servile does not necessarily make them slaves, only more suitable to tyrannical rule. The entire argument is highly abstract, but the explicit association between natural slaves and "barbarians" made it an extremely serviceable category for future generations. The best known case in antiquity is Cicero's discussion of justice in the state in *De Republica*, in which he argues that "the provincials" – that is all those peoples who have been incorporated into the Roman Empire as allies or clients – although they may not be formerly chattels are nevertheless rightly subject to Rome, as they are servile by nature.[25] Again both parties benefit from the relationship, which is why Cicero elsewhere insists, in a passage which was eagerly adopted by the British after the mid-seventeenth century, that the Roman Republic exercised over its provinces not *imperium* but *patrocinium* (protectorate).[26]

Aristotle's account of slavery occurs in a discussion of the household. But Aristotle, as we all know, was Alexander's tutor, and Plutarch – an unreliable source to be sure, but not entirely implausible in this instance – tells us that Aristotle advised his tutee before leaving for the Persian campaigns to treat only the Greeks as humans and all other peoples he might encounter as animals or plants. As later commentators pointed out – something which became one of the arguments used to discredit it – in the theory of natural slavery Aristotle had, in effect, handed his pupil a reason for subjugating the vast Achaemenid Empire, more serviceable than a desire to avenge Xerxes' burning of the Acropolis. (Alexander for his part had other ambitions than to rule over animals and plants and wisely ignored his tutor's advice, as Plutarch pointed out, because otherwise he would have "filled his kingdoms with exiles and clandestine rebellions".[27]) Cicero was explaining the right of Rome to constitute the *orbis terrarum* in its own image. Thus both Aristotle and Cicero bring us to the place where racism would have its most lasting purchase, so to speak; where it would be most urgently needed, but where also, I want to argue, it

[25] In Augustine, *De civitate Dei* XIX. 21. In *De Provinciis Consularibus*, Cicero alludes to the Jews and Syrians as "peoples born to be slaves" which, as Benjamin Isaac says, would hardly have been intelligible to his audience if "a popular version of Aristotle's doctrine of natural slavery had not been common ground for at least a large number of people in antiquity". Isaac, *The Invention of Racism*, p. 225.
[26] Marcus Tullius Cicero, *De Officiis*, II. 27. And see Richard Koebner, *Empire* (Cambridge: Cambridge University Press, 1961), pp. 4–11.
[27] Plutarch, *On the Fortunes of Alexander*, 329b.

would encounter what would in the end prove to be insurmountable difficulties: namely the creation of empires.

II

In 1519 a Scottish theologian at the Collège de Montaigu in Paris, named John Major, or Mair, published a commentary on Peter Lombard's *Sentences*. In discussing the justice of Christian rule over pagans, he made a passing comment on the newly discovered American Indians. "These peoples", he says,

> live like beasts on either side of the equator. And this has now been demonstrated by experience that the first person to conquer them, justly rules over them because they are by nature slaves. As the Philosopher says in the third and fourth chapters of the first book of the *Politics*, it is clear that some are by nature slaves and some are by nature free. On this account the Philosopher says ... that this is the reason why the Greeks should rule over the barbarians, because the barbarians and slaves are the same.[28]

By this argument the inhabitants of the Antilles are barbarians, ergo they are slaves, and ergo it is just that the first people to conquer them – in this case the Spanish – have a right, which might also amount to a duty, to rule over them. This brief comment set in motion an attempt to classify the peoples of the New World as belonging to a quasi-distinct species of man – a race if you will – set down by God in order to perform at least some of the functions without which, as Aristotle had duly observed, the true *polis* could not function adequately.

Here, it seemed, was a category which had been empty since the Greeks (neither Major nor any of those who took up his suggestion mention Cicero) and which could conveniently be used to classify a people who had been unknown to antiquity. (It is not insignificant that the next time this thesis made an appearance, in the context of a "newly-discovered" people, nearly half a millennium later, it is in connection with the Australian aborigines.)

Natural slavery appeared at first to provide a neat argument from an authoritative – indeed *the* authoritative – source to justify the Spanish presence in a part of the world over which neither the Spanish crown nor any other European people had any a priori claim to sovereignty, much less property-rights of the kind which their exploitation of the resources of the Americas would necessarily entail. If the Indians were

---

[28] John Major, *In secundum librum Sententiarum*, second edition (Paris: Veneût apud Iohannem Grãion, 1519), fol. clxxxvijr.

natural slaves they had no claim to possess either sovereign authority over themselves, or rights over the lands on which they happened to reside. The Spanish might, therefore, legitimately conquer and subdue them, deprive them of their goods and lands, and even exploit their labor, in order to introduce them to their proper place in the natural world.

Identifying the Indians as natural slaves, however, posed certain difficulties. Aristotle had argued that external appearances should have been sufficient in order to distinguish the natural slave from the natural master. "Nature would like", he said, "to distinguish between the bodies of free men and slaves, making the one strong for servile labor, the other upright and although useless for service, useful for the political life and the arts of both peace and war". Alas, nature in Aristotle's world was often unable to fulfill her purposes and, as he admitted, "the opposite frequently happens".[29] Despite this note of caution, at least one Spanish "expert" on Indian affairs was gauche enough to inform Philip III that:

> Nature proportioned their [the Indians'] bodies so that they should have strength for personal service. The Spanish, on the other hand, are delicately proportioned, and were made prudent and clever, so that they should be able to lead a political and civil life.[30]

Few were prepared to take such claims seriously. As many Spanish observers pointed out, the Indians could be just as "delicately proportioned" as the Spanish and sometimes a great deal more so. The absence of any secure exterior markers – the color, size and physiognomy of the Indians only becomes of any real concern in the eighteenth century – once again threw all those who hoped to identify the Indians as "natural slaves" back upon some version of the items on Regino's list: "custom, language and law".

One of the earliest commentators on the condition of the Indians, and the earliest to recognize the full implications of Major's suggestion, was the jurist Juan López de Palacios Rubios. In 1512, at the request of King Ferdinand, he wrote an opinion on the legal status of the Spanish Crown in America. The Indians, he said, on the evidence which he had read, appeared to be "rational, gentle and peaceful men capable of understanding our faith". They owned no property and apparently dwelt in peace with nature. "They loved the birds and the animals, as if they were children, and they would not eat them, for that would have been as if they devoured their own offspring." An ideal world it would seem – all

---

[29] Aristotle, *Politics*, 1254[b] 27f.

[30] Quoted in Anthony Pagden, *The Fall of Natural Man: The American Indian and the Origins of Comparative Ethnology* (Cambridge: Cambridge University Press, 1986), p. 46.

peace and light and harmony, not too far removed from the image which some sentimentalists have tried to paint of modern Amerindian tribes.

But Palacios Rubios was no sentimentalist, and America was no Eden. In the real world after the Fall, such behavior indicated not an admirable oneness with nature, but only ineptitude. In the real order of things, ownership was a mark of humanity and animals were for eating not for play. And if the Indians did not understand that, it was hardly surprising that they also did not understand the vastly more complex laws and customs which governed human societies. Look again, said Palacios Rubios, and you will see behind this apparently Edenic exterior a world in which everyone went naked and the men took several wives; in which the women "gave themselves readily considering it shameful to deny themselves". It was hardly surprising, therefore, that they also failed to observe the limits of consanguinity – sisters mating with brothers, daughters with fathers, had no religion worth the name, and in their daily lives were simple hedonists. Thus, he stated, they "are so inept and foolish that they do not know how to rule themselves". History, furthermore, had contrived to pass them by. Had they been a more worthwhile people, would not God have sent them news of the arrival of Christ before now, as he had sent St. Paul to the Corinthians and St. Augustine to the English?[31] Such a people, he concluded, were therefore, "broadly-speaking called slaves as those who are almost born to serve and not to rule".[32]

The theory of natural slavery was widely used to bolster Spanish claims to the Indies, most famously by the humanist Juan Ginés de Sepúlveda. It was certainly important enough for a number of prominent intellectual figures close to the court, notably the theologians Francisco de Vitoria, Domingo de Soto and Melchor Cano, to spend a good deal of time publicly refuting it. The implication, made explicit by some, that if these Indians were such a race of men, they must also lack immortal souls, or at least the ability to understand the teachings of the Gospels, so alarmed the Papacy that in May 1537 Paul III issued a Bull, *Sublimis Deus*, denouncing the idea that "the Indians of the West and South, and other people of whom We have recent knowledge should be treated as dumb brutes created for our service" as the invention of the Devil, and confirming

---

[31] Juan López de Palacios Rubios, "Insularum mari Oceani tractatus", in Augustín Millares Carlo (ed.), *De las islas del mar Océano*, first edition (Mexico City: Fondo de Cultura Económica, 1954), p. 24.

[32] *Ibid.*, p. 127: "quapropter largo modo possunt dici servi, quasi nati ad serviendum, non autem ad imperandum". The highly qualified phrasing is significant. Few even at this early stage, before the discovery of Mexico and Peru had revealed the existence of highly complex Amerindian cultures, were prepared to accept the full force of Aristotle's claims.

their rationality, their humanity and thus "that they may and should, freely and legitimately, enjoy their liberty and possession of their property".

It was also never adopted as a justification for conquest without considerable qualification, and never once appears in any official description of the Indians. Even those who were most convinced of the Indians' natural deficiencies, even Sepúlveda – who described them as *homunculi*, and compared them to pigs and monkeys – even he, in the end, backed away from claiming that these slavish beings constituted a wholly different sub-species of humanity.

There were two immediate and obvious reasons for this reluctance. The first was simply the evidence. The Tainos and the Arawak of the Antilles, with whom Major and Palacios Rubios had some, albeit fragmentary and frequently fantastical, knowledge, might conceivably seem to conform to some notion of creatures without deliberative capacities. But this could hardly be said, for all their "barbarism", of the Aztecs and the Incas. Ethnography disproved the case (from which some concluded that Aristotle's had been a purely hypothetical category: there might still exist natural slaves in the world, but if so they were still awaiting discovery).

For the Christian, who believed in the existence of a single and remote creator, the very existence of inferior races also posed an insuperable problem. Another expert to give his opinion to Ferdinand in 1512 was Bernardo de Mesa, later bishop of Cuba. He shared all Palacios Rubios's generally dismal view of the behavior of the Indians, but drew a very different conclusion from it. "The incapacity we attribute to the Indians", he wrote, "contradicts the bounty of the creator, for it is certain that when a cause produces its effects so that it is unable to achieve its end, then there is some fault in the cause; and thus there must be some fault with God".[33] How could a being with no deliberative faculty possibly be described as having been made in the image of his creator, if that creator was the Christian God? The possibility of the existence of races, of separate and distinct groups of peoples, who stand in an evaluative relationship to one another, is, obviously, an inescapable threat to the existence of a single human species. True, the harmonious and perfect natural world this God had created was capable of throwing up the odd anomaly – madmen, dwarves, etc. But to conceive of an entire continent, or possibly, since

---

[33] Quoted in Pagden, *The Fall of Natural Man*, p. 50. Compare the declaration made by the World Council of Churches in 1968: "Racism is a blatant denial of the Christian faith. (1) It denies the effectiveness of the reconciling work of Jesus Christ ... (2) it denies our common humanity in creation and our belief that all men are made in God's image." Quoted in Kidd, *The Forging of Races*, p. 274.

there was still a lot of the world to be discovered, *continents* filled with people who had no moral agency, who merely shared in reason, but did not possess it, who were only "a living but separate part of their master's body", would be to imagine an imperfect creation. It would also have made the work of Christ, who had been sent to save *all* mankind and not just a favored part of it, similarly incomplete. And both were, of course, unthinkable.

There was a further dimension to this story. The American Indians were not only socially anomalous beings, supposedly capable of unthinkable crimes – human sacrifice, cannibalism, incest, bestiality and so on – they also had no obvious place in any known historical account of the origins of humanity. The diversity which existed between the various "nations" of the world had hitherto been explicable in terms of two Biblical myths: the Tower of Babel and the separation of the sons of Noah, Shem, Japhet and Ham, after the Flood. Shem had repopulated Asia, Japhet Europe, and Ham Africa. The story of Noah's curse on Ham, that his son, Canaan, and all his descendants, should be "a servant of servants unto his brethren", had been used to account for the blackness of the Africans and, by implication, their inferiority to the peoples of Asia and Europe, and for the subsequent identification of the sons of Ham with the Africans.

None of this could be made to apply in any obvious way to the American Indians, nor later to the peoples of the South Pacific. Neither, clearly, were the descendants of Ham, yet it was by no means clear whose descendants they were. Surely, said Jacques Cartier in 1534, when he reached the inhospitable coast of Labrador as his ships stuck fast in the ice, their flimsy wooden hulls cracking like nuts, this must be the land to which God had banished Cain, a land of perpetual wandering in whose soil nothing would grow. But no one took him up on the idea if only because the "land of Nod" was to the east – not the west – of Eden.

If the integrity of the Biblical account of the peopling of the world was to be maintained, the Indians had to have come from some region of the Old World. Could they possibly be the descendants of shipwrecked Carthaginians, alluded to in a popular pseudo-Aristotelian text, *De mirabilibus ausculationibus*, or Vikings or, as the Dutch humanist, Hugo Grotius supposed, the Tartars, or – one of the most enduring suppositions – the descendants of the Ten Lost Tribes of Israel?[34] (This last idea, quite apart from the geographical and chronological difficulties it presented, finally

---

[34] An old but serviceable account of these may be found in Lee E. Huddleston, *Origins of the American Indians: European Concepts, 1492–1929* (Austin, TX: University of Texas Press, 1967). For Grotius's suggestions that the various Indian groups came from different parts of the Old World see Joan-Pau Rubies, "Hugo Grotius's Dissertation on the Origins of the American Peoples, and the Use of Comparative Method", *Journal of the History of Ideas* 52 (1991), 221–244.

faltered on the fact that, as the Jesuit comparativist Joseph François Lafitau noted in 1724, it was inconceivable that two of the tribes of Israel had lost nothing of their Judaism despite centuries of dispersion and persecution, while the other ten, on reaching America, had shed all trace and all memory of their ancestry.)

The uncertainty over the origins of the Indians could perhaps only be resolved by answering another question: how had they come to America? Had they, as some suggested, drifted there on rafts or perhaps even been carried across by angels? And if that were the case, how then could you explain all that proliferation of non-human life, the anacondas and the pumas, not to mention the tarantulas, and a thousand different kinds of venomous snakes? Surely no man, nor angel, in his right mind would have taken the trouble to transfer such creatures from the Old to the New World?

The problem had, in fact, been solved in the late sixteenth century by a number of writers, the most influential being José de Acosta, who had come to the conclusion that the presence in the American continent of any life form which could not be accounted for by spontaneous generation, could only be explained by the existence of a northern land-bridge – whose precise location was yet to be discovered – which joined, or at least had once joined, America to Asia.[35] Today we know, from the fossil record, that this is broadly speaking true. The peoples of the Americas, in fact, migrated across what is now called the Bering Strait in successive waves, probably (though this is hotly contested) beginning sometime between 12,000–13,000 years ago. (It is a striking case of true conclusions arrived at from entirely false premises. It is also significant that it was only in the late eighteenth century, with the arrival of a true physiological racism, that the physical similarities between the peoples of eastern Mongolia and the American Indians became a factor in the debate.)

But although Acosta's solution gradually gained acceptance and indeed became the basis for a substantial diffusionist literature throughout the eighteenth century, it did not entirely dispel the suspicion that the peoples

---

[35] José de Acosta, *Historia natural y moral de las Indias, en que se tratan de las cosas notables del cielo, elementos, metales, plantas y animales dellas, y los ritos y ceremonias, leyes y gobierno de los Indios* [1590], revised edition by Edmundo O'Gorman (Mexico City: Fondo de Cultura Económica, 1962), pp. 324–330. See Saul Jarcho, "Origin of the American Indian as suggested by Fray Joseph de Acosta", *Isis* 59 (1959), 430–438. As Joan-Pau Rubies has pointed out, Acosta's account, despite his claim to originality, in fact follows that of the chronicler-royal, Juan López de Velasco, *Geografía y descripción universal de las Indias* of 1574. A northern land-bridge also appears on maps from 1550 by the Venetian cosmographer Giacomo Gastaldi. Rubies, "Hugo Grotius's Dissertation", 224–225. But almost every learned man in Europe had read Acosta, whereas very few had read Velasco, and fewer still had seen Gastaldi's maps.

of America might be some quite different species of human being. What if the Biblical account were simply wrong or perhaps incomplete? Few if any Spaniards dared contemplate such a move. But in the ecclesiastically more relaxed circles of Italy and northern Europe, the possibility came increasingly to seem the only acceptable answer. In 1537–8, in two works on astronomy, the German doctor-magus Theophrastus Bombast, known as Paracelsus, considered the question. "We are all", he wrote "descended from Adam, and are those creatures called men, whose ancestor was generated directly by God, without the intervention of the stars." But, he went on,

We must not forget those who have been discovered on remote islands, many of which are still hidden, and are still to be discovered ... It cannot be demonstrated that the men that occupy these unknown lands derive from Adam [for] no one can easily believe that they are the line of Adam, since the sons of Adam could not have reached such remote places.[36]

Therefore, he concluded, it must be accepted that "the sons of Adam do not occupy all the earth". This, he explained elsewhere, did not deny them a soul, only a common ancestor with the rest of the species.

So, if they were not the descendants of Adam, who were they? Two alternative versions presented themselves. Aristotle had argued that certain lower creatures, insects, reptiles and fish might have generated either from the soil or from putrid matter. The orthodox view was that this excluded all higher animals and in particular humankind – a point on which Aquinas had insisted – since man was the only creature to be endowed with an immortal soul. But there were those who thought otherwise. One was the Bolognese Aristotelian Pietro Pomponazzi. Had not God himself made Adam out of "the dust of the ground", he asked? And if that were the case, why should not humanity also have been created, as Plato had claimed, *ex putri materia* – from rotting matter? Plato, knowing nothing of the Bible, had assumed that it had been the stars which had been responsible for the final act of generation. We, said Pomponazzi, now know better. But the fact that Adam and his descendants had been created by the hand of God, did not necessarily exclude the possibility of later non-divine acts of creation. "That man is perfect and thus cannot be generated out of rotting matter," he told his students, "is a probable argument, but it does not exclude the possibility that it might occur."

---

[36] Quoted in Giuliano Gliozzi, *Adamo e il nuovo mondo: La nascita dell'antropologia come ideologia coloniale, dalle genealogie bibliche alle teorie razziali (1500–1700)*, (Florence: Nuova Italia Editrice, 1977), pp. 309–310.

The theory of spontaneous generation was taken up by the physicians who found in it a satisfyingly economical solution to the problem of polygenesis, by Paracelsus himself, by Girolamo Cardano, by Andrea Cesalpino – who believed that the climate had something to do with it: "in the torrid zone", he claimed, "perfect animals are constantly generated spontaneously" – and by the arch-magus Giordano Bruno, who was burned at the stake partly for harboring such beliefs. Had the Americans (and who knew who else besides) been the product of spontaneous generation, this might explain their servility, since it was hard for any of these authors to escape the conclusion that even if the higher animals could be generated from putrefaction they were not, for that very reason, of an inferior kind to those which had stepped out of the Ark. The Americans on this calculation became not merely a race, but in effect an entire species apart.

There was, however, another more benign explanation for their origins and incidentally for the origins of other remote peoples such as the Chinese. In 1655 a treatise entitled *Prae-Adamitae* by Isaac La Peyrère, a nominally French Huguenot, of Jewish descent, was published in Holland (having been refused a license by Richelieu ten years earlier).[37] Based on a detailed analysis of the account of the creation in Genesis – and a stray comment from St. Paul's Epistle to the Romans (5.14) – La Peyrère persuaded himself that what the Book of Genesis contained was not one, but two accounts of creation: the first (1:27) speaks of the simultaneous creation of Adam and Eve, "male and female created he them"; the second (2:7, 21–2) describes the creation of Adam, and *then* of Eve from Adam's rib. (La Peyrère was not the first, nor the only, exegete to notice this. Furthermore, the existence of two similar but often contradictory stories is not unusual in creation myths. The *Timaeus*, for instance, also offers two contrasting versions.)[38] The claim that Adam was "the first man" should be understood in the same sense as the claim that Christ was "the second man" (or the second Adam) not literally, but figuratively. Adam and Christ are archetypes each of whom contains within himself the whole of humankind.[39] God had also charged Adam with naming everything on earth. But that, reasoned La Peyrère, would have been impossible given the variety of the species and the huge distances which

---

[37] The volume was made up of two works, the *Preadamitae, sive Exercitatio super Versibus duodecimo, decimotertio, et decimoquarto, capitis quinti, Epistolae D. Pauli ad Romanos, quibus inducuntur Primi Homines ante Adamum conditi*, and the longer *Systema theologicum ex Praeadamitarum hypothesi*.

[38] See the brilliant comments on this and its implications for our conceptions of time in Aldo Schiavone, *Storia e destino* (Turin: Einaudi, 2007), pp. 14–19.

[39] *Preadamitae*, cap. xxiii.

separated them. Therefore there must have been two creations divided by a vast amount of time.

The races of Europe and Asia were the obvious descendants of the better-documented of the two Adams, and all the other peoples of the earth, of the other, earlier, Adam. This theory proved instantly controversial and also immensely popular. Within a year of its publication *Prae-Adamitae* was translated into English, elicited at least a dozen refutations, was condemned by the Parlement of Paris, and burnt by the public executioner. La Peyrère himself went on to become perhaps the most celebrated heretic of his day, and although his work has now been entirely forgotten the controversy it aroused rumbled on well into the eighteenth century.[40] For those who were prepared to ignore its obvious heterodoxy, it had a lot going for it. It provided an answer to those who were already beginning to recognize that no species could have been created from a single pair, and it solved not only the American question, but also the increasingly troubling Chinese question. It also did something else. The traditional Biblical chronology had set the date of the creation at 5199 BC which does not allow much time in which to compress the whole of human pre-history. In the sixteenth century, furthermore, the Jesuits had discovered that the Chinese had sacred books which recorded far longer periods of time. (La Peyrère seems to have believed that the American Indians had similar records.) Voltaire over-optimistically thought this would put an end to the presumption of the Church once and for all. (It did not. But it seriously upset the Church's sense of its hold over human history and, via Leibniz and others, launched the Sinophilia of the eighteenth century, which argued that Confucius was the witness to a theological tradition which pre-dated Moses.)

By positing the existence of two creations, separated by perhaps thousands of years, La Peyrère had effectively resolved this difficulty. It was not something which any traditional Christian theologian could make use of, but it was to have a marked influence on a slightly later generation of English deists, William Petty and Thomas Burnet in particular, who in 1681 linked for the first time what might be described as a theory of race with an attempt to re-evaluate the geological history of the earth.

By establishing two distinct descent groups for all humankind, La Peyrère had, in effect, divided the species into two separate "races". In itself La Peyrère's thesis was not, in any obvious modern sense, "racist". It was strictly non-evaluative, since both Adams and their progeny were treated as exactly equal, insofar as their mental and moral capacities were concerned. If

[40] For his life and work see Richard Popkin, *Isaac La Peyrère (1596–1676): His Life, Work and Influence* (Leiden: Brill, 1987).

anything, at a time when antiquity could establish authority, the peoples of America and China might be thought to be superior to those of Europe and Asia, west of the Himalayas, by virtue of their greater age.

However, the separation of what would come to be called the "white" races into one descent group, and of all the others into another, had obvious racial implications. There was a further point. If there were two Adams, it was clear that only the second had fallen into original sin – at least in the way it was described in Genesis. This did not imply that the descendents of the first were without sin (for if they were so, then they could only be angelic beings, something which no one was prepared to sustain) but rather that they could not have benefited from Christ's sacrifice. To get round this problem, La Peyrère had insisted that God's grace had been extended "mystically" to the descendants of both Adams, and that the Chinese, and the American Indians, although denied immediate access to the Gospel because of the distance between them and Palestine, could be counted as beings in the same condition as those – the "virtuous pagans" – who had led blameless lives before the birth of Christ. Not much attention, however, was paid to this part of La Peyrère's argument, while the idea that all those people who had not originated somewhere west of the Euphrates were not merely descended from a separate progenitor, but had also been excluded by God from grace, appealed strongly to later racial theorists who were also lumbered with being Christian fundamentalists and anti-Darwinians.

All three of these claims – that the Indians were natural slaves, that they had been generated spontaneously or that they were the descendants of another Adam – led inexorably to a conclusion that even the most virulent of their detractors could not quite bring themselves to accept. For not only did all three propositions threaten the idea of a single humankind; they also had the effect of placing those races outside the course of human history – the *operatio Dei*, in Augustine's words, which ran from a single act of creation until the end of human time. And although this might serve the purpose of later exclusionists – true racists, that is – it was deeply inimical to the early European ideologues of empire, since the only ethical and theological justification for the European expansion overseas had been precisely incorporation. This had been made clear in Columbus's charters. It had been made clear in Alexander VI's Bulls of Donation of 1493. It was set out in the Laws of Burgos of 1513, reiterated in *Sublimis Deus* and remained right until the end the sole justification for the conquest.[41] Even slavery was conceived as a means to make the enslaved more

---

[41] Article 4 of an amendment to the Laws of Burgos dated July 28, 1513 reads, "Whereas it may so happen that in the course of time ... the Indians will become so apt and ready to

like their masters, not as Aristotle had conceived it, as a way of rectifying a discrepancy in the natural order. As the Spanish-Netherlandish humanist Sebastian Fox Morcillo pointed out in 1536, the Spanish had conquered America not to exploit or denigrate its inhabitants, but in order that they "should be civilized by good customs and education and led to a more human way of life".[42] And by making them more civilized they would be made fit to take their place in the course of human history.

This is why, in the end, even Ginés de Sepúlveda was prepared to concede that "now that they have received our law, our rule and our customs and have been imbued by the Christian religion" they were as unlike their former selves "as human men are to barbarians, as those with sight to the blind, as savages are to the gentle, as the pious are to the impious and, I say again, almost as men are to beasts".[43]

This remained the case until the collapse of the European empires in the twentieth century. Even when some notion of a civilizing process came to replace the Christian mission, any theory which implied that the conquered peoples of Europe's overseas empires belonged to a distinct race – defined in terms of psychology, descent or origin – ran directly counter to the ideological interest of the colonizing power. So long as they were committed either to evangelizing, or to preparing the non-Christian, non-European subjects for what the British called "self rule", the modern apologists of empire were also, inescapably, committed to a single indivisible human nature. Any claim that the colonized peoples might belong to separate, and inferior, races, necessarily excluded them from history, whether it was conceived as divine or – in terms of the history of "civilization" – secular. And, as even so firm a champion of the political rights of the American Indians as Bartolomé de las Casas had insisted, the entire course of the Spanish overseas empire could only be justified on the grounds that it had brought these "countless peoples" into history, that Columbus's voyages had "broken the locks that had held the Ocean Sea fast ever since the Flood". Had the Indians been a race apart, natural

---

become Christians, and so civilized and educated, that they will be capable of governing themselves and leading the kind of life that the said Christians lead ... [they] shall be allowed to live by themselves and shall be obliged to serve in those things in which our vassals in Spain are accustomed to serve." Text in Charles Gibson (ed.), *The Spanish Tradition in America* (New York: Harper & Row, 1968), p. 81. Their juridical status, furthermore, as Francisco de Vitoria insisted, even in their "uncivilized" state, was no different from that of other vassals of the Spanish crown.

[42] Sebastián Fox Morcillo, *Brevis et perspicua totius ethicae, seu de moribus philosophiae descriptio* (Basle: [s.n], 1566), p. 252.

[43] Juan Ginés de Sepúlveda, "Democrates secundus, sive de justis causis belli apud Indos", in Angel Losada (ed.), *Democrates Segundo, o Justas Causas de la Guerra contra los Indios*, translated by Angel Losada (Madrid: Consejo superior de investigaciones cientificas, 1951), pp. 33, 120.

slaves or the sons of another Adam, their history would have been very different, and there could have been no justification whatsoever for the European attempt either to Christianize or to civilize them. For this reason, paradoxical though it may seem, "race" plays no part in the early-modern ideologies of empire. That is not of course to deny that there were many serving the interests of the European overseas empires who were, by any understanding of the term, the most virulent racists. Nor is it to deny that there were many who sought to justify the European exploitation of non-Europeans on grounds which were, under any heading, clearly racial. But none of these voices, loud though they were, ever received official recognition. The imperial ideologies of Spain, Britain, France and Portugal were grounded upon the assumption of a single human nature; and while such a nature can be divided – to return one last time to Regino of Prüm's list – by "custom, language and law", it cannot be divided by "descent" – that is, in the modern sense of the term, by "race".

15 Demons, stars, and the imagination: the early modern body in the Tropics

Jorge Cañizares-Esguerra

During the 1680 *auto-da-fé* in Madrid, in which a ritual of collective exorcism also took place, 21 of the 117 accused were condemned to be burned at the stake. Of that number, 16 remained unrepentant, while 5 accepted Christ at the very last minute (and consequently were mercifully garroted before being thrown into the flames). José del Olmo, an inquisitor and master of the Royal Chamber of Charles II, paused to describe the differences in the countenance of these two groups:

> Truly if attention is paid to external signs, observed by everyone, the effects of piety could be told, for it was noticed, to the great awe of all witnesses, that there was a great difference between those who turned to the lord (*reducidos*) and those who remained obdurate, not unlike [the difference to be observed] between the saved and the damned. [The obdurate] walked [to their deaths] with their faces in a horrible colour, with disturbed eyes, almost gushing out flames, with the typical aspect of those of their faith [*toda la fisionomia de los rostros*], so much so, that they looked possessed by the devil. Those who converted went [to their deaths] with such humility, resignation, conformity and spiritual happiness that the grace of God could be seen [in their faces].[1]

The idea that the Devil transformed countenances was the reason why Martin Luther's followers rushed to draw the image of the Reformer's face when he passed away in 1546. Lucas Fortnagel's portrait emphasized Luther's peaceful encounter with the Lord, for a contorted face in

---

[1] "Y verdaderamente si se atiende a las senas esteriores, en que todos hicieron reparo, se puede discurrir mui de parte de la piedad, porque con universal admiración se notó una diferencia tan grande entre los reducidos y pertinaces, como entre los escogidos y réprobos. Estos iban con horrible color en los semblantes, con los ojos turbados y casi brotando llamas, y toda la fisonomía de los rostros, de tal suerte, que parecian poseidos del demonio. Pero los conversos iban con tal humildad, consuelo, conformidad y espiritual alegría, que pareció que casi se les traslucia la gracia de Dios." José del Olmo, *Relación histórica de Auto General de Fe que se celebró en Madrid este ano de 1680* (Madrid: Rico de Miranda, 1680), parte II, p. 76.

pain would have been evidence that Luther was the creature of the Devil, not of God.[2]

But the Devil could do far more than simply transform the aspect of one's face. He could also transform the entire body. When Gregorio López arrived in Mexico in the mid-sixteenth century to become a hermit, he chose the northern frontier, a land teeming with "bloodthirsty" Chichimec. In this inhospitable wilderness López often came to blows with demons; his spiritual battles had concrete bodily manifestations. On one occasion, the battle was so fierce that he bled through his ears and nose.[3] The early-modern world was one suffused with demons that entered human bodies at will. Once inside a body, demons not only caused bleeding in their hosts or anguished deathbed countenances, but they could also leave objects behind. In 1691, for example, the city of Queretaro witnessed the awesome power of demons over the body. One afternoon, as the possessed beata Juana de los Reyes was exorcised by the Franciscan Fray Pablo Sarmiento, she ejected "three avocado stones" and had an unusually large toad pulled out of her mouth. On other occasions Juana expelled an "iron spindle" and "paper bag with twenty pins" from her vagina while coughing up a "bundle of black wool" from her lungs. Juana finally one day delivered a baby, for the devil had impregnated her.[4] The early-modern body was not a well-enclosed space designed to remain stable over generations.

The case of the demons that caused López to bleed and Juana to eject toads ought to be taken into account in any explanation of "race" in the early-modern world, for demons seemed also to have been capable of producing lasting change over generations. Take for example the case of Francisco de La Cruz, a leading Dominican theologian in the Viceroyalty of Peru and a contemporary of Gregorio López. One day Cruz was called to exorcise María Pizarro and noticed that one of the spirits possessing the maiden was not the devil but the archangel Gabriel. After long sessions of intimate conversations with the Archangel, which were also opportunities Cruz used to get María pregnant, the Dominican proceeded to articulate a radical millenarian vision for the Peruvian church and polity. Cruz's plans for Peru included declaring Rome the Antichrist, abolishing celibacy for the clergy, legalizing polygamy for the laity,

---

[2] Heiko A. Oberman, *Luther; Man between God and the Devil*, translated from the 1982 German original by Eileem Walliser-Scharzbart (New Haven: Yale University Press, 1989), pp. 5–7.

[3] Francisco Losa, *Vida del siervo de dios Gregorio López* (Madrid: Imprenta de Juan de Ariztia, 1727), 14.14.

[4] Fernando Cervantes, *The Devil in the New World: The Impact of Diabolism in New Spain* (New Haven: Yale University Press, 1994), pp. 117, 121.

founding the original Israelite church in the Indies, and declaring himself, like David and Solomon, head of both the church and the state. The Inquisition swiftly put Cruz out of circulation as a minion of Satan. In 1578, after a trial that lasted six years, the inquisitors sent him to the stake. What is interesting about the trial is that the Inquisition took the opportunity to punish the son Cruz had with María as well as any of the potential descendants of the child. The Inquisition legally barred the newborn and the yet-to-be-born from any church or state position and from membership in any trade or guild. It also prohibited them from ever wearing any mark of wealth or distinction, including riding horses, carrying swords, or sporting jewelry.[5]

There is nothing in the inquisitorial proceedings to explain the logic of such measures against both a newborn and the unborn. But the Inquisition operated as if Cruz's blood and that of his actual and potential descendants had been permanently transformed by the Dominican's prolonged encounter with the Devil. The connection between heresy and the perceived permanent demonic transformation of the body of the heretic is something scholarship has not as yet sufficiently explored. The heretic was treated as the traitor had been in Roman law: even the innocent family of the accused was considered guilty, everyone's property and rights were taken away. Since heresy was a condition that could be passed down to infants in secrecy, inquisitors could not really be sure that the descendants of heretics, including third and even fourth generations, were not already "contaminated." Punishment of heretics, therefore, included the marginalization of the entire multigenerational household, as explicitly requested in Exodus 20:5: "Thou shalt not bow down thyself to them, nor serve [any graven image]: for I the LORD thy God am a jealous God, visiting the iniquity of the fathers upon the children unto the third and fourth generation of them that hate me."[6]

Christian views on the body and on inheritance lie at the core of this discourse on heresy. The doctrine of original sin considered that derelict

---

[5] "Y declaramos los hijos del dicho Fray Francisco y sus nietos por la línea masculina, ser inhábiles e incapaces, y os inhabilitamos para que no puedan tener ni obtener dignidades, beneficios no oficios, así eclesiásticos como seglares, ni otros oficios públicos y de honra, ni poder traer sobre si ni en sus personas oro, plata, piedras preciosas, ni corales, seda, chamelote ni paño fino, ni andar a caballo, ni traer armas, ni ejercer ni usar de otras cosas que por derecho común (leyes y pragmáticas de estos reinos, instrucciones y estilo del Sancto Oficio a los semejantes inhábiles) son prohibidas." "Sumario de la sentencia del proceso contra Fray Francisco de la Cruz, 13 abril 1578," in Alvaro Huerga (ed.), *Historia de los alumbrados*, 5 vols. (Madrid: Fundacion Universitaria Española, 1986), vol III: Alumbrados de Hispanoamérica, p. 473.

[6] Kenneth Pennington "'Pro Peccatis Patrum Puniri': A Moral and Legal Problem of the Inquisition'," *Church History* 47 (1978), 137–154.

Adam and Eve had set in motion processes of unparalleled cosmic decay: their bodies, as well as those of their descendants, had permanently been transformed by their sin. According to St Augustine, in the wake of the Fall, humans became mortal, weak of will, forever subordinated to their bodily wants, constitutionally sinful.[7] The transformation of an individual's lineage by moral lapses is a ubiquitous trope in Genesis: it happens to Adam and Eve; to Ham, Noah's son (Genesis 9:18–28); and to Issachar, Jacob's son (Genesis 49:15). The story of Noah's curse of Ham's descendants to be slaves was deployed in the ancient, medieval, and early modern worlds to explain both race and slavery. It allowed the medieval European nobilities to justify both the subordination of the peasantry and of the Jews and the Christian enslavement of Africans.[8] In the Atlantic world, the narrative of Noah's curse also did its dirty ideological work.[9]

Jacob's curse on Issachar (he and his descendants were condemned to labor as enslaved donkeys) is a tradition whose uses, however, are not as well known. In Spanish America, references to Issachar surface repeatedly to justify the *encomienda* system. Take, for example, the case of the influential commentary on the laws on *encomiendas* by the *converso* Antonio de Leon Pinelo, *Tratado de las Confirmaciones Reales de Encomiendas* (Madrid 1630).

In his frontispiece Leon Pinelo presents the tributary conditions of the Indians of New Spain, represented here by a fully clad woman flanked by a condor and the arms of Tenochtitlan, as the fulfillment of Deuteronomy 20:11: *cunctus populus qui in ea est salvabitur et serviet tibi sub tributo* (that all the people that is found therein shall be tributaries unto thee, and they shall serve thee). More tellingly, Leon Pinelo presents the Indians of Peru as the descendants of Issachar: an Inca carrying a replica of Potosí and flanked by the arms of Peru and a llama, stands on top of

---

[7] Paula Fredrikson and Tina Shepardson, "Embodiment and Redemption: The Human Condition in Ancient Christianity," in Robert C. Neville, John Berthrong, and Peter Berger (eds.), *The Human Condition: A Study of the Comparison of Religious Ideas* (Albany: SUNY Press, 2000), pp. 133–156.

[8] Paul Freedman, *Images of the Medieval Peasant* (Stanford: Stanford University Press, 1999); David M. Goldenberg, *The Curse of Ham: Race and Slavery in Early Judaism, Christianity, and Islam* (Princeton: Princeton University Press, 2005).

[9] Benjamin Braude, "The Sons of Noah and the Construction of Ethnic and Geographical Identities in Medieval and Early Modern Periods," *William and Mary Quarterly* 54 (1997), 103–142; A. J. R. Russell-Wood, "Before Columbus: Portugal's African Prelude to the Middle Passage and Contribution to Discourse on Race and Slavery," in Vera Lawrence and Rex Nettleford (eds.), *Race, Discourse, and the Origins of the Americas: A New World View* (Washington, DC: Smithsonian Institution Press, 1995). See also Colin Kidd, *The Forging of Races: Race and Scripture in the Protestant Atlantic World, 1600–2000* (Cambridge: Cambridge University Press, 2006).

Fig. 15.1 Frontispiece. Antonio de Leon Pinelo, *Tratado de las Confirmaciones Reales de Encomiendas* (Madrid, 1630). John Carter Brown Library.

the extract from Genesis 49:15: *subposuit umerum suum ad portandum factusque est tributis serviens* (and bowed his shoulder to bear, and became a servant unto tribute). In the 1620s in New Spain the Barefoot Carmelite, Antonio Vázquez de Espinosa, applied the curse of Issachar more widely to explain the servile condition of all Amerindians.[10]

It would however be a mistake to consider these early-modern religious interpretations of the collective inheritance of heresy and servitude as "racial." Take for example the case of the discourse on heresy as it was applied to both *conversos* and *moriscos* in Spain and to Amerindians and Africans in Spanish America. In Spain Christians whose ancestors had been Jews or Muslims were deemed unreliable, potentially dangerous vectors of enemy faiths, carrying the latent seed of their ancestral religions. By the early sixteenth century, lay and clerical institutions began to develop systems to screen out these potentially dangerous members of the community.

Yet inquiries on "clean blood lines" were easily subject to manipulation. In order to work, the most rigorous of these institutionalized queries, *Probanzas* developed by the Inquisition, depended on keeping detailed multigenerational genealogical records and archives of every locale and family in the land. Most archives, however, did not go beyond three or four generations. *Probanzas*, therefore, became oral inquiries to probe through the testimonies of elderly witnesses the reputation of individuals within a community. This system, reportedly set up to weed out heresy and enemy faiths by tracing "racial" lineages, was actually used to bolster or undermine individual reputations within communities. Inquiries on "*limpieza de sangre*" in Spain became a way for individuals to cleanse guilty memories of their own Jewish and Muslims backgrounds, not a means to identifying racialized religious miscreants.[11]

María Elena Martínez has shown the relevance of these doctrines on heresy and "purity of blood" for understanding the first early-modern colonial "racial" classifications introduced in the Americas, namely the *casta* system. Clerical and lay institutions in Mexico also instituted screenings to guarantee the religious "purity" of their members. Here, however,

---

[10] Antonio Vázquez de Espinosa, *Descripción de la Nueva España en el Siglo XVII* (Mexico City: Editorial Patria, 1944), pp. 41–45.

[11] Albert A. Sicroff, *Los Estatutos de Limpieza de Sangre: Controversias entre los Siglos XV y XVII* (Madrid: Taurus, 1985); Ruth Pike, *Linajudos and Conversos in Seville: Greed and Prejudice in Sixteenth- and Seventeenth-Century Spain* (New York: Peter Lang, 2000); Gretchen D. Starr-LeBeau, *In the Shadow of the Virgin: Inquisitors, Friars, and Conversos in Guadalupe, Spain* (Princeton: Princeton University Press, 2002); David Coleman, *Creating Christian Granada: Society and Religious Culture in an Old-World Frontier City, 1492–1600* (Ithaca: Cornell University Press, 2003).

the system became slightly more complicated, for in addition to the many *conversos* and *moriscos* there were peoples whose faiths were equally suspect, namely Amerindians and blacks.

According to Martínez, Amerindians became a very peculiar religious category capable of being both "impure" and "pure" at once. Natives were considered a separate republic, vassals of the king, who paid tribute and willingly embraced Catholicism. Amerindian elites had to prove their cleanliness to be elected to positions of power within their communities. Native rulers boisterously embraced the new Spanish ways and strengthened their ancient culture of keeping genealogies. Native elites became as obsessed as their Spanish counterparts with developing a discourse on *limpieza* of "Old Christian Indian" blood as well as archives to prove it.

Yet the natives did mix promiscuously with both Spaniards and blacks. Moreover, for Creole and Spanish theologians, Amerindian "idolatry" became the equivalent of heresy. Thus having Amerindian blood worked in conflicting and contradictory ways for *castas* struggling to prove purity. Sometimes, *mestizos* drew on their dual Spanish and Indian roots to claim a surplus of purity. In other cases, *mestizos* were marginalized from positions of prestige due to their stained (black) and idolatry-prone (Indian) religious backgrounds.

Being black in the New World was the equivalent to being a *converso* or a *morisco* in Spain. Blacks were all considered tainted, with blood doubly contaminated by Noah's curse and Islam. Moreover proving "blackness" was much easier than documenting Jewish and Muslim ancestries, for phenotypical appearances, not genealogical archives, sufficed. Yet there were plenty of mulattoes who manipulated the system. Through oral testimonies documenting Old Christian reputations, many mulattoes cleansed their lineages. Martínez demonstrates that in Mexico both Indian and Spanish communities worked to cleanse memories of black backgrounds in the same way as Iberian communities had cleansed theirs of Jewish and Arab ancestry.[12]

"Purity of blood" and *casta* hierarchies in the Spanish empire were not the early-modern equivalent of race. Although the body was perceived as a permeable object, effortlessly altered by outside forces (e.g., demons; breast feeding by racially alien wet nurses), individuals and communities whose bodies had been permanently altered could not easily be earmarked as outsiders. Despite the fact that the discourse of "purity of blood"

---

[12] María Elena Martínez, "The Black Blood of New Spain: *Limpieza de Sangre*, Racial Violence, and Gendered Power in Early Colonial Mexico", *William and Mary Quarterly* 61 (2004), 479–520, and *Genealogical Fictions: Limpieza de Sangre, Religion, and Gender in Colonial Mexico* (Stanford: Stanford University Press, 2008).

assumed innate racial predispositions, *moriscos*, *conversos*, and *castas* could create networks of patronage through economic success to deny any Moorish, Jewish, Amerindian, or African ancestries. Descendants of perceived heretics and enemies of the faith, regardless of their color or physiognomy, often manipulated the system. Demonstrating high social standing in the community, attesting one's own *calidad*, was often enough for *conversos*, *moriscos*, and *castas* to be considered Old Christians. In the case of blacks and mulattoes, they could even legally prove to be "white."[13]

To understand "race" in the early-modern period we need to put aside our modern definitions of race. In the early-modern period bodies were deemed extremely malleable, crossing boundaries we no longer deem natural. Bodies were thought to change easily due to the effect of climate, diet, constellations, and the maternal imagination. Moreover, as the case of the Spanish empire indicates, racial labels once created did not stick easily; labels were simply a reflection of one's social standing, not a way to record physical descent. The challenge then is to understand the transition away from these conceptions of the early-modern body. Sometime and somewhere bodies suddenly began to be represented differently: they became immutable, tied down through inheritance to the ontological category of race.

The usual explanation maintains that the turning point occurred some time in the eighteenth century as a result of major economic and political transformations. As African black slaves arrived to work in sugar, rice, coffee, and tobacco plantations in America, the merchants to whom the slave belonged set in motion economic processes on a scale that brought prices of staples down, steadily incorporating the European poor as consumers. The cycle turned the plantations into industries and the slaves into chattels, objects upon which Atlantic capital accumulation was made possible. The enslaving of millions and the consumer revolution coincided with the crumbling of the old political order based on social estates, hereditary privileges, and religion. New social formations emerged based on the principles of citizenship, natural rights, and secular political authority. It was at this juncture that "white" European males located in "race" (and the science of innate gender differences) the ideological justification to

---

[13] Ann Twinam, "Racial Passing: Informal and Official 'Whiteness' in Colonial Spanish America", in John Smolenski and Thomas J. Humphrey (eds.), *New World Orders: Violence, Sanction and Authority in the Colonial Americas* (Philadelphia: University of Pennsylvania Press, 2005), pp. 249–272.

prevent women, slaves, former slaves, and non-Europeans from sharing in their newly acquired political rights.[14]

Yet the switch to "race" as an ontological property of the body was a protracted event that originated in the "peripheries" of the Atlantic world, as the ideological underpinnings of the European expansion to America and Africa proved insufficiently coherent for Creole settler societies to embrace. The story can be summarized this way: Europeans set sail assuming that there were unknown islands and continents teeming with slaves and gold in the middle of the ocean. A century of expansion to Africa had taught them to expect new lands full of gold, plants, and slaves in the "Tropics." The balance of earth to water in the ancient and medieval geocentric models predicted abundant new land in the Atlantic antipodes and the equator. According to these theories, lands closer to the sun produced gold, spices, and particularly slavish dark populations. Thus, from the very beginning, America was seen as a southern tropical continent that, like Africa, was capable of producing precious metals and dark, slavish populations.[15]

Europeans quickly justified slavery in the New World on the climatological, cosmographical assumptions: the natives needed to be put to work to offset the degenerating effects of the Tropics. Such ideology, however, did not fit well with the Creole settlers. Casting the indigenous populations as having tropical complexions that required the establishment of forced labor systems (including the *encomienda*, the *mita*, and the *repartimiento*) was one thing; claiming that all those who lived in the Indies could potentially become degenerate Amerindians was another. While Creole settlers benefited from the ideology of the degenerate, servile Amerindians, this very ideology cast Creoles as inferiors to their European brethren. Creole intellectuals therefore put together a defense of the climate and constellations of America to spare the descendants of the conquistadors from the charges of environmentally induced

---

[14] Michael Banton, *The Idea of Race* (London: Tavistock Publications, 1977); Nancy Stepan, *The Idea of Race in Science: Great Britain, 1800–1960* (Hamden: Archon Books, 1982); Nicholas Hudson, "From 'Nation' to 'Race': The Origin of Racial Classification in Eighteenth-Century Thought," *Eighteenth-Century Studies* 29 (1996), 247–264; Ivan Hannaford, *Race: The History of an Idea in the West* (Baltimore: Johns Hopkins University Press, 1996); Dorinda Outram, *The Enlightenment* (Cambridge: Cambridge University Press, 1995), pp. 74–79, 94–95; and Alden T. Vaughan, "From White Man to Redskin: Changing Anglo-American Perceptions of the American Indian," *American Historical Review* 87 (1982), 917–953. On the role of New World plantations and slavery in the creation of Europe's consumer-industrial revolution and the growth of racial prejudice, see Robin Blackburn, *The Making of New World Slavery: From the Baroque to the Modern 1492–1800* (London: Verso, 1997).

[15] Nicolás Wey Gómez, *The Tropics of Empire: Why Columbus Sailed South to the Indies* (Cambridge: MIT Press, 2008).

degeneration. This defense, however, could not include the Amerindians, for the settlers had to justify their own rule over the natives. The solution was to do away with the age-old representation of the body as malleable clay, easily transformed by demons, stars, and the maternal imagination. Creole scholars invented the discourse of ontologically different bodies: under the influences of the tropics natives degenerated into servile labor, while Creoles mutated into beings even more virile and intelligent than their European ancestors.[16]

The invention of ontological bodily differences along "racial" lines, however, did not spread beyond the discourse of Creole degeneration. Thus the thesis of a malleable body persisted. It indeed took the global, momentous transformations of the eighteenth century to slowly put an end to the idea of the body as pliable clay, easily modified by outside forces. It was the massive presence of "black" bodies working as slaves in plantations all over the New World that forced the change. The transition was full of contradictions and no two contemporary sources are the same. Take for example, on the one hand, the writings of the Spanish Jesuit Joseph Gumilla, head of the Jesuit missions in mid-eighteenth century Orinoco. Gumilla explained "racial" differences using the discourse of the fully malleable body. Eighteenth-century *casta* paintings, on the other hand, were based upon an interpretation of the black body as immutable.

In 1745 Gumilla reported an extraordinary event that drew the attention of the city authorities and hundreds of curious people in Cartagena: a black woman had given birth to a speckled (white and black) child. The event was extraordinary because the dog the woman owned shared with the newborn the exact same distribution of spots over the body. For Gumilla this was a ringing confirmation of the influence of the maternal imagination in cross-color generation. Gumilla considered the body as a malleable object, easily transformed by outside forces. He argued that the imagination of the black mother had transformed the daughter inside the womb into a speckled creature. Since the woman had been too close to her pet during pregnancy, her imagination had caused the skin color of her child to resemble the dog's spots.[17] In order for his interpretation to work, Gumilla drew on the theory of cross-color generation that had for centuries considered the imagination of pregnant women to be the cause of world-wide differences in skin color. The theory, in turn, originated in a

[16] Jorge Cañizares-Esguerra, "New Worlds, New Stars: Patriotic Astrology and the Invention of Indian and Creole Bodies in Colonial Spanish America 1600–1650", *American Historical Review* 104 (1999), 33–68.
[17] Joseph Gumilla, *El Orinoco ilustrado, y defendido, historia natural, civil, y geographica de este gran rio, y de sus caudalosas vertientes*, second edition, 2 vols. (Madrid: M. Fernández, 1745), pp. 97–98, 109–115.

learned commentary on Genesis 30:25–43, which recounts how Jacob transformed the white goats of Laban into a new speckled breed by manipulating the imagination of the white goats during the mating season.[18] A Jesuit contemporary of Gumilla, Joseph François Lafitau, used the same theory to explain the "reddish" colour of the Caribbean natives: "The flesh of these people is very reddish: it is so naturally, less because of the nature of the climate than through the imagination of their mothers who, finding beauty in this colour, transmit it to their offspring."[19]

But how was one to explain the stability of skin color over generations? Gumilla argued that since individuals shunned those who looked different and were attracted to those who looked like them, mothers were rarely exposed to outsiders during pregnancy. Occasionally, however, the grip of aesthetics over the imagination and thus the stability of skin color over generations broke down: pregnant women had dreams and imaginary encounters with individuals of different colors and had children of different color. True to this theory of cross-color generation, Gumilla suggested that all blacks were the descendants of an original white woman who had imagined a black during conception.[20] Gumilla, therefore, considered the bodies of whites, Amerindians, and blacks to be essentially the same. Not surprisingly, Gumilla assumed that the offspring of Amerindians who mated with "Europeans" for three continuous generations shed off their Indianness, becoming fully white. This also held true for blacks.[21]

Eighteenth-century *casta* paintings document a different view of the world. *Castas* were the various hybrid populations that demographically began to dominate urban life in Spanish America over the course of the seventeenth century, the product of the miscegenation of poor whites, freed blacks, and uprooted, migrant Amerindians. Authorities saw these mixed groups with distrust, considering them threatening, rebellious and

---

[18] Wendy Doniger and Gregory Spinner, "Misconceptions; Female Imaginations and Male Fantasies in Parental Imprinting," *Daedalus* 127 (1998), 97–130.

[19] Joseph François Lafitau, *Customs of the American Indian Compared with the Customs of the Primitive Times*, translated by William N. Fenton and Elizabeth L. Moore (eds.), 2 vols. (Toronto: The Champlain Society, 1974), vol. I, p. 44.

[20] Gumilla, *El Orinoco ilustrado*, vol. I, pp. 88–89, 98–109.

[21] Ibid., vol. I, pp. 82–86. Gumilla was not alone; the Virginia planter, William Byrd II, shared the same ideas: "A wicked West Indian boasted that he had washt the Black … White, and being askt by what art, he did it, he replyd, that in his youth he had an Intrigue with an Ethiopian Princess, by whome he had a Daughter that was a Mulatto. Her he lay with, believing no man had so good a right to gather the Fruit as he who planted it. By this he had another Daughter of the Portuguese complection and When she came to be 13 years old he again begot Issue Female upon her body, that was perfectly white; and very honourably descended." See William Byrd II, Kevin Berland *et al.* (eds.), *The Commonplace Book of William Byrd II of Westover* (Chapel Hill: University of North Carolina Press, 2001), pp. 139–140. I owe this reference to Professor Mechal Sobel.

Fig. 15.2 Casta image from "Of Spanish and Albino: A Throwback."
Pedro Alonso O'Crouley, *Idea compendiosa del reino de la Nueva Espana*
[1774] (Mexico City, 1975).

promiscuous. The efforts to control these groups led to an explosion of
taxonomical categories seeking to trace the genealogies of such mixed
people. *Casta* paintings offered concrete visual representations.[22]

Relevant to our discussion however is the fact that *casta* paintings documented limits to the early-modern malleability of the body. On the one
hand, the paintings confirm Gumilla's thesis of whitening by consecutively
marrying white Europeans for three generations. Thus the paintings show
that an Amerindian who married a Spaniard begot a *mestiza*, that the
mestiza who married a Spaniard begot a *castiza*, and, finally, that the *castiza*
who married a Spaniard begot a Spaniard. Yet the very *casta* paintings that
present the body of an Amerindian slowly mutating into that of a white
Spaniard, also demonstrate that a similar transformation of the black
body could not take place. All series show that a black who married a
Spaniard begot a *mulatta*, that the *mulatta* who married a Spaniard begot
a *morisca*, that the *morisca* who married a Spaniard begot an *albina*, and,
finally, that the *albina* that married a Spaniard begot a "*torna atrás*," that is,
a black child. The lesson that *casta* painting conveyed on racial mixing was
clear: by the third generation, the dilution of black blood seemed so

---

[22] On the genre, Ilona Katzew, *Casta Painting: Images of Race in Eighteenth-Century Mexico*
(New Haven: Yale University Press, 2004).

thoroughly complete that the albino child could not be any whiter. Yet the process was a delusion, for once the *albina* married a Spaniard blackness reasserted itself and a "step-backwards" child was born.

What is remarkable about these paintings is that they show that in mid-eighteenth-century Spanish America there was already in place a search for laws of racial inheritance and that an impervious, non-malleable black body had finally been invented. This invention, in turn, was part of much larger cultural transformations in the Atlantic world, as Dror Wahrman has suggested.[23] In the early-modern period, individuals could comfortably assume manifold identities. But this carnivalesque mutability gave way by the late eighteenth century to a "modern regime of selfhood," one obsessed with fixation and stability.

---

[23] Dror Wahrman, *The Making of the Modern Self: Identity and Culture in the Eighteenth-Century England* (New Haven: Yale University Press, 2004).

Index